The Industrial
Organization of
Futures Markets

The Industrial Organization of Futures Markets

Edited by
Ronald W. Anderson
Columbia University

LexingtonBooks
D.C. Heath and Company
Lexington, Massachusetts
Toronto

Library of Congress Cataloging in Publication Data
Main entry under title:

The Industrial organization of futures markets.

"This book grew out of a conference entitled 'The industrial organization
of futures markets: structure and conduct' held on November 4 and 5, 1982,
sponsored by the Center for Futures Market Studies at Columbia University
Graduate School of Business"—CIP pref.
    1. Commodity exchanges—Congresses. 2. Industrial organization
(Economic theory)—Congresses. I. Anderson, Ronald W., 1946-
II. Columbia University. Center for Futures Market Studies.
HG6024.A3I52   1984   332.64'4   83-48029
ISBN 0-699-06836-5

Copyright © 1984 by D.C. Heath and Company

Published simultaneously in Canada

Printed in the United States of America

International Standard Book Number: 0-669-06836-5

Library of Congress Catalog Card Number: 83-48029

Contents

Preface

Ronald Anderson

This book grew out of the conference "The Industrial Organization of Futures Markets: Structure and Conduct" held November 4 and 5, 1982, sponsored by the Center for Futures Market Studies at Columbia University Graduate School of Business. The purpose of the conference was to mobilize the efforts of a group of academic economists to attack the conceptual issues that underly the evaluation of performance of futures markets and their regulation. The conference was the culmination of a year and half of research and discussions that involved not only the authors but other academics, regulators, and people working in the futures industry.

The chapters in this book are revised versions of the papers presented at the conference and their formal discussion. Generally, one discussion represents the academic perspective and a second gives a nonacademic perspective. The chapter by Saloner was written independently; however, because it fits with the conference papers, it has been included here. The survey in chapter 1 was written after the conference and is an attempt to give some structure to a new, previously undefined field called the industrial organization of futures markets. In writing this essay I have tried to place the chapters in this volume in the context of a program of research. There remains much to be done in this program. It is hoped that this volume will help to stimulate further work toward building a solid economic foundation for the understanding of futures market institutions.

This volume would not have been possible without the support of the Columbia Futures Center and thus indirectly its two principal donors, the Commodity Exchange Inc. and the Chicago Mercantile Exchange. We have also incurred an intellectual debt to many individuals in the futures industry and government who have given informed and constructive comments along the way. Finally, the director of the Center for the Study of Futures Markets at Columbia University, Frank Edwards, and his staff of Francoise Lamberston and Megan Foehr are to be thanked for providing administrative help in organizing the conference and preparing this book.

1

The Industrial Organization of Futures Markets: A Survey

Ronald W. Anderson

This chapter surveys industrial organization issues dealing with futures markets. Because there is presently no well-developed field called "the industrial organization of futures markets" and because the field of industrial organization has traditionally been concerned with the structure and conduct of manufacturing industries, a definition is in order. By industrial organization of futures markets we mean the study of the nature of competition in futures markets, the relation of futures industry members and their customers, and the organization of futures exchanges.

This definition is broad; however, it does exclude most of the large and rapidly growing literature on futures markets. The vast majority of economic studies of futures markets explicitly or implicitly assume that competition is perfect in the sense that agents possess no market power and that there is free entry. Although such an assumption may be adequate for some purposes—for example, in providing a framework for studying the behavior of futures prices—it casually dismisses many issues that concern futures traders, hedgers, and regulators among others. Examples of the many such issues include the processing of commission orders by brokers, the workings of the cash market for goods that meet the precise delivery condition specified in a futures contract, the approval of an exclusive right to trade a specific contract on a designated futures exchange, and establishment of limits on speculative position sizes to prevent the concentration of open interest in a few hands. Although these issues are important and pose a host of challenging questions, they have been relatively neglected by academic economists. One exception is a small number of careful students who have based their work on a detailed understanding of futures market institutions. The second exception are the contributors to this volume; their work has been gathered together purposely to expand the academic study of futures markets into what we have called here the industrial organization of futures markets.

The author has benefited from discussions with many people including, in particular, the participants of the conference. Conversations with Steve Salant regarding manipulations have been especially useful. Financial support by the Columbia Futures Center, which sponsored the conference, is gratefully acknowledged. The author alone is responsible for errors.

Part of the motivation for taking up this study is to provide the basis for addressing public policy for futures markets and particularly the governmental regulation of futures trading. Thus, regulatory issues are discussed to the extent that they help in identifying significant industrial organization issues. However, we do not attempt to survey the literature on futures market regulation. Edwards (1981) and Johnson (1982) provide general introductions to the area of futures market regulation.

Futures markets are well-defined and easily recognizable entities. They are organizations with members who meet for the purpose of trading at a specific location—the trading floor of an exchange. Thus, with a certain justification, one could argue that the industrial organization of futures markets should be confined to dealings of futures exchanges and its members. However, such a narrow perspective would be severely distorted because futures markets derive their vitality from the relationship of futures trading to the other activities of the participants in the markets, particularly the hedgers and arbitrageurs. Holbrook Working (1953b) has emphasized that many traders hold futures contracts as a temporary substitute for an eventual cash trade (that is, a bilateral merchandising contract). Thus the interaction of cash and futures markets is an essential matter for our study.

This survey is organized as follows. The first section considers the contribution of futures markets to the functioning of cash markets and starts with a brief review of some claimed benefits of competitive futures markets. It then considers a variety of possible market failures, including noncompetitive price determination and manipulations. The second section addresses principal/agent issues that arise from the fact that the general public can trade futures only through exchange members who, as a group, hold a monopoly in futures transacting. The third section is devoted to futures exchanges themselves, including consideration of contract design, market microstructure, and exchange membership.

Market Performance

Results on Competitive Futures Markets

Before taking up the question of possible market imperfection, it is useful to recall the contributions futures markets are thought to make when they work well. Perhaps the most widely accepted view is that they play a role in allocating resources and risks. In the familiar state-preference terminology, economic uncertainty can be characterized as agents in the present facing many possible future states of the world (such as high rainfall or drought). In general, goods are distinguished by the state in which they are consumed (for example, a bushel of wheat in times of abundant rainfall is a different good than in time of drought). If, in the present, agents could exchange state-contingent claims (that is, an asset that has a payoff if and only if a specific state occurs) they would be able to exchange risks in ways that may be collectively beneficial. Formally, the competitive equilibrium will be Pareto-efficient if there is trading in state-contingent claims for all possible states (see Debreu 1959). This is the well-known optimality of competition when markets are complete. If markets are incomplete, as will be true if trade is limited to spot markets (that is, trading occurs only after the state is known), there generally will be untapped potential gains from trade.

An obstacle to achieving complete markets is the difficulty of writing and enforcing contracts for state-contingent claims. As a result, it is natural to ask whether having other kinds of financial markets is sufficient to make the markets effectively complete. Markets will be effectively complete if at prevailing prices an agent could purchase alternative portfolios of assets each of which replicates the payoff of a state-contingent claim. Townsend (1978) shows that a rich set of forward markets in combination with spot markets can be sufficient to effectively complete the markets. Because in Townsend's setting a forward contract is very similar to a futures contract, he provides a general case for the desirability of futures trading.

This view of the beneficial aspects of futures trading is tempered if one asks, following Arrow (1981), if futures markets are necessary to achieving efficient risk-sharing. A number of authors have shown that securities or options are capable of providing effectively complete markets, so that from this general perspective there is nothing unique about futures contracts. Further, the importance of all these results is limited by the fact that for markets to be effectively complete there must be as many assets as states of the world. A bit of reflection leads many people to doubt that this situation could ever occur, in which case, markets are necessarily incomplete.

In stating the contribution of futures trading in a world of incomplete markets, we find the results are more modest and tentative than those for complete markets. Hart (1975) shows that at present there is no rigorous justification of futures trading with incomplete markets based on general equilibrium. What can be said in a partial equilibrium setting?

First, futures trading clearly can be an effective means of reducing risk. When a producer holds a known amount of the commodity specified in the contract, it is argued, risk can be eliminated by hedging in the futures market. If the futures price differs significantly from the expected cash price, the producer's short sale will not exactly equal his cash position. Still, the producer will generally hedge some amount of his output and, because he is maximizing expected utility, it is clear that given prices the individual is made better off by futures trading.

The foregoing summarizes the partial-equilibrium argument for futures trading stated by Keynes (1923) and restated and expanded many times since. In particular, the argument can be extended to allow for the fact that the hedger does not hold the precise good specified in the futures contract and thus faces basis risk (see Stein 1979) or to allow for uncertainty with respect to quantity as well as price (see Anderson and Danthine, 1983 and Newbery and Stiglitz, 1981). These studies show that it is generally beneficial for individual producers to use futures markets when they exist. This statement falls short of showing that it is desirable for these markets to exist. Recently, Magill and Cheng (1982) have shown that a rational expectations equilibrium in a futures market maximizes expected consumer plus producer surplus. In a related but independent study Stein (1981) shows that, if demand and supply take a simple linear form, expected consumer plus producer surplus is maximized if the futures price is an unbiased predictor of the eventual spot price. These two studies give a tentative indication of the social desirability of futures trading when markets are incomplete.

The preceding discussion implicitly treats futures and forward markets as though they were identical. In fact, the high degree of standardization of a futures contract means that hedgers who use these contracts will face basis risk whereas those holding forward contracts generally will not, which would seem to argue more for forward contracting than for futures trading. The case for futures versus forward trading was made first by Working (1953b) who emphasized that agents hold futures contracts as a temporary substitute for an eventual cash market transaction which could be a forward contract. This point has been expanded by Telser and Higinbotham (1977) who emphasize that, because they are guaranteed by a clearing association, futures contracts do not involve default risk. Consequently, they facilitate trade among strangers and thus allow active secondary trading to grow. The resulting liquidity is an important advantage of futures trading over forward contracting. More generally, it has been pointed out by Townsend (chapter 9) that the liquidity of futures trading is a benefit of a market form that uses a third party to internalize an externality of bilateral exchange.

The preceding discussion leads to a presumption that competitive futures markets are socially beneficial. Whether a specific market is beneficial depends on the extent to which the reality of the institutions correspond to the assumptions of the theoretical constructs used above. Further, it remains unclear the extent to which the desirable properties of futures markets are lost if traders are imperfectly competitive. We now turn to these issues.

Noncompetitive Price

Although the generally favorable view of futures trading in the preceding section probably represents the consensus among economists, it is by no means universally accepted. Public mistrust of futures trading is widespread.

In the United States, a major expression of that mistrust is the Commodity Exchange Act of 1936 that, with amendments, is still the basis of governmental regulation of futures trading. This act states that, despite of the fact that futures trading takes place in large volume and that futures prices are freely quoted, futures markets are prone to speculation, manipulation, and control that result in unreasonable prices. Economists have generally tended to dismiss this view as a product of misunderstanding of competitive price determination. This view may be correct; however, the mistrust of futures trading is so deepseated and so longlived as to warrant careful consideration. In what follows we survey the relatively few attempts in this vein. We consider first how price may be controlled by agents possessing sustainable market power, leaving to subsequent sections more transient forms of market power giving rise to manipulations and the possibility that speculation may be excessive.

Agents may possess market power when there is a significant obstacle that inhibits new entry into the market. Anyone who can afford a minimum margin requirement can buy or sell a futures contract through a broker. This ease of entry by new participants contributes to the competitiveness of futures price determination. However, all futures transactions (with very few exceptions) must be carried out on the floor an exchange by exchange members. The fact that there is a barrier to new entry in futures market transacting (as opposed to position holding) potentially gives floor traders a degree of market power.

Working (1953a) drew attention to the influence of floor traders by describing the bi-valence of price that prevails in the market. At any given time, outside purchase orders will be transacted at one price (the floor traders' asking price), while sell orders will transact at a lower price (the floor traders' bid price). The spread between the bid and the ask represents a cost of trading futures for participants off the exchange which is paid to the population of floor traders. The style of trading used to extract this payment is widely known as scalping and has been described by Working (1954) and Hieronymous (1977), among others. In scalping a trader tends to take a position temporarily, working in reaction to the flow of outside orders into the pit. A buy order will be met by a scalper's sale at a price slightly above the immediately preceding transaction price. Under normal circumstances, the next few outside orders will contain a sell order that a scalper will meet by buying at a price below that of the preceding trade. This pattern of "up a tick, down a tick" arises from the fact that trading takes place continuously on a futures exchange, while the flow of outside orders into the pit is intermittent. Empirical evidence of the pervasiveness of scalping has been provided by Working (1954) and (1967) and more extensively by Martell and Helms (1979). The latter examine transaction prices (that is, the prices of all transactions in the order in which they occur) for various delivery months in

1974 and 1975 for seven commodities traded at the Chicago Board of Trade and find widespread evidence of significantly negative first-order autocorrelations as would be expected if scalpers earn a positive return.

The determinants of scalping profits have not been thoroughly studied. Three factors appear to be most important—the volume of outside orders, the number of pit traders processing trades, and distribution of new information flow into the market. The only formal analysis in this area has been by Telser (1981a) who posits a model in which there is a sequence of draws from a fixed population of purchase and sale orders. The dispersion of prices around an asymptotic equilibrium price corresponds to what we have called the bid/ask spread. This dispersion is shown to be a decreasing function of the number of bids or offers. Telser emphasizes that his model does not imply that the dispersion is small only when volume is large; however, the extensive, if informal, observations among futures traders suggest that in fact the bid/ask spread is a decreasing function of volume. How the bid/ask spread is affected by the number of floor traders has not been studied directly. The obvious conjecture is that, all things being equal, the fewer the traders the wider the spread; however, this notion has neither been formalized nor empirically tested. Empirical tests are difficult because, although the number of seats on an exchange is fixed over brief periods, the number of traders active in a given pit is variable and may well be directly related to the volume of commission orders flowing into a pit. Finally, any scalper who takes a position hoping to offset quickly at a slightly advantageous price runs the risk that significant news will change the average price at which transactions take place. If the market is such that new information is received frequently or has a large impact, this risk is relatively great and the bid/ask spread would be expected to be correspondingly large. To date, this issue has not been investigated carefully.

If scalping is a well-understood form of floor trader market power, it is also widely tolerated, for there is no regulatory impediment to deriving profits in this way. In contrast, other manifestations of floor trader power are prohibited by law. The Commodity Exchange Act prohibits such noncompetitive practices as wash sales, cross trades, or accommodation trades. Although the exact meaning of these terms is not made clear in the act and is not totally resolved in the related case law (see Johnson 1982), it is reasonably clear that these transactions are intended to establish a publicly recorded transaction price without resulting in a change in the position of the transacting parties.

There may be a variety of motives for undertaking such transactions. For example, if (as was formerly the case on many American exchanges) the closing price is used to determine the daily flow of margin money among holders of open positions, it would be in the interest of two floor traders who were both long (short) to attempt a pair of transactions just at the close at a price that is as high (low) as is possible. The pair of transactions, each trader buying in one and selling in the other is required to result in no change in either trader's net position. However, much the same result could be accomplished with a single transaction if the number of contracts traded were small relative to the trader's open position sizes. This observation suggests that the existing legal criterion for establishing such trades—namely no change in the trader's net position—is not particularly useful in eliminating the practice. Probably a more effective curb was the establishment of settlement processes that determine margin flows.

Another allegedly noncompetitive practice is to bid prices up or down to induce trading by traders off the floor of the exchange. It is not difficult to give an account of the reasons for such attempts. Traders off the floor of the exchange commonly attempt to reduce the delay in responding to new price information by leaving standing stoploss orders with their brokers. These orders take such forms as "buy at market if a price of $3.00 or higher is touched." If floor traders cooperated to raise prices sufficiently during light volume periods, they could trigger a wave of buy orders that—barring the chance arrival of large sell orders—will be serviced by sales by floor traders at relatively elevated prices. After the stop purchases are processed, it is hoped that the price returns to the initial levels and the acquired short position can be worked off with a profit. Alternatively, the floor traders could then attempt to drive the price down to touch the standing sell-stop orders, thus leaving the floor traders neutral. These are two examples of the practices, allegedly widespread among floor traders, that have been ignored in scholarly work on futures markets. Formal analysis would be useful in establishing which rules, if any, are desirable for floor trader conduct. In addition, better understanding of the behavior of floor traders is fundamental to understanding exchange self-regulation (see the last in this chapter). Such an analysis would include three crucial elements: first, the fact that floor traders as a group possess a monopoly in carrying out transactions; second, transaction prices with low volume can have the same informational impact as transactions with high volume; and third, floor traders possess a significant advantage over the general public in the speed with which they can respond to price changes. The last point is important; it means the general public may rationally wish to leave standing orders with their brokers even though they can be occasionally exploited as a result.

The kind of market power possessed by floor traders permits them to influence transaction prices around some average or equilibrium price. A separate issue is whether any agents have significant market power in influencing the equilibrium price. To prevent arbitrage the price of a futures contract at the expiration date must equal the cash price for the good specified in the contract. Before delivery, the futures price will be tied to the cash price through the participant's expectations and, if the good is storable, through storage arbitrage. Thus, even though there is easy entry in taking futures positions, an agent can have a significant influence on the futures price if he is powerful in the cash market.

The fact that many commodities are governed by international stabilization agreements that act much like producer cartels means that several futures markets exist for goods with imperfectly competitive cash markets (examples are cocoa, coffee, and, recently, crude oil). For other commodities, primary supply is highly concentrated so that a few producers may influence price (for example, gold). In other instances, individual countries may have a national acquisition program and may have a significant share of total world trade (for example, the Soviet Union in the grain market). In all these cases, our understanding is impaired, perhaps significantly, if we attempt to analyze these markets using conventional models that assume both the futures and the cash markets are perfectly competitive. Perhaps as important a reason for considering views of futures trading that allow for cash market power is to discover whether there is any necessary connection between the degree of cash market competition and the viability of futures trading. At times, exchanges support their cases for new contract markets before the regulatory authorities by stating that the cash market is highly competitive, perhaps implying that imperfections in cash market competition represent obstacles to futures trading.

Despite the significance of the question, only Anderson and Sundaresan (chapter 3) and Newbery (chapter 2) have addressed the relationship of cash market power and futures trading. Both studies consider the implications of trading a futures contract that calls for the delivery of a perishable good produced under conditions of imperfect competition and of allowing producers to trades futures. Anderson and Sundaresan assume the good is produced by a monopolist. They find that the amount produced is an increasing function of the monopolist's sales of futures. In an extreme case with sufficiently large futures purchases by the monopolist, he produces zero output thus extracting the maximum profit from the futures market. This result partially characterizes a market "corner." Given this range of possible outcomes, Anderson and Sundaresan ask what are the equilibrium futures positions and find that, if the monopolist is risk-averse or the users of the monopolist's product hedge, there is a tendency for the monopolist to be short futures. Thus there is private demand for futures contracts for non-competitive goods when there is a significant hedging motive. Furthermore, in this setting, futures trading tend to be socially beneficial in the sense of increasing expected output.

Newbery's analysis differs from the Anderson and Sundaresan model in that the good is produced jointly by a dominant, risk-neutral firm and a competitive, risk-averse fringe. In this setting, the competitive producers tend to be short futures and the large producer tend to be long futures, thus leading to a reduction in the large producer's output. These tendencies are counterbalanced by the fact that the large firm's futures purchases raise the futures price and indirectly raise the output of the competitive fringe, thus reducing the cash market power of the large producer. Newbery concludes that a futures market would be a manipulative tool in the hands of a dominant producer. It is clear from a comparison with Anderson and Sundaresan, however, that allowing for risk aversion by the dominant producer or for hedging by end-users would modify Newbery's conclusion.

These studies consider two rather similar forms of imperfect competition and come to quite different conclusions. Consequently, further studies of other cash market structures are needed to provide a comprehensive basis for making broad statements of policy. For example, an important, nontrivial extension would be to allow for the good in question to be storable. Further, it may be important to consider market alternatives to futures and spot markets. For example, in his comment on Newbery in chapter 2, Phlips points out that dominant producers sometimes engage in price listing, a practice that could remove the incentive to trade futures. An interesting, open question is when, if ever, such a practice would dominate trading futures for a monopolist.

An extension in a different direction is suggested in Rosenthal's comment on Anderson and Sundaresan. He points out that Anderson and Sundaresan assume that the large producer takes into account the impact of his futures trading on the futures price, whereas the other traders are price-takers in the futures market (this comment is true also of Newbery's analysis). Rosenthal argues that it may be more satisfactory to assume all traders can potentially affect the futures price, which might be accomplished by modeling futures trading as a market game (see Shapley and Shubik 1977). However, it remains to be seen if this framework, which is designed to describe disequilibrium price adjustment, can yield a clear characterization of market equilibrium. Finally, both Anderson and Sundaresan and Newbery analyzed public information rational expectations equilibria. Clearly dominant firms may have informational advantages as well as market power based on size. Extending the analysis to allow for private information could produce significant additional insights.

Manipulation

There appears to be a widespread belief that futures markets are prone to manipulation. As mentioned previously, this belief clearly motivated the U.S. legislators in writing futures market regulations. Unfortunately, neither common usage nor specific legislation makes clear what exactly is involved in a futures market manipulation. And, although futures market practitioners are reasonably consistent in applying this term to certain problems that can arise when a futures contract approaches the delivery date, outsiders, including legislators and academics, are probably ignorant of this usage. It seems appropriate, then, to attempt to clarify what is meant by a futures market manipulation.

If we apply a dictionary definition of manipulation to futures markets, we would say it involves cleverly influencing futures prices. This very vague usage does make clear, however, that for a manipulation to occur someone (perhaps a group of firms) must have the power to influence market prices. In this sense, models of futures markets with powerful agents, such as those in Anderson and Sundaresan (chapter 3) or Newbery (chapter 2), are models of manipulation. However, because these models assume perfect information, no particular cleverness is involved; a producer is simply dominant, and he exploits this advantage as best he can. Cleverness and power come together in the usage of Chichilnisky (chapter 6) who, following the literature on noncooperative games with imperfect information, considers a market manipulation to be the strategic use of information or market signals. Stated in this way, we may imagine that manipulation would be the rule rather than the exception when agents' information differ; indeed, Chichilnisky does report a result that establishes the general existence of manipulation in such markets. It remains to be seen whether the institutions of futures markets specifically promote differential information and thus are more susceptible to being manipulated than other markets.

In the United States it is a criminal offense to manipulate futures markets. Not surprisingly then, the law contains the most extensive efforts to determine what constitutes a futures market manipulation. The definition of a futures market manipulation is not stated in the Commodity Exchange Act and thus has been left to the courts. In surveying the relevant case law, Johnson (1982) states that the proof of a futures market manipulation involves establishing that an alleged manipulator had the ability to set an artificial futures price, that he intended to bring about such a price, and that such a result has occurred. From the perspective of an economist, the crucial element in this is the notion of price artificiality. Although as a matter of principle, an artificial price is thought by the courts to be one that does not reflect the forces of supply and demand, in practice the test of an artificial price generally involves demonstrating that normal price relationships have been disturbed.

Several kinds of price relations have been used successfully in establishing manipulation. In some cases when the price of a futures contract immediately prior to delivery is high relative to the price of the delivered good immediately after delivery, the futures prices have been considered artificial. An alternative is to show that futures spreads have been distorted, particularly that the price of the contract in its delivery month is high relative to the price of a deferred contract. A third method is to show that the cash price of goods that are deliverable under the terms of the contract are high relative to the cash price of nondeliverable goods. This case is distinct from a fourth method that involves demonstrating that when multiple types of grades can be delivered under the contract, the price of the good that is normally cheapest to deliver is bid up to the price of goods normally more expensive to deliver. This last method (the disturbance of normal relations among the prices of deliverable grades) may seem a relatively lenient standard of price artificiality, and historically it may have been adopted in part to compensate for the difficulty of proving intent in manipulation. Nevertheless, it can be justified by an explicit model of futures trading as seen in Kyle (chapter 5) discussed later.

These tests of price artificiality differ significantly; however, they all share the common element that they concern relatively transient aberrations that are associated with meeting the delivery terms of a maturing futures contract. Thus a large producer who routinely uses his size to advantage in influencing a futures price clearly, on this account, is not manipulating the futures market. Even limiting the term manipulation to delivery month aberrations still covers some rather diverse phenomena, as can be illustrated by briefly reviewing some recent, alleged manipulations.

In March 1979 the Commodity Futures Trading Commission (CFTC) suspended the trading of the expiring wheat futures contract at the Chicago Board of Trade. The primary facts used to justify this action were that:

1. The long open interest in the March contract was concentrated in the hands of a small number of speculative traders.
2. These longs were maintaining these positions even as the delivery date was near.
3. The long open interest exceeded by a wide margin the amount of the good that was in deliverable position.
4. A shortage of transportation and warehouse space made it impossible to bring additional wheat into deliverable position (see Gray and Peck 1981).

These factors were seen as causing the price of the March Chicago wheat futures to be very high relative to the prices of other delivery months and very high relative to the price of cash wheat that was not deliverable because of the shortage of transportation. If these facts are correct, this case had all the ingredients of what is often called a "squeeze"—namely, because of a relative scarcity of deliverable supply the shorts are unable to fulfill all their commitments by delivery and, for the remainder, are obliged either to offset their positions at prices dictated by the longs or to default. In a squeeze the scarcity of deliverable supply does not occur because of any actions by the longs; all the longs need do is to notice the potential and maintain their open positions until late in the delivery period.

A second, alleged manipulation involved the May 1976 Maine potato contract at the New York Mercantile Exchange. During the delivery month, the price of the May futures (relative to other delivery months) fluctuated wildly; at expiration some shorts defaulted by failing to make delivery. As in the wheat situation, long open interest was concentrated in a few hands and exceeded the deliverable supply. In contrast, it was alleged that the longs contributed to the relative shortage by actively attempting to create a shortage of transportation facilities necessary to move potatoes to the delivery location and by spreading rumors with the intent of leading farmers to withhold their potatoes from normal commercial channels. If the longs did actively contribute to the shortage on the cash market, their actions would constitute what is widely called a "corner." The most direct way of attempting to corner a futures market would be to purchase a large amount of the deliverable supply; however, as is clear from the preceding description, it also could be attempted by monopolizing the means of converting non-deliverable goods into deliverable goods. In the 1976 potato contract the sharp fluctuations in price near maturity appeared to reflect a great uncertainty as to the disposition of open interest and of the physical stocks of deliverable goods so that information and, possibly, misinformation had a significant impact on price.

Finally, the fivefold increase of silver prices in 1979 and 1980 and their subsequent collapse is an alleged manipulation that has something in common with the preceding two cases but that differs from them in important respects. Early in this episode a number of buyers led by the Hunt family began to accumulate cash silver in many forms including some, such as silver mines, which were clearly not deliverable on the Commodity Exchange Inc. (Comex) or Chicago Board of Trade silver futures contracts. In conjunction with cash silver, the Hunts accumulated large silver futures spread positions where they were long the near-term contract and short the deferred contact. As contracts matured, the Hunts took delivery on some of these contracts, thus adding to their physical stocks (see Lieb 1981). The prices of silver, both cash and futures, increased in the fall of 1979 as the longs accumulated larger futures positions using the physical silver, valued at elevated prices, as collateral in obtaining the necessary initial margins for these positions. This process continued and accelerated until January 1980. By that time, not only were all silver prices very high by historical standards, but also the price of the Comex March silver was abnormally high relative to the deferred contracts. There followed a number of exchange actions that put downward pressure on prices and forced massive liquidation of the longs' positions and a precipitous decline of prices. The episode was essentially over well before the maturity date of the March contract.

Undoubtedly some consider this case as the most important attempted futures market manipulation in history. However, even this brief summary indicates that much more was involved than just a delivery-related distortion as in the wheat and potatoes cases. The full spectrum of silver prices—futures of all maturities and all cash silver—relative to the general price level was very high by historical standards, clearly reflecting broadbased buying only part of which was carried out by the Hunt family. Because demand for a precious metal such as silver is very largely based on the subjective wish to horde, it is difficult to say that prices did not reflect the forces of supply and demand. In this respect the episode did not involve a manipulation of the futures market in the sense used previously. If it was a temporary aberration it had more in common with speculative bubbles, which are discussed later. Only at the end of the period, when the price relations among silver futures of different delivery dates became distorted, did this episode involve the relative scarcity of deliverable supply and concentrated long open interest associated with the manipulation of futures markets. It is significant that the long open interest in the maturing contract was part of spread positions rather than flat positions, which served two purposes. First, if in advance of the corner, the speculative buying were to stop and silver prices generally were to fall, these spread positions would not have involved any substantial capital loss. Second, the initial margins required for spread positions are smaller than for flat positions so that by using spreads a given amount of capital could support a larger position in the market than would have been possible otherwise.

We have reviewed the legal view of futures market manipulations and have summarized the events in three alleged manipulation cases to delineate futures manipulations as economic phenomena. This indirect route was required because the alternative of surveying established economic theories of futures manipulation was impossible for the simple reason that until recently such theories did not exist. The ambiguity of the legal definitions of manipulations and the undeniable existence of distortions when some futures contracts mature make it clear that a theory of futures markets manipulations is needed. Furthermore, they are helpful in identifying the main ingredients of the needed theory.

The first and perhaps most important requirement for a theory of futures manipulations is that it characterize the delivery process of a futures market. That is, it should recognize that at delivery date the futures price will coincide with the price of an actual good that is specific with respect to grade and location. Such a theory would allow for at least two cash goods and thus at least one price relationship at delivery. Second, a manipulation theory would recognize that agents in these markets can exert market power. There may be a tendency for high concentrations on the long side of the maturing futures markets and perhaps on the short side as well. In general, we expect to characterize such markets as oligopolistic equilibria. For example, the events in the Maine potato case suggest a bilateral monopoly. Third, futures markets manipulations appear necessarily to involve imperfect information. If futures markets are particularly prone to manipulation, it is the result, in part, of the fact that at delivery time this market becomes effectively a local cash good market and is sensitive to detailed aspects of grading, inspection of goods, transportation, and warehouse facilities about which information is often difficult to obtain. Furthermore, imperfect information arises naturally in futures markets because of the anonymity provided by futures trading; large positions can be accumulated through brokers by a single buyer or seller without the knowledge of others in the market. At times, some information about position sizes becomes generally available; however, this information may be purposely leaked or may be misleading. Thus market signals may be very noisy, and there may be an incentive to engage in bluffing. Finally, a theory of manipulations would recognize that the futures markets in advance of delivery provides considerable leverage allowing large positions to be accumulated but at delivery time full payment is necessary requiring a buyer either to obtain financing for the stocks acquired or to resell these stocks immediately on the cash market.

Given a theory that incorporates these features, what questions should it address? First, what is a manipulation, or, alternatively stated, how does a manipulated futures market differ from a normal one? Second, can a manipulation arise in a market where rational agents voluntarily enter? This question is important because public policies aimed at correcting market failure generally differ from those intended to restrain the market participation of irrational agents. Third, what are the social costs of manipulations? In particular, it is important to distinguish transfers of wealth that may be undesirable on the basis of fairness from losses in welfare in the Pareto sense. The preceding discussion suggests that a manipulated market may well be a Pareto-inferior outcome because it often involves needless conversions of nondeliverable goods into deliverable goods through transportation or other means. (Sterling silverware was melted for bullion during the 1979–1980 silver episode.) Fourth, what policies are effective in reducing the frequency of manipulations? Current U.S. regulations that limit speculative position sizes are intended to reduce market manipulability. Margin requirements have been altered by exchanges during alleged manipulations. Futures contracts calling for cash settlement as opposed to physical delivery have recently been introduced, in part, because it is thought that these contracts are not prone to manipulation. The theoretical underpinnings for all these measures is currently not well understood. Finally, the economic bases for the legal test in manipulation cases need to be clarified. In particular, can an unambiguous meaning be given to the term "artificial price"?

Kyle presents a theory of futures markets manipulations in chapter 5 that incorporates some of these features and uses it to address some of the same public policy questions. Although Kyle provides a good discussion of the general issues that arise in futures markets' manipulations, his formal analysis is devoted to a particular model of squeezes involving two goods that are deliverable against a futures contract with one of them normally being the cheaper to deliver. There are three kinds of agents. Hedgers hold stocks of the cash goods and sell futures. Aggregate hedging takes on two levels, high and low. Speculators buy and sell futures. By assumption they are risk-neutral so that the futures price equals their expectation of the futures price at delivery. The only other agent is the squeezer who is like the speculators in that he deals only on the futures market, but unlike the speculators and hedgers, he has privileged information prior to trading about the size of aggregate hedging.

Kyle's chapter shows how the anonymity of futures trading provides a means for the squeezer to profit from his superior information. He recognizes that, if he holds long positions greater than the total supply of the cheaper-to-deliver good, he can force the price of the futures contracts to equal the price of the more expensive-to-deliver good—the essence of a squeeze. Under certain circumstances the squeezer can trade in such a way that he disguises his privileged information and squeezes the market when hedging is low. Specifically, when hedging is high the squeezer goes short futures; when it is low he goes long. The squeezer's positions are chosen so that the combined futures positions of the hedgers and the squeezer are the same in both cases; thus the speculators are unable to deduce the state of hedging from the aggregate trades they see in the market. Consequently, the price at which the speculators absorb this net supply of futures is a weighted average of the squeeze and no-squeeze prices. The squeezer makes money by squeezing the market because, after the state of hedging eventually becomes known, the futures price will rise and produce a profit for his long positions. Perhaps surprisingly, he also makes money when hedging is high and he does not squeeze, for then the price falls and his position is short.

Kyle's analysis shows that this pattern can emerge as a market equilibrium with all agents behaving rationally given their information. Furthermore, in this model a squeeze is apparent by the fact that the futures price at delivery equals the price of the more expensive-to-deliver grade, in which case the price could unambiguously be considered artificial. The profits earned by the squeezer represent a cost of dealing in futures for hedgers and induces less hedging than would occur otherwise. This is a social cost because hedgers bear risk that they would not if squeezes never occurred; as a result, they tend to produce less.

Kyle considers possible remedies to squeezes and argues that exchanges may be able to reduce the probability of squeezes through the choice of additional delivery locations and grades, although the solution to the problem is by no means obvious. Further, he shows that the imposition of position limits can sometimes, but not always, mitigate the consequences of squeezes. Position limits have the disadvantage that they still permit a squeeze to be engineered by a group of agents with privileged information who collude. Kyle argues that cash settlement does not eliminate the incentive to manipulate the futures market. Under cash settlement the maturing futures price is a function of more than one cash price. When one of the goods entering this calculation is in low supply an agent with privileged information would have the incentive to go long futures and then enter the cash market to bid up the price of the low-supply cash good. Although Kyle's argument has merit, it should be pointed out that to effect the manipulation the agent must act on the cash market after accumulating the futures position (in this sense it would be a corner); this may make it easier to establish willful manipulation after the fact and thus to impose penalties that remove the attractiveness of the manipulation. Finally, although he does not discuss it, Kyle's analysis clearly shows that a policy making the state of aggregate hedging public information would remove the possibility of profitably squeezing the market—for example, a disclosure law that makes all individual agents' positions public information.

Salant (chapter 5) shows that Kyle's game-theoretic analysis can be given a more familiar interpretation as an oligopolistic equilibrium where the informed agent maximizes profits by equating marginal revenue and marginal cost for a particular equilibrium price function. He then poses the interesting question of whether, under existing U.S. laws, the squeezer in Kyle's model does anything illegal. Although not coming to a definite conclusion, Salant suggests that, because the informed agent just maximizes profits given the price schedule he faces, he does not willfully deceive and thus may not have an intent to manipulate the market. Under existing laws, then, he would not have manipulated the market. This may be true, but a test of intent based on so intangible a thing as an equilibrium price function might have little impact in court. It seems more direct to reason that, if the squeezer arranges his trades so that they are imperceptible to other traders, presumably he is aware that he can profitably squeeze the market, which then suggests his intent to squeeze. Furthermore, as previously noted, the price that prevails in a squeeze is artificial by one of the standards that have been applied in actual manipulations cases. Therefore, it seems that Kyle's squeezer is guilty of manipulating the market under existing laws when he squeezes the market. On the other hand, even though he profits from his privileged information in the no-squeeze case, it appears he has not manipulated the market because the futures price at maturity is not artificial under current standards. Finally, as noted by Salant, Kyle's analysis does not take into account the effect of legal penalties for squeezing the market. Clearly, a lump-sum cost to squeezing could eliminate the incentive to squeeze; Kyle's analysis shows that the expected value of this penalty must exceed the probability-weighted average of both the squeeze profits and the no-squeeze profits if it is to be effective.

Both Kyle and Salant stress the special assumptions involved in the analysis. Consequently, considerably more work is needed before we can feel confident in the policy prescriptions that emerge from this line of work. In particular, it would be interesting to consider informed agents' multi-period strategies that involve taking cash as well as futures positions. This information seems necessary to characterize episodes like the 1979–1980 silver market.

Undesirable Speculation

In this section we survey research on the question of whether speculation on futures markets is socially undesirable. The issue of the desirability of speculation transcends the institutions of futures markets. The distinguished literature on the subject, which goes back at least to J.S. Mill, is too large to be thoroughly reviewed here. We focus primarily on those contributions devoted to futures speculation and group them into two categories: those favorable to speculation and those unfavorable to speculation.

Noneconomists generally have difficulty in understanding the workings of the invisible hand, so it is perhaps not surprising that economists have devoted considerable energy and imagination to explaining how the obvious greed of speculators is channeled by the market into socially beneficial activities. Some of these arguments have already been discussed. Another faction holds that speculation promotes price stability and is therefore desirable (this argument waives the issue of whether price stability promotes the optimal allocation of resources and risks).

Two related but distinct arguments can be made to show that futures trading promotes price stability. The first holds that by transferring risk it encourages storage, thus reducing the average intra-crop-year price variability for annually harvested, storable goods. The second is that a futures price tends to be a more accurate signal in formulating production plans than a producer's expectation of the spot price, which would determine production if there were no futures trading. These risk-transfer and informational arguments for the stabilizing effect of futures trading have been stated in a variety of ways and have been tested in several markets. (An excellent review of this literature is given in Kamara 1982.) On balance this literature presents a clear consensus view among economists that futures trading does not destabilize prices. It is notable that such relative harmony among economists has done little to modify the noneconomist's perception that futures speculation promotes unstable prices. To understand this entrenched view it is more instructive to consider the relatively small number of serious arguments less favorable to futures speculation.

In this vein it is useful to contemplate two facts that might convince some that futures speculation can sometimes destabilize prices. First, a significant proportion of futures market speculators use technical methods that extrapolate past price movements and consciously do not attempt to forecast fundamental supply and demand factors. Second, futures markets occasionally give rise to price "bubbles"; that is, prices rise sharply and steadily for a period immediately followed by a period of sharp, steady price declines. These facts could be interpreted as evidence of significant speculative behavior that tends to buy as a result of a price rise and sell as a result of a price fall and that could exaggerate price fluctuations initiated by the reception of information about fundamental supply and demand.

The idea that the presence of traders who follow trends may give an incentive to speculation to destabilize prices has been considered by a number of economists (see Hart 1977 for a rigorous treatment of the problem and references to earlier literature). Hart shows that when the asset demand is a function of present and lagged prices, a sufficient but not necessary condition for a speculator to find it desirable to perturb prices is that the demand function be dynamically unstable. Thus even if demand functions are stable, as we might plausibly expect, speculation could be destabilizing. The essence of a destabilizing strategy is to exploit properties of the asset demand function, in particular the cross-elasticies of price and lagged price. For example, if starting from an initial steady state, asset demand is an elastic function of spot price, a speculator can purchase a large amount while causing prices to rise only slightly. If later, in response to the initial small price change, demand became inelastic, the speculator could drive prices high with small purchases. Finally, if still later, the demand were to become elastic, the speculator could sell without depressing prices too severely, thus reaping a profit.

This description raises the obvious question (typically not addressed in this literature) of what forms of individual behavior could generate market demand functions that are exploitable in this way. It might be conjectured that it necessarily involves agents lacking the foresight to see through the speculator's strategy. Benninga (chapter 4) has argued that the daily pressures of marking to market naturally force futures traders to focus on recent price changes; he has constructed a model of futures price determination that assumes myopic behavior. The problem with such an approach is that it omits any incentive to trade to achieve risk transfer and thus does not seem to characterize hedging behavior (see Danthine 1983). Furthermore, there are unexploited riskless profit opportunities so that the agents do not appear to satisfy the standard properties of rationality (see Futia 1983).

The preceding discussion might be interpreted as saying that when some futures traders are irrational, it may be rational (that is, profitable) for other futures traders who recognize this irrationality to destablize prices. This interpretation raises a related but distinct issue of whether the presence of irrational speculators may in itself increase the variability of prices. Stone (1982) is explicitly concerned with this issue; he proposes raising margin requirements to discourage speculation by small, nonprofessionals. Stein (1983a) presents a formal model in which one group of speculators trades randomly while another trades on the basis of rationally formed expectations. He shows the variance of cash price is an increasing funcion of the number of irrational speculators.

If irrational speculation destabilizes prices, what is the empirical evidence supporting the existence of such speculation? However, this question may not be well posed for empirical research, for one might argue that any sequence of futures purchases and sales is consistent with some preferences and some information set. Stein (1983b) again considers a model with two speculator types but here all speculators are rational in the sense that on average their expectations about prices coincides with the true population mean. They have differential forecasting ability in the sense that one group's forecast error variance is less than the second's. He shows that under certain circumstances increasing the number of poor-forecasting speculators increases the variance of cash price. However, the variance-minimizing mix of speculators includes some of the poor forecasters; this is because the two groups' forecast errors are independent, presumably reflecting an assumption that they base their forecasts on separate information sets. Finally, ill-informed speculators contribute to price stability in the model of Kyle (1981) by providing an incentive for smart speculators to invest in costly information that is reflected in futures prices, thus ultimately inducing beneficial real allocation decisions.

Principal/Agent Problems

The Chain of Obligation in Futures Markets

In this section we consider relationships that permit one individual or firm (the principal) to arrange for a second individual or firm (the agent) to carry out actions on the principal's behalf. This process includes but is not limited to the relationship between an investor and his broker.

In a typical futures transaction, an investor can give orders to a futures commission merchant (FCM), the FCM in turn forwards the trade instructions to a floor broker who carries out the trade in the pit, and at the end of the day the floor trader clears this trade through a member of the clearing association. This chain can be more complicated; for example, the investor may delegate the responsibility of giving instructions to a commodity trading advisor or a commodity pool operator. In this process individuals who are initially agents become principals with respect to the individual encountered next in the chain.

Two basic problems arise in these relationships. First, how can one structure the relationship so that the agent has an incentive to work in the principal's best interest? Second, how can the agent assure the principal will fulfill his commitments? Under the first heading we briefly discuss fraud and dual trading. Under the second we discuss default risk, particularly focusing on the use of margins in futures markets.

Fraud

Fraud involves actions by one individual aimed at deriving benefit from deceiving and harming another individual. In futures trading, fraud does not generally involve an exploitation of the market as a whole. Consequently, until now it has been viewed exclusively as a question of law. However, the economic dimension to fraud in futures markets is worthy of study but has been entirely neglected by economists.

As is true for manipulations, the social cost of futures market fraud is that it discourages use of futures markets; thus, some hedgers bear unnecessary price risk. The legal remedy to fraud is to assess penalties for those cases which are detected, but penalties may be an ineffective deterrent if detection is difficult. Altering the structure of the principal/agent relationships may be a more effective means of reducing the frequency of fraud. Potentially, the theory of optimal contract design may clarify this issue (see Townsend, chapter 9), particularly in determining whether any third party intervention (for example, by the government) is necessary.

It might be argued that professionals in futures markets benefit from increased participation in the markets and thus have an incentive to structure trading relationships in a way that minimizes the probability of fraud. For certain kinds of fraud, such as individual misrepresentation where detection after the fact is relatively easy, this reasoning may be true. However, other cases may provide an incentive to make an already difficult detection problem even more difficult. The practice of churning an account (that is, inducing an investor to trade frequently to generate commissions) may be an example. When an investor deals directly with an FCM, he will be aware of the reasons for a series of trades and may recognize that the FCM induced him to trade more frequently than was in his interests. The perception of abuse is made more difficult if the investor participates in a commodity pool; in this case, he may be unable to determine whether the pool operator and the FCM have any arrangement for sharing commission income. Detection of fraud is also difficult in the allocation of trades. The potential for abuse arises because often an FCM will process a number of virtually simultaneous orders with a few trades for large blocks of contracts (see Johnson 1982, section 5.48). Because these trades normally occur at different prices, it is inevitable that some investors will receive less advantageous prices than others. It would be difficult for an investor to detect that an FCM had purposely given a favored account (perhaps a proprietary one) the best price while he had received a relatively unfavorable price.

Dual Trading

In U.S. futures markets the same individuals who act as agents in carrying out trades for others often trade for their own accounts. A number of regulations are intended to limit the actions of dual traders; however, the questions remain open whether the potential for abuse justifies these regulations and whether the regulations are effective. These issues have not yet been addressed in a rigorous manner.

The main abuse that dual trading invites is to use knowledge of customer orders to establish positions that derive profit at the detriment of the customers. The most direct form occurs when the agent takes the other side of the customer's trade without entering the public market; thus, the broker could sell to the customer at a relatively high price and later close out the position at the lower market price. To avoid this practice, U.S. regulations require all trades of a given futures contract to be executed in the pit of the designated exchange. The only significant exception is exchanges of cash positions for futures (Johnson 1982, section 1.13). This rule has the implication of largely preventing off-exchange and off-hours trading, which is widely practiced in American securities markets.

A less direct form of dual trading abuse occurs when brokers take positions in the market after receiving but before processing a customer's order (that is, the trader buys contracts on his own account immediately after receiving a large buy order). To prevent such trading, U.S. regulations require FCMs and floor brokers to process all customer orders before making any proprietary trades. However, enforcement of this rule is extremely difficult because it requires verifying what information the broker or FCM had at the time the proprietary trades took place. A U.S. regulation that requires floor brokers to record to the nearest minute the time of all transactions has received enormous industry opposition and has never been enforced. Even if transaction time records could be kept, the task of reconstructing the exact order of information receipt and trade execution still would be difficult without heavy surveillance.

Perhaps the most convincing evidence of dual trading abuses is the fact that many large commercial users of futures buy seats on the exchange and have all trades executed by employees who are prohibited from trading futures. Because this alternative is feasible for only a handful of users, it appears a safe assumption that other futures users sometimes do lose as a result of dual trading abuses. However, there is clear need for better information on the extent of such abuses. Furthermore, the issue of how a dual trading abuse may be detected without heavy cost is completely unresolved. Finally, there has been no serious attempt to assess the impact of banning dual trading on the viability of futures trading.

Default

In principle the risk of default in a market for deferred delivery is either that the seller of the contract will fail to deliver the goods specified or that the buyer will fail to make payment for the goods. If, after the contract is established, the spot price rises (falls), there is an incentive for the short (long) to default. In informal forward contracting, default risk is controlled by (1) dealing only with traders who have secure financial reputations, (2) demanding partial prepayment, or (3) requiring collateral. In futures markets, default risk is controlled principally by (1) a clearing association standing as a third party to each trade, thus pooling risks much as an insurance company does, and (2) marking all positions to market—that is, when the market price rises the sellers are required to pay the buyer an amount equal to the price rise times the quantity involved in the contract. The role of the clearing associations in reducing default risk faced by individuals has been emphasized by Telser (1981b); in his view this feature creates the high liquidity of futures markets. In fact, the institution of marking to market is crucial to reducing the individual incentives to default and indirectly the aggregate default risk.

When positions are marked to market, a party defaults if he fails to make the required cash payment; upon default, his position is liquidated by an offsetting trade. If this process occurs continuously, the incentive to default is reduced to the minimum increment of price. To reduce transaction costs, marking to market takes place discontinuously (at the level of the clearing association it is typically done daily; although, when price changes are large, it can occur more frequently). Consequently, even when positions are marked to market there does remain a nonnegligible incentive to default. This residual risk is controlled by requiring margins to be posted.

Margins in futures markets are performance bonds (in the form of cash or securities) required of both buyers and sellers; these bonds are relinquished in the case of default. They have been discussed extensively by Telser (1981a). As described earlier in this section, a futures transaction usually involves an extended chain of obligations; there is a risk of nonperformance at each link of the chain. Consequently, at each link the agent will require the principal to post a margin. Thus, the clearing association requires margin of the clearing member, the clearing member requires margin of the nonclearing member, and so on. Generally, the amount of margin posted will be mutually negotiated by the principal and agent in light of the perceived financial standing of the agent. For example, an FCM will require an investor to keep a balance in his account above a maintenance level. (He may request an additional amount as a cushion to avoid the necessity of communication and transactions for minor fluctuations of price.) This maintenance margin will typically differ from the amount of margin required by the clearing association or (if the FCM is not a member of the clearing association) by the clearing member servicing the FCM. However, futures exchanges (as distinct from clearing associations; see the discussion later in this chapter) set minimum margins that the FCMs must require of their customers (see Johnson 1982, section 2.43). This form of self-regulation is important in futures markets; it implies that restricting default risk carries a external benefit in the form of promoting confidence in the markets as a whole. With few exceptions, margins in futures markets are not now subject to governmental regulation.

Although margins in futures markets have been studied in the past, a number of unresolved questions concerning default risk merit further work. For example, what is the risk of default in futures markets and who bears that risk? A common assumption is that, because the clearing association gives a third-party guarantee, default risk is negligible for the individual. In fact, the clearing association reduces the risk, but its guarantee is limited and not fully specified in advance. Thus in the May 1976 Maine potato market, when the shorts failed to deliver the potatoes, the clearing association settled with the longs by making a cash payment based on a price that reflected supply and demand conditions as perceived by a special exchange committee. Furthermore, if price changes are sufficiently dramatic and swift, individual defaults may be so large that a clearing association itself may default. This possibility was discussed in relation to the 1979–1980 silver bubble.

Edwards (chapter 7) has examined the various forms of clearing associations in a way that helps in assessing the likelihood of their default. His analysis shows that the risk of a clearing association default depends on the size of the clearing association margin requirements; whether the association uses a gross or net margin system (in a net margin system, a member FCM posts the absolute value of the difference of the margins for long positions and the margins for short positions); capital requirements for clearing members; and the size of the association's guarantee fund. He demonstrates that in the event of a clearing association default the non-defaulting individual will look to his FCM for performance, so that the creditworthiness of the FCM is potentially important. This study raises many issues that were previously swept aside by a vague allusion to third-party guarantees and that show in futures markets financial obligations involve brokerage houses and the banking system as well as the clearing associations.

An open public policy issue concerning margins is whether minimum margins should be set by governmental regulation. From a theoretical perspective, this comes down to asking whether there is any externality in setting margins which is not effectively internalized by self-regulation at the level of the futures exchange. The argument in favor of government margin-setting is not that current margins permit excessive default risk-taking but rather that higher margins would limit the participation of ill-informed speculators (see Stone 1982). Even if such limits are desirable (which may be open to question; see the discussion earlier in this chapter), the effectiveness of minimum margins as a barrier to market participation may be limited because margins can be posted in the form of interest-bearing securities (see Anderson 1981). Finally, this issue has been given another dimension the fact that futures contracts are now traded for securities; the cash market trading of securities is subject to minimum margins set by the U.S. Federal Reserve Board (FED). Because trading a security and a futures on that security may hold similar risks, some have been led to argue that FED margin requirements should apply to certain futures contracts. This reasoning begs the question of whether FED margin requirements are justified in the first place and ignores the fact that the margin system for securities differs markedly from that in futures markets. Nevertheless, the proposal has considerable political appeal, which in turn raises a significant practical question: what are the consequences of imposing FED margin requirements for futures trading?

Futures Exchanges

The Product of an Exchange

In this section we focus on futures exchanges themselves, specifically their economic efficiency. We start by clarifying what is meant by the product of a futures exchange. Telser stresses that a futures market is distinguished from a forward market by the former's relatively higher liquidity. Thus we could say that the product of a futures exchange is liquidity in price risk shifting. Although this definition is somewhat vague, it makes clear that the reduction of transaction costs is at the heart of futures trading. Perhaps because of the complexity of the issues involved, economists have tended to neglect the questions of how exchanges go about providing liquidity in risk shifting and the role of exchange competition in this process. The exception is the widely noted tendency for a futures contract for a given product to be traded only at a single exchange. This tendency results from the fact that when facing similar futures contracts both hedgers and speculators will tend to select the market with the higher volume because it is more liquid. Thus when a significant difference in liquidity exists between very similar futures, almost inevitably, the liquid one will dominate and the less liquid market will fail. The cases where more than one market for a good exist are usually explained by significant differences in the delivery specifications (for example, the wheat contracts on the Chicago Board of Trade, Kansas City Board of Trade, and the Minneapolis Grain Exchange). The rule "one good, one future market" reflects what might be regarded as a natural monopoly in providing futures for a given good.

Turning to the issue of how futures exchange provide liquidity in shifting the price risk, it is useful to consider three concrete means: contract designs, transaction technologies, and speculative services of exchange members. All aspects other than price of a futures contract are fixed by the futures exchange. In selecting a type of good, the quantity, grade, the delivery means, location, and date, the exchange attempts to make a futures contract attractive to a large number of hedgers and speculators. The same aim motivates the design of the exchange floor, communications facilities, and trade reporting means that determine the transaction technology. By using these methods to promote a high volume of trading, exchanges reduce the bid/ask spread and thus the cost of transaction (see the discussion in the first section of this chapter). In supplying speculative services, the incentives for the exchange may run in the opposite direction.

The exchange affects the supply of speculative services principally in determining the number of exchange memberships. In making this decision, an exchange will reflect the interests of floor trading members that membership be restricted so that a nonzero bid/ask spread is preserved. The membership decision of an exchange is complicated in that it must weigh the implications of an additional member on competition among floor traders in the exchange and on competition with other exchanges. In chapter 8, Saloner proposes a model of a futures exchange that addresses these issues. He shows that given the size of the membership, competition among exchange members determines the bid/ask spread; therefore a futures exchange that seeks to maximize total exchange member profits will set the number of memberships such that the bid/ask spread exactly equals the full value of risk reduction that hedgers achieve by trading futures. Finally, he shows that competition among exchanges does not eliminate the full extraction of the surplus by the futures exchange. That is, when two exchanges trade the same futures contract, many equilibria are possible; however, all equilibria have the property that the total number of seats on the two exchanges combined equals that number such that the bid ask/spread is same as that selected by a single exchange. This modifies the view expressed previously that there is a natural monopoly in futures trading for a given good; it shows that more than one exchange may trade the good but that the bid/ask spread on all exchanges will equal the monopoly solution.

Saloner's work is an important first attempt at modeling the behavior of futures exchanges. However, it is based on a number of simplifications that ideally should be relaxed in further work. For example, he assumes that exchange members earn profits only from the bid/ask spread. In fact, some members earn income from commissions as FCMs. Because an investor's transaction cost includes both the commission and the bid/ask spread, it is in the interest of the FCMs to see that the exchange membership be so large as to drive the bid/ask spread to zero, thus increasing the amount that can be charged in commissions. This division of preferences raises the issue of exchange governance (see the following discussion). A further complication is that members typically are free to trade all the contracts at an exchange and that the external demand for these contracts randomly changes over time, which introduces a dynamic joint-product aspect to the problem that may modify the results significantly.

If the preceding discussion tentatively shows that, in the provision of floor trader services, futures exchanges tend to act as monopolists, it raises the question of whether this implies any market failure and, if so, whether this inefficiency may be corrected by regulatory intervention. Although this is an interesting, unexplored question, a proper answer would consider other forms of exchange competition. In particular, costly competition among exchanges in the development of new contracts or in new transaction technologies may offset the transaction profits earned by exchange members so that the social benefits are equated with social costs.

The most important study of competition in futures contract innovation is Silber (1981). He considers new contracts introduced on American futures exchanges from 1960 to 1980. He finds that the pace of innovation was high (130 new contracts or significant modifications of old contracts); the failure rate was high (75 percent had a volume of less than 10,000 contracts in the third year following the innovation); imitative contract designs are very likely to fail; and apparently slight differences in contract design can determine whether the contract succeeds or fails. He concludes that despite the oligopolistic structure of the futures industry, rivalry among exchanges effectively promotes new contract innovations. Further, he sees no reason for public regulation of new contracts.

Although Silber discusses case studies that demonstrate that the success of a contract can turn on detailed aspects of contract design, he does not attempt to state the determinants of success in a futures contract. Despite the obvious importance of the question no comprehensive analysis of the issue has been attempted. Most of the serious thinking about this question has been done at the economics departments of futures exchanges, and the oral tradition that has emerged suggests the elements which should be incorporated in a theory of new contract innovation.

Factors affecting the likelihood of success in a futures contract innovation fall into three categories: economic environment, contract specification, and management of the new contract in its infancy. One obvious precondition for the successful introduction of a futures contract is that there be significant price uncertainty for the good specified in the contract. If prices vary little, hedgers have no incentive to shift risks and speculators perceive no potential gains in trading futures. Next, the hedgers' demand for a contract is likely to be affected by the availability and cost of alternative forms of risk transfer. For example, if forward contracting is highly liquid in the cash market, demand for futures may be slight unless futures trading involved significantly lower transactions costs. A related point is that hedging demand for futures will be affected by the degree of vertical integration in the relevant sector. The heaviest commercial users of futures markets are typically cash good merchandisers. Thus when the various stages of handling, shipping, and processing the good are carried out by the same firm, hedging demand for futures may be slight.

The design of a futures contract involves a large number of detailed specifications, which, as noted by Silber, may prove to be important in determining the probability of its trading successfully. Beyond identifying the good to be delivered, the contract will specify quantity and grade. Despite their apparent triviality, for goods where there are no established industry standards, these aspects may prove to be stumbling blocks for a new contract. Similarly, selecting delivery location can be decisive. In any of these matters there is a tradeoff between having a broadly defined contract permitting delivery of a variety of grades or at a variety of locations and having a narrowly defined one. Because when multiple deliveries are possible the exact choice is an option for the short, broad contracts generally would be thought to favor the shorts at the expense of the longs; however, this point is mitigated by the fact that the shorts may pay a premium for this option in the form of a downward bias to the futures price (see Yamey 1971 for a discussion of this point). Furthermore, the success of the contract may be affected by the precise means of performance. Seevers (1981) notes the differences between a contract that requires the short to deliver physical goods versus one that allows him to deliver a warehouse receipt that is a claim on physical goods. Also, certain recently introduced contracts dispense with the delivery of assets entirely and instead call for cash settlement based on some reference price or some index of reference prices (see Jones 1982).

Finally, even if an attractively specified contract is introduced when the economic environment is receptive, success may still require proper management by an exchange during the early stages of trading. In part this may be a matter of education. Perhaps even more important is the extent that the new contract is supported by floor speculators. If only a few, relatively undercapitalized floor traders are active in a new contract, the bid/ask spread will be large and prospective off-exchange users will be discouraged from entering the market. Consequently, an established futures exchange with an existing pool of large floor traders may have an advantage in introducing new futures contracts. The high failure rate for new futures exchanges (as opposed to contracts; see Silber 1981) may be evidence of this tendency. However, further study of this issue is needed.

Market Microstructure

U.S. futures markets share a common method of transacting that differs from the method of transacting in either U.S. stock exchanges or commodity futures markets outside the United States. It is characterized by trading taking place in a centralized pit as a continuous, bilateral auction. The important role of the scalper in this process has been discussed previously. Why this trading system has emerged and its merits relative to alternative systems are interesting issues that deserve serious study.

Two comparative studies would be particularly interesting. One would compare the futures trading method with that used in U.S. stock markets. In the latter the specialist serves as market maker and establishes the bid/ask spread. The issue is whether this system tends to promote greater or smaller transactions costs than scalping. The second study would compare U.S. futures trading with the forward trading practiced at the London Metal Exchange (LME). In contrast with U.S. futures where trading may occur continuously during the trading session, formal trading among LME dealers is concentrated daily at two brief sessions or "rings," along with less formal trading outside these sessions. An open question is whether such discontinuous trading gives rise to different price behavior (for example, in the bid/ask spread) than continuous trading.

Two structural aspects of U.S. futures markets deserve study. First, most futures markets impose daily price limits (a maximum increase or decrease over the previous day's settlement price) to prevent excessive price swings. However, whether limits effectively stabilize prices is open to question. Further, how to best determine the limits has not been addressed. Second, most futures markets use a settlement process to determine the price of the day's final transactions and the price to be used for marking positions to market. This process involves some averaging of bids and offers in the closing moments of trading; however, the details of the process differ from exchange to exchange and, despite the importance of the outcomes to all futures participants, are little understood outside the community of floor traders.

Many other interesting aspects of marketing microstructure have not been studied, such as the relationship of spread trading sessions with trading for level positions. Finally, a potentially controversial issue is the feasibility and desirability of new trading technologies. In particular, advances in telecommunications raise the prospect of replacing the trading floor and market-making speculators with a computerized marketplace where principals would trade directly. Such a technological innovation could affect futures trading profoundly. The main questions are whether the change is desirable and whether it can be expected to emerge from the existing futures market institutions.

Exchange Organization

In this section we consider the active role of futures exchanges in determining the character of futures trading. In the United States, futures exchanges are nonprofit corporations whose owners (called members) have the exclusive rights of executing trades on the floor of the exchange and of participating in exchange decisionmaking. There have been few economic studies of futures exchanges themselves; however, a number of interesting questions are worthy of investigation. These can be grouped under three headings: membership, exchange structure, and exchange decisionmaking.

The only study of exchange memberships is Saloner (1983), discussed previously, who addresses the issue of how an exchange determines the number of memberships. The composition of the membership has not been studied, and an obvious but unanswered question is: who are the existing futures exchange members? Because one of the main privileges of membership is the right to trade on the exchange floor, an important type of member is the floor speculator. Remaining members are drawn from other futures market participants, including commission houses, pool operators, and commercial hedgers. There appears to be an informal consensus that floor speculators have a dominant say in exchange affairs, which suggests that this group may hold the most memberships. An empirical study of the composition of membership is needed to verify this conjecture.

A separate set of issues arises if membership is viewed as an asset and its price is considered. One line of inquiry would be to derive an appropriate asset valuation model that could be used to consider whether seat memberships are priced efficiently. Alternatively, by considering the effect of regulatory changes on membership values, we could shed light on the question of whose interests futures market regulation promotes.

The organization of futures exchanges can illuminate their functions.

U.S. futures exchanges separate the function of ensuring contract performance from other activities. The former is the responsibility of the clearing association; in some cases this association is a division of the futures exchange and in others it is a distinct legal entity. In all cases membership in the clearing association is more restrictive than membership in the corresponding exchange. In chapter 7, Edwards studies the organization of futures market clearing associations and finds significant differences among the various associations with respect to financial requirements for members, types of assets accepted as margin, the mode of calculating margin requirements (for example, net margins vs. gross margins), existence and size of guarantee funds, and rules for the financial liability of members. As discussed previously Edwards clarifies the nature of default guarantees in futures markets. However, he does not address the feasibility of centralized clearing. Under a system of centralized clearing, futures positions at one exchange could be used to offset positions at another exchange. This could be advantageous to users if the futures for the same good is traded on more than one exchange with different trading times and dates.

The organization of futures exchanges themselves as distinct from clearing associations has not been subjected to careful comprehensive study. A study similar to Edwards's would be useful in clarifying the diverse functions of futures exchanges. The management of futures exchanges is carried out both by members through a variety of committees and by nonmember employees of the exchange; however, the exact separation of responsibilities is unclear and may differ across exchanges. Furthermore, it would be useful to know the range of member committees' responsibilities.

In considering decisionmaking at futures exchanges, the overriding question is what is the appropriate paradigm for decisions by an exchange? Is it legitimate to view an exchange as a firm maximizing some objective function? If so, what objective function? One view is that the exchange may maximize the value of an exchange membership; this problem would become well defined only when we had a clear understanding of the determinants of the price of a membership. Saloner (chapter 8) views the exchange as maximizing the aggregate of trader profits earned from the bid/ask spread. This perspective implicitly assumes the validity of the conjecture that floor speculator interests dominate those of other member groups in exchange decisionmaking. The idea that some exchange members may have interests in conflict with other members suggests that exchanges may face a problem of social choice.

In principle, this does not necessarily distinguish exchanges from business firms because when markets are incomplete the latter are also characterized by potential conflicts of interest among shareholders (see Grossman and Hart 1979). However, the separate interests of floor speculators, FCMs, and commercial hedgers are so apparent as to raise the possibility of another paradigm for exchanges that would put primary emphasis on conflict. If this view is adopted, the natural question becomes what determines which interests will prevail or how compromises emerge? Seevers (1981) has expressed the view that exchanges are essentially political organizations but that they tend to overrepresent the interest of floor speculators and underrepresent the interest of hedgers. This view appears to be an underlying motivation for public regulation of contract design and other exchange functions. Because the appropriateness of such regulation is a matter of current public policy debate, it is clearly important to learn more than we currently know about how decisionmaking actually takes place at futures exchanges.

Conclusion

In surveying the industrial organization of futures markets, we have shown that a diverse range of topics that largely falls outside the mainstream of past studies offers many opportunities for innovative research. A few topics, such as scalping, have already been studied, and the state of knowledge is reasonably advanced. More often, work on a topic has just began. For example, the recent contributions on decisionmaking by exchanges suggest many potentially fruitful avenues of study. Some topics, such as dual trading, have not been touched at all. Consequently, our survey has been as much a program for research as it has been a literature review.

These topics are both intellectually interesting and—for example, because of advances in the theory of information economics and the theory of imperfect competition—can now be addressed more successfully now than would have been possible a decade ago. This is not the only reason that the time is right for research on the industrial organization of futures market. Many of these topics are directly relevant to current public policy debate concerning futures markets. Since 1972, there has been enormous price volatility on the one hand and unprecedented growth of futures trading on the other. Has the increased futures trading exacerbated the price volatility? Has the expansion of futures trading into new economic sectors been desirable? Do existing rules and regulations for futures trading work in the public interest? These are some of the questions now being discussed. The outcome of the debate could be significant changes in regulations that may affect the institutional environment of futures trading for decades to come. The role that economists play in these public policy discussions will depend in part on their ability to address convincingly the issues we have surveyed.

References

Anderson, R.W. (1981). "Comment on 'Margins and Futures Contracts,' " *Journal of Futures Markets*, vol. 1, pp. 259–264.

————. and Danthine, J.P. (1983). "Hedger Diversity in Futures Markets," *Economic Journal*, vol. 93, pp. 370–389.

Arrow, K.J. (1981). "Futures Markets: Some Theoretical Perspectives," *Journal of Futures Markets*, vol. 1, pp. 107–115.

Debreu, G. (1959). *The Theory of Value*. New York: Wiley.

Edwards, F.R. (1981). "The Regulation of Futures Markets: A Conceptual Framework," *Journal of Futures Markets*, vol. 1, pp. 417–439.

Gray, R.W., and Peck, A.E. (1981). "The Chicago Wheat Futures Market: Recent Problems in Historical Perspective," *Food Research Institute Studies*, vol. 18, pp. 89–115.

Grossman, S.J., and Hart, O.D. (1979). "A Theory of Competitive Equilibrium in Stock Market Economies," *Econometrica*, vol. 47, pp. 293–329.

Hart, O.D. (1975). "On the Optimality of Equilibrium when the Market Structure is Incomplete," *Journal of Economic Theory*, vol. 11, pp. 418–443.

————. (1977). "On the Profitability of Speculation," *Quarterly Journal of Economics*, vol. 90, pp. 579–597.

Hieronymous, T.A. (1977). *Economics of Futures Trading*, 2d ed. New York: Commodity Research Bureau.

Johnson, P.M. (1982). *Commodities Regulation*. Boston: Little, Brown.

Jones, F. (1982). "The Economics of Futures and Options Based on Cash Settlement," *Journal of Futures Markets*, vol. 2, pp. 63–82.

Kamara, A. (1982). "Issues in Futures Markets: A Survey," *Journal of Futures Markets*, vol. 2, pp. 261–294.

Keynes, J.M. (1923). "Some Aspects of Commodity Markets," *Manchester Guardian Commercial*. European Reconstruction Series, section 13, pp. 784–786.

Kyle, A.S. (1981). "An Equilibrium Model of Speculation and Hedging" (unpublished dissertation, University of Chicago).

Lieb, B. (1981). "The Aftermath of Hunt: A New Look at Speculation, Manipulation, and the Regulation of the Futures Industry" (unpublished B.A. thesis, Princeton University).

Magill, M.A.J., and Cheng, H-C. (1982). "Futures Markets, Diversification of Risk and the Optimality of Production," USC Department of Economics, *Working Paper* 8216.

Martell, T.F., and Helms, B.P. (1979). "A Reexamination of Price Changes in the Commodity Futures Market," *International Futures Trading Seminar, Proceedings*. Chicago Board of Trade, pp. 136–152.

Newbery, D.M.G., and Stiglitz, J.E. (1981). *The Theory of Commodity Price Stabilization*. Oxford: Oxford University Press.

Seevers, G. (1981). "Comment on 'Innovation, Competition and New Contract Design in Futures Contracts,' " *Journal of Futures Markets*, vol. 1, pp. 157–159.

Shapley, L.S., and Shubik, M. (1977). "Trading Using One Commodity as a Means of Payment," *Journal of Political Economy*, vol. 85, pp. 937–968.

Silber, W.L. (1981). "Innovation, Competition, New Contract Design in Futures Contracts," *Journal of Futures Markets*, vol. 1, pp. 123–155.

Stein, J.L. (1979). "Spot, Forward and Futures," *Research in Finance*, vol. 1, pp. 225–310.

———. (1981). "Speculative Price: Economic Welfare and the Idiot of Chance," *Review of Economics and Statistics*, vol. 63, pp. 223–232.

———. (1983a). "Rational, Irrational, and Overregulated Speculative Markets," *Research in Finance*, vol. 5, ed. R. Lanzilotti and Y. Peles.

———. (1983b). "Real Effects of Futures Speculation," unpublished.

Stone, J.M. (1982). Letter to the U.S. House of Representatives, Committee on Agriculture.

Telser, L.G. (1981a). "Margins and Futures Contracts," *Journal of Futures Markets*, vol. 1, pp. 225–253.

———. (1981b). "Why Are There Organized Futures Markets?" *Journal of Law and Economics*, vol. 24, pp. 1–22.

———. and Higinbotham, H.N. (1977). "Organized Futures Markets: Costs and Benefits," *Journal of Political Economy*, vol. 85, pp. 969–1000.

Townsend, R. (1978). "On the Optimality of Forward Markets," *American Economic Review*, vol. 68, pp. 54–66.

Working, H. (1953a). "Futures Trading and Hedging," *American Economic Review*, vol. 43, pp. 314–343.

———. (1953b). "Hedging Reconsidered," *Journal of Farm Economics*, vol. 35, pp. 544–561.

———. (1954). "Price Effects of Scalping and Day Trading," reprinted in *Selected Writings of Holbrook Working*, ed. A. Peck. Chicago: Chicago Board of Trade (1977).

———. (1967). "Tests of a Theory Concerning Floor Trading on Commodity Exchanges," *Food Research Studies*, vol. 7 (supplement), pp. 5–48.

Yamey, B. (1971). "Short Hedging and Long Hedging in Futures Markets," *Journal of Law and Economics*, vol. 14, pp. 413–434.

2

The Manipulation of Futures Markets by a Dominant Producer

David M.G. Newbery

The recent development of futures markets in crude oil and oil products raises in an acute form the question of how futures markets operate for commodities whose production is dominated by large producers or cartels. Does the presence of a futures market reduce or increase the market power of the dominant producer? Should consumers encourage the development of such markets or regulate and restrict their operation? Does the market power of the dominant producer in the cash market have any counterpart in the futures market? In particular, does a dominant producer have an incentive to manipulate futures markets? Clearly, these and other questions about the performance of futures markets for imperfectly competitively produced commodities require us to go beyond the standard perfectly competitive models.

The tradition of treating primary commodities as though they are produced and traded under conditions of perfect competition is surprisingly strong and needs questioning quite apart from the case of oil. In the first place, many governments, in both developed and developing countries, intervene in agricultural markets, so that the natural unit of production is arguably the country, rather than the individual farmer or plantation. These countries often produce a significant share of world production. For minerals, the same companies reappear in many different countries, and the largest companies control a significant fraction of world production. Newbery (1981) lists eight commodities for which single countries controlled more than 50 percent of world trade, and another thirteen for which single countries controlled between 25 and 50 percent (averaged over the 1977–1979 period). Interestingly, Saudi Arabian oil just qualified in this period with 26 percent (and may not when 1981–1982 data are reviewed), whereas Brazilian coffee was excluded over this period with only 17 percent.

Second, to the extent that primary producers have long been concerned about both the stability and level of commodity prices, repeated attempts have been made to establish commodity agreements or cartels of varying degrees of formality and durability; such cartels have been potentially large

---

The views expressed here are those of the author alone and do not necessarily reflect those of the World Bank. I am indebted to Ron Anderson for useful discussions on this topic.

35

relative to the market and well placed to trade on the established futures markets. Of the twenty-one commodities with single country trade shares above 25 percent, at least nine have futures markets (table 2–1). In addition, bauxite was one of the commodities, and there is a futures market in aluminum. Copper, coffee, and cocoa, all with active futures markets and moderate producer concentration, did not appear on the original list but are included in table 2–1 for completeness.

It therefore seems important to model the behavior of dominant commodity producers confronted with the choice of trading on futures markets. Apart from any other reason, there are powerful incentives, as mentioned later, for producers to be discreet about any attempt to manipulate futures markets; hence manipulation will be difficult unless the motives and strategies of such agents can be clarified. Finally, there is evidence that the coffee cartel engaged in extensive market manipulation in the 1977–1979 period, so that the subject is of more than academic interest. (See the fascinating accounts in Greenstone 1981 and Edmunds 1982.)

This chapter shows that if all agents have access to the same information and can predict the production and trading strategy of the dominant producer, the dominant producer has an incentive to manipulate the futures market to benefit his position in the cash market, but nevertheless his futures trading activity reduces the bias in the market. Moreover, his market power in the futures market diminishes the more competitive speculators enter the market, and the less averse to risk they are. The second result is that if agents

Table 2–1
Shares of Individual Countries in World Trade of Commodities Traded on Futures Markets
(1977–1979 Average)

Country	Product	Share (%)
USA	Maize	73
Australia	Wool (greasy)	60
Malaysia	Rubber	51
USA	Wheat	39
Malaysia	Tin	36
USA	Cotton	29
Saudi Arabia	Oil	26
Canada	Barley	25
Cuba	Sugar	25
Ghana	Cocoa	23
Chile	Copper	19
Brazil	Coffee	17

Sources: World Bank. *Commodity Trade and Price Trends*. Baltimore: Johns Hopkins University Press (1981);
United Nations. *FAO Trade Yearbook 1979*. Rome: Food and Agriculture Organization.

have the same information but cannot observe the production decision of the dominant producer, that producer may have an incentive to follow randomized production strategy (or to randomize his storage decision.) However, unless fringe producers are very risk-averse, this strategy will an unattractive.

The next section discusses the role of information and the importance of specifying what the different market participants know when making their decisions. It is followed by the model of the futures market and a demonstration that, assuming the dominant producer is less risk-averse than the fringe producers, he would benefit from the collapse of the futures market. The incentives for manipulating the futures market when agents have full information, first as a large speculator, then as a large producer, are described next, demonstrating that the dominant producer benefits from manipulation, no matter what the source of risk. The final section discusses the extent to which the dominant producer can benefit from varying his decisions from year to year when his competitors cannot observe the current decision, but can only predict the average supply.

The Role of Information in the Manipulation of Futures Markets

The simplest model in which to examine the incentives for futures market manipulation is one of a nonstorable agricultural final consumption commodity produced in an annual cycle. At the time of planting the future weather (and hence output) are uncertain, as, consequently, is the post-harvest market clearing price p. Because the commodity is neither stored nor further processed, the only agents concerned are the producers, consumers, and speculators. I shall assume that consumers have no incentive to hedge, and so the only participants in the futures market will be the producers and speculators.[1] The futures market opens at the start of the crop season, and the contract expires after the harvest is in and the spot market clearing price has been established. Thus farmers make their production decisions at the same time as choosing their futures trades and knowing the futures price p^f.

Because we are modeling manipulation by a dominant producer, I assume that there is one dominant producer (to be thought of as the marketing board of a large exporting country, or its counterpart for a cartel) facing a fringe of competititve small producers—the farmers in the rest of the world. The dominant producer is well organized enough to arrange adequate income insurance for its own farmers (for example, through domestic price supports and direct transfers) and larger enough to secure adequate intertemporal income smoothing by borrowing and lending, so that it acts as a risk neutral agent (see Newbery and Stiglitz 1981, pp. 201–204). The fringe farmers are risk-averse.

The first and crucial issue to address in discussing market manipulation is what information the various participants have and what use they make of it in choosing their strategies. It is convenient to distinguish three cases, with very different implications for market manipulability. At one extreme, the dominant producer may hold rational expectations about demand and supply conditions whereas the fringe producers may follow some naive forecasting or decision rule. This implies that the dominant producer knows what this decision rule is and can compute the fringe decisions given information available at the start of the crop year, and, given his own decisions, can predict the joint distribution of his output and the market clearing price (or a sufficient statistic of the distribution—see Newbery and Stiglitz 1981, chaps. 10 and 11). Clearly, the dominant producer is well placed to manipulate futures markets and to exploit his superior information and forecasting ability. Hart (1977) has studied this form of manipulation, which relies on being able to mislead the other agents systematically and hence cause them to make losses. It appears that the alleged coffee market manipulation described by Greenstone (1981) and Edmunds (1982) relied on this strategy, because in 1977 the cartel bought July futures heavily and also bought physical coffee to prevent it reaching the market to squeeze the market. Had speculators possessed the same information as the cartel (in particular, the cartel's plans), this maneuver would not have succeeded.

At the other extreme, all agents may have access to the same information when making their decisions, and hold rational expectations, in the sense that they know the model which describes the (stochastic) determination of market equilibrium. This situation would occur if agents knew the objectives (utility functions), production functions, nature of demand, and the joint probability distribution describing the stochastic elements, and were able to compute the equilibrium choices of all agents. There is thus complete symmetry of information.

The third possibility lies between the two extremes, though closer to the full rational expectations equilibrium just described. Agents have full information about production and utility functions and the nature of risk, but cannot observe production decisions. In an unchanging world in long-run equilibrium, agents could make the same production decisions each year that would then be predictable. Fringe agents, being individually insignificant, would have no incentive not to make such predictable decisions, but the dominant producer may benefit from randomizing his production about some ultimately predictable level to introduce asymmetries into the information system. He would then be better placed to predict futures market clearing prices because he would know his own production decision, and the fringe would face less predictable prices or greater risk.

This chapter ignores the first kind of manipulation because its proper study would require a model of information conveyed by the market. At this stage it does not seem particularly useful to build further models of sophisticated agents playing against naive agents who follow well-defined and systematically incorrect forecasting rules, though it would be very interesting to explore the extent to which a dominant producer can exploit informational advantages over intelligent but less well-informed agents (see, for example, Kyle 1981). Instead, I shall concentrate on the symmetric information rational-expectations case, and discuss the last kind of asymmetry briefly. The reason is simple—if agents can manipulate markets even when other agents know exactly what they are planning to do, then this result is robust because they will presumably have even more incentive to manipulate if they have additional informational advantages to exploit.

Incentives for the Destruction of Futures Markets

In the model just described, a risk-neutral dominant producer facing risk-averse competitors can be harmed by the establishment of a futures market, and hence would have an incentive to undermine or destroy the market. The reason is that futures markets reduce risk and hence induce a positive supply response from the fringe which depresses the market-clearing price and hence reduces the dominant producer's profits. As a risk-neutral speculator he can make a profit on his futures trade by bearing some of the risk of the fringe producers but, unless the futures market is very thin indeed, these profits are not sufficient to outweigh his losses as a producer.

To show that his profits as a producer necessarily fall with the introduction of a futures market, we need to model the production decisions of the farmers and the futures trading decisions of farmers and speculators. Following well-established tradition, assume that agents have constant absolute risk aversion and that prices and quantities are jointly normally distributed. This assumption allows us to use the mean-variance analysis of the standard capital-asset pricing model and gives rise to linear trading rules that can be aggregated and solved in closed form. These admittedly strong assumptions can be defended as second-order approximations to a more complex reality, and should not prove critical in the following analysis.

Suppose that output q after the harvest depends multiplicatively on the weather $\tilde{\theta}$ and the level of inputs x:

$$q = \tilde{\theta}f(x), \quad E\theta = 1, \quad \text{var } \theta = \sigma^2 \tag{2.1}$$

In the absence of a futures market, the farmer's income is

$$\bar{y} = \bar{p}\bar{q} - wx \tag{2.2}$$

where the input price is w, and the output price is $\bar{p}$, a random variable at the time of planting. If A is the coefficient of risk aversion, and the farmer chooses to maximize expected utility, then his decision problem is equivalent to maximizing

$$W = Ey - \tfrac{1}{2} A \text{ var } y \qquad (2.3)$$

(for example, see Newbery and Stiglitz 1981, p. 85). Thus the farmer's choice of x satisfies

$$\hat{p}f'(x) = w \qquad (2.4)$$

where

$$\hat{p} = Ep\theta - Af \text{ var } p\theta \qquad (2.5)$$

is the action certainty equivalent price (that is, the price that, in the absence of uncertainty, would lead the farmer to choose the same action or level of input x).

If there is a futures market the farmer can, in addition, choose his level of futures sales z, in which case his income will be

$$y = \bar{p}\bar{q} + z(p^f - \bar{p}) - wx \qquad (2.6)$$

and his objective is to maximize

$$W = Epq - wx + z(p^f - \bar{p}) - \tfrac{1}{2}A\{\text{var } pq - 2z \text{ cov } (p, pq)$$
$$+ z^2 \text{ var } p\} \qquad (2.7)$$

where $\bar{p} = Ep$ is the expected postharvest price. If z can be positive or negative (that is, forward purchases are also possible), the expected utility maximizing choice of z is

$$z = \frac{\text{cov } (p, pq)}{\text{var } p} - \frac{\bar{p} - p^f}{A \text{ var } p} \qquad (2.8)$$

Speculators, on the other hand, have no risky production or other sources of risky income, and sell z^s forward (or, more accurately, buy $-z^s$ forward) to maximize

$$W^s = z^s(p^f - \bar{p}) - \tfrac{1}{2} A^s z^{s2} \text{ var } p$$
$$z^s = - \frac{\bar{p} - p^f}{A^s \text{ var } p} \qquad (2.9)$$

This has the same form as the second term in equation 2.8, which allows us to interpret that term as the speculative component, whereas the first term is the hedging component. In our simple model, the speculators can only be persuaded to take a long position (in which they provide the forward purchases that balance the farmers' forward sale) if p^f is below the expected future price. The normal backwardation provides the risk premium that covers the cost of transferring risk from farmers to speculators. However, even in this simple model in which there are no processors or stockholders whose hedging needs might complement those of the farmer's, it is still possible for p^f to equal or exceed the expected future price. To see this we need to look at equilibrium in the futures market, in which net futures sales must be zero. Without any other agents, equilibrium implies that the sum of sales of farmers and speculators must be zero, or, if all agents share common beliefs and face the same risk θ:

$$0 = \sum (z^s + z) = \frac{\operatorname{cov}(p, p\theta)}{\operatorname{var} p} \sum \bar{q} - \frac{\bar{p} - p^f}{\operatorname{var} p} \sum \left(\frac{1}{A} + \frac{1}{A^s} \right) \quad (2.10)$$

Let α measure the effective degree of risk aversion of the market as a whole:

$$\frac{1}{\alpha} = \sum \left(\frac{1}{A} + \frac{1}{A^s} \right) \quad (2.11)$$

Thus if there are n farmers and m speculators, all equally risk-averse, $\alpha = A/(n + m)$; if any agent is risk-neutral, $\alpha = 0$ and the market acts risk-neutrally. If average total production is $\bar{Q}$, the bias in the futures market, or the extent of normal backwardation, is

$$\bar{p} - p^f = \alpha \bar{Q} \operatorname{cov}(p, p\theta) \quad (2.12)$$

and the equilibrium futures sale by farmers i is, from equations 2.12 and 2.18,

$$z^i = \beta^i \bar{q}^i \frac{\operatorname{cov}(p, p\theta)}{\operatorname{var} p} \quad (2.13)$$

where, for farmer i

$$\beta^i \equiv 1 - \frac{\alpha \bar{Q}}{A^i \bar{q}^i}, \quad 0 \leq \beta^i \leq 1$$

is a measure of the extent to which the farmer is more risk-averse than average (A^i/α) and more exposed to risk than average $(q^i/\bar{Q})$. If all farmers are identical and there are no speculators $\beta = 0$, whereas if there is one risk-neutral speculator, so $\alpha = 0$, then $\beta = 1$. In between, if there are n farmers and n^s speculators, all equally risk-averse, for an average farmer

$$\beta = 1 - \frac{n}{n + n^s} = \frac{n^s}{n + n^s} \tag{2.14}$$

The term β can also be thought of as the extent to which the farmer is able to share the risk with other agents in the economy. The larger the number of speculators, the more the farmer is able to transfer risk to them, and the more heavily he is willing to be involved in the futures market. The less risk-averse speculators are, the smaller will be α, and the more willing they will be to accept the farmer's risk, and again, the more the farmer will be willing to trade these risks in the future markets.

If, as assumed, p and θ are jointly normally distributed, appendix 2A shows that equation (2.13) can be written

$$\frac{z^i}{q^i} = \beta^i (1 + r\sigma/\sigma_p) \tag{2.15}$$

where σ and σ_p are, respectively, the coefficients of variation of output and price, and r is the correlation coefficient between output and price. Clearly, this expression can be negative, in which case from equation 2.12 p^f will exceed $\bar{p}$ and the futures market will exhibit contango instead of backwardation.

When the farmer can hedge on a futures market, his action certainty equivalent price p^f is, from equation 2.7

$$\hat{p}^f = Ep\theta - A\{f \text{ var } p\theta - z \text{ cov } (p\theta, p)\} \tag{2.16}$$

where z is the optimal futures trade, satisfying equation 2.8 or 2.13. Suppose now that a futures market is introduced into an otherwise unstabilized market, and that it has no effect on the beliefs or information about future prices. If it had no effect on the postmarket price distribution, then from equations 2.5 and 2.15

$$\hat{p}^f - \hat{p} = Az \text{ cov } (p\theta, p) = A\beta f \frac{\text{cov}^2 (p\theta, p)}{\text{var } p} \tag{2.17}$$

substituting from equation 2.13. In this case, the futures market unambiguously increases the action certainty equivalent price, which, other things being equal, will induce a supply response and thus lower the average spot price.

The dominant producer will be adversely affected by the increase in fringe supply, though he may be able to make additional profits exercising his market power in the futures market. Whether these will be enough to compensate for the fall in his profits as a producer will be explored in the next section, where it will be shown that unless the futures market is very thin, the dominant producer loses when futures markets are introduced. In such cases he will be hostile to the introduction of futures markets and will have an incentive to destroy them. He would, in particular, have an incentive to play on the populist sentiments of regulators by encouraging them to believe that futures markets can be manipulated to the disadvantage of producers, if he thought this action might provoke moves to restrict or close future markets. He would also have an incentive to convince other potential participants in the market that the market was manipulated or rigged, and hence that the game is unfair and not worth playing. There is some evidence that futures markets known to be dominated by government marketing agencies are unpopular and consequently thin (Gray 1960). Because the dominant producer certainly has an incentive to mislead other agents, it should not be difficult to so convince these agents, and there is the consolation that if an attempted squeeze or other manipulation fails in its primary purpose, it may succeed by discrediting the market.

The remedy for this kind of behavior is to provide as much public information as possible about the actions of the dominant producer to broaden the market and increase the number of traders. From equation 2.17, the fringe supply response increases with β (that is from equation 2.14), with the number of speculators n^s.

Incentives for Manipulating Futures Markets with Full Information

If futures markets are, however, successfully introduced and maintained, they will affect the trading environment of the dominant producer, and he will have an incentive to manipulate the futures market even if all participants know what strategy he is pursuing. In 1977, the Commodities Trading Commission defined manipulation as

conduct intentionally engaged in resulting in an artificial price that does not reflect the basic forces of supply and demand.

A finding of manipulation in violation of the [Commodities Exchange] Act requires a finding that the party engaged in conduct with the intention of affecting the market price of a commodity (as determined by the forces of supply and demand) and as a result of such conduct or course of action an artificial price was created (at 21, 477, CFTC Dkt No. 75-4, Feb. 18, 1977 [1975-77 Transfer Binder], CCH Comm. Fut. L. Rep. |20, 271, cited by Greenstone 1981, p. 11).

This definition seems acceptable if we interpret artificial price as a price differing from the competitive price. Clearly, a large producer will know that his actions will affect the price—the question is whether he takes advantage of this power. The competitive equilibrium in the futures market with a risk-neutral agent is one in which $p^f = \bar{p}$ and the market is unbiased. Any trading strategy that fails to yield this outcome is, in our full information model, evidence of manipulation.

A dominant producer has two different motives for manipulating the futures market. First, as a large agent, he may be able to exercise market power in the futures market quite independently of his activities as a producer. This he does by influencing the spread between the futures price p^f and the expected cash price $\bar{p}$, both directly by trading on the futures market and hence affecting p^f, and indirectly; by changing p^f he can change the action certainty equivalent price $\hat{p}^f$, and hence induce a supply response that affects the cash price $\bar{p}$.

The second way in which the dominant producer can advantageously manipulate the futures market is to change the futures price, and hence, via a change in the action certainty equivalent price, induce a supply response by the fringe that increases the dominant producer's profits. If, for example, he can lower the futures price he will reduce fringe supply and increase his sales price. However, this move is not costless, as he may lose on his futures trading activities, and the extent to which this strategy is profitable requires a careful cost-benefit analysis.

The next two sections consider each of these motives separately in special cases, chosen to yield a quantifiable estimate of the importance of such manipulation. The first simplifying assumption is that both demand and exante supply schedules are linear. If the production function of a representative farmer is

$$f(x) = \frac{1 - \eta}{n} + \surd(2\eta x/n + k) \qquad (2.18)$$

where k is some constant chosen to yield a sensible form for $f(x)$ for low levels of output, then, assuming the input price of x is unity, planned output will be

$$f(x) = \frac{1}{n}\{1 - \eta + \eta\hat{p}\} \qquad (2.19)$$

and aggregate average supply $\bar{Q}$ will be

$$\bar{Q} = 1 - \eta + \eta\,\hat{p} \qquad (2.20)$$

where $\hat{p}$ is again the action certainty equivalent price. If the demand schedule is

$$p = 1 + \frac{1}{\varepsilon} - \frac{\bar{Q}}{\varepsilon} + \bar{u}, \; E\bar{u} = 0 \qquad (2.21)$$

then, in the absence of any uncertainty, market equilibrium in this competitive market would be $p = 1$, $Q = 1$, and ε, η would be the elasticities of demand and (ex ante) supply respectively. For small risk, the market equilibrium will be close to this point, and the elasticities of demand and supply will likewise be approximately ε, η at and near the equilibrium. The two polar cases of risk we shall consider are pure demand risk and perfectly correlated supply risk.

Pure Demand Risk

In this case output is certain so

$$Q = 1 - \eta + \eta \, \hat{p}$$

but the demand is risky, so that the coefficient of variation of price is σ_p, or, from equation 2.21, since $\bar{p} \doteq 1$,

$$\text{Var } p = Eu^2 = \sigma_p^2$$

With pure demand risk, it is true quite generally that the action certainty equivalent price is the futures price (Danthine 1978). The argument goes as follows. Let $U(y)$ be the utility of income y, then farmers choose inputs x and futures sales z to

$$\underset{x,z}{\text{Max}} \; EU \{\bar{p}f(x) - wx - z(\bar{p} - p^f)\} \qquad (2.22)$$

The first-order conditions are

$$f'EU'p = w \, EU'$$
$$EU'p = p^f \, EU'$$

hence

$$p^f f'(x) = w, \; \hat{p} = p^f \qquad (2.23)$$

Perfectly Correlated Supply Risk

If farmers experience perfectly correlated supply risk, so that their output is

$$q^i = \theta f^i(x), \quad E\theta = 1, \quad \text{var } \theta = \sigma^2$$

their action certainty equivalent price $\hat{p}$ is, from equations 2.16 and 2.8:

$$\hat{p} = Ep\theta - Af \left\{ \text{var } p\theta - \frac{\text{cov}^2(p, p\theta)}{\text{var } p} \right\} - (\bar{p} - p^f) \frac{\text{cov}(p, p\theta)}{\text{var } p}$$

For perfectly correlated pure supply risk, the correlation between price and output is $r = -1$, and $\sigma_p = \sigma/\varepsilon$. From appendix 2A

$$\text{var } p\theta = \bar{p} \frac{\sigma^2}{\varepsilon^2} \{(1 - \varepsilon)^2 + 2\sigma^2\} \doteq \frac{\bar{p}^2 \sigma^2}{\varepsilon^2}(1 - \varepsilon)^2$$

$$\text{cov}(p, p\theta) = \frac{\bar{p}\sigma^2}{\varepsilon^2}(1 - \varepsilon) = (1 - \varepsilon) \text{var } p$$

(2.24)

so, ignoring terms in σ^4

$$\hat{p} = Ep\theta - (1 - \varepsilon)(\bar{p} - p^f)$$

$$\hat{p} = (1 - \varepsilon)p^f + \varepsilon\bar{p}(1 - \sigma^2/\varepsilon^2)$$

(2.25)

If producers experience additive risk, however, so that

$$\tilde{q} = f(x) + \tilde{u}, \quad E\tilde{u} = 0$$

then $\hat{p}$ is again p^f, as can be seen from the first−order conditions for the following expected utility maximization problem:

$$\underset{x,z}{\text{Max }} EU[\tilde{p}\{f(x) + \tilde{u}\} - wx + z(p^f - \tilde{p})]$$

(2.26)

which are identical to equation 2.23.

Futures Market Manipulation by a Large Speculator

First, we examine the best trading strategy for a large risk-neutral non-producing speculator in an otherwise competitive market of competitive producers described by equations 2.20 and 2.21, in the simpler case of pure demand risk. (The case of pure supply risk is left as an exercise.) If the large speculator sells S futures, equilibrium in the futures market is, from equation 2.8

$$S + \Sigma z^i + \Sigma z^s = 0 = S + Q + \frac{p^f - \bar{p}}{\alpha \ \text{var} \ p} \tag{2.27}$$

where α is defined in equation 2.11 and production is

$$Q = 1 - \eta + \eta p^f \tag{2.28}$$

The expected price in the cash market $\bar{p}$ is given by equations 2.28 and 2.21:

$$\bar{p} = 1 + \frac{\eta}{\varepsilon} - \frac{\eta}{\varepsilon} p^f \tag{2.29}$$

Competitive equilibrium with a risk—neutral speculator would yield an unbiased futures market $p^f = \bar{p} = 1 = Q = -S$. The expected income of the large speculator is, using equation 2.29:

$$y = S(p^f - \bar{p}) = S(1 + \eta/\varepsilon) \ (p^f - 1) \tag{2.30}$$

Whereas, from equation 2.27:

$$-S = 1 - \eta + \eta p^f + \frac{(1 + \eta/\varepsilon) \ (p^f - 1)}{\alpha v}$$

where v is var p = var u from equation 2.21. Choosing S in equation 2.30 is equivalent to choosing p^f, and the maximizing choice satisfies

$$p^f = 1 - \frac{1}{2\gamma} \tag{2.31}$$

where

$$\gamma = \frac{1 + \eta/\varepsilon}{\alpha v} + \eta$$

From equation 2.29

$$\bar{p} = 1 + \frac{\eta}{2\gamma\varepsilon} \tag{2.32}$$

Note that as α tends to zero, p^f and $\bar{p}$ both converge to the competitive value of unity, as was to be expected. Perhaps more remarkably, the future sales of the large speculator is exactly one-half the competitive level (note that both are negative, and thus purchases of futures).

Although the large speculator manipulates the market when comparing his behavior to the competitive equilibrium, his presence improves arbitrage, or reduces the magnitude of the bias $\bar{p} - p^f$, for in his absence the competition equilibrium could be

$$p^f = 1 - \frac{1}{\gamma}, \bar{p} = 1 + \frac{\eta}{\gamma \varepsilon} \qquad (2.33)$$

The presence of the large speculator clearly harms other speculators (and will thus tend to make the market thinner), but in the present model he induces a positive supply response that benefits consumers. It is a somewhat delicate question whether he benefits or harms other producers because, their average price falls, but they obtain better risk-sharing facilities via the less biased futures market. In appendix 2C the gain to producers of allowing the large speculator to trade is

$$\frac{1}{2\gamma} - \frac{3\eta}{8\gamma^2} - \frac{2(1 + \eta/\varepsilon)^2}{8Av\gamma^2} \qquad (2.34)$$

which is small, but for at least some parameters, positive. Thus, somewhat surprisingly, in this model allowing a large speculator to manipulate the futures market (as opposed to excluding him) can benefit everyone except the existing speculators, assuming all agents have rational expectations. If, however, the futures market is thin and hence quite biased and supply is relatively more elastic than I assumed, then, as appendix 2C shows, producers would benefit from prohibiting the large speculator.

Futures Market Manipulation by a Large Producer

The previous section demonstrated that large risk-neutral agents have a direct incentive to manipulate futures markets. We now ask whether they have an additional incentive if they are large producers. This will be the case if their choice of futures sales (or purchases) depends on their level of production. The intuitive reason why manipulation is beneficial is that by changing the futures price the dominant producer can reduce fringe supply and hence increase his profits as a producer.

To explore this question, we need a slightly different model of supply. Suppose aggregate fringe supply is given by

$$\bar{Q} = \mu(1 - \eta + \eta\hat{p}) \qquad (2.35)$$

(compare equation 2.19. The parameters are chosen so that at an equilibrium quantity and price of unity, the elasticity of fringe supply is η and market share μ. See appendix 2B for details.). Demand is again given by equation 2.21, while the dominant producer's production function is

$$F(x) = m(1 - \lambda) + \sqrt{(2m\lambda x + K)} \qquad (2.36)$$

(The parameters m, λ are to be chosen so that in the absence of risk the market equilibrium price is unity. The parameter λ would then be the elasticity of supply were the producer to behave competitively. K is an arbitrary constant that does not affect the equilibrium output.) Because it is by no means obvious that the dominant producer will benefit from futures market manipulation as a producer (and not just as a risk-neutral agent) it is important to consider different types of risk specification.

Pure Demand Risk

Fringe supply is riskless and equal to

$$Q = \mu (1 - \eta + \eta p^f) \qquad (2.37)$$

If the dominant producer produces q and sells S futures, equilibrium in the futures market requires (compare equation 2.27):

$$S + Q + \frac{p^f - \bar{p}}{\alpha v} = 0 \qquad (2.38)$$

which, substituting for Q, gives

$$p^f = \frac{\bar{p} - \alpha vS - \mu\alpha v (1 - \eta)}{1 + \mu\alpha v\eta} \qquad (2.39)$$

and hence

$$Q = \frac{\mu \{1 - \eta + \eta (\bar{p} - \alpha vS) \}}{1 + \mu\alpha v\eta} \qquad (2.40)$$

Equilibrium in the cash market requires the average price to satisfy

$$\bar{p} = 1 + \frac{1}{\varepsilon} - \frac{1}{\varepsilon}(q + Q) \tag{2.41}$$

which, with equation 2.40, gives

$$Q = \frac{\mu\left(1 + \dfrac{\eta}{\varepsilon} - \dfrac{\eta}{\varepsilon}q - \eta\alpha v S\right)}{1 + \mu\left(\alpha v\eta + \eta/\varepsilon\right)} \tag{2.42}$$

The dominant producer's expected profits are

$$y = \bar{p}q - wx + S(p^f - \bar{p})$$

which, from equation 2.38, can be written

$$y = \bar{p}q - wx - \alpha v S(S + Q) \tag{2.43}$$

Because, from equation 2.42, Q is linear in q and S, so is $\bar{p}$.

Consequently expression 2.43 contains terms in Sq, and hence the optimizing choice of S will depend on q, and vice versa. Therefore the producer's choice of future trades S will depend on his choice of output q and vice versa. To quantify this interdependence, maximize y in equation 2.43 with respect to S

$$\frac{\partial y}{\partial S} = 0 = q\frac{\partial \bar{p}}{\partial Q}\frac{\partial Q}{\partial S} - \alpha v\left(2S + Q + S\frac{\partial Q}{\partial S}\right) \tag{2.44}$$

where, from equation 2.41, $\partial\bar{p}/\partial Q = -1/\varepsilon$. This can be solved to yield

$$S = -\tfrac{1}{2}\left(\frac{\eta + \varepsilon}{\eta + \varepsilon/\mu}\right) + \frac{\mu\eta q}{\varepsilon + \mu\eta} \tag{2.45}$$

When $\mu = 1$, $q = 0$ so that there is no dominant producer, the result collapses into the previous case of a large speculator, for whom $S = -\tfrac{1}{2}$.

The expected profit-maximizing choice of input x satisfies

$$\frac{\partial y}{\partial x} = 0 = \left\{\bar{p} + q\frac{\partial \bar{p}}{\partial q} - \alpha v S\frac{\partial Q}{\partial q}\right\}F'(x) = 0$$

where the term in braces is the dominant producer's action certainty equivalent marginal revenue MR. Substituting for $\bar{p}$ and $\partial \bar{p}/\partial q$ this can be written

$$MR = 1 + \frac{1}{\varepsilon} - \frac{1}{\varepsilon}(q + Q) - \frac{q}{\varepsilon}\left(1 + \frac{\partial Q}{\partial q}\right) - \alpha v S \frac{\partial Q}{\partial q}$$

while from equation 2.36

$$q = m(1 - \lambda + \lambda MR)$$

These two equations can be solved to yield

$$2\mu\eta\alpha v S = \left\{\left(\frac{\varepsilon}{\lambda m} + 2\right)\phi - \frac{2\mu\eta}{\varepsilon}\right\} q + \mu\left(1 + \frac{\eta}{\varepsilon}\right) - \left(1 + \frac{\varepsilon}{\lambda}\right)\phi \quad (2.46)$$

where $\phi = 1 + \mu(\alpha v\eta + \eta/\varepsilon)$.

Equations 2.45 and 2.46 can be solved for S and q, but one conclusion is immediate; S increases with q. The previous section we proved that a large speculator would still be a net futures buyer, so S would be negative. If he is also a producer, then he buys fewer futures. The effects of this, from equation 2.42, is to reduce Q and hence increase his market power in the cash market.

The Consequences of Excluding the Dominant Producer from the Futures Market. If the dominant producer is somehow excluded from the futures market, then the market equilibrium can be found from equation 2.46 and 2.42 by setting $S = 0$. The dominant producer acts rather like another competitive speculator (so far as arbitraging prices) provided $S < 0$.

If on the other hand $S > 0$, the dominant producer would be amplifying the bias in the futures market, to the disadvantage of consumers and possibly producers.[2] In such a case, banning the dominant producer from trading may improve matters. However, it can be shown that it is never desirable for the producer to be a net futures seller, and so, perhaps surprisingly, allowing the dominant producer to trade on the futures market always reduces the degree of bias of the market in this model (see appendix 2A). There is another or additional way of reducing the bias, and that is to reduce α, the measure of market risk aversion, by increasing the accessibility of the market and reducing transactions or entry costs.

Numerical Example. If $\mu = 1/2$, $\varepsilon = \eta = 1$, $\lambda = 1$, $m = 3/4$, then in the absence of risk, $p = 1$, $q = 1/2$, $Q = 1/2$, and the market would be equally shared between the fringe and the dominant producer. If now $\alpha v = 1/20$, the manipulated equilibrium is:

$$q = 0.5, \ S = -0.1667, \ Q = 0.4945,$$
$$\bar{p} = 1.0055, \ p^f = 0.9891, \ y = 0.3388$$

If the dominant producer is prevented from trading, the equilibrium is

$$q = 0.5020, \ Q = 0.4911,$$
$$\bar{p} = 1.0069, \ p^f = 0.9823, \ y = 0.3375$$

Perfectly Correlated Supply Risk

As the other extreme polar case, suppose all producers experience perfectly correlated supply risk θ and no demand risk, so that u (equation 2.21) is identically zero. Average fringe supply is, from equations 2.2 and 2.25:

$$\bar{Q} = 1 - \eta + \eta \ (1 - \varepsilon) \ p^f + \varepsilon\eta \ (1 - \sigma^2/\varepsilon) \ \bar{p} \qquad (2.47)$$

Equilibrium in the futures market in which the dominant producer sells S requires (from equation 2.10 and 2.24)

$$S + \bar{Q} \ (1 - \varepsilon) + \frac{p^f - \bar{p}}{\alpha v} = 0 \qquad (2.48)$$

(compare equation 2.38). Eliminate p^f between equations 2.47 and 2.48 to give

$$\bar{Q} = \frac{1 - \eta + \varepsilon\eta \ (1 - \sigma^2/\varepsilon) \ \bar{p} - \alpha v\eta(1 - \varepsilon)S}{1 + \alpha v\eta \ (1 - \varepsilon)^2} \qquad (2.49)$$

The average cash market clearing price satisfies

$$\bar{p} = 1 + \frac{1}{\varepsilon} - \frac{1}{\varepsilon}(\bar{Q} + \bar{q})$$

so

$$\bar{p} \ \{1 + \alpha v\eta(1 - \varepsilon)^2 + \eta(1 - \sigma^2/\varepsilon)\} = \{1 + \alpha v\eta \ (1 - \varepsilon)^2\} \ (1 + \frac{1}{\varepsilon} - \frac{\bar{q}}{\varepsilon})$$

$$- \frac{1}{\varepsilon} \{1 - \eta - \alpha v\eta(1 - \varepsilon)S\}(2.50)$$

The dominant producer again wishes to maximize expected profit

$$y = \bar{q}Ep\theta - wx + S(p^f - \bar{p}) \tag{2.51}$$

Equation 2.51 can be written, using equation 2.48, as

$$y = \bar{q}\bar{p}(1 - \sigma^2/\varepsilon) - wx - \alpha vS\{S + \bar{Q}(1 - \varepsilon)\} \tag{2.52}$$

Again, because $\bar{p}$ and Q are linear in $\bar{q}$ and S from equations 2.49 and 2.50, y contains terms in $\bar{q}S$, and hence the profit-maximizing choice of futures sales S depends on planned production $\bar{q}$ and vice versa. Thus the dominant producer does not act just as a large speculator, but chooses his speculative position to benefit his role as a producer. It is clear that this argument is robust, for it merely require $\partial^2 y/\partial q\partial S$ to be non zero, which, given that income is bilinear in prices and quantities and that prices depend on quantities, is virtually guaranteed. Because this is true in the simplest linear examples, we can conclude that the futures and cash markets positions of the dominant producer are generally interdependent.

The next question to resolve is whether the dominant producer's interventions reduce or increases the bias in the futures market. The simplest test of his position is to ask in which direction he wishes to move starting with zero futures sales—that is, what is the sign of

$$\frac{\partial y}{\partial S}\bigg|_{S=0} = \bar{q}(1 - \sigma^2/\varepsilon)\frac{\partial \bar{p}}{\partial S} - \alpha v(1-\varepsilon)\bar{Q} \tag{2.53}$$

from equation 2.52. Equation 2.50 shows

$$\frac{\partial \bar{p}}{\partial S} = \frac{\alpha v\eta(1 - \varepsilon)}{\varepsilon\psi}, \quad \psi = 1 + \alpha v\eta(1 - \varepsilon)^2 + \eta(1 - \sigma^2/\varepsilon)$$

After some manipulation, this can be written

$$\frac{\partial y}{\partial S}\bigg|_0 = \frac{-\alpha v(1-\varepsilon)}{\psi}\left[1 - \eta\varepsilon\left\{1 - \frac{\sigma^2}{\varepsilon}\left(1 + \frac{1}{\varepsilon}\right)\right\}\right. \tag{2.54}$$
$$\left. - (1 - \sigma^2/\varepsilon)(1 + \eta/\varepsilon)q\right]$$

which has the sign of $-(1 - \varepsilon)$. It follows from equation 2.48 that the dominant producer is on the opposite side of the futures market to the hedging element of the fringe farmers—that is, if the farmers are hedging by selling futures, which they will if the market is inelastic ($\varepsilon < 1$), then the dominant producer will be buying futures, and vice versa if $\varepsilon > 1$. Thus the effect of the dominant producer is again to further arbitrage prices, and, assuming this to be desirable, his presence is welcome (provided, of course, that everyone shares the same information and knows his objectives). Moreover, as equations 2.49, 2.50, 2.52, and 2.54 show, as the futures market becomes more efficient (as its risk aversion α tends to zero), the manipulative power of the dominant producer in the futures market goes to zero (see especially equation 2.54, where $S = 0$ if $\alpha = 0$.)

The Benefits to the Dominant Producer of Eliminating the Futures Market

Calculating the effect on the dominant producer's profits of eliminating the futures market is straightforward, for if $n^s = 0$ in equation 2.14, then equation 2.13 shows that, provided the dominant producer does not speculate on the futures market, the fringe producers will not trade either, and hence the market will be inactive. For example, if the number of speculators n^s were equal to the number of farmers n in the previous numerical example, the equilibrium without the futures market is the same as the equilibrium with a a futures market, but the value of αv is twice as large—that is, $\alpha v = 1/10$. In this case, the equilibrium with $S = 0$ is

$$q = 0.5077, Q = 0.4664,$$
$$\bar{p} = 1.0250, y = 0.3490$$

and the dominant producer's profit y is larger without the futures market than with it, even when he is manipulating it to yield maximum total profit.

This same argument shows that if in fact the relative number of speculators $n_s/(n + n_s)$ is zero or small, it would pay the dominant producer to allow the futures market to set up, provided he were allowed to manipulate it. The argument of appendix 2A shows that the dominant producer would never choose a zero futures trade if the futures market were open, even if all other traders were inactive. In other words, he would always choose to make an existing but inactive market active. Using the same parameters as before, if $n_s = 0$ but $\alpha v = 1/20$, without the futures market the dominant producer's profit is 0.3375, as shown previously, whereas with the futures market his profit from production is 0.3361 (which is lower, as argued in the previous section), and from manipulating the futures market is 0.0027, yielding a total of 0.3388 as shown, larger than without the futures market.

Conclusions

Even when all agents share the same information and hence can predict his strategy, the dominant producer still has an incentive to manipulate the futures market beyond the point he would choose if he were merely a large speculator. Nevertheless, his intervention always has the effect of reducing the bias on the futures market (though not as much as if he either acted competitively or as a large speculator), and hence excluding him from the futures market would, on the assumption here of full information, reduce the efficiency of the futures market. Finally, his market power in the futures market diminishes with the risk aversion of that market (that is, as the number of speculators increases or their risk aversion decreases).

Incentives for Destabilizing Markets

If dominant producers can predict planned fringe supply (or can do as well as the fringe farmers can), but fringe farmers cannot observe the dominant producer's current production plans but only his average planned production, the dominant producer might have an incentive to randomize his supply. This incentive is easiest to study in the absence of futures markets and storage, but the argument carries over to these complex cases. For example, where the dominant producer stores, he may have an incentive to randomize his storage decision, and where there is a futures market, he may benefit from further destabilizing the cash market. In all cases, the motive is the same—instability is costly to fringe producers who will respond by reducing their supply to the benefit of the dominant producer. However, it is also costly to the dominant producer and will not necessarily be worthwhile (in contrast to futures market manipulation discussed above, which is always worthwhile).

We shall examine a model with demand risk and no futures market in which the dominant producer can choose his average output q and the magnitude of the variation about this θ measured by its variance s^2. The total price variance is, from equation 2.21, $v = \text{Var } u + s^2/\varepsilon^2$, on the reasonable assumption that demand and supply risk are uncorrelated. Demand and certain fringe supply can be written

$$p = 1 + 1/\varepsilon + \bar{u} - \frac{1}{\varepsilon}(q + \theta + Q), \quad Eu^2 = \sigma^2, \quad E\theta = s^2, \quad E\theta u = 0$$

$$Q = \mu(1 - \eta + \eta\hat{p})$$

where the action certainty equivalent price is

$$\hat{p} = Ep - A Q \text{ var } p, \quad \text{var } p = \sigma^2 + s^2/\varepsilon^2 \equiv v$$

Thus

$$Q = \frac{\mu(1 - \eta + \eta\bar{p})}{1 + \mu\eta vA} , \qquad (2.55)$$

$$\bar{p} = \frac{\left\{1 + \dfrac{1}{\varepsilon}(1 - q)\right\}(1 + \mu\eta vA) - \dfrac{\mu}{\varepsilon}(1 - \eta)}{1 + \mu\eta vA + \mu\eta/\varepsilon} \qquad (2.56)$$

The dominant producer chooses q (or more correctly Ex average input) and s^2 (determined by the variance of input) to maximize expected profit:

$$y = Ep(q + \theta) - Ewx$$

$$= \bar{p}q - \frac{s^2}{\varepsilon^2} - Ewx$$

where, from equation 2.36, if, as assumed, $w = 1$

$$Ewx = \frac{s^2}{2\lambda m^2}$$

The key question is whether destabilizing behavior is profitable—that is, whether

$$\frac{\partial y}{\partial s^2}\bigg|_0 > 0 \quad \text{or} \quad q\frac{\partial\bar{p}}{\partial v} \cdot \frac{\partial v}{\partial s^2} - \frac{1}{\varepsilon^2} - \frac{1}{2\lambda m^2} > 0 \qquad (2.57)$$

Now, from equation 2.56

$$\frac{\partial\bar{p}}{\partial v} = \frac{\mu\eta A\left\{1 + \dfrac{1}{\varepsilon}(1 - q)\right\} - \bar{p}\mu\eta A}{1 + \mu\eta vA + \mu\eta/\varepsilon}$$

which, if risk is small, has $\bar{p}$ - 1, and $1 - q$ - μ, so

$$\frac{\partial\bar{p}}{\partial v} \simeq \frac{\mu^2\eta A/\varepsilon}{1 + \mu\eta vA + \mu\eta/\varepsilon}$$

Hence, a necessary condition for profitable destabilization is

$$\frac{(1 - \mu)\mu^2\eta A}{\varepsilon^3(1 + \mu\eta vA + \mu\eta/\varepsilon)} > \frac{1}{\varepsilon^2} + \frac{1}{2\lambda m^2}$$

or

$$A > \frac{(1 + \mu\eta vA + \mu\eta/\varepsilon)}{(1 - \mu)\mu^2\eta}\left\{\varepsilon + \frac{\varepsilon^3}{2\lambda m^2}\right\} \qquad (2.58)$$

Thus, if fringe producers are sufficiently risk-averse, it will be desirable for the dominant producer to exploit this risk aversion by destabilizing the market. Because A is not dimensionless, it is best replaced by $R = A\pi$, where π is fringe income, approximately $\mu/2$ near $Q = \mu$, $p = 1$, and R is the coefficient of relative risk aversion. Then the condition becomes

$$R > \frac{1 + \mu\eta/\varepsilon + 2\eta vR}{2\mu(1 - \mu)\eta}\left\{\varepsilon + \frac{\varepsilon^3}{2\lambda m^2}\right\}$$

Taking the rather favorable (for destabilization) parameters used before, $\mu = 1/2$, $\varepsilon = \eta = 1$, $\lambda = 1$, $m = 3/4$, $v = 1/10$, then the initial value of R is 9.107, which is very high (empirical estimates cluster around values of 1 to 2; see Newbery and Stiglitz 1981, chap. 7).

Conclusions About Destabilizing Markets

For destabilization to be profitable, fringe producers must be more risk-averse than some critical level, which, in the absence of storage, is implausibly high. In the presence of a futures market, destabilization is likely to be even less attractive as fringe producers are partially insured, and the costs to the dominant producer are of the same magnitude as before. Similarly, destabilizing storage is, at the margin, presumably as costly as destabilizing future supply (because they are, at the margin, substitutes). Hence this form of market manipulation appears a theoretical rather than a practical possibility.

Notes

1. If the commodity is further processed, processors will also hedge and experience different risks than producers, as will stockholders for storable

commodities. Modeling this behavior is important for some questions—notably whether futures markets are biased—but are not obviously relevant for market manipulation. See Stein (1979) and Anderson and Danthine (1983) for models with processors and stockholders.

2. As shown previously, reducing the bias reduces producers' risk but may, via the supply response, reduce their income and lower utility. See appendix 2A.

References

Anderson, R.W., and Danthine, J.-P. (1983). "Hedger Diversity in Futures Markets," *Economic Journal*, vol. 93, pp. 370–389.

Danthine, J.-P. (1978). "Information, Futures Prices, and Stabilizing Speculation," *Journal of Economic Theory*, vol. 17, pp. 79–98.

Edmunds, J.C. (1982). "A Comment on Greenstone's "The Coffee Cartel: Manipulation in the Public Interest"," *Journal of Futures Markets* (2:1), pp. 19–24.

Gray, R.W. (1960). "The Characteristic Bias on Some Thin Futures Markets," *Food Research Institute Studies* (November).

Greenstone, W.D. (1981). "The Coffee Cartel: Manipulation in the Public Interest," *Journal of Futures Markets* (1:1), pp. 3–16.

Hart, O.D. (1977). "On the Profitability of Speculation," *Quarterly Journal of Economics*, vol. 91, pp. 579–597.

Kyle, A.S. (1981). "Market Structure, Futures Markets and Price Formation," mimeo. Princeton University, Department of Economics.

Newbery, D.M.G. (1981). "Commodity Price Stabilization in Imperfectly Competitive Markets," Development Research Center *Discussion Paper* 32. Washington, D.C.: World Bank.

———. and Stiglitz, J.E. (1981). *The Theory of Commodity Price Stabilization*. Oxford: Oxford University Press.

Stein, J.L. (1979). "Spot, Forward and Futures," in *Research in Finance I*, ed. H. Levy, Greenwich: JAI Press, pp. 225–310.

Appendix 2A

Properties of Joint Normal Distributions

If x and y are jointly normally distributed about the origin with standard deviations σ_1, σ_2, and correlation coefficient ρ, write this

$$N(0, 0, \sigma_1^2, \sigma_2^2, \rho).$$

The moment-generating function (m.g.f.) is

$$M(t_1, t_2) = \exp \{\tfrac{1}{2}(\sigma_1^2 t_1^2 + 2\rho\sigma_1\sigma_2 t_1 t_2 + \sigma_2^2 t_2^2)\}$$

and then

$$\mu_{rs} = Ex^r y^s = \text{coefficient of} \frac{t_1^r t_2^s}{r!s!}$$

in the expansion of the m.g.f. Therefore

$$\mu_{11} = \rho\sigma_1\sigma_2; \quad \mu_{22} = (1 + 2\rho^2)\sigma_1^2\sigma_2^2; \quad \mu_{12} = \mu_{21} = 0$$

To evaluate $Ep\theta$, var $(p\theta)$, cov $(p, p\theta)$, write

$$p = \bar{p}(1 + x), \quad \theta = 1 + y$$

$$Ep\theta = \bar{p}E(1 + x)(1 + y) = \bar{p}(1 + \mu_{11}) = \bar{p}(1 + \rho\sigma_1\sigma_2)$$

$$\text{var}(p\theta) = \bar{p}^2 E(1 + x + y + xy - 1 - \rho\sigma_1\sigma_2)^2$$

$$\text{var}(p\theta) = \bar{p}^2 \{\sigma_1^2 + 2\rho\sigma_1\sigma_2 + \sigma_2^2 + (1 + \rho^2)\sigma_1^2\sigma_2^2\}$$

$$\text{cov}(p, p\theta) = \bar{p}^2 Ex(x + y + xy - \rho\sigma_1\sigma_2)$$

$$\text{cov}(p, p\theta) = \bar{p}^2(\sigma_1^2 + \rho\sigma_1\sigma_2)$$

Finding Market Equilibrium without Risk

Equations (2.37) and (2.41) together with $p = \bar{p} = p^f$ imply

$$p = 1 + \frac{1}{\varepsilon} - \frac{q}{\varepsilon} - \frac{\mu}{\varepsilon}(1 - \eta + \eta p)$$

or

$$p(1 + \mu\eta/\varepsilon) = 1 + \frac{1}{\varepsilon}(1 + \mu(1 - \eta)) - q/\varepsilon$$

This gives the net demand facing the dominant producer, for whom marginal revenue is

$$MR = 1 + \frac{1 - \mu - 2q}{\varepsilon + \mu\eta}$$

But

$$q = m(1 - \lambda + \lambda MR) = 1 - \mu \text{ in equilibrium}$$

so

$$\frac{1}{m} = \frac{1}{1 - \mu} - \frac{\lambda}{\varepsilon + \eta\mu} \qquad (2A.1)$$

This determines m given μ, λ, ε, and η.

The Welfare Effect of Speculative Manipulation

With pure demand risk and optimal hedging the farmer's welfare is

$$W = \bar{p}q - wx + z(p^f - \bar{p}) - \frac{1}{2} Av(q - z)^2,$$

$$q - z = \frac{\bar{p} - p^f}{Av}, \quad v = \text{var} p = \text{var} u$$

From the production function with n identical farmers

$$wx = \frac{\eta(p^f)^2}{2n} - \frac{nk}{2\eta}$$

and

$$nq = 1 - \eta + \eta p^f$$

Hence, to an arbitrary constant, aggregate producer welfare is

$$nW = p^f \left(1 - \eta + \frac{\eta}{2} p^f \right) + \frac{(\bar{p} - p^f)^2}{2av}$$

where $a = A/n \cong 2R$ is a measure of risk aversion (where R is the dimensionless coefficient of relative risk aversion, $-y\ U''(y)/u'\ (y) = Ay$, and each farmer has net income of roughly $n/2$ in equilibrium for small risk).
    In the absence of the large speculator

$$p^f = 1 - \frac{1}{\gamma}, \quad \bar{p} = 1 + \frac{\eta/\varepsilon}{\gamma}, \quad \bar{p} - p^f = \frac{1}{\gamma}(1 + \eta/\varepsilon),$$

$$\gamma = \frac{1 + \eta/\varepsilon}{\alpha v} + \eta$$

whereas with the large speculator

$$p^f = 1 - \frac{1}{2\gamma}, \quad \bar{p} = 1 + \frac{\eta/\varepsilon}{2\gamma}, \quad \bar{p} - p^f = \frac{1}{2\gamma}(1 + \eta/\varepsilon)$$

Let m, c superscripts denote the manipulated and competitive equilibria, then

$$n(W^m - W^c) = (1 - \eta) \left(\frac{1}{2\gamma} \right) + \frac{\eta}{2} \left\{ \left(1 - \frac{1}{2\gamma} \right)^2 - \left(1 - \frac{1}{\gamma} \right)^2 \right\}$$

$$+ \frac{(1 + \eta/\varepsilon)^2}{2av} \left(\frac{1}{4\gamma^2} - \frac{1}{\gamma^2} \right)$$

$$= \frac{1}{2\gamma} - \frac{3\eta}{8\gamma^2} - \frac{3(1 + \eta/\varepsilon)^2}{8\gamma^2 av}$$

For an agricultural commodity, plausible values for the parameters might be $\eta = 0.5, \varepsilon = 0.5, R = 1, a = 2, v = 0.1, \alpha = 0.5,$ and $\gamma = 20.5$ (where we have assumed that small speculators contribute as much risk-sharing as the farmers—that is, $m = n$). In this case the expression is positive, but it would be negative if

$$4\gamma av < 3 (1 + \eta/\varepsilon)^2$$

or

$$\frac{n + m}{n}(1 + \eta/\varepsilon) + 2Rv\eta < \frac{3}{4}(1 + \eta/\varepsilon)^2$$

This is quite possible with elastic supply η, inelastic demand ε, and few speculators m, relative to farmers n, and small risk v, or risk aversion R.

Proof that the Dominant Producer Is a Net Purchaser of Futures

Proof by contradiction. Consider the boundary case $S = 0$. From equation 2.45:

$$q = \frac{1}{2}(1 + \varepsilon/\eta), \text{ so } \varepsilon < \eta$$

Substitute for q and m in equation 2.46 and rearrange to solve for λ

$$\lambda\left\{\frac{2\mu(1 - \eta/\varepsilon)}{\varepsilon} + \frac{1 + \mu(\alpha v\eta + \eta/\varepsilon)}{\varepsilon + \eta\mu}\right\} = \frac{1 + \mu(\alpha v\eta + \eta/\varepsilon)}{1 - \mu}$$

Since $\eta > \varepsilon$

$$\lambda > \frac{\varepsilon + \eta\mu}{1 - \mu}$$

which implies from equation 2A.1 that

$$m < 0$$

which is impossible, therefore $S < 0$. (The same argument hold with greater force if it is assumed that $S > 0$).

Comment

Louis Phlips

Chapter 2 compares the competitive equilibrium of a futures market for a nonstorable agricultural final consumption commodity with the equilibrium that arises when there is a dominant producer who can act both as a big speculator would and as a big producer would. It is shown, in a convincing and technically brilliant way, how—on balance—his presence will reduce the bias $\bar{p} - p^f$ (where $\bar{p}$ is the expected postharvest price and p^f is the futures price), so that it is better to let him do whatever he does, rather than to exclude him from the futures market. The argument is counterintuitive in its policy implications and therefore provocative.

The case considered is a narrow one. Rather than delving into the algebra, I thought it might be of some interest, for the purpose of the present discussion, to ask what would happen if the case considered were somewhat broader.

Indeed, while reading the chapter, I was surprised in two ways. My first surprise stemmed from the absence—from the title and the content—of the word "storage." There is only a brief appearance of the word "storage" in the final section, where the implausible possibility of destabilizing the market is analyzed. My second surprise was the result of the expectations raised by Newbery's insistence in his introduction on the need to reason in terms other than perfect competition and to take the monopoly power of governments and cartels into account. My expectations were not fulfilled entirely. Indeed, Newbery's dominant producer basically continues to act as a speculator would—a big speculator admittedly. He is annoyed by the fact that the futures market increases the supply of the competitive fringe, by its very existence, which in turn depresses the spot price. And he is happy to discover that it is in his interest, as a speculator, to be a net buyer in case of normal backwardation and thus to reduce the magnitude of the bias. This reduction is a happy consequence of his being there, but is not of direct interest to him as such. (If he is also a producer, he will buy less futures, but the net—indirect—result is the same.)

It seems to me that, if the commodity were storable, the situation would be different in that the dominant producer would have a personal direct interest in reducing the bias. In fact, we would have a situation that looks like the asymmetric oligopoly case described by Salant (1976) in his paper on OPEC and the world oil market, except for the fact that the storable commodity considered here is reproducible rather than exhaustible.

The fringe and the dominant producer would have conflicting interests in that their profit-maximizing conditions are different. The fringe's production and storage policy would obey

$$p^f - p^c = - \text{bias} = C' \qquad (2B.1)$$

and

$$k^f - k^c = C' \qquad (2B.2)$$

where p^f is the price expected to prevail in the future (reflected in a futures price if there is a futures market). p^c is the current price (or the expected spot price $\bar{p}$, if there is a futures market), k is the marginal cost of production (strictly increasing, to make storage profitable) and C' is the marginal cost of storage. The latter includes the marginal interest cost, the marginal physical costs of storage, a risk premium (if there is no futures market) and a negative convenience yield, so that normal backwardation remains possible.[1]

The dominant producer, to the contrary, can influence the market price, so that he will want[2]

$$MR^f - MR^c = C' \qquad (2B.3)$$

where MR designates his marginal revenue, in addition to equation 2B.2. As a result, he will want.

$$p^f - p^c < C' \qquad (2B.4)$$

I suppose that the fringe and the dominant producer have the same C' curve, so that the latter's only advantage is his market size. (If storage costs reduce to interest costs, then equation (2.B4) is formally the equivalent of Hotelling's rule for a monopolistic producer of an exhaustible commodity).

If now there is a futures market, the large producer can no doubt act for the two motives described by Newbery. But he will also have a direct interest in reducing the bias, because a more stable futures price increases his profits. In reducing $p^f - p^c$, he will push the fringe producers down their production and storage cost curves, thus reducing directly the production and the quantity stored by the fringe. It might then be in the long-run interest of the fringe, and possibly of the final consumer, to have the dominant producer excluded from the futures market.

But why should he bother to act through the futures market? In Newbery's world, he is driven by risk neutrality. In my world, he has a powerful additional incentive to eliminate the futures market entirely and to replace it by another pricing system. He, the large producer, could simply announce the future (monthly, quarterly, and so forth) prices due to prevail, thus eliminating the risk for the competitive fringe, and fix himself the time spread from period to period (that is, the amount of the monthly or quarterly bias). Because the commodity is not exhaustible, the fringe could not use its stock to influence the time spread, in contradistinction with the Salant model. My guess is that the dominant producer would fix a spread such that the fringe could just survive.

At any rate, that is exactly what happened in a number of European fertilizer markets in the 1930s, under the combined action of national cartels and national governments.[3] Since then, an intertemporal equilibrium of the Stackelberg type prevails. Even the farmers' unions clearly prefer this type of certainty (monthly retail prices are announced each year, in July, for the twelve coming months) to the reduction of risk through futures markets, as was the case in the beginning of the century. Which type of risk reduction would be in the consumers' interest is another question, one that is outside the scope of the present discussion.

Notes

1. See Brennan (1958).
2. Equations 2B.1, 2B.2, and 2B.3 can be derived from equations 11a and 11b in Phlips and Thisse (1981).
3. See Phlips and Thisse (1981) and Phlips (1962, chapter 10) for more details.

References

Brennan, M.J. (1958). "The Supply of Storage," *American Economic Review*, vol. 48, pp. 50–72.
Phlips, L., and J.F. Thisse (1981). "Pricing, Distribution and the Supply of Storage," *European Economic Review*, vol. 15, pp. 225–243.
Phlips, L. (1962). *De l'intégration des marchés*. Nauwelaerts, Louvain.
Salant, S. (1976). "Exhaustible Resources and Industrial Structure: A Nash-Cournot Approach to the World Oil Market," *Journal of Political Economy*, vol. 84, pp. 1079–1093.

Comment

Lawrence J. White

David Newbery has written an interesting chapter offering good insights. He shows that the behavior of a dominant participant—one who has market power but who is less risk-averse than the other participants—in a sector with both a spot market and a futures market is likely to benefit both himself and others as well.

At the beginning, though, I should state that I am not comfortable with his use of the term "manipulation." I usually associate this term with active movement and changes in the values of variables, possibly accompanied by deception. Instead, Newbery uses the term to mean simply behavior that diverges from that which a competitive market would yield—such as the static price-quantity behavior chosen by a monopolist. He reserves the term "destabilization" for the activities that I would group under the term "manipulation." The reader may want to keep these distinctions in mind.

Let me now summarize Newbery's model. At the heart of the model are a group of competitive fringe producers of a product (such as farmers), a separate group of competitive fringe speculators, and a dominant producer-speculator. The fringe producers and speculators are risk-averse, and Newbery uses an Arrow-Pratt certainty equivalence formulation to represent this risk averison. This mean-variance approach allows easy mathematical manipulation. But it ignores higher moments; I am uncomfortable with this approach, because skewness (or the perception of skewness by participants) may be quite important in futures markets. Still, the gains in tractability are substantial.

Crucial to Newbery's model is the assumption that the dominant producer-speculator is less risk-averse than are the fringe participants. In the formal model, the dominant firm is wholly risk-neutral (which, again, makes the model tractable). But Newbery's general propositions almost certainly hold for the less stringent assumption that the dominant firm is simply less risk-averse than is the fringe.

Newbery first explores the nature of equilibrium in the spot and futures markets in the absence of the dominant firm. Price uncertainty can arise either because of fluctuations in demand or fluctuations in production functions. The production supply curve by the fringe producers is initially derived in the absence of a futures market. This supply curve and an exogenous demand curve yield a price-quantity equilibrium in the spot market.

The opinions expressed in this paper are those of the author and do not necessarily represent the views of the Department of Justice. I wish to thank David Newbery for his suggestions on an earlier set of comments.

Then, the possibility of a futures market (which clears prior to the producers' making their production decisions) is introduced, and Newbery shows (equation 2.8) that an individual producer will have a supply curve of futures contracts that can be represented as

$$z = \frac{\text{cov}(p, pq)}{\text{var } p} + \frac{p^f - \bar{p}}{A \cdot \text{var } p}$$

where z is the quantity of futures contracts supplied, p is the spot price, q is the quantity produced by an individual producer, p^f is the futures price, p is the expected spot price at the time of future sale (for example, at harvest), and A is the measure of risk aversion. Newbery points out that the first term represents the pure hedging motive of a producer and the second term is the pure speculative motive of a producer. The second group in the model, the fringe speculators, have no production, so they have no hedging motive. They only speculate, so their supply of futures contracts is represented solely by the second term. If $p^f < \bar{p}$, the speculators' supply will be negative—that is, they will demand futures contracts. Equilibrium in this market can be represented by figure 2C–1.

Newbery also shows that the presence of the futures market reduces risk for the producers, inducing a greater supply and causing a lower spot price than would occur in the absence of the futures market. Consumers are better off, and producers may or may not be better off, depending on the shapes of the demand and supply curves. The presence of the futures market, though, does represent an unambiguous potential Pareto improvement, in the Hicks-Harrod sense that the gainers could compensate the losers and still be ahead.

Newbery next introduces into the model a large dominant risk-neutral firm—initially solely as a speculator. Because this firm is risk-neutral, it has an infinite demand for futures contracts at the point at which the future price equals the expected spot price at the time of future sale—that is, at the point at which

$$p^f - \bar{p} = 0$$

This demand is represented in figure 2C–2. (The model assumes zero transactions costs.)

If this dominant firm were to ignore its market power and behaved in the futures market as if it were a competitive entity, the intersection of this demand curve with the supply curve of the producers would produce an equilibrium involving a volume of futures contracts indicated by z_2 in figure 2C–2. But if the dominant firm recognizes its market power, it will realize that it has monopsony power in the futures market. In terms of figure 2C–2,

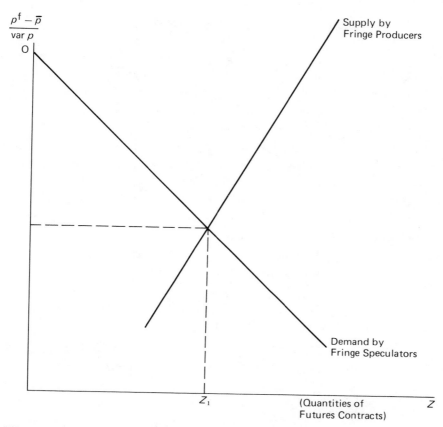

Figure 2C–1. Futures Market Equilibrium without a Dominant Producer/ Speculator

the dominant firm faces as its supply curve the excess supply curve yielded by the difference between the fringe speculators' demand curve and the fringe producer's supply curve (above point A); this excess supply curve can be represented by curve BC. Because the dominant firm recognizes its monopsony market power, it realizes that this supply curve has a marginal cost of supply schedule represented by curve BE.

The profit-maximizing outcome for this firm, then, is yielded by the intersection of this marginal cost of supply schedule with the firm's demand curve; that is, the dominant firm demands a volume of z_3 futures contracts. This intersection can then be shown to yield an outcome of a volume of z_4 futures contracts being traded (with fringe speculators demanding $z_5 = z_4 - z_3$ contracts and the dominant firm earning monopsony profits of

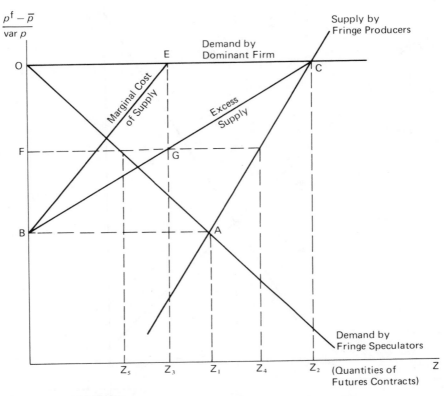

Figure 2C–2. Equilibrium with a Dominant Firm

OEGF). Point F on the price axis represents a narrower spread between the futures price and the expected spot price for future sales than occurs in the absence of the dominant firm (but, of course, the spread would be zero if the dominant firm somehow were to behave in a competitive fashion). I strongly suspect (but have not proved) that this narrower spread yielded by the presence of the dominant firm represents another potential Pareto improvement.

Thus, even if the dominant firm exercises its market power ("manipulates," in Newbery's term), society is better off with its presence than with its absence (though, of course, society would be yet better off if the dominant firm were to ignore its market power and would behave competitively). This improvement in social welfare occurs because the dominant firm has an efficiency advantage over the other actors in the model: its lower level of risk aversion.

Newbery next allows the dominant firm to be a dominant producer as well as a dominant participant in the futures market. It is clear that, in its role as a producer, the dominant firm gets larger profits from wider (negative) spreads between p^f and p, because a wider spread will cause its risk-averse fringe competitors to reduce their supply (whereas the dominant firm, because it is risk-neutral, does not care about this spread from its perspective as a producer). But, in its role as speculator, it maximizes profits at the spread indicated by point F in figure 2A–2. Accordingly, the dominant firm faces a tradeoff between the larger profits in production yielded by a wider spread and the smaller profits yielded in speculation from this wider spread. The equilibrium for the dominant firm will now clearly involve a wider spread than that indicated by point F; that is, the dominant firm will reduce its demand for futures contracts (as compared with the situation in which it is only a speculator). But, again, the spread is nevertheless narrower than if the dominant firm were not present at all and social welfare is improved (though, again, not by as much as if the dominant firm behaved competitively). Again, the reason for the improvement in social welfare is the presence of a more efficient, less risk-averse participant.

Finally, Newbery asks if the dominant producer would find destabilization (or, what I would term true "manipulation") worthwhile. He explores this question in the context of a pared-down model that involves no futures market and involves only fluctuations in demand. He asks whether it would be worthwhile for the dominant firm to shift its supply curve randomly, sacrificing short-run profits in the hope that the extra risk would cause the fringe producers to reduce their supply and thus raise the overall profit level for the dominant firm. Newbery finds that this outcome is a theoretical possibility, but realistic values for the key parameters indicate that it is unlikely in practice.

The reasons for this last outcome are not intuitively clear. Unfortunately, the uncertainty imposed on the demand curve complicates the model needlessly. I can suggest (though I have not solved) a simpler model that may allow a clearer and more intuitive understanding of whatever outcome emerges. In figure 2C–3, there is an overall demand curve for the commodity and a rising supply curve by the group of fringe producers. The demand curve facing the dominant producer is simply the difference between the overall demand curve and the fringe supply curve—this is, a residual demand curve. If the dominant producer recognizes its market power, it will normally produce at the point at which the marginal revenue schedule of this residual demand curve intersects the producer's marginal cost curve (as-sumed to be horizontal in figure 2C–3)—that is, at point Q_1. The interesting question is whether, by introducing variance into its production decision (by varying output around Q_1) and thus sacrificing short-run profits, the domi-

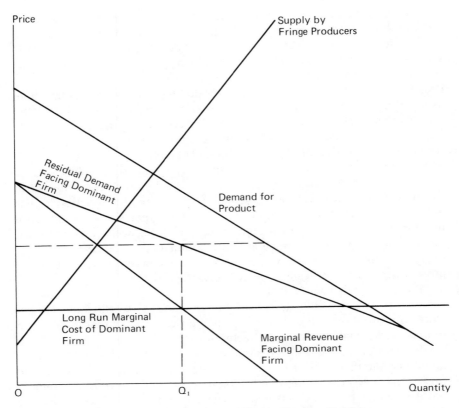

Figure 2C-3. Dominant Firm's Output Decision

nant firm can cause the fringe suppliers to perceive greater risk, consequently to reduce their supply, and thus to increase the residual demand for the dominant firm's output sufficiently to raise that firm's overall level of profitability.

What suggestions can I offer for future research? First, the destabilization question could be explored in the context of a simpler model. Second, one could ask what happens in the basic model if the dominant firm has the same degree of risk aversion as the other participants in the market. (I am not convinced by Newbery's arguments that the dominant producer is likely to be less risk-averse.) I will briefly sketch my suspicions as to what this revised model would yield. Because the dominant firm has no advantage in risk averision, it has no special role to play if it is only a speculator in the futures market. But suppose it has a special efficiency advantage in production that allows it to be a dominant firm (but not a monopolist). Now it will want to enter the futures market and sell futures, so as to hedge and reduce risk, just like other risk-averse producers. This risk reduction will cause it to increase its output. But the same act that reduces risk for the dominant firm—selling futures contracts—also depresses the futures price (as compared with the absence of the dominant firm from the futures market) and reduces the expected return to the fringe of competitive producers. They in turn will reduce their output, which will yield yet greater profits for the dominant firm. Thus, another forum for the exercise of the dominant firm's market power is in the futures market.

Still, the interesting question is whether society is better off or worse by allowing the dominant firm to transact in the futures market. This question, in turn, seems to hinge on whether total production (the dominant firm's increased output less the fringe firms' reductions) increases or decreases. The degree of risk aversion, the elasticities of supply, and the market share of the dominant firm appear to be the crucial parameters. I do not know the answer to this question, but it is conceivable that (contrary to the conclusions of Newbery's model) society could be better off by keeping the dominant firm out of the futures market (though, of course, its special production advantage makes it a welcome participant in the spot market).

Third, as I have noted, Newbery's models do not really address the question of manipulation: dynamic activities by the dominant firm in the futures market. Unfortunately, a truly dynamic model would be quite complex and unwieldy. But an approximation to a model involving manipulation might be achieved by modifying Newbery's model in a simple way: allow the futures market to clear after the production decisions have been made, rather than before. Without a dominant firm, an assumption of rational expectations would probably cause the equilibrium to be similar to that of Newberry's model. And a dominant firm (either risk-neutral or risk-averse), behaving statistically, would probably also yield results similar to Newbery's model (or to my suggested modified model for the case of the dominant firm that is just as risk-averse as the other participants). But now the dominant firm has an extra opportunity: it can create noise in the futures market (for example, by nonsystematic purchases or sales of contracts), which would increase the perceived risk by the fringe producers and cause them to reduce their supply and so forth. A model of this sort would, I believe, come closer to conveying a sense of (and the possible consequences of) manipulation in the futures market.

3 Futures Markets and Monopoly

Ronald W. Anderson and
Mahadevan Sundaresan

Organized futures markets are widely regarded as being perfectly competitive. The fact that anyone may buy or sell futures contracts for homogeneous goods in centralized markets at publicly quoted prices suggests that these markets come close to fulfilling the standard criteria for perfect markets. Economists have memorialized this fact by studying thoroughly the theory of the competitive futures market. By design, this theory cannot address issues of individual agents possessing market power; however, market power is often a real concern to those who deal in futures markets. At least three forms of market power are potentially important for the study of futures markets:

1. An agent may control the supply of or demand for the good called for delivery in the futures contract.
2. There may be private information concerning supply or demand.
3. A limited number of market makers may be able to benefit from a bid/ask spread.

This chapter is concerned with the first type of market power; it presents a theory of futures markets when the deliverable good (called the cash good) is produced by a monopolist. A monopolistic cash market is the polar opposite of a competitive cash market; many other forms of cash market power are possible and are deserving a study. However, to the extent that few sellers approach a cooperative solution, these outcomes can be described by the monopolistic paradigm. In this sense the model in this chapter is the natural complement of the theory of competitive futures markets. Several specific questions motivate our work. First, what are the characteristics of positions held and prices in futures markets for goods that are produced under imperfect competition? Second, is cash market power increased or decreased by the existence of the corresponding futures market? Third, to what extent can the nonexistence of futures markets for some

The authors have benefited from the comments of James Hayes, David Newbery, Louis Phlips, Bob Rosenthal, and Steve Salant. All errors are the responsibility of the authors. Financial support from Columbia Futures Center is gratefully acknowledged.

goods be attributed to the fact that the goods are produced under imperfect competition?

There are a number of active futures markets for goods that are produced by a few large agents who may recognize the interdependence of their production decisions. For example, tin, coffee, and cocoa production is dominated by a relatively small number of countries who control export through national marketing boards.[1] The primary supply in U.S. grain trade is highly disperse, but export demand is important and is concentrated in a relatively few Communist bloc countries.[2] In other cases a futures contract may involve a partially processed good where the intermediate stage of production is competitively organized (or relatively so) but where the primary good is not—for example, the heating oil futures contract.

Clearly then, there are futures markets for noncompetitively produced goods, and the model investigated here is intended to shed light on these markets. It also addresses the many cases of noncompetitively produced goods for which futures contracts are not available. Many such goods are highly differentiated and are obviously poor candidates for futures trading. Others may have stable demand and production conditions so that prices are stable over time. Certain markets—such as plastics—are highly concentrated but do have homogeneous products for which production conditions are unstable. The observation that there are no futures markets for such products despite the fact that the participants in the market face significant price risk raises the question of whether it is imperfect competition alone that inhibits futures trading.

Almost all theories of futures markets, from Keynes (1923) to the present, implicitly or explicitly assume that the underlying cash good is competitive and therefore do not address these concerns. Newbery (chapter 2, this volume) is an exception. His framework of a dominant firm and a competitive fringe differs from ours, and his analysis relies on some strong assumptions concerning functional forms; this contribution is discussed further following the analysis. A governmental market board that pursues price stabilization is an example of cash market power. Salant (1983) has studied the interaction of this market power and speculation, thus touching on issues that arise in our analysis; however, the analyses differ in that he does not specifically allow for futures trading and we do not treat durable goods and thus cannot discuss buffer stock schemes.

The problem of market power obtained through agents' holding private information has been treated in the context of futures markets by Grossman and Stiglitz (1975), Danthine (1977), and Bray (1981). Each addresses the question is private information revealed through equilibrium prices? The answer is that for some structures the information is revealed in a rational expectations equilibrium whereas for other, more general structures it is not. Many issues in this area remain to be investigated; particularly interesting from our perspective is the question of how private information interacts with cash market power of the type we analyze.

The return earned by a limited number of market makers has been treated in the analysis of market liquidity (Telser and Higinbotham 1977) and margin requirements (Telser 1981). Finally, in his study of private information Kyle (1981) presents an interesting model that manifests all three sources of market power.

The Setting and Cash Market Equilibrium

The model is a standard static partial equilibrium treatment of a monopolistic producer of a perishable good, with the modification that prior to the meeting of the goods market there is trading of futures contracts for the monopolist's good. In this section, we show that the monopolist's futures trading directly affects his output because in this way he can indirectly affect his return from the futures market. If the monopolist has sold futures, he produces more than if he had no futures position. If he has purchased futures, he produces less. If his futures purchase is sufficiently large, he removes the cash good entirely from the market to gain the maximum possible return from futures trading. In this case he corners the futures market. Thus when agents with market power trade futures for their goods, real resource allocation is affected in important ways. Accepting the limitations of the partial equilibrium setting, the producer's futures sales reduce the social costs of monopoly; whereas producer's futures purchases increase these costs. In section 3 we turn to the question of what is the equilibrium futures position of the monopolist.

The structure of the model is similar to the competitive equilibrium analysis of Anderson and Danthine (1983) in that agents are differentiated as primary producers, processors, and speculators; however, here there is a single producer. There are two trading dates.[3] At time 0 agents, including the monopolist, trade in futures contracts that are unconditional promises to deliver at time 1 the monopolistically produced good in return for payment at the futures price p^f that is determined at time 0. At time 1, the monopolist facing a known technology and a known demand for his product makes the production decision that determines the cash market price p. At the same time the monopolist's production decision determines the outcome in the futures market because the agents with short positions must purchase the good from the monopolist (or, equivalently, all agents close out their futures commitments with offsetting trades at the price p).[4] The profit relation of the monopolist is:

$$\pi = pq - c + (p^f - p)f_m \qquad (3.1)$$

where π is the monoplist's profits, q is his output, c is the cost of production, and f_m is the size of his short futures position ($f_m < 0$ if he is long).

The monopolist's technology is represented by the cost function $c(q, \varepsilon)$, where ε is a factor such as input price or weather outside the monoplist's control. At time 0 this factor may be a random variable; that is, we allow for general production uncertainty. However, given realizations of this factor, marginal cost is positive and increasing

$$c_1(q, \varepsilon) > 0 \quad \text{and} \quad c_{11}(q, \varepsilon) > 0$$

for all $q \geqq 0$ and all ε.

The demand for the monopolist's product is represented by the inverse demand curve $p = g(q, \eta)$ where η is a factor such as taste or price of a substitute outside the monopolist's control. We assume the function $g(\cdot)$ is known by the monopolist. There may be demand uncertainty in the sense that the noncontrollable factor is a random variable $\tilde{\eta}$ at time 0; however, at time 1 this factor is known. We assume that the demand curve is everywhere downward sloping, $g_1 < 0$ and that $g_2 > 0$. Furthermore, we assume that the price is bounded above by $\bar{g}(\eta) = g(0, \eta) < \infty$. This assumption is important for the following analysis because it is in this way that profits from a monopolist's long futures position will be bounded. It is clear we could accomplish the same thing by assuming that the futures price is bounded above while the cash price is not.[5] The analysis would be slightly different; however, the conclusions would be the same.

With these specifications we can rewrite the monopolist's profit as

$$\pi(q, f_m) = \pi^c(q) + \pi^f(q, f_m)$$

$$\pi^c(q) = g(q, \eta)q - c(q, \varepsilon) \qquad\qquad 3.2$$

$$\pi^f(q, f_m) = [p^f - g(q, \eta)]f_m$$

where $\pi^c(q)$ may be interpreted as the monopolist's cash market profit function and $\pi^f(q, f_m)$ is his futures profit function. The latter depends on the monopolist's output, but the former does not depend on his futures position. We restrict the curvature of $g(\cdot)$ and $c(\cdot)$ so that cash market profit is concave

$$\pi^c_{11}(q) < 0, \quad \text{all } q$$

At time 1 all uncertainty has been resolved, so we assume the monopolist maximizes profits. Specifically, the problem is to maximize $\pi(q, f_m)$

with respect to $q \geqq 0$ given f_m. The first-order necessary condition for this is

$$g_1 q + g - c_1 - f_m g_1 \leqq 0 \qquad (3.3)$$

where the equality holds for an interior solution ($q > 0$). In equation 3.3, arguments of the demand and cost functions have been omitted to simplify the notation. Now, for this problem f_m is an arbitrary fixed number. An inspection of equation 3.3 suggests that, since $g_1 < 0$, the corner solution ($q = 0$) may be optimal if f_m is sufficiently negative (that is, the monopolist has to take a sufficiently large long position). This supposition is in fact correct. Figure 3–1A plots the cash market profit function. An interior point $q^0 > 0$ maximizes the cash market profit; if the monopolist had no futures position, q^0 would be his optimal choice.

In figure 3–1B the futures profit function has been plotted for a long position ($f_1 < 0$) and a short position ($f_2 > 0$). All such curves pass through the point $g^{-1}(p^f)$, which is the output that would result in the cash price equal to the futures price. The intercepts are drawn on the assumption that $p^f < \bar{g}$, which is the only economically interesting case. Thus the futures profit function for a long position has a positive intercept and is monotonically decreasing. Furthermore, the intercept is linearly decreasing in f_m. Consequently, it is clear for a sufficiently large long position π^f will dominate π^c, resulting in a total profit function as depicted in figure 3–2. Here the corner solution $q = 0$ dominates the point $q^* > 0$, which is the local maximum ($\pi(0, f_m) > \pi(q^*, f_m)$). For small long futures positions or for short positions, some positive output will be chosen. We can formalize the relationship between the monopolist's output and his futures position as follows.

Define $f^* < 0$ as a long futures position such that the monopolist is indifferent between producing nothing and producing some positive output. That is, f^* solves

$$\pi(0, f^*) = \pi(q^*, f^*)$$

where the interior local maximum $q^* > 0$ satisfies equation 3.3 with equality, or $\pi_1(q^*, f^*) = 0$. We can interpret f^* as a corner threshold as is made clear by the following proposition.

PROPOSITION 1. *Given η and ε there is a unique $f^* < 0$ such that the optimal $q = 0$ for all $f_m < f^*$ and optimal $q > 0$ for all $f_m > f^*$.*

Proof. Let $\phi(f)$ be the local interior maximum corresponding to f (that is, $\pi_1(\phi(f), f) = 0$). Define the function

$$\Gamma(f) = \pi(0, f) - \pi(\phi(f), f)$$

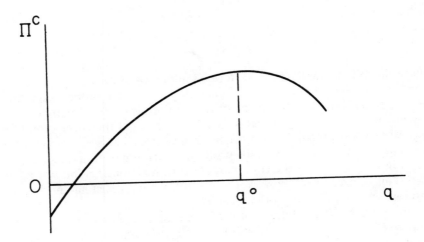

Figure 1a

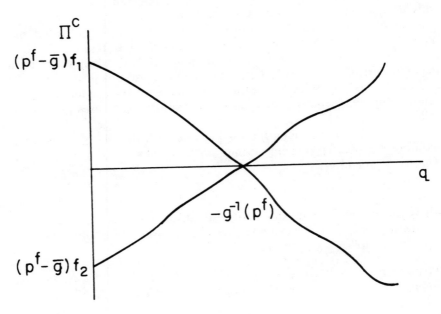

Figure 1b

Figure 3-1. Cash and Futures Profits

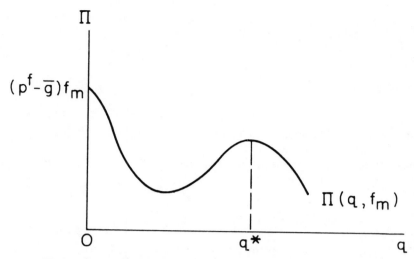

Figure 3-2. Profit Function with a Long Futures Position

Clearly, for some $f' < 0$, $\Gamma(f') > 0$. It is also clear that $\Gamma(0) < 0$. The proposition is proved by showing that $\Gamma(\cdot)$ is continuously decreasing in f. Differentiating totally with respect to f

$$d\Gamma = [\pi_2(0, f) - \pi_1(\phi(f), f)\phi_1 - \pi_2(\phi(f), f)]df$$

But by the assumption of an interior solution $\pi_1(\phi(f), f) = 0$. Now, $\pi_2(0, f) = (p^f - \bar{g})$ and $\pi_2(\phi(f), f) = (p^f - g(\phi(f)))$. Thus collecting results

$$\frac{d\Gamma(f)}{df} = g(\phi(f)) - \bar{g} < 0$$

where the inequality follows from the definitions of $\bar{g}$ and $\phi(\cdot)$.

PROPOSITION 2.   *The monopolist's optimal output is a nondecreasing function of f_m.*

Proof. By proposition 1 for $f_m < f^*$ the corner solution $q = 0$ obtains and small increases of f_m would have no effect on q. For $f_m \geq f^*$ the optimal q is an interior solution satisfying $\pi_1 = 0$. Differentiating the first-order condition totally with respect to q and f_m

$$\frac{dq}{df_m} = -\frac{\pi_{12}}{\pi_{11}}$$

Now, from equation 3.3, $\pi_{12} = -g_1 > 0$. And $\pi_{11} < 0$ by the second-order condition for an interior maximum. Consequently, $dq/df_m > 0$.

PROPOSITION 3.   *Let q° be optimal conditional on $f = 0$. If q^* is the unconditional maximum then*

$$q^* \gtreqqless q^\circ \quad \text{as} \quad f_m \gtreqqless 0$$

Proof. If $f_m < f^*$, then from proposition 1 $q^* = 0 < q^\circ$. Otherwise f_m is an interior solution and thus satisfies

$$\pi_1^c(q^*) = f_m g_1(q^*)$$

Because $g_1 < 0$, then as $f_m \gtreqqless 0$ we have

$$\pi_1^c(q^*) \lesseqqgtr 0 = \pi_1^c(q^0)$$

The proposition follows immediately from the concavity of $\pi^c(\cdot)$.

Propositions 1 to 3 completely characterize the relationship of the monopolist's output and futures position. The relationship is shown in figure 3–3. There is a positive association between q and f_m. If the monopolist has sold short ($f_m > 0$), he produces more than the amount he would have produced in the absence of futures (q°). In this range the difference between the monopolist's price and his marginal cost ($g - c_1$) is less than at q°. In this sense, social costs of monopoly are reduced by the monopolist's futures sales. If he is long futures he produces less than q° and thus price exceeds marginal cost by more than it would in the absence of futures. If he has long futures beyond the corner threshold ($f_m < f^*$), he cuts his output to zero to corner the futures market. In this case, futures trading leads to the maximum possible misallocation of resources in this market.

    In view of this wide range of possible consequences for resource allocation, the important question becomes in the futures market equilibrium is the monopolist long or short? We investigate this in the following section.

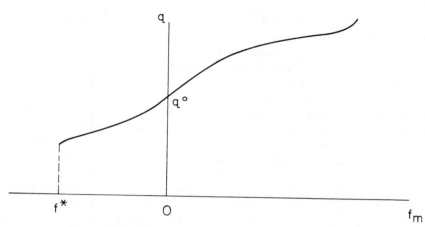

Figure 3-3. Output as a Function of Futures Sales

Futures Market Equilibrium

The General Case

The futures market that meets at $t = 0$ is assumed to be perfectly competitive in the sense that entry and exit are free. The monopolistic producer of cash good has no direct power to manipulate the futures market and affects futures prices only through the size of his own futures position.[6] Aside from the monopolist there are other agents trading in futures. Let f_i be the futures short sales of agent i, then the futures market clearing condition is

$$f_m = - \sum_i f_i \tag{3.5}$$

In equilibrium, the monopolist's futures market sales equals the net futures purchases of all other agents. In view of the monopolist's large size in the spot market (which is equivalent to the futures market one period later), it is natural to assume that the monopolist recognizes this futures market equilibrium condition and thus that he may influence the futures price. We further assume that the monopolist recognizes that his futures choice will affect his production decision at $t = 1$ and thus the distribution of the cash price. The monopolist's preferences are represented by the cardinal utility function $u(\cdot)$ with $u' > 0$ and $u'' \leq 0$. This last assumption allows us to consider either risk-averse or risk-neutral behavior. Formally, the monopolist's problem at $t = 0$ is to choose f_m so as to maximize $Eu(\pi)$ subject to the profit relationship in equation 3.2, the cash market optimality condition 3.3, and the futures market equilibrium condition 3.5

All other agents are assumed to be price-taking, risk-averse expected utility maximizers.[7] The nature of these agents' futures demand depends on their profit functions. If trading in futures markets is the only random source of income these agents will be pure speculators; if there are other random income sources, their trades in futures will generally reflect some hedging motive. These two cases are discussed later separately. In all cases, the competitive agents' demands for futures will depend importantly on their spot price expectations. Some of the results that follow hold for arbitrary expectations. Other results will hold for expectations that reflect the structure of cash market, in which case the disposition of information becomes important. In such cases we assume full public information, which implies, in particular, that competitors know the monopolist's cost function and observe the monopolist's futures position.

Formally, each competitor chooses, f_i to maximize the expected utility of income given p^f. In rational expectations, this problem is modified to incorporate the constraint that the cash price is distributed according to $g(\bar{q},\bar{\eta})$, where q will be chosen to satisfy condition 3.3. The solution will depend on p^f; thus, assuming this relationship is one to one we can aggregate using equation 3.5 and invert to obtain the futures market inverse demand function

$$p^f = h(f_m) \qquad (3.6)$$

In the following discussion, we will assume $H(\cdot)$ is continuously differentiable and that $h' < 0$.

In view of the discontinuity in the relationship of q and f_m (and thus of p and f_m) noted in the previous section, these assumptions deserve some comment. With rational expectations, competitors' futures demands would be discontinuous in f_m if the moments of the probability distribution of p were discontinuous in f_m. However if η and ε are continuous random variables, the moments of the induced distribution of $\bar{p}$ will be continuous in f_m. One way to see this is to note that, if $m(f_m)$ is a central moment of the distribution of p conditional on f_m we can generally write

$$m(f_m) = \rho(f_m)m_1(f_m) + (1 - \rho(f_m))m_2(f_m)$$

where $\rho(f_m)$ is the probability that $q = 0$ (that is, the probability of a corner), m_1 is the moment corresponding to m of the distribution of p conditional on $q = 0$, and m_2 is the corresponding moment of the distribution of p conditional on $q \neq 0$), and f_m. Now, conditional on an interior solution ($q \neq 0$), q is continuous in f_m; consequently, so are p and m_2. Similarly, for m_1. Finally, for continuous random variable η and ε the probability of a corner $\rho(f_m)$ will be continuous in f_m. Since ρ, m_1, and m_2 are continuous, so will be m.

Given the continuity of $h(\cdot)$, the further assumption of differentiability is unrestrictive, for any continuous function can be accurately approximated by a differentiable function. Finally, the assumption of a downward sloping futures demand curve is fairly weak. Given expectations, competitors' futures sales will be increasing in p^f; consequently, increases in f_m can be accommodated only by decreasing p^f. Allowing the expected cash price to be a decreasing function of f_m strengthens this effect. As a matter of principle, it may be possible to find cases where increases in f_m increase the variance or otherwise affect the cash price distribution sufficiently to offset the effects just described; however, such pathological cases would be of little interest. In the next section, we derive the inverse futures demand curve for a parametric special case and demonstrate that it obeys our assumptions.

We assume the monopolist knows $h(\cdot)$ and thus recognizes the effect of his futures position on the current futures price. With this structure it is clear that the monopolist's futures choice is rather complicated, reflecting the fact that his choice will affect his cash market profits and also the distribution of returns from futures trading both through p^f and the distribution of p. The characterization of the problem is further complicated by the fact that, in view of the discontinuity of q in f_m noted earlier, the profit function will not be differentiable at certain points. We can proceed as follows.

Earlier, we defined the corner threshold f^* conditional on realizations of η and ε; we may denote this relationship as $f^*(\eta, \varepsilon)$. In view of our assumption $g_2 > 0$, we assume $f_1^* < 0$. Define $\eta^*(f, \varepsilon)$ implicitly by $f^*(\eta^*(f,\varepsilon),\varepsilon) = f$; that is, η^* is the realization of η such that, given ε, f is a corner threshold. With this notation the monopolist's expected utility of profits can be written as

$$Eu(\pi) = \int_0^\infty \left\{ \int_0^{\eta^*(f,\varepsilon)} u(\pi^f(0, f))dG_\eta + \int_{\eta^*(f,\varepsilon)}^\infty u(\pi(q, f))dG_\eta \right\} dG_\varepsilon$$

where G is the joint cumulative distribution function of (η, ε). By the definition of η^*, $\pi^f(0, f)$ is differentiable for $\eta \varepsilon (0, \eta^*)$. Similarly, $\pi(\cdot)$ and q are differentiable for $\eta \varepsilon (\eta^*, \infty)$. Consequently, the necessary condition for optimal f_m is given by differentiating each component of $Eu(\pi)$ to obtain

$$\int_0^\infty \left\{ \int_0^{\eta^*} u'\pi_2^f dG_\eta + \eta_1^*[\pi^f(0, f^*) - \pi(q^*, f^*)] \right. $$
$$\left. + \int_{\eta^*}^\infty u'\left[\pi_1 \frac{dq}{df} + \pi_2\right]dG_\eta \right\} dG_\varepsilon = 0$$

Now recall by the definition of f^*, $\pi^f(0, f^*) = \pi(q^*, f^*)$. Furthermore, for $\eta \in (\eta^*, \infty)$ q is an interior solution, and then $\pi_1 = 0$. Finally, $\pi_2 = \pi_2^f = h + h'f - g$. Using all these results, the necessary condition for optimal f_m can be rewritten as,

$$Eu'(\pi)[h'f_m + h - g] = 0 \qquad (3.7)$$

In general, equation 3.7 determines the optimal futures position of the monopolist and through equation 3.6 the equilibrium futures price. The solution will depend on the monopolist's expectations and preferences and on the expectations, preferences, and cash market positions of the competitive futures traders. In subsequent subsections we analyze the solution under alternative specifications of these factors.

Equilibrium in the Absence of Hedging

In this subsection we consider futures market equilibrium assuming the monopolist is risk-neutral so that he maximizes the expected value of period 1 revenues and that for the competitive agents in the futures market the only source of risk is their futures position. Consequently, neither the monopolist nor the competitive agents will view the futures market as a hedging instrument; in this version of the model the futures market may be viewed as providing a means of speculative side bets. In such a framework the monopolist has a position of power in the ostensibly competitive futures market and that he will generally choose a finite futures position despite his risk neutrality. Furthermore, despite the interaction of the monopolist's cash and futures positions, the monopolist will always choose a futures position such that the expected return from futures trading is greater than zero. Consequently, in public information and rational expectations equilibrium all agents will select zero positions in futures; the futures market will be inactive. We now turn to the modification of our model to reflect these assumptions and then demonstrate the points explicitly.

If futures trading is the only source of risk for the competitive agents, given expectations, by the assumptions of risk aversion and expected utility maximization the ith agent's futures sales can be written as

$$f_i = \psi_i(p^f - E_ip), \ \psi'_i > 0; \ \psi_i(0) = 0$$

where E_ip is the agent's expectation of the time 1 cash price (see Anderson and Danthine 1983 for a derivation of these results). That is, the agent will be short (long) if and only if the futures price exceeds (is less than) cash price he expects to prevail next period. Now if expectations of competitive agents are homogeneous, their individual positions and thus their aggregate positions will be zero if and only if the futures price equals their expected spot price, $\bar{p}_c$. Consequently, if the competitive agents are pure speculators and have homogeneous expectations, the monopolist's inverse futures demand function has the property

$$\bar{p}_c = h(0) \tag{3.8}$$

Next, we impose the assumption that the monopolist is risk-neutral. If $u'' = 0$ everywhere then u' is nonstochastic and the monopolist's futures choice condition in equation 3.7 becomes

$$h(f_m) + f_m h'(f_m) - Eg = 0 \tag{3.9}$$

This expression bears a striking resemblance to the usual optimality condition for a static monopolist and demonstrates that the monopolist's power in the cash market endows him with power in the competitive futures market for his good. We can interpret equation 3.9 as "marginal revenue equals marginal cost" where the first two terms on the left side correspond to the marginal revenue from futures sales and the expected cash price (Eg) is the cost of a futures sale.

Expression 3.9 shows that it will generally pay for the monopolist to deal in futures and that the optimal position will depend on the characteristics of the futures inverse demand curve including its location and elasticity. Without specifying the competitive agent's expectations we are unable to provide a definite answer to the question of whether the monopolist goes long or short. Loosely put, if the competitors expect a high cash price, their demand for futures will be great and the monopolist will go short. If they expect a low cash price, the monopolist will go long. Consequently, the monopolist's futures position, the futures price, and the effect of futures trading on the allocation of real resources depend crucially on the competitor's expectations.

It is natural in the circumstance to ask what will be the result if expectations are rational in the sense that the competitive agents are systematically fooled neither by nature nor the monopolist. The key to the answer comes from realizing that, from the monopolist's futures optimality condition, the monopolist always chooses a futures position that he expects to have non-negative payoff. That is, using expression 3.9 and the fact that $h' < 0$ implies that $p^f > Ep$ if he is short ($f_m > 0$) so that he expects to make a futures trading profit. Conversely, if he is long ($f_m < 0$), then $p^f < Ep$ so that he expects to make a futures profit. Now if the monopolist knows the true distribution of the random variables affecting the cash market and if a competitive agent realizes this, the competitor cannot rationally expect to make a profit trading against the monopolist. Consequently, the rational competitor will wish to be long when the monopolist is long and short when the monopolist is short. But if all competitors are rational, the only solution that will clear the futures market is one of all agents taking no position.

We can formalize this point as follows. We assume homogeneous expectations for competitors ($h(0) = \bar{p}_c$). Then if the monopolist's expectations are correct and if the competitive agent's expectations are rational, $\bar{p}_c = Eg$. Consequently, $f_m = 0$ is an equilibrium because condition 3.9 is satisfied

$$h(0) - Eg = Eg - Eg = 0$$

Furthermore at $f_m = 0$, the monopolist chooses an interior solution and the derivative q_{f_m} exists and is positive everywhere. Thus because $h' < 0$ and $Eg_1 q_{f_m} < 0$, the left side of equation 3.9 is monotonic decreasing at $f_m = 0$; consequently, this solution is locally unique.[8] In summary, we have proved the following proposition.

PROPOSITION 4. *If the monopolist is risk-neutral and if competitive agents in the futures markets are risk-averse speculators, a unique, rational expectations futures market equilibrium exists. In equilibrium, all agents hold no futures contracts and the futures price equals the expected next-period cash market price.*

This proposition deserves several comments.

1. It can be interpreted as saying that under our assumptions the futures market will not exist. To say also that the futures price is unbiased is not a paradox because what we mean is at any other announced futures price there would be active trading but this would not be an equilibrium.
2. The notion of rational expectations we require is a weak one, $\bar{p}_c = Eg$. That is, the subjective probability distributions of competitors are unbiased. Other moments may not coincide with underlying fundamental distributions. This is compatible with differential information across agents so long as the competitors are correct about the mean price.
3. This result can be viewed as another result on the impossibility of pure speculation in rational expectations (see Kreps 1977 and Tirole 1982). From that perspective, the importance of the result is to demonstrate the robustness of the logic to the introduction of monopoly power into the determination of the uncertain price.

Proposition 4 was established without specific restrictions on utility or production functions or on the nature of the technological or demand uncertainty. Later, we show that changing the timing of the decision so that the monopolist must make his input choice under uncertainty does not essentially alter the result.

Finally, we examine a parametric special case of our model that shows the logic of proposition 4 from an additional point of view as well as compactly illustrates the general structure of our model.

Starting with the cash market problem, we assume the monopolist has the production function

$$q = x^{1/2} \tag{3.10}$$

where x is the quantity of input whose unit price is r and faces the inverse demand function

$$\bar{p} = \bar{a} - bq \tag{3.11}$$

where the "choke" price a is random at time 0 but is known at time 1. We assume the support of a is the interval $(\underline{a}, \bar{a})$. Then profit maximization leads to the output

$$q = \frac{a + bf_m}{2(r + b)} \quad f_m \geqq f^* $$
$$= 0 \quad f < f^* \tag{3.12}$$

where the corner threshold f^* is uniquely given by $f = -a/b$ (proposition 1). Note q is nondecreasing in f_m (proposition 2) and exceeds the no-futures output when the monopolist is short (proposition 3). Turning to the futures market problem, we assume competitive agent i maximizes the expected utility of profits, $\tilde{\pi} = (p^f - \bar{p})f_i$ where preferences are of the constant absolute risk-aversion type

$$E_i u_i(\tilde{\pi}_i) = E_i \tilde{\pi}_i - \frac{1}{2}\lambda_i \text{var}_i \tilde{\pi}_i \tag{3.13}$$

Then an individual competitor's demand for futures is

$$f_i = \frac{p^f - E_i \bar{p}}{\lambda_i \text{var}_i p} \tag{3.14}$$

We assume all competitors expect the same cash price to prevail ($E_i \bar{p} = \bar{p}_c$). Then using this in equation 3.14, inserting this into the market clearing condition 3.5, and inverting yields the inverse demand function

$$p^f = \bar{p}_c - Rf_m \tag{3.15}$$

where

$$R = \{\sum_i [1/(\lambda_i \text{ var}_i p)]\}^{-1}$$

is a market measure of risk aversion and perceived riskiness. Conditional on expectations $\partial p^f/\partial f_m = -R < 0$. If we assume competitors' expectations are rational and f_m is observable to them, the distribution of the cash price depends on f_m. Inserting equation 3.12 into 3.11, Var p, and thus R in equation 3.15, does not depend on f_m. Furthermore, then taking expectations and differentiating reveals that

$$\frac{\partial \bar{p}_c}{\partial f_m} = -(1 - \rho(f_m))\beta$$

where $\beta = b^2/2(r + b)$ and

$$\rho(f_m) = \int_{\underline{a}}^{-f_m b} dG_a$$

for $(-\bar{a}/b) < f_m < (-\underline{a}/b)$, $\rho(f_m) = 0$ for $f_m > (-\underline{a}/b)$, and $\rho(f_m) = 1$ for $f_m < (-\bar{a}/b)$. Thus under rational expectations, the future inverse demand curve $h\,(\cdot)$ is everywhere downward sloping. Furthermore, assuming the probability density function G_a exists, it is clear that $\rho(f_m)$ and thus $h(\cdot)$ are differentiable. This demonstrates that the properties assumed for $h(\cdot)$ in the first section hold for this parametric example.

To find the monopolist's optimal futures position we must consider $E\pi$ piecewise. If $f_m < (-\bar{a}/b)$, the monopolist will always corner the market so that expected profits are $E\pi = (\bar{p}_c - Rf_m - Ea)f_m$. For $\bar{p}_c$ sufficiently high, an f_m in this range may be optimal; however, under rational expectations $\bar{p}_c = Ea$ so the $E\pi = -Rf_m^2 < 0$, which is unambiguously worse than taking no futures position. For long positions satisfying $(-\bar{a}/b) < f_m < (-\underline{a}/b)$, the monopolist sometimes but not always corners the market, and the analysis is somewhat more complex. However, making the rational expectations assumption, it is possible to show for large markets (that is, R is sufficiently large) the derivative of expected profit is strictly positive in this entire range and thus cannot be optimal. Finally, in the range $(-\underline{a}/b) < f_m$, the interior solution always holds. Then, differentiating expected profits and solving yields,

$$f_m = \frac{1}{2} \left| \frac{\bar{a} - \dfrac{\bar{a}b}{2(b + r)} - \bar{p}_c}{\left(\dfrac{b^2}{4(b + r)} - R\right)} \right| \tag{3.16}$$

The monopolist's position is zero if $\bar{p}_c = Ea(1 - b/2(b + r))$. Inserting equation 3.16 in the inverse demand function 3.11 and taking expectations shows that competitors' expectations will be rational if and only if $Ep = \bar{a}(1 - b/2(b + r))$. Consequently, in rational expectations equilibrium the monopolist takes a zero position and, from equation 3.15, the futures price equals the expected spot price (proposition 4).

Monopolist's Risk Aversion

In the preceding subsection we analyzed the purely speculative equilibrium of a futures market for a monopolistically produced good; that is, we did not consider the role of futures for hedging either by the monopolist or by competitive traders. In this subsection, we consider hedging by the monopolist still assuming that the competitive futures traders are risk-averse speculators.

The implications of these assumptions for the futures market equilibrium are seen by reconsidering the monopolist's futures optimality condition in equation 3.7. If the monopolist is risk-averse ($u''(\pi) < 0$) but if other futures traders are pure speculators, this condition is

$$[h(f_m) + h'(f_m)f_m]Eu'(\tilde{\pi}) - E[u(\tilde{\pi})g] = 0$$

or rearranging this we have,

$$h(f_m) + h'(f_m)f_m = E\tilde{g} + \frac{\text{Cov}[u'(\tilde{\pi}), \tilde{g}]}{Eu'(\tilde{\pi})} \tag{3.17}$$

Before we proceed to study the qualitative properties of this expression, it is useful to compare the equilibrium pricing specification in equation 3.17 with similar results obtained by Cox, Ingersoll, and Ross (1981) and Richard and Sundaresan (1981). In the absence of stochastic variations in the term structure of interest rates, these papers establish the following relationship:

$$p_t^f(T) = E_t[g(T)] + \frac{\text{cov}_t[u'(\tilde{c}(T)), \tilde{g}(T)]}{E[u'(c(t))]}$$

In the preceding equation, $T > t$ represents the maturity date of the futures contract and t represents the current date. Although relationship 3.17 bears a formal resemblance to their specifications, the framework in this chapter, in purpose and spirit, differs substantially from theirs. Their intertemporal models assume that all agents are competitive and identical so that futures contracts are redundant assets. By construction their models address pricing relationships and are not designed to characterize any agent's position size. In this framework, however, futures contracts are nonredundant assets in general. The absence of trading in this model under rational expectations and risk neutrality of the monopolist is by choice, not by design. Our model can be used to obtain the equilibrium specification of these competitive models as a special case. For instance if the monopolist perceives the inverse futures demand function $h(\cdot)$ as a competitor so that $h' = 0$, then equation 3.17 collapses to the preceding expression. In this sense our static monopoly model complements their dynamic competitive models.

Condition 3.17 states that the monopolist should adjust his futures position until the marginal revenue from futures sales equals the expected cash price plus a risk premium that depends upon the covariance of the monopolist's marginal utility and the cash price. If $cov(\bar{u}', \tilde{g}) = 0$ the risk premium vanishes, equation 3.17 collapses to 3.9, and all the results of the previous section, including the nonexistence of futures trading in rational expectations equilibrium, would hold. With the monopolist's risk aversion, generally $cov(\bar{u}', g) \neq 0$ so that in rational expectations equilibrium agents will hold nonzero futures positions. Under rational expectations with competitive speculators $h(0) = E\tilde{g}$, which implies the monopolist's marginal expected utility $f_m = 0$ is just $-cov(\bar{u}', g)$. Consequently, if cash price and marginal utility are negatively correlated, the monopolist is made better off by selling futures. When the cash price and marginal utility are positively correlated, the monopolist will take a long position. To say more requires an examination of the determinants of $cov(\bar{u}', \tilde{g})$—namely, the monopolist's preferences and production technology, the shape of the demand function, and the relationship of demand and technological uncertainty.

In general, the interaction of all the factors affecting the risk premium will be quite complicated; however, we can assess those which are likely to be of relatively greater importance if we consider the following approximation. First, expand around $\bar{\pi} = E\tilde{\pi}$, dropping third- and higher-order terms to find as an approximation

$$cov[\bar{u}'(\pi), g] = u''(\bar{\pi}) \, cov(\bar{\pi}, \tilde{g}). \tag{3.18}$$

Because $u'' < 0$, the sign of the risk premium depends upon the correlation of the monopolist's profits and his cash price. Next, with the ambiguous but convenient notation $\bar{\pi} = \bar{\pi}(\tilde{q})$ we can expand around some fixed output, $q°$ to find approximately

$$cov(\bar{\pi}, \tilde{g}) = E\bar{\pi}(q°)(\tilde{g} - E\tilde{g}) + E\left(\frac{\partial\bar{\pi}(q°)}{\partial q}(\tilde{q} - q°)(\tilde{g} - E\tilde{g})\right) \tag{3.19}$$

The second term on the right side is a third-moment term that we might expect to be small. This expectation is very likely to be true because, using equation 3.3, for $q°$ in the neighborhood of the optimal outputs

$$\frac{\partial \bar{\pi}(q°)}{\partial q} = 0$$

approximately. Concentrating then on the first term on the right side of equation 3.19, using equation 3.2, we can write this as

$$E\bar{\pi}(q°)(\tilde{g} - E\tilde{g}) = (q° - f_m)\text{var}(g|q°) - \text{cov}(c, \tilde{g}|q°) \qquad (3.20)$$

Combining equations 3.18, 3.19, and 3.20, the risk premium is approximately

$$(Eu')^{-1}u''(\bar{\pi})[q° - f_m)\text{var}(g|q°) - \text{cov}(c, g|q°)] \qquad (3.21)$$

The leading term $(Eu')^{-1}u''$ is a measure of the monopolist's risk aversion and is strictly negative.[9] The more risk averse the monopolist, the larger the coefficient of risk aversion in absolute value and, other things equal, the greater the equilibrium futures position in absolute value. The sign of the futures position will depend on the term in brackets in equation 3.21.

If the factors affecting demand are stochastically independent of those affecting costs, in the neighborhood of $f_m = 0$ the expression 3.21 is unambiguously negative. Consequently, in this case there is a rational expectations equilibrium that involves the monopolist taking a short position in futures. If the monopolist's costs and demand are negatively correlated the risk premium, equation 3.21 will be even more negative, thus representing a stronger inducement to the monopolist taking a short position. On the other hand, positively correlated costs and demand exert an opposite influence, tending to reduce the monopolist's short sales and, if very strong, inducing a long position.

To obtain specific results on the risk premium we have resorted to second-order approximations. Although the results in this context are only approximate, many of our conclusions could be established without approximation using a continuous time methodology in an intertemporal setting. In a continuous time setting the portfolio revision horizon is small and in the limit the horizon approaches zero. In such a context the only parameters of the distribution that are relevant at each instant are the vector of mean returns and the variance-covariance matrix (see Samuelson 1970 and Ohlson 1975). As a result, these approximations may be reasonable.

To summarize the results of this section, when the monopolist is risk-averse there will be a hedging motive for trading futures. In equilibrium, agents will generally hold futures positions even if expectations are rational. The size of the futures positions taken is an increasing function of the monopolist's coefficient of risk aversion. Whether the monopolist goes short or long depends on a complex of factors. This question cannot be definitively resolved on theoretical grounds and generally should be viewed as depending upon the particulars of the good in question. However, based on some Taylor series approximations, the principal factors are the variance of the cash price and the correlation of demand with the monopolist's costs. If costs and demand are unrelated or are negatively correlated, the monopolist holds short positions in a rational expectations equilibrium and the futures price is less than the expected cash price. In this case, the monopolist's hedging tends to increase his next-period production. Furthermore, in this case there is no risk that the monopolist will elect to corner the market by producing zero output. Only if the monopolist's costs and demand are highly positively correlated would his hedging induce him to hold a long position in equilibrium. Barring this case, futures trading plus monopolist's risk aversion tend to undercut the monopolist's cash market power.

Competitors' Hedging

In this subsection we allow for the possibility that the competitive agents who trade futures with the monopolist will choose positions partly to hedge other random income sources. For example, the competitors could be speculators holding a portfolio of assets that will select a futures position on the basis of its expected return and its contributions to the riskiness of the overall portfolio. Alternatively, the users of the monopolist's product may seek to reduce price risk by trading futures. We view the latter as the more likely source of hedging interest in futures and explore this case in greater detail.

We assume that the competitive agent i has a random income $\bar{y}_i$ apart from futures trading income so that his total period 1 income is

$$\bar{\pi}_i = \bar{y}_i + (p^f - \bar{p})f_i$$

If this agent chooses his futures position f_i at time 0 to maximize the expected utility of $\bar{\pi}_i$, the resulting futures position is generally decomposable into a hedging component and a pure speculation (see Anderson and Danthine 1983 for a discussion). The hedging component will generally be nonzero so long as $\bar{y}_i$ and $\bar{p}$ are not stochastically independent. The speculative futures short will be an increasing function of $(p^f - E_i\bar{p})$ and will be zero when $p^f = E_i\bar{p}$. In view of the hedging demand for futures, the agent's total futures position will be zero only if p^f differs from $E_i\bar{p}$ sufficiently to induce an exactly offsetting speculative component.

Competitors' hedging has immediate implications for the inverse futures demand curve faced by the monopolist and thus on the equilibrium in the futures market. If we assume homogeneous competitors' expectations ($E_i\bar{p} = \bar{p}_c$, all i), the monopolist would induce a futures price equal to the competitor's expected spot price only by taking a futures position that exactly meets the competitor's aggregate hedging demand. Alternatively stated,

$$\bar{p}_c \neq h(0) \qquad (3.22)$$

(Compare equation 3.22 with equation 3.8.) Property 3.22 generally will be sufficient to induce futures trading even if the monopolist is risk-neutral and expectations are rational.

To explore this, let us assume temporarily that the monopolist is risk-neutral so that equation 3.9 characterizes the monopolist's futures choice and the futures market equilibrium. Under rational expectations ($\bar{p}_c = Eg$), we see immediately that competitor's hedging implies $f_m = 0$ is not an equilibrium because at that point the left side of equation 3.9 is $h(0) - Eg$, which is not zero if equation 3.22 holds. If the competitors' aggregate hedging demand is long, $h(0) > Eg$; in rational expectations equilibrium the monopolist holds a short futures position. If the competitor's aggregate hedging position is short, $h(0) < Eg$; in the rational expectations equilibrium, the monopolist is long futures.

When the monopolist is risk-averse, hedging demand for futures originates from two sources. The equilibrium condition is then equation 3.17, which accepting the approximation 3.21, is

$$h(f_m) + h'(f_m)f_m - E\tilde{g} - \frac{u''(\bar{\pi})}{Eu'}((q^\circ - f_m)\text{var }\tilde{g}$$
$$- \text{cov}(\tilde{c}, \tilde{g})) = 0 \qquad (3.23)$$

Whether the equilibrium involves the monopolist going long or short depends on the sign of the risk premium and the direction of the competitor's hedging demand. If competitive hedging is long ($h(0) > Eg$) and the monopolist's costs are not positively correlated with demand, at $f_m = 0$ the left side of equation 3.23 is unambiguously positive and in rational expectations equilibrium the monopolist holds short futures positions. Either short competitive hedging ($h(0) < Eg$) or negatively related costs and demand ($\text{cov}(\tilde{g}, \tilde{c}) < 0$) exert the oppositive influence; if they are strong they may be sufficient to induce an equilibrium with the monopolist long futures positions.

It is of some importance then to determine whether competitive hedging interest is generally long or short. We now consider this issue in some detail for the case where the typical competitive agent's nonfutures income $\bar{y}_i$ is derived from buying the monopolist's good, processing it, and selling it to some agents farther along the chain of production, possibly the end-users. Specifically, we assume that at time 1 the competitor purchases amount q_i of the monopolist's good (taking the announced price as given), processes it according to some production function $\gamma_i(\cdot)$ (with $\gamma_i' > 0$ and $\gamma_i'' < 0$), and sells it at some given price s_i. Then the agent's income is

$$\pi_i = s_i \gamma_i(q_i) - pq_i + (p^f - p)f_i \qquad (3.24)$$

At $t = 1$ the agent's problem is to choose q_i to maximize π_i given s_i, p, p^f, and f_i.[10] The necessary condition is

$$s_i \gamma_i(q_i) - p = 0 \qquad (3.25)$$

In view of the properties of $\gamma(\cdot)$ the competitor's input demand is given by some $\theta_i(\cdot)$

$$q_i = \theta_i \left(\frac{p}{s_i} \right) \qquad (3.26)$$

It is useful to we consider the concentrated profit function obtained by inserting equation 3.26 in 3.24:

$$\pi_i = s_i \gamma_i \left(\theta_i \left(\frac{p}{s_i} \right) \right) - p\theta \left(\frac{p}{s_i} \right) + \left(p^f - p \right) f_i \qquad (3.27)$$

This function shows that the marginal effect on competitor's profits of a change in the monopolist's price is

$$\frac{\partial \pi_i}{\partial p} = \gamma_i' \theta_i' - \frac{p\theta_i}{s_i} - \theta_i - f_i = -(\theta_i + f_i) \qquad (3.28)$$

where the second equality follows from equation 3.25. Similarly, the effect of a change in selling price can be shown to be

$$\frac{\partial \pi_i}{\partial s_i} = \gamma_i \qquad (3.29)$$

At $t = 0$ the agent faces an uncertain income $\tilde{\pi}_i$. In addition to $\tilde{p}$ we assume his selling price $\tilde{s}_i$ is random. (The case of random production $\tilde{\gamma}_i$ is very similar and offers no additional insights.) His problem at $t = 0$ is to choose f_i to maximize $E_i u_i(\tilde{\pi}_i)$ where $u_i(\cdot)$ is the agent's utility function ($u_i' > 0$, $u_i'' < 0$). The necessary condition for this problem can be written as

$$p^f - E_i \bar{p} - \frac{\text{cov}(u_i', p)}{E u_i'} = 0 \tag{3.30}$$

As for the risk-averse monopolist's optimality condition (3.17), expression 3.30 involves a risk premium that depends on the covariance of marginal utility and the price of the monopolist's good. To focus on the principal determinants of the competitor's risk premium, we make the following approximations. First, expand around $\bar{\pi}_i$, retaining up to second-order terms

$$\text{cov}(\tilde{u}_i', \bar{p}) = u_i''(\bar{\pi}_i)\text{cov}(\tilde{\pi}_i, \bar{p})$$

Next, writing $\pi_i = \pi_i(p, s_i)$ we can expand around $Ep = \bar{p}$ and $Es_i = \bar{s}_i$ to find approximately

$$\text{cov}(\tilde{\pi}_i, \bar{p}) = \frac{\partial \pi_i(\bar{p}, \bar{s}_i)}{\partial p} \text{var } p + \frac{\partial \pi_i(\bar{p}, \bar{s}_i)}{\partial s_i} \text{cov}(s_i, p)$$

Combining these approximations and substituting equations 3.28 and 3.29, equation 3.30 can be written as

$$p^f - Ep - \frac{u_i''}{E u_i'} \left[- (\theta_i + f_i)\text{var } p + \gamma_i \text{cov}(s_i, p) \right] = 0 \tag{3.31}$$

We can solve this expression for the competitor's optimal futures position

$$f_i = \left(-\frac{E u_i'}{u_i''} \right) \left(\frac{p^f - E_i p}{\text{var } p} \right) + \frac{\gamma_i \text{cov}(s_i, p)}{\text{var } p} - \theta_i \tag{3.32}$$

The first term in equation 3.32 is the competitor's speculative supply of futures; as stated, it is increasing in $(p^f - Ep)$ and vanishes when the futures price is unbiased. The remaining terms are the agent's hedging component. The term $-\theta_i$ is just minus the competitor's planned purchases of the monopolist's good. The term $\gamma_i \text{cov}(s_i, p)/\text{var } p$ is his planned output times the theoretical regression coefficient of his selling price on the monopolist's price. If $\text{cov}(s_i, p) \leq 0$, the competitor's hedging demand for futures is unambiguously long; when his input and output prices are unrelated, his pure hedge consists of his planned purchases of the monopolist's output. If $\text{cov}(s_i, p) > 0$ so that the agent is able to pass along price increases at least partially, his long hedge will be less than his planned output, and if $\text{cov}(s_i, p)$ is sufficiently large it could involve him taking a short position.

What will determine $\text{cov}(s_i, p)$? If the monopolist's product is used in a wide variety of end uses and if these goods are not close substitutes then we would expect $\text{cov}(s_i, p)$ to be positive but negligibly small. At the opposite extreme, if the monopolist sells to producers of a single homogeneous good $(s_i = s$, all $s)$, then $\text{cov}(s, p)$ will depend on the elasticity of demand for the competitor's good. If this demand is highly elastic, $\text{cov}(s, p)$ will be small. Only if the demand for the competitor's good is very inelastic will $\text{cov}(s, p)$ be very large.

To summarize the results of this section, hedging by competitive futures traders alters the futures market equilibrium in important ways. In general, there will be futures trading even in a rational expectations equilibrium with a risk neutral monopolist. If the competitors' trading futures are the users of the monopolist's good, unless their output price is very highly correlated with the monopolist's output price, there is a tendency for the competitors' hedging demand to be long. Only if the final good price is very highly correlated with the monopolist's price could competitors conceivably engage in short hedges. Combining the results of this and the previous subsection we see that under what appears to be the most normal circumstances, futures hedging by the monopolist producer and by competitive users of the monopolist's product tends to result in an equilibrium with the monopolist holding short positions in futures and competitors holding long positions. In this circumstance, expected output of the monopolist is unambiguously increased by futures trading. Futures trading here has a beneficial effect on resource allocation as well as permits risk reduction for individual agents including the monopolist. Finally, if in equilibrium the monopolist's short sales exactly equals the competitor's long hedge, the resulting futures price coincides with the current expectation of the monopolist's cash price.

Simultaneous Production and Futures Choices

The model that has been analyzed to this point assumes the futures market meets prior to the cash market so that at $t = 0$ the monopolist is not committed to any particular production level. It might be thought that the results obtained may depend crucially on this feature and would be altered significantly if the monopolist committed himself at $t = 0$, for example, through a real investment decision. In this section we show that the earlier result—namely, the inactivity of the futures market in a speculative, rational expectations equilibrium—holds when the monopolist chooses his output level at $t = 0$.

Formally, we assume, as above, that the monopolist is risk-neutral and competitive speculators risk-averse, except that the monopolist chooses f_m and q simultaneously. If the monopolist commits himself at $t = 0$ to produce q, this decision constitutes a parameter for the competitors' problem. An important issue then is what is the information structure concerning q? We explicitly assume q is known by all agents. Thus we characterize a public information equilibrium. How this case differs from an equilibrium in which there is private information—for example, if the monopolist knows q but the competitors do not—is a question for future investigation.

If the competitors know q, this information will condition their expectations of the $t = 1$ cash price. That is, their futures demands will now be of the form

$$f_i = \psi_i[p^f - E_i(\tilde{p}|q)]$$

Consequently, the monopolist will recognize that his output choice will affect the futures demand; the equilibrium futures price will be given by an equation of the form

$$p^f = h(q, f_m) \qquad (3.33)$$

where $h_1 < 0$ and $h_2 < 0$.

Assuming he is risk-neutral, the monopolist's problem is to maximize $E\pi \equiv \bar{\pi}(q, f_m)$ with respect to q and f_m subject to the constraint $q \geqq 0$ and the definition in equation 3.2. Using equations 3.2 and 3.33, the necessary conditions for a stationary point are

$$\bar{\pi}_1 = Eg(q, \eta) + Eg_1(q, \eta)\,(q - f_m) - Ec_1(q, \varepsilon)$$
$$+ f_m h_1(q, f_m) \leqq 0 \qquad (3.34)$$

$$\bar{\pi}_2 = h(q, f_m) + f_m h_2(q, f_m) - Eg(q, \eta) = 0 \qquad (3.35)$$

The inequality in equation 3.34 reflects the fact that $q = 0$ may be a solution. Thus the fact that the monopolist chooses his output simultaneously with his futures position does not eliminate the possibility that the monopolist will produce zero output in an attempt to gain the maximum return from his futures position. Because we again assume that the curvature of the cash demand cost functions are such as to assure a unique interior solution q^* when $f = 0$, it is clear from equation 3.34 that the possibility of a corner solution depends on the expectations reflected in $Eg_1(q, \varepsilon)$ and $h_1(q, f_m)$. For arbitrary expectations little can be said. However, we will show that

$q = q^*$ and $f_m = 0$ constitute a locally unique rational expectations equilibrium.

Formally, we must show that $(q^*, 0)$ satisfies condition 3.34 with a strict equality (equation 3.35) and the second-order conditions for a locally unique maximum—namely: $\bar{\pi}_{11} < 0$, $\bar{\pi}_{22} < 0$, and $\bar{\pi}_{11} \bar{\pi}_{22} - (\bar{\pi}_{12})^2 > 0$.

If competitors are speculators who observe q and whose expectations are rational, they will be willing to hold a futures position only if the futures price differs from the cash price rationally expected given q. Thus rational expectations implies

$$h(q, 0) = Eg(q, \eta) \quad \text{all } q \tag{3.36}$$

Now, by assumption, the (q, f_m) pair $(q^*, 0)$ satisifies equation 3.34 and $\bar{\pi}_{11} < 0$. Furthermore, by equation 3.36 we see immediately that $(q^*, 0)$ satisfies 3.35. Furthermore

$$\bar{\pi}_{22}(q, f_m) = 2h_2(q, f_m) + f_m h_{22}(q, f_m)$$

so that $\bar{\pi}_{22}(q^*, 0) < 0$ since $h_2 < 0$. Finally,

$$\bar{\pi}_{12}(q, f_m) = h_1(q, f_m) + f_m h_{12}(q, f_m) - Eg_1(q, \eta)$$

But by equation 3.36, $h_1(q, 0) = Eg_1(q, \eta)$ for all q so that $\bar{\pi}_{12}(q^*, 0) = 0$ and thus $\bar{\pi}_{11}(q^*, 0) \cdot \bar{\pi}_{22}(q^*, 0) - [\bar{\pi}_{12}(q^*, 0)]^2 = \bar{\pi}_{11} \bar{\pi}_{22} > 0$. This shows that $(q^*, 0)$ is a locally unique solution to the monopolist's problem under equation 3.36 and thus constitutes a locally unique rational expectations equilibrium.

If the monopolist is risk-averse, the fact that he must commit himself to a production level q at $t = 0$ will affect his use of futures as a hedging instrument. Consequently, the discussion earlier in this section must be modified if we allow for the simultaneous choice of f_m and q. It should be clear, however, that the general conclusion will still hold—namely, that there will be an active futures market when the monopolist is risk-averse even in a rational expectations equilibrium. The characteristics of his futures position will differ; however, we do not pursue these details here.

Conclusion

In this chapter we examine prices and resource allocations in futures markets when the cash good is produced under imperfectly competitive conditions. In this sense, we reconsider, in the setting of a static monopolist, results that were previously obtained in static competitive equilibrium.

Unlike the competitive case, we find futures trading affects resource allocation independently of any risk reduction because the monopolist will choose
an output level in part for the effect it will have on his futures trading profit.
If he has sold futures, it will result in greater output than would otherwise
prevail. If he has bought futures, output is reduced. In an extreme case,
when the monopolist has accumulated a sufficiently large long futures
position, he will elect to produce nothing, thus cornering the futures market
and obtaining the maximum possible futures trading profit. The outcome
that prevails depends on the expectations of the market participants; we
devote particular attention to the case of rational expectations with full,
public information. Specifically, we show that, when the futures market is
viewed as an arena of pure speculative side bets, rational expectations
preclude any trading at equilibrium prices. On the other hand, when the
monopolist or the competitors wish to hedge, generally there is trading in
rational expectations equilibrium.

If both the monopolist and the purchasers of his product hedge, the
equilibrium that emerges depends on the elasticity of supply of primary
inputs and of demand for the final product as well as on the degree that
agents are risk-averse. Thus despite the differences these results are completely analogous to the competitive analysis of Anderson and Danthine
(1983). Accepting some second-order approximations and excluding some
extreme forms of primary supply and final demand, we see that the situation
when both the monopolist and his customers hedge futures trading is socially
beneficial in the sense that expected output is increased and private risks are
reduced.

This rather benign view of futures markets and monopoly may be rather
surprising, especially in contrast with Newbery (chapter 2) who finds a
futures market provides a dominant producer with an additional means of
exercising market power. Our results clearly indicate that Newbery's conclusions follow his assumption that the dominant producer is risk-neutral
and the competitive hedgers are producers of the good. In this case dominant producer tends to go long futures and reduce his physical output. The
supply effect (because the hedgers are also producers), noted by Newbery
but excluded from our discussion by the assumption of monopolistic production, is a partial counterbalance to the socially harmful effect of the larger
producer's long speculation.

A potentially important public policy question is whether futures trading should be permitted for goods produced under imperfect competition.
This analysis suggests that there is no general case to be made against futures
trading in such industries. Futures trading of monopolist goods can be
beneficial when there is sufficient long hedging or the monopolist is risk-
averse. An important concern then is whether, in a particular case, an
imperfectly competitive producer will behave in a risk-averse or risk-neutral

manner. If the producer is a broadly held corporation or is internally well diversified, it might be argued that they will act to maximize expected profits. On the other hand, for a very large producer of a commodity (such as Brazil's production of coffee), risks associated with price fluctuation may be so large as to be undiversifiable. In that case, the producer may be risk-averse and our analysis suggests that in giving an outlet for hedging a futures market will improve the allocation of resources. However, this conclusion is based on the assumption that the imperfectly competitive producer does not possess informational advantages.

The analysis in this chapter also has implications for the design of new contracts. Specifically, futures contracts for goods produced under imperfect competition are similar to the competitive case. The potential for futures trading exists if there is a hedging demand. Whether or not there is a hedging demand for a futures market depends in part of the extent of the risk aversion of producers and users, as well as the availability of alternative methods of risk-shifting. The only financial instrument explicitly present in this analysis is a futures contract; it would be interesting to reconsider the problem, still in an incomplete markets setting, but with such alternative commercial arrangements as price-listing. Without hedging demand, the only rational reason for trading is differential information or "price discovery" as it is called in the industry.

What tasks remain for future research? Competitive models of futures trading and futures pricing have been extended to intertemporal settings to study many interesting questions such as the time pattern of hedging, price volatility, normal backwardation, and the like. A natural extension of this study would be to model the dynamic monopolist who trades futures. In this setting we could study such issues in the context of an imperfectly competitive market.

For simplicity, the good in this chapter was assumed to be perishable. In a more general setting the precise nature of the cash good might be an important determinant of the nature of equilibrium. Bulow (1982) and Stokey (1981) among others have shown that when the good is durable, monopoly power is somewhat mitigated. It is possible that with a durable cash good, the trading of futures might be a means of assuring precommitment and may restore some of the monopolist's power. The basis risk associated with the quality differentials in the good produced by the monopolist relative to that in the second-hand market is yet another dimension of interest.

Through this chapter we assumed that homogeneous information was available to all participants without cost. In reality, the anonymity of traders in futures markets makes private information a real possibility. For instance, if the monopolist can participate in the futures market anonymously and his position size is not public information, the equilibrium implications of such markets can be quite different. Another source of differential information may be that the monopolist may have a more precise idea about the realization from the production technology than other participants. In these cases it may be thought that the monopolist may be able to exploit his private information in futures trading. The question then becomes: will anyone be rationally willing to trade with the monopolist in the futures market? In this setting a nonexistence of speculation result similar to proposition 2 may be obtained. Even if there is trading in the futures market, it may be that all information will be revealed in static equilibrium prices as in Danthine (1977) and Grossman and Stiglitz (1975). Alternatively, fully revealing prices may emerge in the limit of an infinitely repeated, asymmetric information game.

Notes

1. For a discussion of the coffee cartel see Greenstone (1981).

2. It is also true that export merchandising is concentrated in a small number of large grain companies. See Morgan (1979) for a description of the grain companies and an analysis of grain exports.

3. The two trading dates assumption implies that there is no distinction between futures prices and forward prices. The differences between forward prices and futures prices are discussed in Cox, Ingersoll, and Ross (1981) and Richard and Sundaresan (1981).

4. A third interpretation is that the futures market does not call for the delivery of the monopolist's product but rather for a monetary payment proportional to the differences between the futures price at time 0 and the price of the monopolist's good at time 1. A number of existing futures markets call for cash settlements of this sort. We have placed no bounds on the futures position size so the monopolist's output may be less than the aggregate sales in the futures market. It might be thought that this implies that the futures market in our model must be of the cash settlement type. In fact, we can accommodate futures sales exceeding total output within the context of a traditional physical delivery market if we imagine the same physical good may be retendered several times in the cash good's secondary market, which is precisely what happens in the delivery process of many existing futures markets.

5. In reality, the payoff in a futures contract is bounded even if the cash price is not because a short position holder has the option of defaulting on the contract. In such case, an exchange will follow a default settlement procedure that typically calls for a cash payment which reflects normal equilibrium price under the circumstance. For example, the Maine potato default of 1976 was settled in this way. We have eschewed modeling futures

contract defaults explicitly but have assumed a bounded cash price, which permits an equivalent but less cumbersome analysis.

6. Direct monopoly power in futures markets may take many forms. Access to information about outstanding orders is an example. This type of monopoly power is not the focus of our study.

7. As a matter of principle, with a finite number of agents the equilibrium condition 5 implies that the decision of each agent will affect the futures price. We have assumed this effect is negligible for all agents except the monopolist.

8. So long as h'' is not too large in absolute value, the equilibrium will be globally unique. This is true for example with linear futures demand ($h'' = 0$).

9. This measure of risk aversion coincides with the coefficient of absolute risk aversion ($-u''/u'$) except that in equation 3.21 the numerator is the function evaluated at the mean profit $\bar{\pi}$, whereas the denominator is the mean expected marginal utility.

10. Alternatively we could assume that q_i must be chosen at $t = 0$, perhaps because of a binding forward commitment or technological requirements. The analysis would be much the same. Anderson and Danthine (1983) and Stein (1979) discuss this kind of long hedging. Our formulation of the competitor's problem imposes no wealth constraint. If such a constraint were imposed, as would be the case if competitors were consumers who allocated their predetermined income among many goods including the monopolist's, their profits or losses from futures trading would directly affect their demands for the monopolist's product. Consequently, f_m would enter directly into the inverse cash market demand function $g(\cdot)$. This complication is not explored in this chapter.

References

Anderson, R.W., and J.P. Danthine (1983). "Hedger Diversity in Futures Markets," *Economic Journal*, vol. 93, 370–389.

Bray, M. (1981). "Futures Trading, Rational Expectations, and the Efficient Market Hypothesis," *Econometrica*, vol. 49, pp. 575–596.

Bulow, J.I. (1982). "Durable Goods Monopolist," *Journal of Political Economy*, vol. 90, pp. 314–332.

Cox, J.,J. Ingersoll, and S.A. Ross (1981). "The Relation Between Forward Prices and Futures Prices," *Journal of Financial Economics*, vol. 9, pp. 321–346.

Danthine, J.P. (1978). "Information, Futures Markets, and Stabilizing Speculation," *Journal of Economic Theory*, vol. 17, pp. 79–98.

Greenstone, W.D. (1981). "The Coffee Cartel: Manipulation in the Public Interest," *Journal of Futures Markets*, vol. 1, pp. 3–16.

Grossman, S.J., and J.E. Stiglitz (1976). "Information and the Competitive Price System," *American Economic Review, Proceedings*, vol. 66, pp. 246–253.

Keynes, J.M. (1923). "Some Aspects of Commodity Markets," *Manchester Guardian Commercial*.

Kreps, D.M. (1977). "A Note on 'Fulfilled Expectations' Equilibria," *Journal of Economic Theory*, 14, pp. 32–43.

Kyle, A.S. (1981). "An Equilibrium Model of Speculation and Hedging," Unpublished dissertation, University of Chicago.

Morgan, D. (1979). *Merchants of Grain*. New York: Viking Press.

Ohlson, J.A. (1975). "The Asymptotic Validity of Quadratic Utility as the Trading Interval Approaches Zero," in *Stochastic Optimization Models in Finance*, ed. W.T. Ziemba and R.G. Vickson. New York: Academic Press.

Richard, S.T., and M. Sundaresan (1981). "A Continuous Time Model of Forward Prices and Futures Prices in a Multigood Economy," *Journal of Financial Economics*, vol. 9, pp. 347–371.

Salant, S.W. (1983). "The Vulnerability of Price Stabilization Schemes to Speculative Attack," *Journal of Political Economy*, vol. 91, pp. 1–38.

Samuelson, P.A. (1970). "The Fundamental Approximation Theorem of Portfolio Analysis in Terms of Means, Variances and Higher Moments," *Review of Economic Studies*, vol. 37, 537–542.

Stein, J.L. (1979). "Spot, Forward, and Futures," *Research in Finance*, vol. 1, pp. 225–310.

Stokey, N.L. (1981). "Rational Expectations and Durable Goods Pricing," *Bell Journal of Economics*, vol. 12, pp. 112–128.

Telser, L.G. (1981). "Margins and Futures Contracts," *Journal of Futures Markets*, vol. 1, pp. 225–254.

———. H.N. Higinbotham (1977). "Organized Futures Markets: Costs and Benefits," *Journal of Political Economy*, vol. 85, pp. 969–1000.

Tirole, J. (1982). "On the Possibility of Speculation Under Rational Expectations," *Econometrica*, vol. 50, pp. 1163–1182.

Comment

Robert W. Rosenthal

The results of chapter 3 are probably sensitive to certain modeling decisions by the authors that, although convenient for purposes of analysis, are not obviously superior to possible alternative decisions as descriptors of reality. The first of these modeling decisions is the treatment of the agents who trade with the monopolist in the futures markets as passive; these agents behave according to some function known to or deduced by the monopolist. It is, of course, familiar from the economics literature that assuming Stackelberg leader-follower behavior generally leads to different results than does a more symmetric (such as Nash) treatment, no matter how rationally the followers' function is selected. Second, chapter 3 assumes that the agents' actions are choices of quantities, a Cournot-like treatment; and it is equally familiar that different action variables for the agents (such as price) can lead to radically different results. Third, the authors assume that the market-clearing price in the cash market is unaffected by what has transpired in the futures market (except indirectly through the monopolist's output), evidently reflecting the attitude that any price that clears the cash market will also clear it when equal amounts are added to both the supply and the demand sides as a consequence of positions taken in the futures market (an attitude that seems to me inconsistent with the Cournot treatment).

To illustrate one instance in which these three assumptions combine to generate a seemingly idiosyncratic analysis, consider the situation in which the monopolist decides to buy futures and produce nothing, intending to squeeze the shorts. In chapter 3, the cash-market price is read from the demand curve *g* independently of, for example, the size of the monopolist's position. In the real world, of course, there must be some bound to the profits that can be generated in a squeeze, and the authors probably intend their treatment as merely suggestive of what arises when additional institutional details are included in the model; but their methods would no longer be appropriate if the cash-market price were to depend in part on the outcome in the futures market or if either of the other two aforementioned assumptions are altered. In fact, it would not seem difficult to produce a model in which, on the basis of plausible assumptions, equilibrium requires that only the monopolist can be short.

Finally, the authors' finding that risk-averse speculators will not trade in the futures market when there is a risk-neutral monopolist in this model is reminiscent of some recent no-trade results in the economics literature which arise even when additional informational disparities among the agents are present.[1] Such sources cite an added disincentive to trade (one that may be interesting in the context of futures markets) because, roughly speaking, the knowledge that some other agent would be willing to trade under certain terms is itself a signal that the terms are less favorable for a given agent that he might otherwise infer.

Notes

1. See Geanakoplos, J., and Sebenius, J.K. (1982), "Don't Bet on It," Cowles Foundation Discussion Paper. New Haven, Conn.: Yale University, 1982; and Milgrom, P., and Stokey, N. (1982), "Information, Trade, and Common Knowledge," *Journal of Economic Theory*, 26. pp. 17–27.

Comment

James Hayes

Major Conclusions

Citing the existence of futures markets for noncompetitively produced commodities like coffee and cocoa, the authors define models of monopolists' behavior in futures markets for commodities and establish optimal conditions for their behavior.

Their first conclusion is, for a single producer with two trading dates (the first trading date is futures trading; the second trading date the setting of cash market price and quantity), that futures trading will induce him to produce more than he otherwise would have produced in the absence of a futures market.

Necessary conditions for an optimum are the subject of the section on futures market equilibrium. For a risk-neutral monopolist and risk-averse competitors, the authors conclude there will be no futures position in a rational expectations equilibrium because competitors wish to be short (long) when the monopolist is short (long). For the risk-averse monopolist optimality conditions are also established. Key terms in these optimality conditions are the covariances of marginal utility of profits and cash price or cost and cash prices. In either case if the covariance is positive (negative) and big enough in magnitude, the monopolist goes long (short) futures. When and if competitive agents of the monopolist have other income and hedge it in the futures market, the authors conclude the optimum futures position has a pure hedge component and a speculative component.

The sign and magnitude of the speculative component turns on the difference, if any, between the futures price and the expected cash price. The key element of the hedge component is the competitive agent's planned output times the partial of his selling price with respect to the monopolist's selling price. The authors point out the similarity of these results to prior literature on optimum hedges.

Finally, the authors examine the impact on a rational expectations equilibrium of the monopolist's choosing cash and futures positions simultaneously. They conclude the futures market will be inactive in a speculative, rational expectations equilibrium.

Critique

I have two general remarks on chapter 3. First, I find propositions about the trading of competitors against monopolists on the one hand and the decomposition of optimum futures positions into speculative and hedge components on the other hand reasonable. I do not know if the particular canonical formulations of the model are necessarily correct, but the results they generate are plausible. In energy futures markets, participants are unwilling to trade against the dominant firm if they think that firm has significant informational advantages over prices. Some companies assert they will not trade heating oil futures as much as they would were it not for the ability of some firms to move both cash and futures markets.

Some energy firms long in the cash market can be simultaneously optimally long or short in the futures market. Firms long cash and long futures in the futures vernacular are said to have "Texas hedges."

Second, some of the presumptions in chapter 3 are not plausible. Working for a commodities exchange, I find it difficult to imagine how an exchange, without extenuating circumstances, would write a futures contract and get it approved by the CFTC if there is only one principal short, the monopolist. Expectations of the high probabilities of a squeeze by the short would prelude a futures contract. If a futures contract had been designed for a more or less competitive market and if that market had changed to become a monopolist's market, the exchange and government regulators would evaluate the probability of squeezes in the market. If the probability were judged to be too great, the futures contract would be redesigned in some manner to neutralize the monopolist's advantages.

Other Issues

My professional contact with oil companies is a basis for an examination of other issues related to but not treated in chapter 3. There is a simultaneous demand for both futures markets and a strategy for organizing and determining optimum futures positions among many oil companies today. Many firms link their decision to trade futures at all with their ability to organize and to gather information for futures trading.

Among other things, commodity exchanges are in the business of supplying futures markets. Long and short hedgers and others are in the business of demanding futures markets. New futures markets are successful, like the energy markets, when companies decide they should trade futures and decide they can effectively organize to trade futures. Once companies decide they have a strategic policy for organizing to trade cash and futures, they put the effort into solving for more precise decision rules for optimal hedges, however defined.

Many companies, in deciding to trade futures, evaluate their use of their forward markets (term-supply agreements) to hedge themselves. If a company has creditworthy trading partners upstream and downstream, they can often be as well hedged in the forward market as they would be in a futures market. Consequently, for some companies futures markets compete with forward markets, not to mention spot markets.

These firms also will decide to trade which market (spot, forward, or futures) depending on which market gives them the best price. One of the reasons the New York harbor heating oil contract is so successful is because heating oil jobbers from time to time along the Eastern seaboard saw the futures market as a cheaper way to get product compared to traditional spot and forward markets.

The New York Merchantile Exchange also attempted recently to trade Gulf Coast heating oil and gasoline contracts. These contracts failed after a short time because, in my view, of vigorous competition with long-term forward markets among upstream producers at the primary distribution level of refined products markets. Many oil people in recent years think they do not need a futures market because they can get product any time they want from their long-term trading partners with little or no credit risk. That these companies perceive little credit risk in the forward markets, other things equal, lessens the economic significance of the credit guarantees offered by clearing houses associated with exchanges.

Many oil companies have begun to trade energy futures for several reasons:

1. The cost of credit has risen in their spot and forward markets.
2. Prices have become more variable.
3. For buying or selling in futures markets there are from time to time better prices than in spot or forward markets.
4. There are opportunities to speculate.
5. Significantly, they fear being left behind, competitively, other firms in the oil industry who use futures markets to solve logistical and marketing problems.

Flexible marketing opportunities for trading wet barrels like hedged fixed-price contracts, basis pricing, or even private options on futures positions are getting increased attention.

These various comments on the demand for futures markets underscore the complexity of how futures markets come into existence and how companies evaluate the prospects for successful trading. Although I believe the authors have presupposed too much about how a monopolist would ever come to find himself in a position to trade a futures market for the commodity he produces, I nonetheless think they have begun to lay the foundation for very interesting future work. For example, their preliminary efforts to model a monopolist's choosing cash and futures positions simultaneously rather than sequentially is an important extension of their model worth exploring further.

I think attention needs eventually be paid to the type of futures contract that even the monopolist might trade. There are three kinds of futures contracts: settlement by the cash commodity, by receipts good for the cash commodity, and cash dollars. Active secondary markets usually develop for the receipts in receipt delivery contracts. A monopolist's decision to trade a receipt contract will not be made for the same reasons as a decision to trade a cash commodity contract because outstanding receipts, having been delivered through a futures exchange, constitute an uncertain draw on production or inventories for the monopolist.

4 Futures Markets when Agents are Myopic

Simon Benninga

Introduction

Futures markets models in the literature are typified by one or more of the following features:

Hedgers are pictured as buying insurance or otherwise protecting existing spot positions (see, for example, Cootner 1960, Johnson 1960, Stein 1961, Telser 1960).

Decisions are defined as taking place over a finite, defined amount of time. The usual framework is a two-period model (Cootner 1960, Grossman 1977, Johnson 1960, Stein 1961).

Something can be said about the statistical properties of futures and other prices in the model (see Grossman 1977 and Johnson 1960; see also the recent symposium in the *Journal of Financial Economics*: Cox, Ingersoll, and Ross 1981; Richard and Sundaresan 1981; Jarrow and Oldfield 1981).

Markets are assumed to equilibrate, and it is the equilibrium properties of futures prices that are discussed.

However, none of these four properties represent very accurately what we know (and it is but little and not organized well) about the way futures markets operate. In the model in this chapter, none of these four properties necessarily hold.[1]

Hedging: Traditional Theory and Observation of Practice

It is well known that the actual activities of hedgers in futures markets coincide but little with the standard textbook examples. Such examples of hedging contain a progression that is well illustrated by Hoffman (1925). After first illustrating a number of perfect hedges (in which the hedger guarantees himself the current price and there is no basis risk), Hoffman discusses basis changes as a function of carrying charges. The first section of the next chapter ("Limitations Affecting Hedging") is entitled "A more

113

extended analysis necessary"—a familiar refrain in the subsequent literature. Hoffman concludes that the spot and the futures prices "frequently get
out of alignment, causing a speculative loss or gain to the hedger."

Other authors have also referred to the speculative aspects of hedging.
Working (1953) concludes that the

> role of risk-avoidance in most commercial hedging has been greatly over-
> emphasized in economic discussions. . . . Hedging in commodity futures
> involves the purchase or sale of futures in conjunction with another
> commitment, usually in the expectation of a favorable change in the rela-
> tion between spot and future prices.

Hieronymus (1963) makes the same point more succinctly; he defines hedging as being speculation on the basis instead of on the cash price. An even
stronger view is expressed by Johnson (1960). After surveying representatives of the coffee trade in New York, Johnson writes:

> The traders in the survey take cognizance not only of expected relative
> price movements but of expected *absolute* price movements as well. Gen-
> erally, if traders expect spot prices to rise they tend to remove hedges and
> increase their inventory holdings. In some cases they take long positions in
> both the spot and futures markets as a more obvious speculative venture.
> On the other hand, if they are bearish they increase their short futures
> positions in excess of hedging requirements. In other words, hedging
> activities get mixed in very closely with speculative operations in the
> accounts of the individual trader.

The salient features of the hedging model of this chapter are well
described in the quotation from Johnson. These features are:

Hedgers make separate decisions on inventory sizes (physicals) and on
sizes of futures positions.

The gains/losses anticipated from these separate decisions are viewed
additively. That is, although the position as a whole may be viewed as a
portfolio, there is no necessity for a hedge ratio of 1.

Decisions are based on expectations of short-term price movements.

The fact that a futures decision is made without necessary reference to
the size of the dealer's inventory raises an obvious question about how
futures markets can clear. For example, imagine that both storers (that is,
consumers with access to storage facilities) and speculators (other consumers) believe that the futures price will rise. If Johnson's description is
correct, the result will be that both speculators and hedgers will wish to be
long in the futures market. An obvious way out of this dilemma is to assume
that futures markets can only clear when there is a difference of opinion

between speculators and hedgers as to the movement of prices. Such an approach, however, means that we are excluding the case where prices are rational. I resolve this problem later in this chapter by assuming that there are both qualitative and quantitative differences between storers and speculators.

Marking to Market: Futures vs. Forward Markets

A second major problem with many models of futures markets is that they in effect have dealt with forward markets. In a forward market it makes sense to speak of two or more defined points in time—the delivery dates for the goods, or the time at which the inventory is purchased and the hedge established and the subsequent time when both these actions are undone. In its simplest versions, a forward market model allows discussion of hedging as arbitrage and speculation as risk-bearing activity for which payment must be made. In more complicated models (for example, Grossman 1977) the forward market mechanism allows discussion of how much one side of the market can learn from the other, more informed side.

The futures market is complicated, however, by the fact that all prices are marked to market daily. Marking to market has a number of effects. First, it is impossible to consider a futures market contract as a simple, two-date arrangement, because the purchaser/seller of the contract must bear considerable intermediate price risks. This fact—and its attendant consequences when something is known about future interest rate movements—has been noted and expanded on the *Journal of Financial Economics* symposium cited above. The results given in that symposium depend critically upon extreme informational assumptions. Second, it has important effects on the budget equations of the purchaser/seller of the contract. Third, it appears to have the effect of shortening the horizon over which speculators (and perhaps hedgers) operated. For example, as Cahnman (1982) notes:

> All analysis must be made on a daily basis. The reason for this is that margin risk is the primary risk associated with commodity trading. . . . In fact, analysis of daily closes may not be sufficient because margin calls can be made at any time during the trading day. Daily highs and lows should be incorporated so as to give margin risk its proper emphasis. I want to emphasize that, in my personal speculation, margin risk is the most important consideration.

The Informational Requirements of Existing Models

Another common property of many futures markets models is the assumption that some information about the statistical properties of futures prices is known. In its extreme form this is taken to mean that the distribution of futures prices (and other relevant prices in the future—for instance, interest rates) is known. This assumption is employed in both portfolio models and in the arbitrage models. A less extreme version is that some of the participants know the statistical properties of the prices and that the function of the markets is to allow other participants to learn these properties (Grossmann 1977).

Existing empirical evidence would seem to indicate that at best participants in futures markets feel that they know some long-term properties of futures prices. Thus Hieronymus (1963) states: "I would like to mention a theoretical basis pattern for a two-year period. In the long run, the cash price of grain will increase by the cost of storing grain for a year." However, because marking to market has the effect of shortening horizons, long-run tendencies of the market are not likely to be significant.

Is a Static Equilibrium a Meaningful Concept?

Finally, it appears to be the intention of many of the model builders in futures markets to construct equilibrium models of pricing. Later, I shall ask if a model in which trading is continuous and both speculators and hedgers are myopic and can observe only local properties of prices can be logically said to have a static equilibrium. It appears that the best one can do in such a model is to discuss some kind of Hicksian "temporary equilibrium" (Hicks 1946). In particular I wish to claim that equilibrium results derived on the assumption of full information make such extreme assumptions about the ability of speculators and hedgers to deal with informational burdens that the results are doubtful.

Preliminaries

The model is an adaptation of Smale's model (1976), in which there is continuous trading at (possibly) out-of-equilibrium prices. Traders are not required to optimize, but a given set of trades will be made at any time t only if those trades are in some sense utility-improving and are market-clearing (technicalities are outlined in later sections).

There are H physical goods, I speculators, and J storers. Time starts at $t = 0$; at $t = t_.$ there is a delivery date for the single futures market of the model. This futures market deals in physical commodity 1 only. Up to time $t_.$ there is continuous trading in both the spot and the futures markets.

Both speculators and storers trade a vector of physical goods that they will eventually consume. Trades affecting this vector are made only if there is a direct utility improvement. In addition both storers and speculators trade futures contracts, and storers—who have access to a storage technology—can acquire inventories (or sell them) of the single good for which a futures market exists. Both storers and speculators are assumed to have knowledge only of the local properties of the commodity and futures prices. The vector of commodity prices at time t will be denoted by $p(t) = (p_1(t), \ldots, p_H(t))$. The futures price at t for the delivery of one unit of good 1 at time $t_\circ$ will be denoted by $F(t)$.

Speculators

By speculators I shall mean all consumers who do not have access to storage facilities. Each speculator is endowed with a utility function U_i defined over the vector of goods $x_i = (x_{i1}, \ldots, x_{iH})$ of goods which the speculator will eventually consume. Initially, consumer i starts off with an endowment of goods $x_i(0)$; he trades this endowment continuously at market prices and his goods vector at time t will be denoted by $x_i(t)$. Given a vector of market prices at time t of $p(t) = (p_1(t), \ldots, p_H(t))$ and given a change $x'_i(t)$ in consumer i's goods vector, the cost of such a change is the dot product of $p(t)$ and $x'_i(t)$

$$p(t)x'_i(t) = \sum_h p_h(t)x'_{ih}(t) \tag{4.1}$$

In addition to trading consumption vectors, speculators may—at any time $s \leq t$—purchase or sell on the futures market at the prevailing price $F(s)$. In this chapter there is a futures market only in the first good; to prevent futures purchases from becoming a substitute for spot purchases, I shall assume that $p_1(s) < F(s)$ for all $s \leq t_\circ$. Denote speculators i's net position in the futures market at time t by $y_i(t)$. Daily settlement means that any position undertaken leads to an immediate profit or loss when futures prices change. Thus, although taking a new position in the futures market has no effect on the speculator's budget, existing positions will effect this budget through marking to market. The instantaneous effect of a change in futures prices on the budget of speculator i is given by

$$y_i(t)F'(t) \tag{4.2}$$

(Proof of equation 4.2 and other technical details are given in appendix 4A.)
    The budget constraint of speculator i is given by the sum of equations 4.1 and 4.2

$$x'_i(t)p(t) + y_i(t)F'(t) = 0 \tag{4.3}$$

Consumers make voluntary changes in their consumption (goods) vectors only to increase their utility (this rule also applies to hedgers, as shown later). On the other hand, it follows from equation 4.4 that a change in the futures price F can force consumers to liquidate part of their consumption vector. If such liquidation is not forced, I assume that changes in the consumption vector are to improve utility:

$$y_i(t)F'(t) > 0 \quad \rightarrow \quad (d/dt)U_i(x_i(t)) > 0 \tag{4.4}$$

How do speculators pick y_i'? This problem is not trivial, because y_i' has no immediate effect either on the budget equation nor on the utility function U_i. I shall assume that speculators choose y_i' to maximize the contribution of the futures position to the budget. Differentiating $y_i(t)F'(t)$ with respect to t gives

$$y_i'(t)F'(t) + y_i(t)F''(t) \tag{4.5}$$

To complete the story, I shall assume that speculators' positions in the futures market are so small that the second term of equation 4.5 is negligible. We then have[2]

$$y_i'(t) \gtrless 0 \quad \text{if and only if} \quad F'(t) \gtrless 0 \tag{4.6}$$

Storage and Hedging

A special set of consumers will be termed storers. Storers have access to a storage technology (that is they own grain elevators, warehouses, or other storage sites) that is exclusive to them and that has linear storage costs. A typical storer j has an inventory of $z_j(t)$ at time t. The cost of purchasing this inventory was

$$\int_0^t z_j'(s)p(s)ds \tag{4.7}$$

Storage costs are assumed to be linear. Denote the cost of storing one unit of good for one unit of time for storer j by c_j. Then total storage costs by time t are

$$\int_0^t c_j z_j'(s)(t-s)ds \tag{4.8}$$

Because the total market value of the storer's inventories at time t is $z_j(t)p(t)$, we may write the net value (at market prices) of the storer's inventories by

$$z_j(t)p(t) - \int_0^t z_j'(s) \{ p(s) + c_j(t-s) \} \, ds \qquad (4.9)$$

Like speculators, storers have access to futures markets. Writing the storer's total futures position at time t by $y_j(t)$, the value of this position is

$$\int_0^t y_j'(s) \{ F(t) - F(s) \} \, ds \qquad (4.10)$$

In the next two subsections, I contrast two possible objective functions for the storer.

The Naive Storer

The naive storer looks only at the delivery value of the goods he has purchased for storage; that is, he treats the futures market as if it were a forward market (he is, in fact, doing what a great many texts tell him to do). The naive storer's total profits at time t are the sum of anticipated receipts from delivering on his futures contracts minus the total costs of purchasing the goods minus total storage costs up to delivery:

$$\Pi_j(t) = - \int_0^t y_j'(s)F(s)ds - \int_0^t z_j'(s) \{ p(s) + c_j(t_\circ - s) \} \, ds \quad (4.11)$$

If we assume that the naive storer sets his short futures position equal to his inventories—that is, $y_j'(s) = - z_j'(s)$ for $0 \le s \le t$— then total profits at t become

$$\Pi_j(t) = \int_0^t z_j'(s) \{ F(s) - p(s) - c_j(t_\circ - s) \} \, ds \qquad (4.12)$$

The naive storer—like all agents in the model—is assumed to be myopic, and he is therefore interested in choosing a purchase/hedging strategy that increases his profits locally. Taking the derivative of $\Pi_j(t)$, we get

$$\Pi_j'(t) = z_j'(t) \{ F(t) - p(t) - c_j(t_\circ - t) \} \qquad (4.13)$$

It is readily seen that a profit-increasing strategy (one can't talk here of a profit-maximizing strategy) for the naive storer is one which sets

$$z_j'(t) \gtreqqless 0 \quad \text{if and only if} \quad F(t) - p(t) - c_j(t_\circ - t) \gtreqqless 0 \qquad (4.14)$$

The naive storer thus builds up inventories when the futures price suffices to cover purchase and storage costs and sells off inventories when the futures price falls below the sum of the current spot price plus storage costs until delivery.

The naive storer's strategy ignores the cost at which inventories were purchased in the past in making the decision to sell them off at time t. The intuition behind this is as follows: Consider goods bought by the storer at time s at price $p(s)$ and hedged for delivery at $t_\circ$ at $F(s)$. At some time t, $s < t < t_\circ$, it may profit the naive storer to sell the goods and lift the hedge. To derive the conditions under which this may be so, consider such a sale. The profit on the sale of the physical goods at t will be

$$p(t) - p(s) \qquad (5.15)$$

and the profit from lifting the hedge will be

$$F(s) - F(t) \qquad (5.16)$$

Total profits from disstorage of one unit of the physical good are the sum of equations 5.15 and 5.16 minus accumulated storage costs:

$$p(t) - p(s) + F(s) - F(t) - c_j(t-s) \qquad (5.17)$$

This option offers greater profits than an alternative strategy of holding the same goods for delivery if and only if

$$p(t) - p(s) + F(s) - F(t) - c_j(t - s) > F(s) - p(s) - c_j(t_\circ - s) \qquad (5.18)$$

or

$$F(t) < p(t) + c_j(t_\circ - t) \qquad (5.19)$$

which is exactly the result derived in equation 4.14.

The following question may be posed at this point. Is the hedging strategy of the naive storer (setting futures positions equal in quantity but opposite in sign to the inventory position) one of the set of strategies that allows $\Pi_j'(t) > 0$? The answer is yes, as can be seen by taking the derivative of equation 4.11.

$$\Pi'_j(t) = -y'_j(t)F(t) - z'_j(t)\{p(t) + c_j(t_\circ - t)\} \tag{4.20}$$

Dividing through by $F(t)$ after setting equation 4.20 greater than zero gives

$$\Pi'_j(t) > 0 \quad \text{iff} \quad y'_j(t) < -z'_j(t)\frac{p(t) + c_j(t_\circ - t)}{F(t)} \tag{4.21}$$

It follows that when $z'_j(t) \gtrless 0, y'_j(t) \lessgtr 0$ is an allowable strategy (in the sense that it gives $\Pi'_j(t) > 0$). To see that $y'_j(t) = -z'_j(t)$ is an allowable strategy, note that this is only true if

$$\frac{p(t) + c_j(t_\circ - t)}{F(t)} \gtrless 1 \quad \text{iff} \quad z'_j(t) \gtrless 0 \tag{4.22}$$

But this is precisely the case. The naive hedger is thus—given that equation 4.11 defines his objective function—following an acceptable strategy, even though it may not be the strategy that causes equation 4.11 to increase at the greatest rate.

The Sophisticated Storer

The naive storer ignores the costs of marking to market in the futures market and treats the futures as if they were forward contracts. A more sophisticated storage-hedging policy takes account of the costs of marking to market. I shall assume that the sophisticated storer uses changes in the current market value of his inventory/futures position as a guide to strategic decisions. The total profits to such a storer from having followed an inventory policy $z'_j(s)$, $0 \le s \le t$ and a hedging policy $y'_j(s)$, $0 \le s \le t$, are the sum of the inventory's current market value minus the total costs of acquiring the inventory, minus total storage costs, and plus the value of marking to market the futures position:

$$\Pi_j(t) = p(t)z_j(t) - \int_0^t z'_j(s)p(s)ds - \int_0^t c_j(t - s)z'_j(s)ds \\ + \int_0^t y'_j(s)\{F(t) - F(s)\}ds \tag{4.23}$$

The first derivative of the total profit function is given by

$$\Pi'_j(t) = z_j(t)\{p'(t) - c_j\} + y_j(t)F'(t) \tag{4.24}$$

The derivative is not a function of any change in either the inventory or the futures position of the storer. The explanation is simple: remembering that $\Pi_j(t)$ = market value of inventory minus storage costs minus purchase costs plus marking to market, it is readily apparent that for new inventory purchased:

Market value = purchase price   (instantaneously)

Storage costs = 0   (instantaneously)

and for any new futures position established

Marking to market = 0   (instantaneously)

The first derivative of the total profit function thus contains no guide for the sophisticated storer of how he should act either with respect to the purchase of new inventories or with respect to establishing new futures positions. In this paragraph I shall try to rationalize $\Pi_j''(t) > 0$ as a worthwhile goal for the sophisticated storer. Note that if the profit function $\Pi_j(t)$ has a positive second derivative, then $\Pi_j(t)$ increases faster when $\Pi_j'(t) > 0$ and $\Pi_j(t)$ decreases slower when $\Pi_j'(t) < 0$ (figure 4–1). The sophisticated storer— realizing that he has no control over the instantaneous rate of change of his total profits—is thus acting rationally when he tries to fix his policies so that this rate of change is faster when it is increasing and is slower when it is decreasing.[3]

Taking the second derivative, we find:

$$\Pi_j''(t) = z_j(t)p''(t) + z'_j(t)p'(t) + y'_j(t)F'(t) + y_j(t)F''(t) \qquad (4.25)$$

The contributions of $z_j'(t)$ and $y_j'(t)$ are separate and additive. There is thus no reason for a storer to engage in a hedging strategy for the inventories he purchases. The contribution of $y_j'(t)$ to the storer's profit function (or its

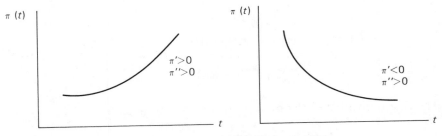

Figure 4–1. Paths of Storer's Profits

derivatives) is the same for the storer and for the speculator. Unless there is some qualitative or quantitative difference between the storer and the consumer, therefore, the admissable strategies for both will be the same, with the result that there is no reason to expect the futures market to clear. That is, without some additional differences between speculators and hedgers, both will want to be short (or long) in futures at the same time. The difference I shall invoke will be that storers have large enough futures positions to take advantage of second-order effects, while speculators do not.

From equation 4.25, conditions may be derived under which an increase in inventories ($z'_j(t) > 0$) and a corresponding short sale in the futures market ($y'_j(t) < 0$) increase $\Pi''_j(t)$. First note that $z'_j(t) > 0$ increases $\Pi''_j(t)$ if and only if

$$z_j(t)p''(t) + z'_j(t)p'(t) > 0 \qquad (4.26)$$

To interpret this condition, suppose that $z_j(t) > 0$. Then equation 4.26 holds if

$$z'_j(t) \quad \begin{matrix} > & \dfrac{-p''(t)z_j(t)}{p'(t)} & \text{if } p'(t) > 0 \\[2em] < & \dfrac{-p''(t)z_j(t)}{p'(t)} & \text{if } p'(t) < 0 \end{matrix} \qquad (4.27)$$

From the top line of equation 4.27 it follows that when $z_j(t) > 0$ and $p'(t) > 0$, inventory buildups will increase $\Pi''_j(t)$. However, if $p''(t)$ is negative, inventory buildups may have to occur at a very high rate in order that Π''_j increase.

From the bottom line of equation 4.27 it follows that if prices are falling, inventory buildups by storers can occur if $p''(t)$ is positive—that is, the price trend is as shown in figure 4–2. The size of such buildups depends on the total size of holdings $z_j(t)$; those storers with large holdings will be able to increase their inventories faster than storers with small holdings when $p'(t) < 0$.

To derive the conditions under which $y'_j(t) < 0$ increases $\Pi''_j(t)$, recall that $\Sigma_j y'_j(t) < 0$ must mean that $F'(t) > 0$, because if hedgers are short, speculators must be long. From equation 4.25 it thus follows that $y'_j(t) < 0$ increases $\Pi''_j(t)$ if and only if

$$y'_j(t) > \frac{-y_j(t)F''(t)}{F'(t)} \qquad (4.28)$$

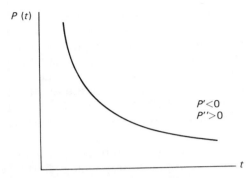

Figure 4–2. Path of Prices

A storer who is short in the futures market at t (that is, $y_j(t) < 0$) must thus expect $F''(t) < 0$ to justify an additional short sale in the futures market. In order for $y_j'(t) < 0$, therefore, futures prices must be locally concave if $y_j(t) < 0$.[4]

Equilibrium

The concept of an equilibrium as it is usually employed in the standard Arrow-Debreu model or in, for example, the Sharp-Lintner-Mossin model of a financial equilibrium is obviously inadequate to describe the equilibrating process in a model whose agents were described in the previous two sections. In this section I shall define a kind of equilibrium that is possible in this model. The spirit of the definitions is very much that of the temporary equilibrium concept of Hicks (see Grandmont 1977) and the exchange process model of Smale (1976). The basic idea is as follows. Because agents know only the local properties of the price vectors and have no idea of what will happen in the future, there is no possibility of discussing behavior that is locally maximizing for each agent. The best we can hope for is a process by which agents trade and through which agents reach some kind of an equilibrium. At no point in this process will prices and allocations necessarily represent an equilibrium. All I shall ask is that at every point in the process, trading bring some improvement in agents' objective functions and that markets clear.

DEFINITION. *An exchange process consists of prices $p(t)$ for commodities $F(t)$ for the futures price of the single commodity for which a futures market exists, and the assignment of a pair $\{x_i(t), y_i(t)\}$ (a commodity vector, and a futures position) to each of I speculators, and the assignment of a triplet $\{x_j(t), y_j(t),$*

$z_j(t)\}$ *(a commodity vector, a futures position, and an inventory/storage position) to each of J storers. The process must obey the following axioms:*

Property 1. Budget conditions for speculators and storers:

$$p(t)x_i'(t) + y_i(t)F'(t) = 0 \quad \text{(speculators)}$$

$$p(t)x_j'(t) + z_j'(t) + y_j(t)F'(t) = 0 \quad \text{(storers)}^5$$

Property 2. Local properties of x_i' and y_i':

$$y_i(t)F'(t) \geq 0 \rightarrow (d/dt)U_i(x_i(t)) \geq 0$$

$$y_i'(t) \neq 0 \longleftrightarrow y_i'(t)F'(t) > 0$$

Property 3. Local properties of x_j' and y_j' and z_j':

$$x_j'(t) \neq 0 \rightarrow (d/dt)U_j(x_j(t)) > 0$$

For naive storers: $y_j'(t) = -z_j'(t)$ and $z_j'(t) \neq 0 \rightarrow z_j'(t) \{ F(t) - p(t) -c_j(t - t_\circ) \} > 0$
For sophisticated storers[6]: $(y_j'(t), z_j'(t)) \neq 0 \rightarrow \Pi''(t) > 0$

Property 4. Market-clearing conditions:

$$\sum_i x_i'(t) + \sum_j x_j'(t) + \sum_j z_j'(t) = 0 \text{ for all } t$$

$$\sum_i y_i'(t) + \sum_j y_j'(t) = 0$$

Property 5. Price changes for commodities: Consider the vector of shadow prices for the commodities, $q_i(t) = (q_{i1}(t), \ldots, q_{iH}(t))$, where these prices are derived from the following maximization problem:

$$\max U_i(x)$$

$$\text{s.t.}$$

$$xp(t) = x_i(t)p(t) + y_i(t)F'(t)$$

Then

$$q_{ih}(t) = \left. \frac{\partial U_i/\partial x_{ih}}{\lambda} \right|_{x^*(t)}$$

where $x^*(t)$ is the solution to the problem and λ is the appropriate Lagrange multiplier.

For storers, the shadow prices are defined similarly, except that the budget equation becomes

$$xp(t) = x_j(t)p(t) + y_j(t)F'(t) + z_j(t)(p(t) - c_j)$$

The axiom for price changes for commodities says if for any commodity h

$$q_{ih}(t) \gtreqless p_h(t) \text{ and } q_{jh}(t) \gtreqless p_h(t) \text{ for every } i \text{ and } j$$

then

$$p'_h(t) \gtreqless 0$$

Note: The axiom describes how prices change over time; the condition is very weak. It says: Any price change is acceptable as long as, when all consumers are in agreement that the price of a given commodity is too low (high), that price moves up (down).

Property 6. Price changes for the futures. $F'(t)$ obeys:

$$F(t) \geq p(t) \text{ for all } t \leq t_o,$$

$$F(t) \to p(t) \text{ as } t \to t_o,$$

Note: The first condition was discussed in the previous section and is designed to prevent futures from being a substitute for the physical good in the consumption vector. The second condition guarantees that the naive and sophisticated hedging strategies coincide if the sophisticated storer delivers on all of his futures contracts (that is, if we set $z'_j(t) = -y'_j(t)$, and let $t \to t_o$, then equation 4.23 becomes equation 4.12.

Property 7. Continuity. All variables—$x_i(t)$, $x_j(t)$, $z_j(t)$, $p(t)$, $F(t)$, $y_i(t)$, $y_j(t)$—are twice continuously differentiable.

Property 8. Existence of trading. If there exists some vector $\{x'_i(t), x'_j(t), z'_j(t), y'_i(t), y'_j(t)\} \neq 0$, which satisfies properties 1–4, then there will exist some trade. Thus trading stops only when there is—for some t—no possibility of arranging a set of trades that is market-clearing, fulfills the budget conditions, and gives rise to a local improvement in utility.

DEFINITION. *An exchange process will be said to have reached a temporary equilibrium at time t if* $\{x'_i(t), x'_j(t), z'_j(t), y'_i(t), y'_j(t)\} = 0.$

Note that by property 8 a temporary equilibrium means that given market prices $p(t)$ and $F(t)$, there exist no set of market clearing trades which satisfy both the budget conditions (property 1) and the locally utility-improving conditions (properties 2 and 3). In this sense, a temporary equilibrium is similar to the spirit of an Arrow-Debreu equilibrium. However, there is no guarantee that if we have reached a temporary equilibrium at t, this will be the case for any time close to t. On the other hand, a temporary equilibrium must have $F'(t) = 0$, because otherwise there will be liquidation or acquisition of commodity vectors by consumers and storers.

The existence of a temporary equilibrium need not imply that futures prices necessarily reflect storage costs—that is, that $F(t) = p(t) + c_j(t_0 - t)$ for all storers j. This problem is not merely related to the artificial assumption of linear storage costs; these could easily be replaced with some more flexible assumption that would allow—in principle—for equal marginal storage costs among storers. When futures prices stand still, consumer will wish to trade only if their marginal rates of substitution are not equal to commodity prices. If rates of substitution are equal to prices and consumers as a result do not wish to trade, then producers could still have $F(t) \neq p(t) + c_j(t_0 - t)$. All that can really be said of a trading process in which storers are naive is that the existence of trading in which there is inventory accumulation means that futures prices cover storage and acquisition costs. Clearly if some storers are sophisticated, even this need not be true.

Empirical Implications of the Model

The model described earlier has at least two immediate empirical implications that may be tested.

1. When $\Sigma_j y'_j(t) \gtrless 0, F'(t) \lessgtr 0$. This follows from the discussion in equation 4.6. If speculators have small positions (so that they ignore the influence of F''), an increase in short hedging by storers must be correlated with an increase in the futures price.

2. When $\Sigma_j y'_j(t) < 0$, $F''(t) < 0$, if storers are sophisticated. This follows from equation 4.28. As long as speculators need an increase in the futures price to absorb extra hedging activity, storers (who do not ignore the influence of F'') will demand that $F''(t) < 0$.[7]

I know of no research that deals with the second question; however, Jaffe and Margrabe (1978) examine the first question and find results which coincide with the model. Specifically, Jaffe and Margrabe, after examining the statistics for wheat and corn from 1948 to 1969 conclude: "An unanticipated drop in the corn futures price accompanies a simultaneous unanticipated increase in hedging activity." Similar results are reported for wheat.

Furthermore, the correlation coefficients between futures prices and either hedging positions or speculative positions at nearly all leads and lags are small and insignificant (the only significant coefficient are in wheat for lags of two and six weeks, "suggesting that hedging activity *follows* price movements. However, . . . the coefficients for all leads are small. . . . ").

Market Power and Hedging

The model above describes a nonmanipulable trading process; neither storers nor speculators have any power to influence the course of prices. It is easy to modify the description of the trading process to give an indication of how hedgers can have power in futures markets. This section explores such a modification and its policy implications. A conclusion is that the disclosure of hedging positions in futures markets may be of considerable importance.

Recall first that it is a consequence of our description of a trading process that where

$$\sum_j y'_j(t) < 0$$

it must be that $F'(t) > 0$. In a market with hedging power, we assume that speculators cannot directly observe y'_j, and that they are partially dependent for information on signals sent by storers. Denote these signals by $\bar{y}'_j(t)$, and assume that F' has the functional form

$$F'(\sum_j y'_j(t), \sum_j (\bar{y}'_j(t) - y'_j(t))) \qquad (4.29)$$

where

$$\frac{\partial F'}{\partial y'_j(t)} > 0 , \frac{\partial F'}{\partial(\bar{y}'(t) - y'(t))} > 0 \qquad (4.30)$$

$$y'(t) = \sum_j y'_j(t), \bar{y}'(t) = \sum_j \bar{y}'_j(t)$$

Intuitively, our story is as follows: The change in futures prices depends on both actual changes in futures commitments by hedgers and on signals sent by hedgers. This supposition does not necessarily contradict the empirical results related in the last section.

In this version of the trading process, storers have some influence on prices, and they can—if they are sophisticated—now directly influence Π' (equation 4.24). In particular it will now be in the interest of sophisticated storers who are net short (that is, $y_j'(t) < 0$) to minimize current changes in their hedging commitments. This will tend to depress F' and will raise profits.

If storers are naive and if F' obeys equations 4.29 and 4.30, the story is somewhat different. That is, the pattern of futures prices desired by every naive storer is one in which—initially—futures prices are high enough to cover storage costs (the higher the futures price, the better), and in which—at some point before the delivery date $t_.$—futures prices drop below the spot price plus storage costs. Earlier I showed that inventory acquired and hedged by the naive storer when the futures price covered the spot price plus storage costs could subsequently be disposed of (before delivery and with a lifting of the hedge) at a greater profit if the futures price dropped below spot plus storage. If F' follows equations 4.29 and 4.30, naive storers can directly influence F, and it follows from the first part of this paragraph that initially they will wish to exaggerate the size of their inventory build-ups to drive the futures price up during the phase where inventories are indeed being built up. Later, they will wish to drive down the futures price so that inventories can be profitably disposed of in the spot market and hedges lifted; to this end it will serve their purpose to exaggerate the speed with which inventories are going down.

The foregoing has sketched the informational strategies of both sophisticated and naive hedgers in futures markets where futures prices are at least partially affected by signals from hedgers about their futures commitments. Although the strategies were shown to be diametrically opposite for naive and sophisticated storers, the conclusion for policymakers is the same. To prevent the transfer of profits from speculators to storers, the latter should be made to reveal their true futures markets commitments.

Notes

1. I have benefitted from comments made by Jean-Pierre Danthine and Carl Futia. Remaining errors and infelicities of expression are mine.

2. Another way to view the consumer's problem is to consider a consumer who trades his consumption vector at intervals of ε at the current market prices. Thus at time t the consumer's problem is to exchange $x_i(t - \varepsilon)$ for some vector $x_i(t)$ subject to the budget constraint

$$\{x_i(t) - x_i(t - \varepsilon)\}p(t) + y_i(t - \varepsilon)\{F(t) - F(t - \varepsilon)\} = 0$$

Here, $y_i(t - \varepsilon)$ is the futures position established by consumer i at time $t - \varepsilon$. This position affects the budget constraint at time t and a new position $y_i(t)$ will affect the budget only at $t + \varepsilon$.

If the consumer uses F' to predict futures prices, the last term on the left side becomes

$$y_i(t - \varepsilon)\varepsilon \, F'(t - \varepsilon)$$

and it follows that a utility-improving choice of $y_i(t - \varepsilon)$ is one such that

$$y_i(t - \varepsilon) \gtreqless 0 \quad \text{if and only if} \quad F'(t - \varepsilon) \gtreqless 0$$

The view of consumer behavior embodied in this paper is thus one which incorporates myopia (consumers consider only very short-term movements in futures prices); inability to speculate in commodities directly (consumers do not use any information about commodity prices to predict the future course of prices); and limited use of information, even about futures prices (consumers do not use the second derivative of futures prices).

3. Another way of viewing the sophisticated storer follows the scenario of note 1. The sophisticated storer is myopic in choosing his consumption vector, but uses p', F', and F'' to predict price movements for the purpose of storage and hedging.

4. If a storer has $y_j(t) > 0$, then y_j' can be negative if $F'' > 0$. The behavior of $\Sigma_j y_j'(t)$ thus depends on how many storers have positive total futures positions at t and whether storers are sophisticated or naive.

5. For internal consistency in the model, storage costs are assumed to occur as the instantaneous deterioration of supplies over time, so that they have no effect on the budget equation.

6. This implicitly assumes that the storer will liquidate his inventory position before selling part of his consumption vector x_j.

7. This assumes that storers are generally holders of negative futures positions (see note 4).

References

Cahnman, R. (1982). *Review of Research in Futures Markets*, 1 (1), pp. 18–19.

Cootner, P. (1960). "Returns to Speculators: Telser versus Keynes," *Journal of Political Economy*, vol. 68, pp. 396–404.

Cox, J.C., J.E. Ingersoll, and S.A. Ross. (1981). "The Relation between Forward Prices and Futures Prices." *Journal of Financial Economics*, vol. 9 pp. 321–346.

Grandmont, J.M. (1977) "Temporary General Equilibrium Theory," *Econometrica*, vol. 45, pp. 535–572.

Grossman, S.J. (1977) "The Existence of Futures Markets, Noisy Rational Expectations and Informational Externalities," *Review of Economic Studies*, vol. 44, pp. 431–449.

Hicks, J. (1946). *Value and Capital*, 2d ed. Oxford: Clarendon Press.

Hieronymus, T.A. (1978). "Basic Patterns," in *Views from the Trade*, ed. A. E. Peck. Chicago: Chicago Board of Trade, pp. 45–56.

Hoffman, G.W. (1925). *Hedging by Dealing in Grain Futures*. Philadelphia: University of Pennsylvania.

Jaffe, J.J., and W. Margrabe. (c. 1978). "Hedgers, Speculators, and Efficiency in the Commodities Futures Market," undated working paper.

Jarrow, R.A., and G.S. Oldfield. (1981). "Forward Contracts and Futures Contracts." *Journal of Financial Economics*, vol. 9, pp. 373–382.

Johnson, L.L. (1960). "The Theory of Hedging and Speculation in Commodity Futures." *Review of Economic Studies*, vol. 27, pp. 139–151.

Richard, S.F., and M. Sundaresan. (1981). "A Continuous Time Equilibrium Model of Forward Prices and Futures prices in a Multigood Economy." *Journal of Financial Economics*, vol. 9, pp. 347–372.

Smale, S. (1976). "Exchange Processes with Price Adjustment." *Journal of Mathematical Economics*, vol. 3, pp. 211–226.

Stein, J.L. (1961). "The Simultaneous Determination of Spot and Futures Prices." *American Economic Review*, vol. 51, pp. 1012–1025.

Telser, L. (1958) "Futures Trading and the Storage of Cotton and Wheat." *Journal of Political Economy*, vol. 66, pp. 233–255.

Working, H. (1953). "Futures Trading and Hedging." *American Economic Review*, vol. 43, pp. 314–343.

Appendix 4A

To establish equation 4.2, note that the value of the futures position at time t (assuming daily settlement) is

$$\int_0^t y_i'(s) \{ F(t) - F(s) \} \, ds = y_i(t)F(t) - \int_0^t y_i'(s)F(s)ds$$

Differentiating this gives

$$y_i'(t)F(t) + y_i(t)F'(t) - y'_i(s)F(s)|_0^t$$
$$= y_i'(t)F(t) + y_i(t)F'(t) - y_i'(t)F(t) = y_i(t)F'(t)$$

which is equation 4.2.

To establish equation 4.24, differentiate equation 4.23. By integration by parts

$$d/dt \{ c_j(t - s)z_j'(s)ds\} = d/dt \{ tc_jz_j(t)\} - d/dt \{ c_jsz_j(s) |_0^t$$
$$- \int_0^t c_jz_j(s)ds\}$$
$$= c_jz_j(t)$$

Using expression 4.3, $\Pi_j'(t)$ thus becomes

$$\Pi_j'(t) = p'(t)z_j(t) + p(t)z_j'(t) - z_j'(t)p(t) - c_jz_j(t) + y_j(t)F'(t)$$

which reduces to equation 4.24.

Comment

Jean-Pierre Danthine

To ascertain what one can hope to achieve with a model of the type proposed by S. Benninga, it is useful to start by outlining some features of a more traditional class of models well represented in the futures literature. In such models, futures markets are described as markets where risks or information are exchanged among different types of agents, often grouped as hedgers and speculators. These traders may be differently risk-averse and have different information sets. Most important, hedgers are viewed as having to bear risks from their activity in other markets. Exchange take place at equilibrium prices. An equilibrium corresponds to a state of rest of the system; however, a continuous flow of net hedging interest and information ensures that such a state is ephemeral.

Theories built on variations of such a model are mostly hedging theories, which does not mean that hedgers will not speculate. In fact, we know that all rational agents making decisions under uncertainty speculate to some degree. But nothing much can be said on the speculative portion of a hedger's futures position, or, for that matter, on speculative strategies because these are essentially determined by the characteristics of agents' subjective probability distributions. Information on prices or price differences is the essence of speculation. Admitting that everyone may have his own source of information prevents the outside observer from going very far in predicting behavior; the methodology of economics is not very powerful once it can be asserted with some plausibility that a phenomenon's explanation lies mostly in changes in preferences. By contrast, interesting results can be obtained about the characteristics of optimal hedging strategies in a variety of circumstances.

The view emerging from this type of model suggests hedgers make simultaneous decisions on inventory sizes and futures position sizes. The decisions can be revised over time and need not correspond to routine hedges. This plausible middle-of-the-road view can be contrasted with the strawman Benninga sets up to criticize—hedging is taking a futures position equal in size but opposite in sign to preestablished cash position (routine hedging)—and the feature he proposes for his model: "Hedgers make separate decisions on inventory sizes and on sizes of futures positions."

The major motivation for Benninga's model is apparently his opinion that marking to market forces market participants to concentrate on short run strategies and, for that reason, that information possessed by futures market participants with a number of other behavioral and conceptual changes (some by the information structure and the hypothesis of continuous trading), Benninga corners himself into a model that has lost all of the substance of the more traditional models without much to show in return. Thus, if all agents are myopic according to his definition—that is, if all they know of the future as of time t is the derivative at t_o of prices viewed as functions of time—they have necessarily homogeneous expectations, and information differences play no role in explaining futures trades.

Furthermore, with only this kind of instantaneous information, there is no meaningful statistical relationship between futures and spot prices to take advantage of; consequently, there is no hedging in this model. What are called hedgers (storers) are individuals who speculate in two markets simultaneously but independently. From the point of view of futures trading, they are exactly in the same position as speculators (this comment applies to sophisticated storers; naive storers, by definition, hedge routinely).

Finally, the objective function of the two types of agents—that is, they choose policies so that the second derivative of profit as a function of time is positive—does not allow for differences in risk aversion. Thus, the proposed model includes none of the differences in information, risk, or risk-taking behavior that fuel trading in the traditional models. It is no surprise that trading will be scarce in this world.

Indeed the only source of trading lies in the postulated difference in position sizes between speculators and storers. Storers are assumed to take larger futures positions than speculators. The reason for this assumption is not clear because storer's futures positions are taken independently of the size of their inventories. In any case, the assumed implication is that speculators can ignore the second derivative of the futures price with respect to time while storers don't. Thus speculators choose $y_j'F' > 0$, while sophisticated storers choose y_j' so that $y_j'F'' > 0$, the term y_iF'' being ignored by speculators.

There are at least two problems with this view. First, it leads to very implausible conclusions. Trade can only occur if $y_jF'' > 0$ (to compensate for the fact that $y_j'F' > \rightarrow y_j'F < 0$ because speculators and storers must necessarily be at the opposite ends of any trade). This means that if storers are short $(\sum y_j < 0)$ (long) trade can occur only if the futures price is a concave (convex) function of time. In figure 2A−1, for a hypothetical configuration of $F(t)$, there is no trading possible in time intervals t_1,t_3 and t_5,t_7 if storers are sophisticated and short. Furthermore, if there is trade in t_0,t_1 and t_4,t_5 speculators must be selling and in t_3,t_4, they must be buying. It is obvious that these empirical implications of the model are too mechanistic to be plausible.

Second, it is difficult to see why storers would want to trade even in time intervals like t_3,t_5—that is, when $F'' < 0$. Indeed if they like $\prod''$ to be positive, it is realistic to assume they want it larger than smaller. But then the better strategy when $F'' < 0$ (and they are short $y_j < 0$), it would be to set

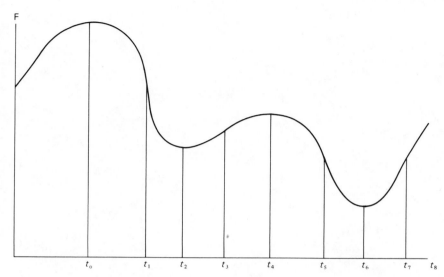

Figure 4A–1. Path of Futures Price

$y'_j = 0$ (refuse to trade) and enjoy a $\prod'' = y_j F''$ positive and large. Accepting to trade means, for storers, accepting a decrease in $\prod''$ since $y'_j F$ must be negative to induce speculators in the exchange. Thus we are left with a model of futures markets where there is never any trade unless one wants to appeal to the presence of naive storers hedging routinely.

A last comment on the notion of equilibrium is called for. In the present context, equilibrium is unimportant conceptually as well as rare empirically. Indeed, on one hand, nothing that has been said thus far depends on whether there is an equilibrium or not, or whether the system is in equilibrium or not; on the other hand, marking to market implies that equilibrium can occur only if $F'(t) = 0$—that is, if the futures price is at a point of stationarity (in figure 4A–1 only t_0, t_2, t_4, t_6 are candidates for equilibrium). The question is what makes the equilibrium temporary (as opposed to permanent)? Indeed, an equilibrium is a situation with no trade and a stationary futures price. But, even forgetting these objections, trade will resume only in the futures price starts to move again. Thus, the only possibility in this world, to avoid a permanent no-trade–fixed-price equilibrium is to assume—as is done—that the price of futures contracts will start changing autonomously and independently of changes in the supply and demand for futures.

Comment

Carl A. Futia

I have two basic remarks to make about Professor Benninga's chapter. He defines an equilibrium as a kind of limit point of what he calls an exchange process. An exchange process is a deterministic path of spot and futures prices and quantities that satisfies a number of local conditions. Because exchange processes play a pivotal role in his equilibrium concept, I think it fair to ask for some argument that shows that such processes in fact exist for some set of initial conditions. Professor Benninga provides us with no such argument and I suspect the matter is not a trivial one to resolve.

Of course, the existence of nontrivial exchange processes may be inessential for the main point of the chapter. Indeed, the only implications of Professor Benninga's model appear in the last section and they apparently depend only on the instantaneous market-clearing hypothesis. If so, the whole concept of an exchange process seems to be a bit of a red herring; it is then fair to ask why the reader is forced to grapple with it when none of Professor Benninga's results depend upon this concept.

A more worrisome feature of Professor Benninga's model is that there can be exchange processes that entail profit opportunities which remain unexploited by the model's market participants. Such opportunities would occur when the rate of change in the futures price $F'(t)$ deviates from the instantaneous riskless rate. Because $F'(t)$ itself it assumed to vary continuously, any such deviation would imply (in chapter 4's deterministic world) the existence of a riskless asset (that is, a futures position) that dominates the originally hypothesized riskless asset. This is inconsistent with any sort of instantaneous market-clearing condition.

This sort of inconsistency is particularly worrisome in any model of the futures markets. In the world of futures trading in the United States, thousands of traders and money managers attempt to exploit and profit from information about departures of $F'(t)$ from the riskless rate by using so-called moving-average trading systems. From the apparent fact that not many of them succeed over an extended period of time, one suspects that an equilibrium $F'(t)$ must satisfy more constraints than are set down in chapter 4.

5

A Theory of Futures Market Manipulations

Albert S. Kyle

The great liquidity of futures markets and the anonymity that goes along with futures trading make it feasible for one large trader to acquire a substantial long position without having a large effect on prices and without being noticed by the other traders in the market. If a large trader in this position subsequently pushes prices higher by either threatening to take delivery or actually doing so, then we have a market manipulation, which is usually called a corner or a squeeze.

This chapter develops a simple model of futures trading in which market manipulations, which take the form of squeezes, discourage the use of futures markets by increasing the cost of hedging. The model contains three kinds of traders: hedgers, speculators, and a squeezer. In a well-functioning market where market manipulations do not occur, speculators who are risk-neutral have the risks faced by hedgers transferred to them at unbiased prices. When squeezes become a possibility, speculators bid up futures prices to levels that accurately reflect the probability of a squeeze. In this situation, futures prices, which are unbiased from the point of view of speculators, become biased against hedgers from the point of view of hedgers.

How is it that futures prices which appear unbiased or fair from the point of view of speculators nevertheless are compatible with the squeezer's making profits and hedgers' losing money consistently? The squeezer trades in such a way that speculators cannot tell from observing the trading process how much the squeezer is buying and how much the hedgers are selling. In early trading, the squeezer acquires a large long position when short hedging is active and acquires a large short position when hedging is inactive. To speculators, the amount of trade appears constant; it is thus impossible for speculators to learn whether a squeeze is in the works or not. It becomes apparent whether or not a squeeze is on when hedgers try to liquidate their positions. When hedging is active, the squeezer hangs on to his long positions, the squeeze is on, and hedgers must bid up prices to high levels to get out of their short positions. When hedging is inactive, the squeezer and hedgers both liquidate their positions at lower no-squeeze prices. Because

Financial support from the Center for The Study of Futures Markets is gratefully acknowledged. The views expressed in this paper are those of the author and do not necessarily express those of The Center for The Study of Futures Markets.

initial prices discount the probability of a squeeze, the squeezer makes money both ways. He makes money on the long side as prices rise when there is a squeeze, and he makes money on the short side as prices fall when there is no squeeze. Hedgers, on the other hand, lose money consistently. When hedging is active, hedgers lose money on large short positions; when hedging is inactive, hedgers make money or small short positions. It is the asymmetric size of the positions when gains and losses occur—losses on large positions and gains on small positions—that is responsible for hedgers consistently losing money.

In equilibrium, hedgers adjust the amount of futures trading they do in light of the costs imposed on them by squeezers. The probability of squeezes, on the other hand, depends endogenously on the amount of hedging that takes place in the futures market. The equilibrium level of hedging and the equilibrium probability of squeezes are thus determined simultaneously in much the same way that equilibrium quantities and prices are determined by the intersection of supply and demand curves in the standard theory of supply and demand.

This chapter is organized into several sections. First, I justify using the concepts of liquidity and anonymity to explain squeezes as a futures market phenomenon. I then define corners and squeezes as two different kinds of market manipulations (squeezes are the kind of manipulation discussed here). Then the relationship between squeezes and the cheapest-to-deliver concept of delivery is discussed, followed by a simple model of squeezes, in which hedgers are assumed to behave exogenously. Despite the apparent simplicity of the basic model, the equilibrium is rather tricky to discuss mathematically. It is shown that the probability of a squeeze depends on the amount of hedging and the size of deliverable stocks.

I then show that when delivery is costly, threats to take or make delivery become important but that the model can be applied to the situation in which the squeezer uses threats to obtain the best outcome from his point of view. Next, the equilibrium behavior of hedgers is modelled to allow us to determine simultaneously the amount of hedging and the probability of squeezes in the market. Finally, I examine the effectiveness of various policies to control squeezes, including different delivery differentials, additional deliverable supply, cash settlement, and position limits.

The Role of Liquidity and Anonymity in Squeezes

To explain corners and squeezes as futures market phenomena, it is useful to examine first the features of futures trading that distinguish it from other forms of market organization. Two basic approaches have been used to explain futures trading: the insurance approach and the liquidity approach.

According to the insurance approach, futures markets provide a step toward complete markets—a set of markets in which it is possible to exchange every conceivable kind of risk—by making it possible to exchange risks that would not be possible to exchange using combinations of other kinds of assets. However, the insurance approach, as emphasized by Telser (1981), does not distinguish futures markets from ordinary insurance markets. Insurance markets and futures markets are clearly different forms of market organization, the former distinguished by large numbers of contracts uniquely tailored for specific risks borne by specific firms or individuals in specific situations, the latter distinguished by a small number of contracts, each of which is traded actively by a large number of traders for a variety of reasons. The insurance approach does not help explain why we see one form of market organization in some situations and another form of market organization in another situation.

A better explanation of futures trading is the liquidity approach, advanced recently by Telser (1981) but reminiscent of Working (1953). According to this approach, futures markets are a form of market organization designed, as Telser puts it, to "facilitate trade among strangers," or, as Working puts it, to reduce transactions costs. The advantage of the liquidity approach to futures trading is that it helps explain those institutional features of futures trading which distinguish it from other forms of market organization. These institutional features—small numbers of perfectly fungible contracts with well-defined terms, trading by open outcry on an organized exchange floor under well-defined rules, book-entry accounting of open positions, clearing of trades by a central clearing house, margins and mark-to-market settlement of accounts on a daily basis by a clearing organization, centralized monitoring of the financial positions of member firms—all reduce the costs of trading by centralizing the search, bookkeeping, and credit activities that are part of trading.

A feature of futures trading closely connected with liquidity is anonymity, a fact reflected in Telser's statement that futures markets "facilitate trade among strangers." The organizational structure of futures trading makes it unnecessary for traders to know individually the principals on the other side of their transaction, because the brokers on the trading floor bring traders off the floor together behind a wall of anonymity and because the clearing house of the exchange guarantees the integrity of positions on both sides of the market. In fact, the anonymity of futures trading is closely related to its low transactions costs, in that the high costs of trading in other markets are in large part the result of the costs of keeping detailed records of positions with a large number of trading partners and the cost of assessing the financial integrity of each of then.

The anonymity of futures markets tends to change the nature of the market dramatically, because knowledge of who is trading what is in many cases a valuable commodity itself. Traders sometimes go to great lengths to conceal their identities while simultaneously going to equally great lengths to figure out what other traders in the market are doing. It is clear that both liquidity and anonymity make futures markets an attractive form of market organization.

In our model, we assume that hedgers, who are basically buyers of insurance, use futures contracts because of their liquidity. Implicitly, we assume that cash markets are too costly to be used as a hedging device but that futures markets are, at a transactional level, essentially costless. Thus, hedgers use futures markets even though the risk and delivery characteristics of the contracts do not mesh perfectly with the hedger's inventories. As we shall see, this imperfect fit between inventories and futures positions is important when thinking about squeezes because a hedger who is persuaded by the liquidity of the market to short a futures contract against a cash market position that is not most deliverable leaves himself in a vulnerable position when the longs in the market decide to take delivery.

Although hedgers are attracted to the futures market mainly because of its liquidity, the squeezer is attracted mainly because of its anonymity. It seems clear that if the rest of the market knew what the squeezer was up to, prices would adjust quickly to levels such that the squeezer could not engineer a squeeze in which he expected to make a profit.

Distinguishing Between Corners and Squeezes

In a market manipulation, prices are manipulated not because supply is prevented from being equal to demand but because the manipulator holds positions that, at the margin, could be liquidated at current prices and reacquired later at more favorable prices (even after adjusting for storage and interest costs). A perfect competitor would not be willing to hold a position in this situation because it would be unprofitable, but an imperfect competitor may be willing to do so if it enables him to liquidate his inframarginal positions at better prices.

The terms corner and squeeze are often used interchangeably to describe the market manipulations in futures markets. However, it is useful to distinguish between these two different kinds of market manipulations. In a corner, the manipulator acquires control over large enough stocks to set up a temporary monopoly in the commodity. He then supplies stocks to the market gradually, keeping prices high by exploiting intertemporal elasticities in demand and supply. In a squeeze, the manipulator exploits the delivery mechanism of the futures contract by taking advantage of the fact that not all stocks of the commodity are easily available for delivery on favorable terms. The squeezer makes his profits either by threatening to take delivery and thereby forcing shorts to bail out at high prices to avoid the high costs of bringing supplies into deliverable position or by taking delivery of so much of the commodity that the shorts must deliver goods that would not ordinarily be cheapest to deliver.

The difference between a corner and a squeeze is that a squeeze, which exploits the delivery mechanism, is essentially over once delivery is made. In contrast, a corner, which exploits intertemporal elasticities of supply and demand, is in some sense just getting started when delivery is made. In a squeeze, the prices that have been bid up for specific qualities and locations (the ones treated most favorably by the futures contract) fall quickly back to normal levels once delivery is made. In a corner, a generalized rise in the price of all qualities and locations occurs, and prices fall back more slowly once delivery is made, as the cornerer works off his stocks slowly at high prices.

The distinction between a corner and a squeeze is not sharp. Individual market manipulations may have characteristics of both corners and squeezes. In this chapter, market manipulations are modelled as squeezes because we are concerned with the transactions technology of futures markets and the delivery mechanism of the futures contract rather than with the underlying fundamentals of demand and supply. However, the mathematics of a model of a corner would be similar to the mathematics of a model of a squeeze.

Squeezes and the Delivery Mechanism

In most futures contracts the cash prices and futures prices are tied together at delivery by the cheapest to deliver concept. To explain how the cheapest to deliver concept works, suppose that there are two qualities of the asset, quality one and quality two. Let p_1^M and p_2^M denote the market prices of these qualities at the time of delivery in a market where no squeeze takes place. We call these no-squeeze prices. Let p^F denote the futures price at the time of delivery. Let p_1^D and p_2^D denote the prices at which the different qualities can be delivered against the futures contract. The prices p_1^D and p_2^D are determined in the specifications of the contract as functions of the futures prices p^F. We will assume that the delivery prices are determined by adjusting the futures price p^F by adding constants Δ_1 and Δ_2, so that

$$p_1^D = p^F + \Delta_1$$

$$p_2^D = p^F + \Delta_2$$

defines the delivery prices. The quantities Δ_1 and Δ_2 are part of the specifications of the futures contract. Positive values of Δ_1 and Δ_2 denote premiums and negative values denote discounts.

In most futures contracts, the seller has the option to decide what qualities are delivered. This option is given to the seller because the flexibility made possible by this option makes it more difficult for the buyer to squeeze the seller by insisting on the delivery of particular qualities. If sellers have the option to choose the quality delivered, and if there is at least one competitive trader in the market, the relationship between cash prices and futures prices will be determined according to the cheapest to deliver concept, which states that the seller breaks even by delivering at least one quality and does not make a profit delivering any quality. Mathematically, this relationship can be written

$$\max(p^F + \Delta_1 - p_1^M, p^F + \Delta_2 - p_2^M) = 0$$

If good 1 is the cheapest to deliver, then $p_1^M = p^F + \Delta_1 = p_1^D$ and $p_2^M \geq p^F + \Delta_2 = p_2^D$. The cheapest to deliver constraint makes it possible to calculate the equilibrium futures price p^F given equilibrium cash prices p_1^M, p_2^M and contract specifications Δ_1, Δ_2. The equilibrium futures price p^F is by definition the price at which no arbitrage is possible.

The delivery mechanism creates an opportunity for squeezes in the following way. Suppose for simplicity that it is known that good 1 will be cheapest to deliver and let d denote the cost advantage of delivering good 1 instead of good 2 when cash prices are determined under the assumption that there will be no squeeze. Then it is straightforward to show that

$$d = (\Delta_2 - \Delta_1) - (p_2^M - p_1^M)$$

that is, d is the difference between the arbitrary contract relationships used for delivery purposes and the basis relationships prevailing in the open market. It is also clear that the equilibrium futures price is given by

$$p^f = p_1^M - \Delta_1$$

that is, the futures price is perfectly correlated with the cash price for good 1 and differs from the cash price by the delivery adjustment Δ_1. Let x_1 and x_2 denote the supplies of good 1 and good 2 available for delivery against the futures contract.

The possibility for a squeeze exists if a trader can purchase such large quantities of futures contracts at prices close to p^F that the shorts are forced to deliver underlying qualities which would not otherwise be cheapest to deliver. If a position whose size is in excess of x_1 (the total available supply of cheapest to deliver quality) can be acquired, then the trader, by taking delivery of his contracts, can force the shorts to deliver expensive to deliver good 2 on some of the contracts. If the trader purchases the futures contracts at price $p_1^M - \Delta_1$, and sells the qualities he has delivered at prices p_1^M and p_2^M, then the trader breaks even on deliveries of good 1 and makes a profit of d on deliveries of good 2. (If the trader purchases positions in excess of the total available supply $x_1 + x_2$, the shorts must either cover at prices dictated by the squeezer or default on some contracts.) Thus, if the squeezer acquires at no-squeeze price a position of size x, where $x_1 \leqslant x \leqslant x_1 + x_2$, the squeezer's profits are $(x - x_1)d$.

When a squeeze is on, the no-squeeze prices p_1^M, p_2^M will not be the ones prevailing in the market. Because during a squeeze there is not enough of the cheapest to deliver quality available to make all of the deliveries necessary, the shorts will bid up the cash market price of the cheapest to deliver qualities to a point where both qualities are equally deliverable. This bidding up of cash market prices on cheapest to deliver qualities, which occurs in line with the bidding up of futures prices, will only occur on cash market forward contracts that settle on or before delivery of the futures contract. For cash market transactions with delivery after this point, there will be no bidding up of prices. Implicitly, the market is expecting the spot prices of the cheapest to deliver quality, which have been run up sharply before delivery, to collapse immediately after delivery back to the no-squeeze levels (assuming another squeeze is not expected at maturity of the next futures contract.)

If traders expect spot prices for the cheapest to deliver quality to collapse immediately after delivery is made, why will any competitive trader be willing to hold inventories of the cheapest to deliver quality during the delivery period? In fact, only the squeezer himself will be willing to do so, because he is the only trader who is not a perfect competitor. He is willing to hold inventories of the cheapest to deliver commodity and take a loss on them, because doing so allows him to acquire the expensive to deliver quality at favorable terms—which is essentially what the squeeze is all about.

The squeezer is in effect able to internalize an externality that crops up in the delivery mechanism. To explain this externality, we compare the price a competitive short is willing to pay to buy back his position with the price a competitive long is willing to accept to liquidate his short. The marginal cost of making delivery is the price at which the short breaks even delivering the expensive commodity, because the cheapest to deliver commodity is also bid up before delivery to this level. As a result, a competitive short is willing to pay anything up to this price to liquidate his short position.

A competitive long, on the other hand, looks at the value of the delivered qualities after delivery. Because the cheapest to deliver quality will have fallen back to its no-squeeze value at this point, he is looking at lower prices than a short. Let us suppose that the delivery mechanism works as follows. During delivery the qualities that the shorts tender for delivery are allocated randomly to the longs, and no bargaining is allowed between shorts or longs over the question of who gets delivered what. Then the value to the long of taking delivery is the weighted average value of the qualities delivered, where the cheapest to deliver quality has its lower, post-delivery value. A competitive long is willing to sell at any price greater than this weighted average value.

Because the marginal cost of taking delivery for the competitive long is less than the marginal cost of making delivery for a competitive short, the longs are better off liquidating at prices close to the marginal cost of making delivery for the shorts than by taking delivery. As a result, the only trader left on the long side of the market will be the squeezer.

The nature of the externality present during a squeeze is now clear. When an extra long position and an extra short position are created during a squeeze, the marginal quality delivered by the short is the expensive quality but the marginal quality delivered to the long is the average of the qualities delivered. The extra delivery of the expensive quality at the margin tends to raise average quality, but almost all these benefits of improved quality are captured by the inframarginal longs already present in the market and not by the long with whom the trade occurs. This externality discourages accumulation of open interest and in fact causes open interest to liquidate. The only trader with no incentive to liquidate is the squeezer. He has no incentive to liquidate because he internalizes the externality by also holding all of the inframarginal long positions and takes this into account in making his trading decisions.

A Simple Model

In this section we examine a simple model of squeezes that has many of the properties discussed intuitively in the preceding sections. Assume that futures trading takes place in two trading periods, at equilibrium prices p_1^F, p_2^F. Before trading in the first period, there is no open interest, and the open interest remaining after trading in the second period is liquidated through delivery. The exogenous deliverable supply consists of z_1 units of quality 1 and z_2 units of quality 2. Immediately after delivery, quality 1 will have a value of $\bar{v}$ and quality 2 will have a value of $\bar{v} + d$, where d is a positive constant known by all traders and $\bar{v}$ is a random variable. During the first period of trade, traders know the distribution of $\bar{v}$ but not its outcome. During the second period of trade, the outcome $\bar{v}$ is known with certainty by all traders. Both qualities of the commodity can be delivered against the futures contract (with no differentials). Thus, good 1 is cheapest to deliver and good 2 is d dollars more expensive.

There are three types of traders: hedgers, speculators, and a squeezer. The model is a game played by speculators and the squeezer. In this game, hedgers' trade is exogenous—that is, hedgers do not trade strategically.

Hedgers trade exogenously by selling a random quantity of contracts, denoted $\tilde{H}$, in period 1 and purchasing back the $\tilde{H}$ contracts in period 2. the random variable $\tilde{H}$, which is distributed independently of $\tilde{v}$, assumes two outcomes, H_0 and H_1, where

$$\tilde{H} = \begin{cases} H_0 & \text{with probability } 1 - \lambda \\ \\ H_1 & \text{with probability } \lambda \end{cases}$$

We assume $0 < H_0 < H_1$, so an outcome of H_0 corresponds to inactive hedging and an outcome of H_1 corresponds to active hedging. (The assumption that the quantities H_0 and H_1 are positive is not actually necessary).

The strategy choice of the squeezer consists of two measurable functions, denoted $\tilde{X}_1(\cdot)$ and $\tilde{X}_2(.\ ,.\ ,.\ )$, where $\tilde{X}_1(\cdot)$ maps the space of real numbers into the space of random variables distributed independently from $\tilde{v}$, and $X_2(\ \cdot\ ,\ \cdot\ ,\ \cdot\ )$ maps R^3 into the space of random variables distributed independently from $\tilde{v}$. The quantities traded by the squeezer in periods 1 and 2, denoted $\tilde{x}_1$ and $\tilde{x}_2$ respectively, are given by

$$\tilde{x}_1 = \tilde{X}_1(\tilde{H}_1)$$

and

$$\tilde{x}_2 = \tilde{X}_2(\tilde{H}_1, \tilde{x}_1, \tilde{v})$$

where positive quantities denote purchases and negative quantities denote sales. This method of defining the trading strategy of the squeezer captures the idea that the squeezer observes the quantity $\tilde{H}$ traded by the hedgers before choosing the quantity he wishes to trade himself. Furthermore, the squeezer is allowed to randomize the quantities he trades in ways that do not anticipate the future spot price $\tilde{v}$. The fact that $\tilde{x}_2$ can depend on $\tilde{x}_1$ and $\tilde{v}$ allows the squeezer to adjust the quantity traded in period 2 in light of the quantity traded in period 1 and in light of the value $\tilde{v}$ revealed in period 2 (but this is not an important feature of the equilibrium).

The behavior of the speculators is specified by two measurable functions $P_1(\cdot)$ and $P_2(\ \cdot\ ,\ \cdot\ ,\ \cdot\ )$, which map R^1 and R^3, respectively, into R^1. The futures prices in periods 1 and 2 are given by

$$\tilde{p}_1^F = p_1(\tilde{x}_1 - \tilde{H})$$

and

$$\tilde{p}_2^F = p_2(\tilde{x}_1 - \tilde{H}, \tilde{x}_2 + H, \tilde{v})$$

In setting $\tilde{p}_1^F$, the speculators observe the aggregate quantity traded in period 1, denoted by $\tilde{y}_1 = X_1(\tilde{H}) - \tilde{H}$, but they do not observe the individual quantities $\tilde{X}_1(\tilde{H})$ and $\tilde{H}$ traded by the squeezer and the hedgers respectively. In setting the price in period 2, the speculators observe trade in period 1, trade in period 2, and the realized value $\tilde{v}$. Although the insider randomizes the quantity he trades, the pricing functions $P_1(\cdot)$ and $P_2(\cdot, \cdot, \cdot)$ are nonstochastic.

Let the notation $\tilde{X}_1$, $\tilde{X}_2$, P_1, P_2 denote in more abbreviated form the strategy choices $\tilde{X}_1(\cdot)$ and $\tilde{X}_2(\cdot, \cdot, \cdot)$ of the squeezer and the choices $P_1(\cdot)$ and $P_2(\cdot, \cdot, \cdot)$ of the speculators. Let $\tilde{\pi}(\tilde{X}_1, \tilde{X}_2, P_1, P_2)$ denote the profits of the insider as a function of these strategy choices. It is clear that $\tilde{\pi}(\tilde{X}_1, \tilde{X}_2, P_1, P_2)$ is a random variable given by

$$\tilde{\pi}(\tilde{X}_1, \tilde{X}_2, P_1, P_2) = \tilde{X}_1(\tilde{v} - \tilde{p}_1) + \tilde{X}_2(\tilde{v} - \tilde{p}_2) + \max\{\tilde{x}_1 + \tilde{x}_2 - z_1, 0\}d,$$

or, expressed explicitly in terms of $\tilde{X}_1$, $\tilde{X}_2$, P_1, P_2, by

$$
\begin{aligned}
\tilde{\pi}(\tilde{X}_1, \tilde{X}_2, P_1, P_2) = {} & X_1(\tilde{H}) \cdot [\tilde{v} - p_1(\tilde{X}_1(\tilde{H}) - \tilde{H})] \\
& + \tilde{X}_2(\tilde{H}, \tilde{X}_1(\tilde{H}), \tilde{v}) \\
& \cdot [\tilde{v} - P_2(\tilde{X}_1(\tilde{H}) - \tilde{H}, \tilde{X}_2(\tilde{H}, \tilde{X}_1(\tilde{H}), \tilde{v}) + \tilde{H}, \tilde{v})] \\
& + \max\{\tilde{X}_1(\tilde{H}) + \tilde{X}_2(\tilde{H}, \tilde{X}_1(\tilde{H}), \tilde{v}) - z_1, 0\}\, d.
\end{aligned}
$$

In this expression, the first term gives no-squeeze profits on trade made in period 1, the second term gives no-squeeze profits on trade made in period 2, and the third term gives additional profits captured when there is a squeeze.

An equilibrium is defined as a set of strategy choices $\tilde{X}_1$, $\tilde{X}_2$, P_1, P_2 such that three conditions hold. For all alternate strategies $\tilde{X}_1'$, $\tilde{X}_2'$

$$E\{\tilde{\pi}(\tilde{X}_1, \tilde{X}_2, P_1, P_2)\} \geq E\{\tilde{\pi}(\tilde{X}_1', \tilde{X}_2', P_1, P_2)\} \qquad (5.1)$$

The function P_1 satisifies $P_1(y) = E\{\tilde{p}_2 \mid \tilde{x}_1 - \tilde{H} = y\}$, or explicitly

$$P_1, (y) = E\{P_2[\tilde{X}_1(\tilde{H}) - \tilde{H}, X_2(\tilde{H}, \tilde{X}_1(\tilde{H}), \tilde{v}) + \tilde{H}, \tilde{v}] \mid \tilde{X}_1(\tilde{H}) - \tilde{H} = y\}$$
$$(5.2)$$

The function P_2 is given by

$$P_2(y_1,y_2,v) = \begin{cases} v & \text{if } y_1 + y_2 \leqslant z_1 \\ v + d & \text{if } y_1 + y_2 > z_1 \end{cases} \qquad (5.3)$$

According to this equilibrium concept, the squeezer maximizes his expected profits, taking into account the effect that a change in his trading has on future prices. Speculators are assumed to trade in such a way that the expected profits of acquiring a futures position at market-clearing prices, then liquidating it later through trade or through delivery, are zero. In effect, we assume that speculators are risk-neutral, perfect competitors who compete with one another so fiercely that their extra profits are driven to zero, but we do not model explicitly the auction process that generates this outcome. To both the speculators and the insider, the equilibrium reflects fulfilled expectations in the sense that traders utilize models which are not contradicted in equilibrium by observations of variables in their respective information sets.

In order to understand this equilibrium concept, it is important to keep in mind two points. First, the squeezer's strategy choices $\tilde{X}_1$ and $\tilde{X}_2$ are not arguments of the speculators' pricing functions p_1 and p_2. That is, we are in effect using a Nash concept of equilibrium rather than a Stackleberg concept in which the squeezer moves first. If the squeezer contemplates changing his strategy $\tilde{X}_1$, $\tilde{X}_2$, he assumes that speculators do not change theirs in response. Instead, the speculators merely react to the actual quantities traded. Because of the Nash equilibrium concept, the squeezer will not follow a random strategy unless the various random outcomes all generate the same expected profits conditional on the squeezer's information. Furthermore, there will be no sense in which the squeezer, say, sacrifices expected profits when hedging is inactive to increase profits when hedging is active because such behavior implicitly assumes that the squeezer gets the speculators to change their strategies in response to changes in his own. Finally, the Nash concept automatically makes the equilibrium dynamically consistent by ruling out credibility issues involving whether the squeezer will still want to follow the second-period strategy $\tilde{X}_2$ after first-period trade has already occurred.

Second, remember the nature of the conditional expectation defining $P_1(y_1)$ in condition 5.2 of equilibrium. The function $P_1(\cdot)$ must be defined for all values of $\bar{y}_1$, where $\bar{y}_1$, the equilibrium quantity traded in period 1, is given by $\bar{y}_1 = \tilde{X}_1(\tilde{H}) - \tilde{H}$. Because $\tilde{H}$ assumes only two outcomes, the equilibrium distribution of $\bar{y}_1$ may well be massed at only one or two points, so almost all of the admissible outcomes of $\bar{y}_1$ will never be realized.

For those sets of outcomes y_1 with probability zero of occurring, the value of $P_1(y_1)$ can be changed without affecting the fact that $P_1(y_1)$ is the conditional expectation because conditional expectations are only defined up to sets of probability zero. Thus, condition 5.2 does not define $P_1(y_1)$ uniquely (except for those values of y_1 which have positive probability of occurring). In equilibrium, however, the prices $P_1(y_1)$ corresponding to values of y_1 that never occur play an important role. The prices corresponding to these y_1 values must be such that for all outcomes $\bar{H}$, the squeezer is never induced to trade in such a way that the corresponding y_1 values are realized. In other words, although almost all values of y_1 will never be realized, the function $P_1(\cdot)$, which is not uniquely defined by condition 5.2, must be chosen in such a way that it sustains the equilibrium in which they are not realized, by making it unattractive for the squeezer to trade in such a way that they are.

In the rest of this section, we show how to characterize the equilibria in this model. We show that an equilibrium exists and also show that except for trivial changes in $\bar{X}_1$, $\bar{X}_2$, P_1, P_2, the equilibrium is unique. In particular, there exists a unique probability that a squeeze occurs and a unique equilibrium pricing process. However, the quantities traded by the insider and the prices that occur with probability zero are not necessarily uniquely defined.

Because of the way in which equilibrium is defined, it is possible to calculate the equilibria for the model by working backward from period 2. As a first step, we show that in any equilibrium, no second-period trading strategy for the squeezer dominates the strategy of not trading.

LEMMA 1. *For all* $\bar{X}_1$, $\bar{X}'_2$, P_1, P_2, *the trading strategy* $\bar{X}_2 = 0$, *defined by* $\bar{X}_2(\bar{H},\bar{x}_1,\bar{v}) = 0$ *with probability 1, has the property that*

$$\bar{\pi}(\bar{X}_1, 0, P_1, P_2) \geq \bar{\pi}(\bar{X}_1, \bar{X}'_2, P_1, P_2)$$

Proof.   From the definition of $\bar{\pi}(\bar{X}_1, \bar{X}_2, P_1, P_2)$, we have

$$\bar{\pi}(\bar{X}_1, 0, P_1, P_2) - \bar{\pi}(\bar{X}_1, \bar{X}'_2, P_1, P_2)$$

$$= \max\{\bar{X}_1(\bar{H}_1) - z_1, 0\} - \max\{\bar{X}_1(\bar{H}) + \bar{X}'_2(\bar{H},\bar{X}_1(\bar{H}),z_1), 0\}d$$

$$- \bar{X}'_2(\bar{H}, X_1(\bar{H}),\bar{v})[\bar{v} - P_2(\bar{X}_1(\bar{H}) - \bar{H}, \bar{X}_2(\bar{H},\bar{X}_1(\bar{H}),\bar{v}) + \bar{H},\bar{v})]$$

We wish to show that the preceding expression is always nonnegative. Letting $x_1 = \bar{X}_1(\bar{H})$, $x_2 = \bar{X}'_2(\bar{H},\bar{X}_1(\bar{H}),\bar{v}$, $\bar{H} = h$, $\bar{v} = v$, the right side of the preceding expression can be expressed as $J(x_1,x_2,h,p)$, where J is defined by

$$J(x_1,x_2,h,p) = \max\{x_1 - z_1, 0\}\cdot d - \max\{x_1 + x_2 - z_1, 0\} \cdot d$$

$$- x_2(v - P_2(x_1 + h, x_2 - h, v))$$

From the definition of P_2 (property 5.3 of the definition of equilibrium), it is a straightforward exercise to show that whenever $x_1 - z_1$ has the same sign as $x_1 + x_2 - z_1$, then $J = 0$, and whenever $x_1 - z_1$ is opposite in sign to $x_1 + x_2 - z_1$, then $J = |x_1 - z_1| \cdot d$. Thus, J is always nonnegative, and the result is proved.

The intuition behind this result is quite simple. Because speculators observe whether or not there will be a squeeze before p_2^F is determined, the squeeze cannot trick the speculators into trading at unfavorable prices in period 2. This being the case, he has no incentive to trade in period 2 at all. The speculator is actually indifferent between trading $x_2 = 0$ and any other x_2 that leaves the sign of $x_1 - z_1$ the same as the sign of $x_1 + x_2 - z_1$. Because there will be a squeeze if and only if $x_1 + x_2 - z_1$ is positive, the squeezer determines whether or not there will be a squeeze by his trading in period 1. In period 2, he does anything that does not alter this determination. Without loss of generality, we can therefore assume $\tilde{X}_2 = 0$, that is, the squeezer does not trade in period 2.

Because P_2 is defined in part 5.3 of the definition of equilibrium and because $\tilde{X}_2$ is (without loss of generality) zero, the problem of characterizing equilibrium collapses back to determining period 1 strategies $\tilde{X}_1$ and $\tilde{P}_1$.

Letting $\tilde{\pi}_1(\tilde{X}_1, P_1)$ denote the profits of the insider with $\tilde{X}_2$ and P_2 substituted out, we obtain

$$\tilde{\pi}_1(\tilde{X}_1, P_1) = \tilde{X}_1(\tilde{H}) \cdot [\tilde{v} - P_1(\tilde{X}_1(\tilde{H}) - \tilde{H})] + \max(\tilde{X}_1(\tilde{H}) - z_1, 0) \cdot d$$

$\tilde{X}_1$ and P_1 generate an equilibrium provided

$$E\tilde{\pi}_1(\tilde{X}_1, P_1) \geq E\tilde{\pi}_1(\tilde{X}_1', P_1) \text{ for all } \tilde{X}_1',$$

$$P_1(y_1) = E\tilde{v} + \text{Prob}\{\tilde{X}_1(\tilde{H}) - z_1 > 0 \,|\, \tilde{X}_1(\tilde{H}) - \tilde{H} = y_1\} \cdot d$$

The conditional expectation in the preceding equation is defined uniquely only up to sets of probability zero.

Now, given the function P, define the functions $\Pi_p(\cdot, \cdot)$, measuring expected squeezer profits when the squeezer trades x and hedgers trade h, and $\Pi_p^*(\cdot)$, measuring maximized profits, by

$$\Pi_P(x, h) = (E\tilde{v} - P(x - h))x + \max(x - z_1, 0) \cdot d,$$

$$\Pi_P^*(h) = \max_X \Pi_P(x, h)$$

For the conditions $E\pi_1(\tilde{X}_1, P) > E\pi_1(\tilde{X}_1', P)$ to hold for all $\tilde{X}_1'$, it is necessary that

$$\text{Prob}\{\Pi_P(\tilde{X}_1(H_i), H_i) = \Pi_P^*(H_i)\} = 1 \quad \text{for} \quad i = 0, 1.$$

As a first step toward characterizing equilibrium, we show that if squeezes occur with positive probability in equilibrium, the squeezer is always short when hedging is inactive.

LEMMA 2. *If prob $\{\bar{X}_1(\bar{H}) - z_1 > 0\} > 0$ in equilibrium, then $\bar{X}_1(H_0) < 0$ with probability 1, $P(\bar{X}_1(H_0) - H_0) > E\tilde{v}$ with probability 1, and $\Pi_P^*(H_0) > 0$.*

Proof. Consider an equilibrium where prob $\{\bar{X}_1(\bar{H}) - z_1 > 0\} > 0$. Because squeezes occur with positive probability, it must be the case that prob $\{\bar{H} = H_0$ and $P(\bar{X}(\bar{H}) - \bar{H}) > E\tilde{v}\} > 0$ since otherwise speculators could infer from $P(\bar{X}_1(\bar{H}) - \bar{H}) > E\tilde{v}$ that $\bar{H} = H_1$, and, knowing that a squeeze was going to occur, would set $P(\bar{X}(\bar{H}) - \bar{H}) = E\tilde{v} + d$; but this would make the squeeze unprofitable for the squeezer and hence cannot be an equilibrium.

Clearly, for the squeezer not to lose money when $P(\bar{X}_1(H_0) - H_0) > E\tilde{v}$, it must be the case that either $\Pi_P^*(H_0) = 0$ (and $\bar{X}_1(H_0) = 0$ when $P(\bar{X}_1(H_0) - H_0) > E\tilde{v}$ or $\Pi_p^*(H_0) > 0$ and $\bar{X}_1(H_0) <$ when $P(\bar{X}_1(H_0) - H) > E\tilde{v}$.

Suppose (to be contradicted) that $\bar{X}_1(H_0) = 0$ when $P(\bar{X}_1(H_0) - H_0) > E\tilde{v}$. For $\bar{X}_1(H_0) = 0$ to be maximizing, it must be the case that $P(y) \leq E\tilde{v}$ for $y < -H_0$; otherwise the squeezer could sell short and make positive profits. Clearly, for $\bar{X}_1(H_0) = 0$ to hold when $P(\bar{X}_1(H_0) - H_0) > E\tilde{v}$, we must have $P(-H_0) > E\tilde{v}$. Since $\bar{X}_1(H_0) = 0$ with positive probability, we must have $\bar{X}_1(H_1) = H_1 - H_0$ with positive probability since otherwise speculators could infer from $\bar{X}_1(\bar{H}) - \bar{H} = -H_0$ that $\bar{H} = H_0$ and $\bar{X}_1(\bar{H}) = 0$, and would thus set $P(-H_0) = E\tilde{v}$. Because of the left discontinuity in $P(y)$ at $y = -H_0$, the squeezer makes greater profits setting $\bar{X}_1(H_1) = H_1 - H_0 - \varepsilon$ for small $\varepsilon > 0$ than from $\bar{X}_1(H_1) = H_1 - H_0$. This contradicts the fact that $\bar{X}_1(H_1) = H_1 - H_0$ maximize profits when $\bar{H} = H_1$; thus original supposition that $\bar{X}_1(H_0) = 0$ when $P(\bar{X}_1(H_0) - H_0) > E\tilde{v}$ must be false.

From this contradiction, we conclude that $\Pi_p^*(H_0) > 0$ and $\bar{X}_1(H_0) < 0$ when $P(\bar{X}_1(H_0) - H_0) > E\tilde{v}$. When futures prices are not greater than $E\tilde{v}$, it is clear that futures prices equal $E\tilde{v}$ since lower prices (with positive probability) are inconsistent with equilibrium. When $P(\bar{X}_1(H_0) - H_0) = E\tilde{v}$, it must be the case that the squeezer engineer a squeeze to achieve strictly positive profits $\Pi_G^*(H_0)$. But this is inconsistent with prices being equal to $E\tilde{v}$. It follows that conditional on $\bar{H} = H_0$, futures prices are greater than $E\tilde{v}$ with probability 1 and $\bar{X}_1(H_0)$ is negative with probability 1—the desired result.

The next lemma amplifies the previous result by showing that in equilibria where squeezes occur, the short position taken by the squeezer when hedging is inactive is unique (nonrandom). Furthermore, whenever the squeezer attempts a squeeze, he purchases a unique (nonrandom) quantity.

LEMMA 3.   *Suppose prob* $\{\tilde{X}_1(\tilde{H}) - z_1 > 0\} > 0$ *in equilibrium. Then there exists a constant* y^* *satisfying* $y^* + H_0 < 0 < z_1 < y^* + H_1$ *such that*

1. Prob $\{\tilde{X}_1(H_0) = y^* + H_0\} = 1$,

2. Prob $\{\tilde{X}_1(H_1) > z_1\} = $ prob $\{\tilde{X}_1(H_1) = y^* + H_1\}$

Proof: Define the function $\pi(\cdot,\cdot)$ by

$$\pi(x,p) = (E\tilde{v} - p)x + \max\{x - z_1, \, 0\}d$$

For equilibrium profit levels $\Pi_P^*(H_0)$ and $\Pi_P^*(H_1)$, define the sets $B(H_i)$, $I(H_i)$, $i = 0, 1$, by

$$B(H_i) = \{(y,p): z_1 - H_1 < y < -H_0, \, \Pi(y + H_i,p) = \Pi_P^*(H_i)\},$$

$$I(H_i) = \{(y,p): z_1 - H_1 < y < -H_0, \, \Pi(y + H_i,p) > \Pi_P^*(H_i)\}$$

We claim that in equilibrium $I(H_0) \cap I(H_1) = \phi$. To prove this claim observe that over x values such that $x = y + H_0$, $z - H_1 < y < -H_0$ implies that $z_1 - (H_1 - H_0) < x < 0$. Since x is negative, $\pi(x,p)$ is strictly quasiconcave in x and p and increasing in p. Thus, $I(H_0)$ is convex if it contains (y,p); it also contains (y,p') for all $p' \geq p$. Similarly, observe that over x values such that $x = y + H_1$, $z_1 - H_1 < y < -H_0$ implies that $z_1 < x < H_1 - H_0$. Since x is greater than z_1, $\Pi(x,p)$ is strictly quasiconcave and decreasing in p. Thus, $I(H_1)$ is convex, and if it contains (y,p) it also contains (y,p') for all $p' \leq p$ (see figure 5–1).

Now suppose (to be contradicted) that $I(H_0) \cap (H_1)$ is nonempty and let $(y,p) \, \varepsilon \, I(H_0) \wedge I(H_1)$. There clearly exists no p' such that $(y,p') \notin I(H_0)$ and $(y,p') \notin I(H_1$ because $I(H_0)$ contains all (y,p') with $p' \geq p$ and $I(H_1)$ contains all p' with $p' < p$. Thus, no matter how $P(y)$ is defined, the squeezer can do better than his equilibrium strategy by choosing $x = y + H_i$ when either $\tilde{H} = H_0$ or $\tilde{H} = H_1$. This is clearly a contradiction, from which we conclude that $I(H_0) \cap I(H_1) = \phi$.

Now it follows from the properties of convex sets that since $I(H_0)$ and $I(H_1)$ do not intersect, their boundaries $B(H_0)$ and $B(H_1)$ intersect in at most one point. Call this point, if it exists, $< y^*,p^* >$. (See figure 5–1.)

We now claim that

$$\text{Prob}\{<\tilde{X}_1(\tilde{H}) - \tilde{H}, P(\tilde{X}_1(\tilde{H}) - \tilde{H}) > \varepsilon \, B(H_0) \cap B(H_1) \, |$$
$$P(\tilde{X}(\tilde{H}) - \tilde{H}) > E\tilde{v}\} = 1$$

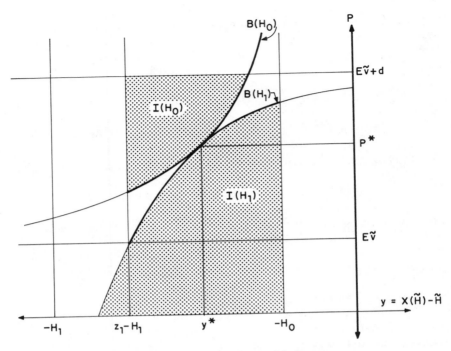

Figure 5–1. Equilibrium with Squeezes

From this claim, it follows that whenever $\bar{p}_1^F > E\tilde{v}$, the observed quantity-price outcome is $< y^*,p^*>$, from which the desired results stated in lemma 3 follow immediately from lemma 2. To prove the claim, observe that a quantity-price outcome consistent with prices greater than $E\tilde{v}$ must be such that it is impossible to infer whether or not there will be a squeeze, since if it is possible to infer that there will be no squeeze (with probability 1), the price would be $E\tilde{v}$; and since if it is possible to infer that there will be a squeeze (with probability 1), the price would be $E\tilde{v} + d$ and the squeezer would be losing money. Clearly, $z_1 - H_1 < y$ and $\Pi(y + H_1,p) = \Pi_P^*(H_1)$ because otherwise it can be inferred that there will not be a squeeze, and $y < H_0$ and $\Pi(y + H_0,p) = \Pi_P^*(H_0)$ because otherwise it can be inferred (from lemma 2) that there will be a squeeze. This is enough to put the price-quantity outcome in the set $B(H_0) \cap B(H_1)$ (with probability 1), which proves the desired claim. This completes the proof of the lemma.

Define the quantity μ^* by

$$\mu^* = \text{prob}\{\tilde{X}_1(H_1) > z_1\}$$

The quantity μ^* is the conditional probability of a squeeze given $\tilde{H} = H_1$. From lemma 3 we can conclude that it is necessary for all equilibria to fall under one of the following three cases, classified according to whether $\mu^* = 0$, $0 < \mu^* < 1$, or $\mu^* = 1$.

Type 1. $\mu^* = 0$: Squeezes occur with probability 0. The equilibrium price is $E\tilde{v}$ with probability 1.

Type 2. $0 < \mu^* < 1$: Squeezes occur with probability $\lambda\mu^*$. There exists a pair (y^*, p^*) such that $z_1 - H_1 < y^* < -H_0$ and

$$X(H_0) \quad = y^* + H_0 \text{ with probability } 1$$

$$X(H_1) \begin{cases} = y^* + H_1 \text{ with probability } \mu^* \\ < z_1 \qquad \text{with probability } 1 - \mu^* \end{cases}$$

$$\tilde{p}_1^F = P(\tilde{X}_1(\tilde{H}) - \tilde{H}) = \begin{cases} p^* = E\tilde{v} + \dfrac{\mu^*\lambda}{1 - \lambda + \mu^*\lambda}d, \text{ when } X_1(\tilde{H}) - \tilde{H} = \\ \qquad \qquad \qquad \qquad \qquad \quad y^*, \text{ which occurs with} \\ \qquad \qquad \qquad \qquad \qquad \quad \text{probability } 1 - \lambda + \\ \qquad \qquad \qquad \qquad \qquad \quad \mu^*\lambda \\ E\tilde{v}, \qquad \qquad \qquad \qquad \quad \text{otherwise} \end{cases}$$

These conditions do not define the distribution of $\tilde{X}_1(H_1)$ uniquely for $\tilde{X}_1(H_1) < z_1$ and do not define the values of the function $P(y)$ uniquely for $y \neq y^*$. In this case, $\Pi_P^*(H_1) = 0$, that is, the squeezer makes zero profits when there is a squeeze. The squeezer makes positive profits by shorting the market when there will be no squeeze.

Type 3. $\mu^* = 1$: Squeezes occur with probability λ. There exists a pair (y^*, p^*) such that $z_1 - H_1 < y^* < -H_0$ and

$$\tilde{X}_1(H_0) = y^* + H_0 \qquad \text{with probability } 1$$

$$\tilde{X}_1(H_1) = y^* + H_1 \qquad \text{with probability } 1$$

$$\tilde{P}_1^F = P(\tilde{X}_1(\tilde{H}) - \tilde{H}) = P^* = E\tilde{v} + \lambda d \qquad \text{with probability } 1$$

These conditions do not define the values of the function $P(y)$ for $y \neq y^*$. Also, the squeezer always expects positive profits—he makes positive profits on the long side when there is a squeeze and positive profits on the short side when there is no squeeze.

We now show that an equilibrium for the model always exists, and that each of the three cases can be an equilibrium, depending on the size of $H_1 - H_0$. As $H_1 - H_0$ increases exogenously, the equilibrium changes from type 1 to type 2 to type 3.

THEOREM. *There exists an equilibrium. Depending on the size of $H_1 - H_0$, the equilibrium is one of the following three types.*

Type 1. $0 < H_1 - H_0 \leq z_1$: Squeezes occur with probability

$$0 \text{ and } \tilde{p}_1^F = E\tilde{v} \text{ with probability } 1$$

Type 2. $z_1 \leq H_1 - H_0 < \dfrac{z_1}{(1-\lambda)^2}$: then $\mu^* = \left[\left(\dfrac{H_1 - H_0}{z_1}\right)^{1/2} - 1\right]\dfrac{1-\lambda}{\lambda}$

$$\tilde{X}_1(H_0) = (H_1 - H_0)^{1/2}z_1^{1/2} - (H_1 - H_0) \text{ with probability } 1$$

$$\tilde{X}_1(H_1) \begin{cases} = (H_1 - H_0)^{1/2}z_1^{1/2} & \text{with probability } \mu^* \\[2mm] < z_1 & \text{otherwise} \end{cases}$$

$$p_1^F = \begin{cases} E\tilde{v} + \left[1 - \left(\dfrac{z_1}{H_1 - H_0}\right)^{1/2}\right]d & \begin{array}{l}\text{when } X_1(H) - H = \\ (H_1 - H_2)^{1/2}z_1^{1/2} - H_1 \\ \text{which occurs with probability} \\ 1 - \lambda + \mu^*\lambda\end{array} \\[6mm] E\tilde{v} & \text{otherwise} \end{cases}$$

Type 3. $\left(\dfrac{z_1}{(1-\lambda)^2}\right) \leq H_1 - H_0$: Then, with probability 1, we have

$$X_1(H_0) = \lambda(H_0 - H_1),$$
$$X_1(H_1) = (1 - \lambda)(H_0 - H_1),$$
$$p_1^F = E\tilde{v} + \lambda d.$$

Proof: Suppose first that $H_1 - H_0 \leq z_1$. Since there exists no y^* such that $y^* + H_0 < 0$ and $z_1 < y^* + H_1$, the conclusion of lemma 3 cannot hold, so any equilibrium must have zero probability of squeezes. To show that such an equilibrium does exist, we must specify functions P and $\tilde{X}$ that generate an equilibrium. One such example is given by

$$P(y) = \begin{cases} E\tilde{v} & \text{if } y \leq -H_0 \\[3mm] E\tilde{v} + d & \text{if } y > -H_0 \end{cases}$$

$$\tilde{X}(\tilde{H}) = 0 \qquad \text{with probability } 1$$

To prove that this is an equilibrium, observe that when $\tilde{H} = H_1$, the squeezer must pay $E\tilde{v} + d$ to buy enough to squeeze, which is unprofitable, and if he does not squeeze, can at best break even by trading at price $E\bar{v}$. When $\bar{H} = H_0$, the squeezer cannot take a short position at any price except $E\bar{v}$ and hence cannot make positive expected profits in this case either. Because the squeezer makes zero profits when $\bar{H} = H_0$ and zero profits when $\bar{H} = H_1$, no strategy dominates the no-trade strategy. Note that the equilibrium P and $\bar{X}$ are not unique. No other equilibrium, however, generates a positive probability of squeezes—that is, all such equilibria are type 1.

Now suppose $H_1 - H_0 > z_1$. We claim that squeezes must have a positive probability of occurring. To prove this claim, observe that for y satisfying $z_1 - H_1 < y < H_0$, we must have $\pi_P^*(H_0) > 0$ unless $P(y) = E\bar{v}$ and we must have $\pi_P^*(H_1) > 0$ if $P(y) = E\bar{v}$. It is thus impossible to have $\pi_P^*(H_0) = \pi_P^*(H_1) = 0$, which is necessary if squeezes never occur.

Because squeezes occur with positive probability, there exists a y^* satisfying lemma 3 and an associated p^* as discussed in the proof of that lemma. Recall that in the proof of lemma 3, it was shown that to satisfy the condition $F\bar{\pi}_1(\bar{X}_1, P) \geq E\bar{\pi}_1(\bar{X}_1', P)$ for all $\bar{X}_1'$, it is necessary that there exist profit levels $\Pi_P^*(H_0) > 0$ and $\pi_P^*(H_1) \geq 0$ such that $\{(y^*, p^*)\}$ is the intersection of the boundaries $B(H_0)$ and $B(H_1)$, and the interiors $I(H_0)$ and $I(H_1)$ do not intersect. For this necessary condition to be sufficient to satisfy the condition $E\bar{\pi}_1(\bar{X}_1, P) \geq E\bar{\pi}_1(\bar{X}_1', P)$ for all $\bar{X}_1'$, we must be able to define the function P such that the following two conditions hold:

1. For the restricted domain $z_1 - H_1 < y < H_0$, the graph of P separates the interiors $I(H_0)$ and $I(H_1)$.
2. For y outside this domain, P must be defined so that the profit levels $\pi_P^*(H_0)$ and $\pi_P^*(H_1)$ cannot be dominated either.

To prove that condition 1 then can be satisfied, we know from the properties of convex sets (the difference curves $B(H_0)$ and $B(H_1)$ are both nowhere vertical) that a linear function P exists, but the actual P chosen need not be linear. To satisfy condition 2, we can choose $P(y) = E\bar{v}$ for $y \leq z_1 - H_1$ and $P(y) = E\bar{v} + d$ for $y \geq H_0$, but again, many other definitions of P work just as well (see figure 5–2).

The (y^*, p^*) combinations consistent with equilibrium lie along a contract curve defined as a set of points (y^*, p^*) satisfying $z_1 - H_1 \leq y^* < -H_0$ and such that there exists a nonnegative profit level $\Pi_P^*(H_1)$ with

$$(y^*, p^*) = \underset{y, p}{\operatorname{argmax}} \{ (E\bar{v} - p)(y + H_0):$$

$$(E\bar{v} - p + d)(y + H_1) - z_1 d \geq \Pi_P^*(H_1) \}$$

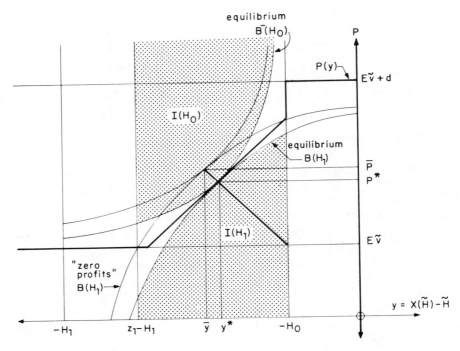

Figure 5–2. Equilibrium Futures Price Function

To calculate the locus of points defining this contact curve, we obtain from the Lagrangian

$$L = (E\tilde{v} - p)\,(y + H_0) - \alpha[\,(E\tilde{v} - p + d)\,(y + H_1) - z_1 d - \Pi^*_P(H_1)\,]$$

(with Lagrange multiplier α) the first-order conditions

$$y^* + H_0 = \alpha(y^* + H_1),$$
$$E\tilde{p} + p^* = \alpha(E\tilde{v} - p^* + d)$$

It is not hard to show that these conditions imply

$$(H_1 - H_0)\,(E\tilde{v} - p^* + d) = (y^* + H_1)d,$$

from which it is apparent that the contract curve is a straight line segment. The left endpoint of the contract curve, denoted $(\bar{y}, \bar{p})$, corresponds to the solution of the maximization problem when $\Pi^*_P(H_1) = 0$, and is given by

$$\bar{y} = (H_1 - H_0)^{1/2} z_1^{1/2} - H_1,$$

$$\bar{p} = E\tilde{v} + \left[1 - \left(\frac{z_1}{H_1 - H_0}\right)^{\frac{1}{2}}\right]d$$

Note that the condition $z_1 - H_1 \leq \bar{y} < H_0$ is satisfied. The right end-point of the contract curve is defined by $y^* = -H_0$, $p^* = E\tilde{v}$. Because we have already shown that the equilibrium condition $E\tilde{\pi}_1(\tilde{X}_1, P_1,) \geq E\tilde{\pi}_1(\tilde{X}_1', P_1)$ for all $\tilde{X}_1'$ is satisified, the points along the contract curve will generate equilibria provided the market-efficiency condition

$$P(y) = E\tilde{v} + \text{prob}\{\tilde{X}_1(\tilde{H}) - z_1 > 0 | \tilde{X}_1(\tilde{H}) - \tilde{H} = y\}\cdot d$$

is also satisfied. There are two cases to consider:

Case 1: $\Pi_P^*(H_1) = 0$. Then we have a type 2 equilibrium with $(y^*, p^*) = (\bar{y}, \bar{p})$. The parameter μ^* gives the probability of a squeeze conditional on $\tilde{H} = H_1$. The market-efficiency condition holds provided first, $p_1^F = E\tilde{v}$ with probability 1 conditional on $\tilde{X}_1(\tilde{H}) - \tilde{H} \neq \bar{y}$ and second

$$\bar{p} = E\tilde{v} + \frac{\mu^* \lambda}{1 - \lambda + \mu^* \lambda} d$$

Condition 1 holds because P was defined so that $P(y) = E\tilde{v}$ for all $y < z_1 - H_1$ (other definitions of P would work just as well). From the definition of $\bar{p}$, condition 2 holds provided

$$\mu^* = \frac{1 - \lambda}{\lambda} \left[\left(\frac{H_1 - H_0}{z_1}\right)^{\frac{1}{2}} - 1\right]$$

Because μ^* is a probability, we must have $\mu^* \varepsilon [0,1]$, which occurs provided

$$z_1 < H_1 - H_0 < \frac{z_1}{(1 - \lambda)^2}$$

Case 2: $\Pi_P^*(H_1) > 0$. Then we have a type 3 equilibrium. The market-efficiency condition holds if and only if $p^* = E\tilde{v} + \lambda d$, from which we obtain $y^* = -\lambda H_1 - (1 - \lambda)H_0$. The point (y^*, p^*) is on the contract curve provided

$$H_1 - H_0 \geq \frac{z_1}{(1 - \lambda)^2}$$

We have now characterized equilibrium when $H_1 - H_0 > z_1$ in a manner consistent with the statement of the theorem. This completes the proof of the theorem.

It is interesting to observe what happens as the size of the market, as measured by $H_1 - H_0$, increases from some small initial value. For $H_1 - H_0 < z_1$, there are no squeezes. When $H_1 - H_0$ gets slightly larger than z_1, squeezes begin to occur occasionally but are never expected to be profitable for the squeezer; however, the bidding up of prices in anticipation of squeezes allows the squeezer to earn positive profits by shorting the market when no squeeze is going to occur. Finally, when $H_1 - H_0 > z_1/(1 - \lambda)^2$, squeezes occur with probability λ.

Now define λ^* by

$$\lambda^* = \min\left(\lambda, \max\left(1 - \left(\frac{z_1}{H_1 - H_0}\right)^{1/2}, 0\right)\right)$$

The quantity λ^* measures the conditional probability of a squeeze given that $\tilde{X}_1(\tilde{H}) - \tilde{H} = y^*$. The expected losses of hedgers, denoted L, are given by

$$L = \lambda^*(1 - \lambda)(H_1 - H_0)$$

and the expected profits of the squeezer are given by

$$E\tilde{\pi}_1(X_1, P) = \lambda^*[(1 - \lambda)(H_1 - H_0) - \mu\lambda z_1]$$

The difference between L and $E\tilde{\pi}_1(\tilde{X}_1, P)$ is the transfer of resources to the holders of the cheap quality because its price is bid up in anticipation of squeezes.

What Happens When Delivery Is Costly?

A typical squeeze situation is often thought to involve a great deal of threatening and bluffing. The squeezer acquires a large long position but does not really want to take delivery. Instead, the squeezer wants to set the futures price at a high level and persuade the shorts to liquidate at the high price that he dictates. If the shorts can be persuaded, the squeeze can be successful, even though few actual deliveries are made.

This threatening and bluffing is missing from the model described in the previous section. It is missing because the marginal qualities involved in the delivery process, which are the expensive qualities, are worth to the squeezer exactly what they cost the shorts to deliver. The squeezer has nothing to lose by taking delivery so he does not need to threaten to do so. In fact, we showed in the previous section that the squeezer is indifferent between taking delivery of all the positions he acquires in period 1 and taking delivery of only slightly more than is necessary to soak up all of the cheap quality. He is indifferent because the difference, which represents the high-quality deliveries, can be liquidated in period 2 at the high squeeze price.

Threats and bluffs enter the picture when it costs the shorts more to make delivery than it is worth to the squeezer to take delivery. It is easy to see how this situation can arise in practice. Contract specifications call for deliverable stocks to be stored at particular delivery points. When stocks at these delivery points are low, shorts are forced to transport the stocks from nondeliverable points to deliverable points, even though at postdelivery prices the value premium for stocks stored at the deliverable points over nondeliverable points may not be enough to cover transportation and other delivery costs. In fact, it is possible that stocks are worth more at nondeliverable points than at deliverable points, when valued at no-squeeze prices, and moving them not only involves a transportation cost but destroys some of their value as well. In this situation, delivery of the commodity is economically inefficient and involves a deadweight cost that must be born by the squeezer or the shorts. With costly delivery, an incentive is created for both sides to liquidate their contracts before delivery. The problem of course, involves setting the price at which liquidation will occur.

The squeezer would like to set a price slightly below what it costs the shorts to make delivery. To do so, he must threaten to take delivery of contracts that will be worth much less to him. The shorts, on the other hand, would like to set a price only slightly above what the contracts would be worth to the squeezer. In doing so, they implicitly threaten to make delivery at a cost that is much higher than this price. The equilibrium price that emerges and the number of deliveries, if any, that are made will be determined in part by the game theoretic structure of the delivery process.

Because the shorts are fragmented competitors, it may seem appropriate to model the delivery process as a game in which the squeezer forces liquidation on his terms. However, if the leader tries to force liquidation on his terms, the shorts may not remain fragmented competitors. Instead, one short may allow the others to buy out of their position at prices slightly lower than the squeezer is offering. It costs him little to do this because he always preserves the option of caving in to the squeezer and taking a small loss. He has a great deal to gain, however, if—having bought out the other shorts—he can use a stronger bargaining position with the squeezer to achieve a better price. This reasoning suggests that open interest on both sides of the market will become concentrated near delivery and that the delivery process should be modeled as a game with a small number of players on both sides of the market. The actual outcome may be indeterminate, in the sense that there is either no equilibrium or are multiple equilibria, but we do not pursue this idea in detail here.

The question remains whether the model discussed in the previous section is relevant at all when there is costly delivery. In fact, that model can be interpreted as modeling a situation in which the shorts cave in to the squeezer and liquidate before delivery on his terms. To make this interpretation, a few trivial changes are needed. First, the underlying value of the expensive qualities $\bar{v} + d$ is interpreted not as its value to the squeezer but rather as its delivered cost to the shorts. For example, we can assume that there is really only one quality and that it is worth $\bar{v}$ regardless of whether it is stored at deliverable or nondeliverable points. Let z_1 denote stocks at the deliverable storage point, let z_2 denote stocks at the nondeliverable point, and let d denote the cost of transporting stocks from one point to another. Then stocks at the nondeliverable point are worth $\bar{v}$ to the squeezer when delivered but cost the shorts $\bar{v} + d$ to deliver.

The second change concerns the second period of trading. In the second period, the squeezer, rather than being indifferent about delivery, prefers not to take delivery and liquidates almost all of his position in excess of z_1 at the squeeze price $\bar{v} + d$, thus cashing in almost all of his profits through liquidation. Taking delivery of slightly more than z_1 units forces the shorts to deliver some expensive stocks and keeps the period 2 price high.

With these minor changes, the period 1 game remains unchanged and prices and profits are exactly the same as discussed in the previous section. Thus, that model remains applicable when there is costly delivery. The model gives the squeezer the power to make a credible threat by forcing him to move first in period 2 and not letting him trade more later.

Endogenous Hedging

The model discussed in the preceding section takes as given the amount of hedging H_0 and H_1. In this section we make the amount of hedging endogenous by constructing a simple model of endogenous hedging.

Suppose that there are N potential hedgers. We suppose that there are two states, where state zero corresponds to inactive hedging and state one corresponds to active hedging. In state i, $i = 0, 1$, a fraction η_i of the hedgers have an inventory of one unit of the commodity and the remaining fraction $1 - \eta_i$ of hedgers have no inventory. We assume $0 < \eta_0 < \eta_1 < 1$, so the states differ only with respect to the percentage of the population of hedgers who have inventories to hedge. The problem for a hedger is to decide how large a futures position to take, given the size of the hedger's inventory. The hedger does not know whether there will be active hedging or inactive hedging, but he can use Baye's Theorem to calculate the probabilities conditional on his inventory as follows:

$$\text{Probability (inactive hedging|one unit)} = \frac{(1 - \lambda)\eta_0}{(1 - \lambda)\eta_0 + \lambda\eta_1}$$

$$\text{Probability (active hedging|one unit)} = \frac{\lambda \eta_1}{(1 - \lambda)\eta_0 + \lambda \eta_1}$$

$$\text{Probability (inactive hedging|zero units)} = \frac{(1 - \lambda)(1 - \eta_1)}{(1 - \lambda)(1 - \eta_0) + \lambda(1 - \eta_1)}$$

$$\text{Probability (active hedging|zero units)} = \frac{\lambda(1 - \eta_0)}{(1 - \lambda)(1 - \eta_0) + \lambda(1 - \eta_1)}$$

From the previous section, expected returns on a futures position between period 1 and period 2 are given by

$$E\left(p_2^F - p_1^F \;\middle|\; \text{inactive hedging}\right) = -\lambda^* d$$

$$E\left(p_2^F - p_1^F \;\middle|\; \text{active hedging}\right) = \frac{\lambda^*}{\lambda}(1 - \lambda)d$$

Using these conditional expectations and the conditional probabilities listed previously, the hedger can calculate the expected return on futures contracts conditional on the information revealed to him by the size of his endowment. These are given by

$$E\left(p_2^F - p_1^F \;\middle|\; \text{one unit}\right) = \frac{(1 - \lambda)\lambda^* d(\eta_1 - \eta_0)}{(1 - \lambda)\eta_0 + \lambda \eta_1}$$

$$E\left(p_2^F - p_1^F \;\middle|\; \text{zero units}\right) = \frac{-(1 - \lambda)\lambda^* d(\eta_1 - \eta_0)}{(1 - \lambda)(1 - \eta_0) + \lambda(1 - \eta_1)}$$

Suppose that each hedger is a risk-averse expected utility maximizer and that each hedger's inventory is a mixture of qualities 1 and 2 held in the same proportions as the other hedgers. Let $S_1(\lambda^*)$ denote the net unhedged position taken (after futures trading) by a hedger with one unit of the commodity and let $S_0(\lambda^*)$ be the position taken by a hedger with no inventory. It can be shown, under reasonable conditions, that $S_1(\lambda^*)$ is positive and increasing in λ^* and $S_0(\lambda^*)$ is negative and increasing in λ^*.

The aggregate futures position taken by the hedgers in the two states H_0 and H_1 is given by

$$H_i = [\eta_i(1 - S_1(\lambda^*)) + (1 - \eta_i)S_0(\lambda^*)]N \quad i = 0,1$$

and the difference in hedging between the two states $H_1 - H_0$ is given by

$$H_1 - H_0 = (\eta_1 - \eta_0) (1 - (S_1(\lambda^*) + S_0(\lambda^*)))N$$

An equilibrium with endogenous hedging is generated by values of λ^* and $H_1 - H_0$ such that the preceding equation holds and such that

$$\lambda^* = \min\left(\lambda, \max\left(1 - \left(\frac{z_1}{H_1 - H_0}\right)^{1/2}, 0\right)\right)$$

(See figure 5–3.) The downward-sloping demand for hedging curve plots the equation for $H_1 - H_0$ above, and the upward-sloping supply of squeezes curve plots the equation for λ^*. The intersection of the two curves, represented by point E in figure 5–3, determines simultaneously the probability of a squeeze λ^* and the difference between active and inactive hedging $H_1 - H_0$.

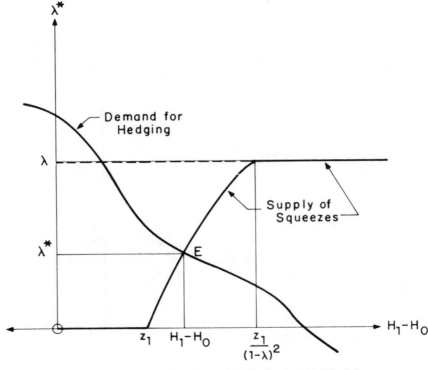

Figure 5–3. Equilibrium with Endogenous Hedging

From this equilibrium model of hedging, it is clear that one of the welfare costs of squeezes is that hedging is discouraged. As a result, risk-averse hedgers bear risk, even though there are other traders in the economy who are risk-neutral. Implicitly, we are assuming that other markets in the economy are not used for hedging. These markets are not used because, for example, the transactions costs of finding trading partners is too high.

Policy Applications

Our model of corners and squeezes shows that when corners and squeezes are possible, the profits of the squeezer come at the expense of hedgers; furthermore, squeezes also create benefits for the holders of the cheaply delivered quality, and these benefits also come at the expense of hedgers. The costs that fall upon hedgers induce hedgers to hedge only part of the risks that would be fully hedged in a futures market without squeezes. The resulting misallocation of risk-bearing represents the social cost of squeezes.

In this section, we examine briefly several policies designed to reduce the effect of squeezes: different delivery differentials, additional deliverable supply, cash settlement, and position limits. These policies might be either the result of government regulation or the result of self-regulation by the exchanges themselves.

Delivery Differentials

A reduction in the delivery differential d between quality 1 and quality 2, holding hedging behavior constant, leaves the probability of squeezes unchanged but decreases their profitability proportionately with the reduction in d. To hedgers, the decreased profitability of squeezes represents a lowered cost of hedging. With endogenous hedging, hedgers expand their hedging activities, and squeezes tend to become more frequent, even though the allocation of risk is made more efficient.

Reduction of d to zero eliminates squeezes entirely. Why, then, are differentials not always set equal to actual market differentials? The reason is that, in practice, market differentials change but their value in any particular case cannot be objectively verified by a government or commodity exchange bureaucracy, even if market participants know what they are. Suppose that the difference in market values $\tilde{d}$ is a random variable whose distribution can be objectively verified but whose outcome in any particular case cannot be objectively verified. Our model then represents a market outcome conditional on a particular outcome of $\tilde{d}$ and a delivery differential of zero. This leads us to pose the following question: What delivery differential d, chosen as a function of deliverable supplies z_1, and z_2 and the distribution of $\tilde{d}$ (but not its outcome), results in the most efficient use of the market as a hedging device? Although this question is well posed, answering it takes us beyond the scope of this paper. Suffice it to observe that the optimal value of d is not the mean or median of the distribution of $\tilde{d}$. It is easy to convince oneself that the optimal differential d depends on the relative supplies of qualities 1 and 2 and that optimal differentials will in many cases be chosen such that the quality in greatest supply is the cheapest to deliver.

Additional Deliverable Supply

If the supply of the cheapest to deliver quality z_1 is increased, squeezes become less profitable and tend to become less likely. Figure 5–4 illustrates the effect of an increase in deliverable supply on λ^*, using the same format as figure 5–3. The increase in z_1 shifts outward the supply curve, which tends to improve the allocation of risk-bearing by increasing the amount of hedging.

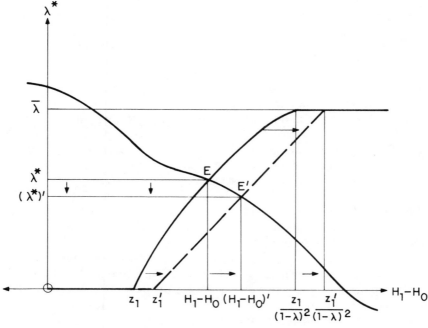

Figure 5–4. Increases of Deliverable Supply

One way to increase deliverable supply in this way is to add delivery points that have the property that quantities delivered to these points have no-squeeze market values which are perfectly correlated with no-squeeze market values of the cheapest to deliver quality. When the new delivery points have values that are perfectly correlated with neither quality 1 nor quality 2, the result is a multiquality model, which again takes us beyond the scope of this paper. Within the context of such a multiquality model, however, choosing the optimal combination of delivery points and delivery differentials for these points is clearly a well-posed problem. Given the joint probability distribution of the vector of market differentials, one suspects that the optimal delivery differentials—chosen as a function of this distribution but not actual outcomes—will in many cases have the property that one cluster of qualities (delivery points) whose values are closely correlated will tend to be cheapest to deliver.

Cash Settlement

Cash settlement has been proposed as a device that eliminates squeezes as an exploitation of the delivery mechanism by eliminating delivery itself. In the context of our model, cash settlement can be modeled in the following way. Instead of liquidating through delivery the open interest remaining in period 2, positions are liquidated at a price that is some function of the cash market prices of qualities 1 and 2, evaluated at the end of period 2. Although various functions can be used (a weighted average is typical), the functions consistent with our delivery mechanism is the minimum of the cash market prices of the two qualities. In the model with delivery, the cash prices at the end of period 2 of qualities 1 and 2 are $\bar{v}_1$ and $\bar{v}_1 + d$ when there is no squeeze and $\bar{v} + d$ for both qualities when there is a squeeze. The price of quality 1 is higher when there is a squeeze because traders with short positions are willing to buy it to deliver it immediately to the squeezer, who immediately suffers a loss d as the price falls back to the no-squeeze price $\bar{v}$.

With cash settlement, traders with short positions would not be willing to pay a premium of size d for quality 1. Does this mean that the cash price of quality one would be $\bar{v}$ instead of $\bar{v} + d$ even in the squeeze situation where the squeezer has a futures position in excess of z_1? It is easy to see that, in this situation, the squeezer himself has an incentive to bid up the price of quality 1, even if this means that he must purchase the entire available supply, z_1. If the squeezer bids the price to $\bar{v} + d$ and purchases the entire deliverable supply z_1, his profits are exactly the same as they would be with delivery. We conclude that cash settlement has no effect on the incentive to engage in squeezes. It only transfers some of the manipulative activity into the cash market.

Cash settlement is also proposed as a method for reducing the costs associated with use of the delivery mechanism. To the extent that transactions costs for utilizing the futures market delivery mechanism play into the hands of the squeezer, cash settlement might be thought to be a way to avoid these costs and reduce the power of the squeezer. In fact, cash settlement merely replaces the cost of using the futures market delivery mechanism with the costs of utilizing the cash market delivery mechanism. If these costs are the same, then cash settlement again has no effect on the incentive to engage in squeezes.

Position Limits

Position limits are often ineffective because it is difficult in practice to tell whether positions owned by different traders are in fact being managed cooperatively. If, however, effective position limits can be devised, our model suggests that they have beneficial effects.

Suppose that a position limit of size x_L is imposed on long positions. If the position limit is less than the available supply of the cheapest to deliver quality, squeezes are eliminated entirely. It can be shown that if the position limit is greater than the supply of the cheapest to deliver commodity, but less than the quantity the squeezer buys when he squeezes, squeezs may—but need not—be, mitigated to some extent (figure 5–5). Without position limits, the equilibrium can be represented as some point along the contract curve $O\bar{E}$, the particular point depending upon the exogenous value of λ. At the equilibrium corresponding to point E, for example, the squeezer buys x_E when $\bar{H} = H_1$, sells $H_1 - H_0$, $-x_E$ when $\bar{H} = H_0$, and the price in period 1 is $p_E = E\bar{v} + \lambda d$. Now suppose that a position limit of size x_L, with $z_1 < x_L < x_E$, is imposed on long positions. Let $\bar{E}_L$ denote the intersection of the vertical line $y = x_L - H_1$ and the concave indifference curve $B(H_1)$ passing through $\bar{E} = (\bar{y}, \bar{p})$. It can be shown (but we do not prove it here) that all equilibria affected by the position limit are in effect replaced by equilibria along the new contract curve $O_L\bar{E}_L$; furthermore, there are two cases to consider, depending on whether the old equilibrium is northwest or southeast of the point M, defined as the point on the old contract curve lying on the horizontal line through $\bar{E}_L$.

Case 1:   For old equilibria lying on the line segment $0M$ (that is, southeast of M), such as point E in figure 5–5, the new equilibrium is the point on the new contract curve lying along the same horizontal line as the old equilibrium (point E' in figure 5–5). The new equilibrium has virtually the same economic properties as the old. In particular, the equilibrium price is the same, the occurrence of squeezes is the same, and the expected profits of

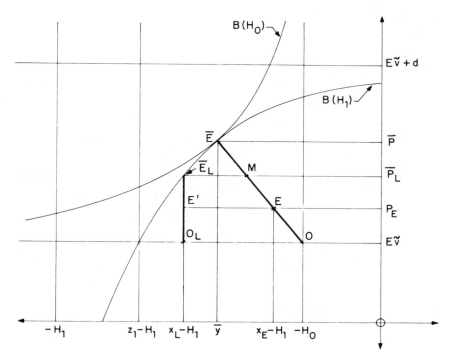

Figure 5–5. Imposition of Position Limits

the squeezer are the same. The only difference is that the squeezer takes a smaller long position when squeezing, thus earning smaller profits, while taking a larger short position when not squeezing, thus earning greater profits.

Case 2: For old equilibria lying on the line segment $M\overline{E}$ (that is, northwest of M), the new equilibrium corresponds to point $\overline{E}_L$. The new equilibrium point $\overline{E}_L$ has quite different economic properties from the old: lower equilibrium prices, less frequent squeezes, and lower expected profits for the squeezer, who now makes all of his profits on the short side when he does not squeeze.

It is clear that in case 2, position limits will have an expansionary effect on hedging because the downward shift in the supply curve in figure 5–6, induces a beneficial downward movement along the demand curve, corresponding to more hedging. In case 1, the downward shift in the supply curve only occurs for points on the supply curve above the equilibrium, and therefore has no welfare consequences.

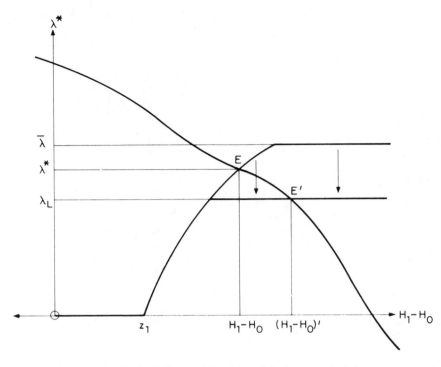

Figure 5-6. Effect of Position Limits on Hedging

Conclusion

Our model is based upon some very special informational and game-theoretic assumptions that might be relaxed in future research. The squeezer, who has private information about what hedgers are doing for example, faces no threat from potential entrants who also have such private information. He earns a rent based on his unchallenged large market power and information about the order flow from hedgers. Other kinds of information, such as inside information (in period one) about the outcome of ˉ might be added to the model. In the hands of a large trader, such information might become more valuable if squeezes are possible. Clearly, the model can be extended by using a more complicated process generating hedge trade, more deliverable qualities, and more trading periods.

   The principle advantage of this simple model is that it illustrates clearly how a large trader with information about the order flow of hedgers can use the anonymity of the trading process to accumulate a large enough position to engineer a successful squeeze. Price fluctuations, which are perceived to be a fair game from the point of view of speculators, are simultaneously perceived to be an unfair game from the point of view of hedgers. As a result, even though prices have the random features of an efficient market from the point of view of speculators, the increased cost of hedging resulting from squeezes reduces the amount of hedging, leads to a misallocation risks in the economy, and calls for some policies designed to make squeezes more difficult.

References

Telser, Lester G. (1981). "Why There Are Organized Futures Markets," *Journal of Law and Economics*, vol. 24, pp. 1–22.

Working, Holbrook. (1953). "Futures Trading and Hedging," *American Economic Review*, vol. 43, pp. 314–343.

Comment

Stephen W. Salant

Futures trading is among humanity's more impenetrable concepts. It involves selling what one does not own and, as a rule, buying what one does not want. It is deeply shrouded in terminology that conceals its meaning. It operates in an arena where opinion is everything, where supply and demand are hard to distinguish from supposition and doctrine and where inherent uncertainty has spawned an endless holy war between two religious sounding antagonists, the "fundamentalists" and the "chartists.". . . Into this world comes the general public, eager to enjoy its riches and often unprepared to become its poor.
—Philip Johnson (*Commodities Regulation*, vol. 2, p. 351)

Chapter 5 is extraordinary. It represents—to the best of my knowledge—the first logically coherent, formal model of a manipulation in the futures market. This model and the successors it will almost surely spawn may some day provide the information that policymakers need to judge in advance how proposed regulations would likely affect the conduct of participants in the futures markets.

Kyle's chapter can be divided into two parts. Two-thirds—composed of eight sections—lucidly motivates the model, summarizes its story, and points out its policy implications. These sections are accessible to any interested reader and by themselves clarify its essential ideas. The lone remaining section—which comprises a full third of the chapter—contains the formal model. Kyle titles the section "A Simple Model"—presumably because it is a simplified representation of the complex behaviors engaged in by commodity traders. However, readers unaccustomed to models with asymmetric information, Nash conjectures, mixed strategies, and separation theorems may not find reading this section simple. One constructive function I can therefore serve is to make this part of chapter 5 more widely accessible. In the next section, I summarize the model so that it is accessible to any reader who understands why a profit-maximizing monopolist equates marginal revenue and marginal cost. After clarifying what is the equilibrium behavior of agents in the model, I turn briefly to a normative evaluation of the squeezer's behavior. I then suggest several promising extensions of the model. Finally, I present a more general characterization of a manipulations and indicate other cases that warrant modeling in the future.

The Simple Model Simplified

Kyle envisions a futures market frequented by three types of agents: hedgers, speculators, and an informed trader. Hedgers make offers to sell contracts for future delivery. The informed trader—with private information about the aggregate size of such offers—decides whether to buy some of the contracts offered by the hedgers or to offer to sell additional contracts himself. Speculators observe the net amount of contracts offered. Using this information, they revise their expectation of the final futures price and bid against each other to purchase the net offering of the hedgers and informed trader. This bidding determines the initial futures price.

The contracts traded specify that the same amount (call it one unit) of either of two grades (call them plain and fancy) can be delivered. To take delivery a purchaser need merely hold his contract to maturity; if no delivery is desired the purchaser offsets his long position in the final (and only other) round of futures trading. Which grade is delivered is up to the short seller. Because the fancy grade under normal circumstances sells on the cash market for d more than the plain grade, shorts will ordinarily find the plain grade the cheaper to deliver. On some occasions, however, the delivery required exceeds the available supplies. Then the price of plain grade is bid up to the price of the fancy grade and the demand in excess of the available plain grade is satisfied with the fancy grade. It is assumed that the supply of the plain grade is inelastic at Z and this information is common knowledge. Moreover, there exists limitless amounts of the fancy grade.

Kyle refers to the informed trader as "the manipulator" but we will adhere to more neutral language. The informed trader places orders to buy or sell futures contracts. Based on his observation of the hedger's offers and his market experience he knows how much he will affect the initial futures price by a given offer to purchase or sell.

The informed trader finds that when hedging is active if he buys enough futures contracts and holds them to delivery he can make a profit—even though his long position drives futures prices up above the price expected for the plain grade. The informed trader makes profits because the futures price he pays for each contract is not driven as high as the expected price of the fancy grade and—for each contract he buys beyond Z—the shorts deliver an additional unit of the fancy grade in fulfillment of their contract. Hence he incurs losses on deliveries of Z units of the plain grade to get deliveries of the fancy grade. In Kyle's model, the prices of the two grades differ by d with the price of the plain grade exogenous and random. Because the informed trader is risk-neutral he would buy infinite amounts of futures contracts to secure title to limitless amounts of the fancy grade if he did not take account of the impact such a long position would have on the initial futures price and hence on his inframarginal costs.

When hedging is inactive, the informed trader finds that the futures price is high relative to what he expects the cash price to be on the plain grade. He finds that by selling futures contracts and then delivering the plain grade he maximizes profits. Again, he restrains his short sales because he takes account of the depressing effect they have on the initial futures price and hence on his inframarginal revenues.

The informed trader faces one schedule for the initial futures price if hedging is active and a different price schedule if it is inactive. Both schedules are increasing functions of his demand for futures contracts. The schedule when hedging is inactive can be derived from the schedule when hedging is active by shifting each point on the latter schedule to the right by a constant amount. It is unnecessary that the informed trader ever noticed this relationship between the two price schedules.

As it happens, the profit-maximizing long position that the informed trader takes when hedging is active and the profit-maximizing short position that he takes when hedging is inactive differ by this same constant. Consequently, the initial futures price that results from each position is identical.

We now formalize the foregoing description of the informed trader's problem. Kyle shows in figure 5–2 how to derive a function whose lateral translations indicate the price in the futures market resulting from a given position when hedging is active on the one hand or inactive on the other. The function is not unique but as all the equilibrium price functions induce the same behavior we choose the simplest—a piecewise linear function. We take this price function as a given throughout this section.[1]

The Informed Trader's Profit Maximization Problem

Whether hedging is active or inactive the informed trader can earn $R(x)$ if he takes delivery on x futures contracts and resells them on the cash market. The price on the cash market is uncertain but the plain grade has mean price EV and the fancy grade normally sells for d more. $R(x)$ is therefore defined as follows:

$$R(x) = \begin{cases} xEV \text{ for } x < Z \\ xEV + (x - Z)d \text{ for } x \geqslant Z \end{cases}$$

That is, if the informed trader takes delivery of less than the deliverable supply of the plain grade, the mean per unit value is merely EV. But each unit in excess of Z that he receives is worth $EV + d$.

Let H_1 (respectively H_0) denote the short position of the hedger when trading is active (respectively inactive) with $H_1 > H_0$. It will be assumed throughout that the deliverable supply of the plain grade is small relative to the variation between active and inactive hedging. In particular.

$$Z \leqslant (1 - \lambda)^2(H_1 - H_0) \tag{5A.1}$$

When the exogenous parameters do not bear this relationship to each other Kyle shows that an equilibrium still exists but its characteristics differ.[2]

Behavior of the Informed Trader When Hedging is Active. When hedging is active, the informed trader faces the following piecewise continuous price function:

$$
P_{H_1}(x) = \begin{cases} EV + d & \text{for } x > x_1^u \\[2mm] \dfrac{dx}{H_1 - H_0} + EV + (2\lambda - 1)d & \text{for } x_1^u \geqslant x \geqslant x_1^l \\[2mm] EV & \text{for } x < x_1^l \end{cases}
$$

where: λ is the probability that hedging is active; $x_1^u = 2(1 - \lambda)(H_1 - H_0)$; and $x_1^l = (1 - 2\lambda)(H_1 - H_0)$. That is, if the informed trader goes very long he will drive the futures price up to the expected price of the fancy grade; if he goes very short he will drive the futures price down to the expected price of the plain grade. And for intermediate positions, larger purchases raise the price at a constant rate.

When hedging is active, the cost of acquiring a position of x is simply $C_{H_1}(x)$:

$$
C_{H_1}(x) = x P_{H_1}(x)
$$

The informed agent's problem is therefore to

$$
\underset{\{x\}}{\text{Maximize}} \ R(x) - C_{H_1}(x)
$$

From the definitions of x_1^u, x_1^l, and equation 5A.1 it is obvious that $x_1^u > Z > x_1^l$. Hence there are four regions to investigate ($x < x_1^l$, $x > x_1^u$, $x_1^u > x > Z$, and $Z > x > x_1^l$). The optimum occurs in the region where $x_1^u > x > Z$—at the point where $MR(x) - MC_{H_1}(x)$. Because $x > Z$ in this region, the informed trader's revenue function is $R(x) = xEV + (x - Z)d$. Since $x_1^u > x > x_1^l$ his cost function is $C_{H_1}(x) = \dfrac{dx^2}{H_1 - H_0} + (2\lambda - 1)xd$ + xEV. By equating marginal revenue to marginal cost, it is straightforward to confirm that a unique local maximum (x_1) is achieved for this subinterval at $x_1 = (1 - \lambda)(H_1 - H_0)$ and results in a profit of $(1 - \lambda)^2 (H_1 - H_0)d - Zd$. This profit is nonnegative by virtue of equation 5A.1. To verify that this is the global optimum we must determine the largest maximized profit achievable across the other subintervals and show that this value is strictly less than the profit at the asserted global optimum. Kyle omits these tedious but necessary details.[3]

To summarize, when hedging is active the price function induces the informed trader to go long by x_1. In doing so he drives the initial futures price to $P_{H_1}(x_1) = EV + \lambda d$.

Behavior of the Informed Trader When Hedging Is Inactive. When hedging is inactive, the informed trader faces the following lateral translation of the previous price schedule

$$P_{H_0}(x) = \begin{cases} EV + d & \text{for } x > x_0^u \\ \dfrac{dx}{H_1 - H_0} + EV + 2\lambda d & \text{for } x_0^l \leq x \leq x_0^u \\ EV & \text{for } x < x_0^l \end{cases}$$

where $x_0^u = x_1^u + (H_1 - H_0) = (1 - 2\lambda)(H_1 - H_0)$

$$x_0^l = x_1^l + (H_1 - H_0) = -2\lambda(H_1 - H_0)$$

When hedging is inactive, the cost of acquiring a position of size x is simply $C_{H_0}(x)$:

$$C_{H_0}(x) = xP_{H_0}(x)$$

The informed agent's problem is therefore to

$$\underset{\{x\}}{\text{Maximize}} \ R(x) - C_{H_0}(x)$$

From the definitions of x_0^u, x_0^l, and equation 5A.1 it is obvious that $Z > x_0^u > x_0^l$ and $x_0^l < 0$. Hence there are again four regions to investigate $(x < x_0^l, \ x > Z, \ Z > x > x_0^u,$ and $x_0^u > x > x_0^l)$. The optimum occurs in the region where $x_0^l < x < x_0^u$ at the point where $MR(x) - MC_{H_0}(x)$. In this region the informed trader's revenue function is $R(x) = xEV$ and cost function is $C_{H_0}(x) = \dfrac{dx^2}{H_1 - H_0} + (EV + 2\lambda d)x$. It can be verified by equating marginal revenue to marginal cost that a unique local maximum (x_0) is achieved for this subinterval at $x_0 = -\lambda(H_1 - H_0) < 0$ and results in a profit of $d\lambda^2(H_1 - H_0)$. To prove that this is the global optimum we must determine the largest maximized profit achievable across the other subintervals and show that this value is strictly smaller than the profit at the asserted optimum.[4]

To summarize, when hedging is inactive the informed trader finds going short to be optimal. In doing so he drives down the price to $P_{H_0}(x_0) = EV + \lambda d$.

Behavior of Speculators

Speculators observe the excess of hedgers' offers over the informed trader's bids, and using this information try to infer whether hedging is active or inactive. Whenever hedging is active they expect the final futures price to be $EV + d$; whenever hedging is inactive they expect the final futures price to be EV. Hence they scrutinize the information at their disposal trying to determine which state has occurred so they can make a profit. When hedging is inactive, the excess of hedgers' offers over the bids of the informed trader is $H_0 - x_0 = \lambda H_1 + (1 - \lambda)H_0$. (This is larger than H_0—reflecting the fact that the informed trader in fact goes short himself.) When hedging is active, the excess of hedgers' offers over the bids of the informed trader is $H_1 - x_1 = \lambda H_1 + (1 - \lambda)H_0$. (This is smaller than H_1—reflecting the fact that the informed trader purchases some of what the hedgers offer.) Because speculators see a net offer of $\lambda H_1 + (1 - \lambda)H_0$ in either situation, they cannot tell whether the hedging offers were active or inactive. Hence the speculators bid the initial futures price to a probability-weighted average ($EV + \lambda d$) of the two possible final futures prices using unrevised priors about the probability of hedging being active. When hedging is active, they gain; when hedging is inactive, they lose. On average, they break even.

What happens on the final round of futures trading is critical to Kyle's story. He shows in lemma 1 that the informed trader can do no better than to refrain from trading on the final period. If the informed trader always does refrain (indeed, as long as he adopts a pure strategy rather than randomizing among any of the equally good alternatives) then the speculators can infer whether hedging was initially active or inactive by observing the hedgers' demands for offsetting contracts.[5] For example, if hedging was active, their demands for offsets will be large (H_1) and speculators will know that a squeeze is in progress. In this case, speculators close out their own limited long positions and hedgers who are unable to settle make deliveries to the informed trader.

At what prices do these exchanges between speculators and hedgers take place in the final period? A hedger trying to offset his short position would be willing to pay as much as $EV + d$—the price he would have to pay if instead he made delivery. A speculator trying to offset his long position would be willing to accept a smaller amount—as little as the market value of the mixture of grades he would expect to receive if instead he took delivery. If there were enough small speculators—each with an infinitesimal portion of the aggregate long speculative position $(H_1 - x_1)$, each of them would be willing to settle for arbitrarily more than EV.[6] Kyle argues that the futures price in the final round would settle at $EV + d$. Certainly, each speculator knows that hedgers will have to pay this amount if they cannot offset and that some hedgers will have to make deliveries. Nonetheless, one might be able to imagine final prices other than the one Kyle posits. Considering how much of the analysis hinges on what price occurs in the final round if a squeeze is in progress, I hope Kyle elaborates on the precise sequence of bargaining moves in subsequent work.

It is important to understand why the speculators—unlike the informed trader—never take delivery. If a squeeze is on and a speculator takes delivery, he is virtually certain to get a mixture of the plain and fancy grades. As long as he can get a strictly better price selling his futures contract than he would expect to get by taking delivery of the mixture of grades and reselling them on the cash market, the speculator will avoid delivery. Because the futures price is driven to $EV + d$ in a squeeze, no speculator would take delivery. As long as he expected any plain grade to be delivered, he would be better off selling his contract. The informed trader no doubt would also like to avoid delivery but realizes that if he unwinds his position the final futures price will collapse. In more familiar terms, the informed trader holds up the price umbrella and the speculators get a free ride under it by unwinding their positions without having either to receive delivery of the plain grade or to cause a collapse of the final futures price.

Behavior of the Hedgers

If the informed trader makes positive expected profits and the speculators break even, someone must make losses. The hedgers are the losers. They cannot do as well as the speculators because of a first-mover disadvantage. It is true that the game is fair to the speculators. But even if the hedgers flipped a coin to determine whether to be active or inactive the informed trader—who acts knowing the outcome of the flip—is in a position to gain at their expense. Every time their flip directs them to take an inconsequential short position, the informed trader also goes short, and the final futures price falls to EV—leaving them with an inconsequential profit. Every time they take a significant short position, the informed trader squeezes, and the final futures price subsequently rises to $EV + d$—leaving them with a significant loss.

Discussion

One nice thing about a theoretical model like Kyle's is that it describes each agent's behavior precisely. No facts can be in dispute. Another nice thing is that the behaviors posited do not conflict with the self-interest of any agent. Hence the scenario described—unlike most hypotheticals about behavior during a manipulation—is not so implausible that it is foolish to consider. Given the clarity of Kyle's description, I would find it immensely interesting to know whether his informed trader is doing something illegal and, if so, what it is. Is he doing something illegal when he shorts the market or only when he squeezes? Suppose there were two informed trader's each unaware of the other's existence. One understands only the mechanics of going short, the other only the mechanics of going long. When hedging is inactive, the first trader goes short and the second trader abstains. When hedging is active, the first trader abstains and the second trader goes long. Both profit when they trade. Are both doing something illegal or only one of them? I do not have the legal training or expertise to answer any of these questions but would like to hear from someone who does.

In the meantime, permit me to play devil's advocate for a moment by emphasizing what—in my opinion—Kyle's informed trader cannot legitimately be accused of. It is true that his informed trader acts in a way that leaves speculators unable to distinguish whether hedging is active or inactive. But as we have seen, he is led to act in this way by the invisible hand and certainly not by any intention to deceive. It is true that no other trader is assumed to have access to information about hedging activity but there is no suggestion that the informed trader is in any way responsible for the failure of others to gain access to the same information. It is true that the informed trader realizes that his initial purchase or sale of futures contracts will affect their price—but so does any intelligent market trader; at any rate, this makes him a garden variety monopolist/monopsonist at worst—but manipulator seems a bit harsh to me. It is true that the informed trader holds contracts that result in delivery of Z units of a grade he does not want in order to acquire $x_1 - Z$ units of the fancy grade. But in doing so, his motives are essentially no different than that of a child who buys a cereal he does not like for the sake of the toy or coupon at the bottom of the box. Our informed trader deceives no one, excludes no one, and does nothing to impede delivery by the shorts. Indeed, he both wants and takes delivery by the shorts. The informed trader may be legally or morally culpable, but not for the foregoing reasons.

There are two aspects of his conduct that seem to me questionable. In part, these are hard to ferret out because Kyle ignores the first altogether and downplays the second. First, who must the informed trader be to acquire information about the offers of hedgers? A broker? A member of the exchange? William Casey? It is possible that the only people with access to such information must either have acquired it illegally or be breaking a law in trading on the basis of it. I can only raise these questions. I lack the requisite expertise to answer them and again defer to the experts.

The second aspect of the informed trader's conduct that I feel warrants closer scrutiny is what he does in the final round of trading. He does nothing. He holds x_1 contracts. If he offset $x_1 - Z - \varepsilon$ of them, the final futures price would remain $EV + d$ and he would earn from his partial offset exactly what he lost by foregoing delivery on those contracts. But if he sold any more, the final futures price would collapse to EV. This is not a situation which a garden-variety monopolist ever faces, let alone engineers.

Extensions

Several extensions of this model are suggested by the previous discussion. The informed trader in Kyle's model does not consider legal consequences when determining his optimal strategy. If he does something that violates current laws, perhaps we should regard the model as describing how the informed trader would have behaved in the absence of such laws. It would then be interesting to ask how the imposition of the current laws alters equilibrium behavior and even whether the benefits of the current regulations are worth the various associated costs. This form of analysis could, of course, lead to use of the model to help design better laws. Here the law would not be judged by its implicit norms but by its positive consequences.

I would be very interested in an extension of Kyle's model in which there are n identical informed traders who move simultaneously. This seemingly innocuous extension might dramatically alter the nature of the equilibrium and would, in any case, clarify the fragility or stability of the manipulation scheme.

For simplicity, suppose these are two informed traders. Suppose that whenever hedging is active they always end the final round of trading with identical long positions. Denote each position as $\hat{x}$. If a profitable squeeze is in effect, $2\hat{x} > Z$. It is straightforward to see that this cannot be a Nash equilibrium for any $\hat{x}$. That is, each informed trader has an incentive to sell additional contracts, thus unilaterally altering his final position. Each trader would conjecture that as long as the other fellow maintained his position, he could reduce his own by $2\hat{x} - Z - \varepsilon$ without causing the price to collapse. For each contract he sold he would get $EV + d$—more than he would get from reselling the hodgepodge he would receive if he took delivery. This is not to say that an equilibrium fails to exist in the final round, but it must either involve asymmetric pure strategies or symmetric mixed strategies. From a policy point of view, what happens in the final round with n informed traders is important because it indicates how fragile this particular manipulation scheme is.

There is another interesting aspect of this extension. By assumption, each of the two informed traders initially observes whether hedging is active or inactive and each moves simultaneously. But neither can directly observe what position the other has taken. Each can, however, make an inference by observing the responses of the speculators to their simultaneous moves. This inference aspect of the problem is absent in the case of a single informed trader.

A final group of extensions warrants mention. Kyle occasionally refers to what the speculators observe as open interest. But open interest reflects completed transactions—not outstanding offers to sell. (To understand why, for example, one cannot interpret what the informed trader sees as completed sales by hedgers it is sufficient to note that—at the time of his observation—neither the informed trader nor the speculators have yet moved and consequently there is no one who could be on the other side of the hedgers' transactions.) Presumably, Kyle has in mind a more complex multiperiod story in which what agents observe is in fact open interest. I would be interested to learn whether squeezes can occur in such a model. In this regard it is important to remember that speculators in reality have access to information on both the volume and the concentration of open interest. It would be interesting to see the characteristics of the equilibrium under the assumption that both types of information are available. Perhaps the concentration data would eliminate squeezes; alternatively in the new equilibrium perhaps the invisible hand would induce the informed trader to use multiple accounts.

Toward an Expanded Theory of Manipulations

In titling his chapter "A Theory of Futures Market Manipulations," Kyle implies that he has not said the last word on the subject. Indeed, despite the importance of this pioneering contribution, I believe some real-world manipulations may fall outside the scope of his model. In this final section, therefore, I broaden my discussion to include other manipulations that may merit future consideration.

In any long squeeze, traders who hold futures contracts succeed in raising the costs that the shorts expect to pay to deliver on their contracts. Given their revised expectations, the shorts then find themselves in a situation where they are willing to pay dearly to offset their positions. Kyle's model fits this characterization. His short hedgers initially expect delivery will cost $EV + \lambda d$ but learn unambiguously whenever the squeeze is on that the true delivery cost will be $EV + d$. The long trader accomplishes the squeeze in Kyle's model by taking delivery on the cheapest to deliver grade and consequently bidding up its spot price.

But the foregoing characterization also fits other situations besides the one envisioned by Kyle. Delivery costs can be bid up without affecting the spot price of the commodity—by increasing packing, shipping, or storage costs. Indeed, such manipulations of the delivery mechanism are a common complaint in squeeze cases. And—if the spot price of the commodity is increased—it can be accomplished without taking delivery. In the May 1976 fiasco in the Maine potato market, for example, the increase in the spot price that competitive holders of the inventory found acceptable during the brief delivery period seemed to be in part related to a timely rumor—reported in local newspapers but apparently without factual basis—that foreign buyers desperate for potatoes were heading toward the port in Searsport, Maine.[7]

Finally, it may be unnecessary for the actual delivery costs of the shorts to increase. A squeeze can occur if the shorts revise upward their expectations of the costs of future delivery. If, for example, the shorts had limited information about future delivery costs but observed some signal that made an upward revision in their cost expectations rational, they might be induced to offset their contracts even if delivery costs did not happen in fact to be higher. One such signal might be relatively high settlement demands by a long known to have superior information. In such situations, there might still be considerable ambiguity about the magnitude of delivery costs at the close of futures trading. This situation differs from the one depicted by Kyle where all such ambiguity is resolved before entry into the delivery period. When such ambiguity persists, we might expect to see wild gyrations in the final futures price, acrimony and charges of bluffing in the final round of trading, and occasional episodes where the shorts go to delivery (and possibly default) in what turns out to be a mistaken belief that delivery costs are in fact low. It is my impression that at least the Maine potato futures market has displayed each of these characteristics.

At the end of chapter 5, Kyle discusses the effects of alternative policy proposals such as cash settlements instead of required delivery, modification of delivery differentials, implementation of position limits, and so forth. I have argued that squeezes other than the type modeled by Kyle merit serious attention in the future. Policies that Kyle finds to be ineffective against his particular form of squeeze may turn out to be effective against other forms of squeeze. For example, in Kyle's model, there is no cost to making delivery except the cost of purchasing the deliverable at the spot price; there is no way for a squeezer to manipulate the delivery mechanism by increasing packing, shipping, or storage costs. Kyle finds that—in his model—implementing a policy of cash settlements at spot prices does not eliminate squeezes. Although it is valuable to discover that least one form of squeeze cannot be affected by a policy of cash settlements, one cannot logically conclude from his analysis that such a policy would be similarly ineffective against every form of squeeze. Until the other forms of squeeze are subjected to a parallel analysis and the relative importance of each assessed empirically, policy recommendations seems premature.

Notes

1. Of the three types of equilibria that Kyle shows can arise for different values of the exogenous parameters, each can be supported by a continuous price function (and its lateral translation) with a constant value of EV to the left of some point, a constant value of $EV + d$ to the right of some point, and a linear segment in between the two points. Such a function can always be parameterized by the two points where the flat segments terminate. For example, consider the following price function $(P_{H_1}(x))$ and its lateral translation $(P_{H_0}(x))$, both of which are parameterized by the numbers x_1^u and x_1^l.

$$P_{H_1}(x) = \begin{cases} EV + d & \text{for } x > x_1^u \\[2ex] \dfrac{xd}{x_1^u - x_1^l} + EV - \dfrac{dx_1^l}{x_1^u - x_1^l} & \text{for } x_1^l \leqslant x \leqslant x_1^u \\[2ex] EV & \text{for } x < x_1^l \end{cases}$$

$$P_{H_0}(x) = \begin{cases} EV + d & \text{for } x > x_0^u \\[2ex] \dfrac{xd}{x_1^u - x_1^l} + EV - \dfrac{d[x_1^l - (H_1 - H_0)]}{x_1^u - x_1^l} & \text{for } x_0^l \leqslant x \leqslant x_0^u \\[2ex] EV & \text{for } x < x_0^l \end{cases}$$

where $x_0^l = x_1^l + H_1 - H_0$ and $x_0^u = x_1^u + H_1 - H_0$. In the discussion, we assume these functions are given by specifying $x_1^u = 2(1 - \lambda)(H_1 - H_0)$ and $x_1^l = (l - 2\lambda)(H_1 - H_0)$. We could alternatively have solved for these two numbers, thereby determining the equilibrium price functions. For any pair of numbers (x_1^u, x_1^l) the optimal positions for the informed trader (x_0, x_1) and the resulting initial futures price in each state can be determined as in the test. x_1^u and x_1^l can then be determined to satisfy the twin conditions that the futures price equal $EV + \lambda d$ in each state. For the two other types of equilibria, corresponding conditions permit determination of x_1^u and x_1^l.

2. As we will see, when equation 5A.1 holds (1) the informed trader goes long by more than Z whenever hedging is active and goes short when-

ever it is inactive; (2) each position depends only on $H_1 - H_0$ and not on Z, and (3) the price in each state is $EV + \lambda d$, As Z is increased within the region (holding $H_1 - H_0$ fixed), profits when hedging is inactive do not change. Profits when hedging is active decline, however, because more of the unchanged optimal position x_1 results in delivery of the plain grade and less in delivery of the fancy grade. In particular, if π_1 denotes profits hedging is active:

$$\pi_1 = \{x_1 EV + (x_1 - Z)d\} - x_1(EV + \lambda d)$$
$$= [x_1(1 - \lambda) - Z]d$$

That is, profits equal revenues (enclosed in curly brackets) less costs. Profits in this state decline linearly as Z increases. Since $x_1 = (1 - \lambda)(H_1 - H_0)$, profits from the long squeeze fall to zero when equation 5A.1 holds with equality.

For larger values of Z, this type of equilibrium cannot exist because the informed trader would prefer not to trade when hedging is active. Kyle shows that another type of equilibrium does exist, however, in which—when hedging is active—the informed trader sometimes goes long and sometimes abstains from trade. Because squeezes are less frequent, speculators bid the initial futures price up by less and the informed trader makes zero profits—instead of losses—when he goes long. As Z increases, the frequency of squeezes must decline so that the initial futures price is lowered and the long squeeze continues to result in zero profits; otherwise it would result in losses. Eventually, the frequency of squeezes reaches zero. Beyond this, we are in Kyle's third region where squeezes never occur.

3. If $x < x_1^l$, $R(x) - C_{H_1}(x) = xEV - xEV = 0$. If $x < x_1^u$, $R(x) - C_{H_1}(x) = xEV + (x - Z)d - xEV - xd = -Zd < 0$. If $Z > x > x_1^l$,

$$R(x) - C_{H_1}(x) = xEV - \frac{dx^2}{H_1 - H_0} - xEV - (2\lambda - 1)xd$$

$$= \frac{dx^2}{H_1 - H_0} - (2\lambda - 1)xd.$$

This function reaches a relative maximum at $\frac{1}{2}x_1^l$.

If $x_1^l > 0$, the relative maximum is not achieved within the interval under consideration and a constrained maximum of zero is achieved at the lower boundary with $x = x_1^l$. If $x_1^l < 0$, the relative maximum is achieved within the interval at a profit of $\frac{d}{4}(1 - 2\lambda)^2(H_1 - H_0) > 0$. Because this is strictly smaller than the profits at x_1, the global maximum occurs at x_1 as asserted in the text.

4. If $x < x_0^l$, $R(x) - C_{H_0}(x) = xEV - xEV = 0$. If $x > Z$, $R(x) - C_{H_0}(x) = xEV + xd - Zd - xEV - dx = -Zd < 0$. If $x_0^u \le x \le Z$, $R(x) - C_{H_0}(x) = xEV - x(EV + d) = -dx \le -dx_0^u$. Maximized profit in these regions equals max $(0, -dx_0^u)$. Because this is strictly smaller than the profits at x_0, the global maximum occurs at x_0 as asserted in the text.

5. If the informed trader does randomize, it is unclear to me whether the speculators could tell whether a squeeze was in progress; if not, perhaps there are other equilibria that have been excluded by the assumption that the informed trader adopts a pure strategy (always abstaining) in the final round.

6. Suppose there were n identical speculators and that all went to delivery. The informed trader is long x_1 contracts. Because the hedgers are short H_1 contracts, speculators collectively are long $H_1 - x_1$ contracts. Hence, each speculator holds $\dfrac{H_1 - x_1}{n}$ of the contracts and expects to receive

$$\left(\frac{\dfrac{H_1 - x_1}{n}}{H_1} \right)$$

of the total deliveries of each grade. Because Z plain grade and $H_1 - Z$ fancy grade will be delivered, the speculator expects to receive a mixture worth

$$\left(\frac{H_1 - x_1}{nH_1} \right)(H_1 - Z) \cdot d + EV$$

on each contract. Hence the expected value per contract to a speculator who takes delivery of the mixture approaches EV if the number of other speculators is large enough.

7. These tentative conclusions are based on telephone and personal interviews in June 1976 with journalists in Maine, Commodity Futures Trading Commission investigators, in Washington, and officials at the port of Searsport.

Comment

Thomas E. Kilcollin

I would like to comment exclusively on the first four sections of Kyle's chapter—that is, up to, but not including, his simple model. Kyle seems to have identified some of the elements of a squeeze but the context is so narrow that it is difficult to see the general nature of a squeeze. Also I take issue with Kyle's hedger/speculator distinction, which is essentially that the hedger loses on average when squeezes are probable while the speculator does not.

I propose to show that the profitability of a squeeze does not depend on the existence of multiple delivery grades of a commodity, nor can a squeeze be profitably engineered only on the long side. In general, a squeeze is possible whenever the demand for and supply of deliveries on a futures contract is less than perfectly elastic, and it can be initiated on either the long or short side. One implication is that hedgers, even if they are all on the same side of the market, need not systematically lose from squeezes. Another implication is that manipulators may not be able to anticipate systematic gain from squeezes.

A General Model of Futures Market Manipulation

It is useful to view a futures contract as, first, creating a delivery market for exchange of the physical commodity during the delivery period and, second, specifying rules for trading before this time. The purpose of the delivery market (or some substitute for it such as cash settlement) is to produce a final settlement price for the futures contract that bears a relationship to cash market prices. The futures price at any previous time simply reflects the current market expectation of the final settlement price.

Figure 5B–1A depicts supply and demand schedules for the delivery market during the delivery period. The position and slopes of these schedules depend on such considerations as the opportunity cost of the commodity in ongoing cash markets (and factors that affect this) and the differential cost of making or taking delivery of a futures contract versus transacting in ongoing cash markets.

Given the demand and supply schedules of figure 5B–1A, the equilibrium price in this market, to which the futures price converges, is p_0 and the equilibrium number of deliveries is q_0. Open interest in the futures market

The views expressed herein are those of the author and do not necessarily represent the views of the Chicago Mercantile Exchange.

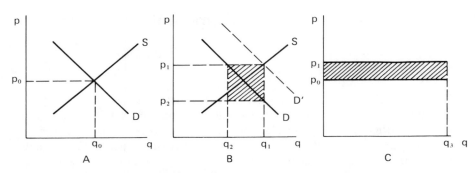

Figure 5B–1. Sequence of Prices in a Manipulation

before delivery is generally much greater than q_0, but open interest in excess of q_0 is closed out before delivery. At open interest greater than q_0 the supply schedule of figure 5B–1A indicates that shorts would be willing to bid a price greater than p_1 to offset their positions rather than make delivery, whereas the demand schedule indicates that longs would be willing to offer prices less than p_0 to offset their positions rather than accept delivery. Because bid prices exceed offer prices at open interest greater than q_0 presumably these offsetting transactions will occur.

As long as the demand or supply schedules in figure 5B–1A are not infinitely elastic, in principle one could increase the equilibrium price in this market and hence the futures price by augmenting demand or by restricting supply. Or one could decrease the equilibrium price by augmenting supply or by restricting demand.

Shifting these schedules to manipulate price is, by itself, unprofitable. For example, by standing for delivery of the quantity $q_1 - q_2$ a manipulator shifts the demand curve to D' in figure 5B–1B. The effect on price of this shift in demand will be muted by the fact that as prices rise normal demand will fall off while total supply will be augmented. In the new equilibrium, the price rises to p_1, normal demand falls to q_2 and total supply rises to q_1. The quantity $q_1 - q_2$ that the manipulator acquires at price p_1 has a marginal value of p_2 so that delivery losses equal to the shaded area in figure 5B–1B are incurred by the manipulator.

However, if the manipulator were able to obtain long futures positions at a price below p_1, it is possible that the profit on these positions as the futures price rises to p_1 might more than offset these delivery losses. For example, if the manipulator acquired q_3 long futures positions at the price p_0 in figure 5B–1C, his futures gain from the manipulation, given as the shaded area in figure 5B–1C, would more than offset his delivery loss indicated by the shaded area in figure 5B–1B.

From here, it is straightforward to show that the manipulator's optimal shift in the supply or demand schedule is directly related to the number of futures positions he holds and that the expected profits from his manipulation is directly related to the size of his futures position, is directly related to his ability to establish futures positions at nonmanipulated prices, and is inversely related to the elasticities of demand and supply for futures deliveries that determine his cost of price manipulation.

Comparison with Kyle's Results

This analysis supports Kyle's contention that anonymity is an important ingredient of a successful squeeze. In this model, knowledge of the manipulator's position reveals the magnitude of the coming squeeze and thereby limits the ability of the manipulator to establish futures positions at nonmanipulated prices. However, nothing in this model suggests that multiple delivery grades have any necessary connection with squeezes. Indeed, Kyle's model is a very special case of a rising supply price for deliveries in which the supply schedule jumps when the supply of the cheapest delivery grade is exhausted.[1]

This analysis also makes clear that squeezes can occur on both sides of the market. For example, to manipulate the market, a normal purchaser in an ongoing cash market might build up large short futures positions, then forego his usual cash market purchases so that cash and futures prices fall. Or a manipulator may accumulate inventory for sudden dumping on the market to produce gains in short futures positions. In both cases, losses from disrupted production, consumption, or inventorying might be more than offset by futures gains.

Recognition that squeezes can occur on both sides of the market brings into question Kyle's general contention that hedgers can systematically be expected to suffer monetary loss from squeezes. In principal, manipulators on the same side of the market as hedgers may be attempting to squeeze speculators or potential manipulators on the other side of the market.

Also with manipulators on both sides of the market, there can be no supposition that futures prices are biased estimates of normal cash market prices. Finally, with the potential for manipulation on both sides of the market a manipulator could not necessarily expect to gain from manipulation because a more powerful manipulator might be on the other side of the market.

Notes

1. Kyle's model does have the interesting but nonessential wrinkle that when the supply schedule rises because a higher quality commodity must be delivered, the manipulator gets some superior quality instead of producing additional rents to the supplier of the inferior quality commodity.

6

Manipulation and Repeated Games in Futures Markets

Graciela Chichilnisky

This chapter analyzes the possibility of manipulation in futures markets, concentrating on the effects that manipulation may have on their informational efficiency. We use the concept of manipulation as it arises in the study of noncooperative games with imperfect information.

Forward and futures markets illustrate sharply many of the issues central to the economics of uncertainty and of imperfect information.[1] Clearly, future economic activity is an area in which conditions of uncertainty and of imperfect information arise quite naturally. With respect to uncertainty about future conditions, the existence of a full set of future markets or the equivalent is seen as a precondition for attaining allocative efficiency. One of the major roles of such markets is to allow agents to trade so as to allocate risks optimally among themselves, according to each agent's attitudes toward risk. In this view, futures markets exist because they allow traders with different risk positions toward the future to trade with each other for mutual gain (see, for example, Edwards 1982).

A second, different, role of futures markets is akin to that of a general financial market. In this role, the futures market is seen as an instrument for gathering and distributing information about future market conditions to other parts of the economy (Grossman 1977). This information is of importance for decision making about inventories, outputs and investment, as well as in financial transactions. The performance of futures markets in this sense is measured by their informational efficiency.

We are concerned here with a particular issue concerning informational efficiency, the manipulation of futures markets. This subject has long been of practical importance, but has not until now commanded attention in the literature. The issue of manipulation arises, for instance, in the study of what are institutionally known as squeezes or corners. In both cases, an implicit assumption is that some agents control certain strategic information and that they may use such control to influence the market to their advantage—for instance, through their impact on prices. We assume that agents are not fully informed about the characteristics of all other traders (such as their de-

A grant from the Center for the Study of Futures Markets, Columbia University, is gratefully acknowledged. I thank R. Anderson, R. Kihlstrom, A Kyle, and G.M. Heal for helpful discussions.

193

mands) and that each agent may use his private information to influence prices to his possible advantage. The context is therefore that of games with imperfect information, and we explore the possibility of manipulation when agents play in a noncooperative fashion—that is, through Nash equilibrium strategies. By manipulation, I refer to the strategic use of information and signals to obtain more advantageous outcomes. I shall illustrate certain examples of manipulation, such as market squeezes: the temporary aberration of the futures prices and spot prices for strategic advantage.

The first section establishes the concepts of games with imperfect information and of manipulation. A brief discussion of the literature is given. A class of games is then used to explore the extent to which the problem of manipulation is likely to arise in these markets. One theorem shows that manipulation arises quite generally, and with it, the informational efficiency in these markets may decrease. Using these games as examples we then set up the problem of manipulation in a repeated game context—that is, games where players are assumed to play repeatedly with each other through time, even ad infinitum (Heal 1976). In this latter case, the incidence of manipulation is greatly reduced. Futures markets become more efficient in their informational role.

We next examine the extent to which a futures market may be viewed as repeated games. This view depends on a number of features, including the degree of anonymity and of restrictions on entry. I argue that these two features are related, in the sense that more anonymity may ease entry. On the other hand, anonymity may prevent the futures market from behaving as a repeated game, thus making it more vulnerable to manipulation.[2]

The problem can be summarized as follows: disclosure that is, less anonymity) may prevent manipulation and therefore improve the informational efficiency of the market. On the other hand, disclosure (less anonymity) may restrict entry, and therefore produce an efficiency loss. There is, in this sense, a tradeoff between informational efficiency and free entry.

It is often argued that the ease of entry in futures markets is a significant improvement from the conditions prevailing in more traditional forward markets. The role of the clearing houses, as discussed in Edwards (9), is in part related to preserving as much anonymity as possible in futures markets. Anonymity and free entry appear to be rather important features of futures markets. It follows that the possibility of manipulation is higher in these markets because they do not easily satisfy the characteristics of repeated games.

The conclusions are that a certain amount of market manipulation can be expected in futures market because of their informational structure, and that manipulation will have some negative effects on the informational efficiency of these markets. Self-policing measures involving some form of disclosure could decrease to a certain extent the incidence of manipulation. However, such measures carry a cost in terms of barriers to entry and the accompanying efficiency losses. It seems therefore that an overall approach to the problem is to seek an optimal tradeoff between the two types of efficiency losses: informational inefficiencies and restrictions to entry.

The Concept of Manipulation

The concept of manipulation has been studied now for a number of years (Chichilnisky and Heal 1982). It arises most naturally in the context of noncooperative games with imperfect information. This section summarizes the conceptual issues involved and describe briefly existing results.

Economic Games

A game is defined here by specifying four objects:

1. The strategies available to each player—that is, the strategy space S.
2. The space of outcomes, denoted X.
3. The payoff function (or game form) g, a function which assigns an outcome to the strategies played by the individuals.
4. Individual characteristics, such as preferences over outcomes, that determine the strategic behavior of the players.

The term "game with imperfect information" denotes a game in which the players are not fully informed about one or more of the aspects of the game. For instance, players may be aware only of some of the strategies available to them, so they do not know their strategy space S accurately. Another typical incidence of imperfect information is when each agent is not fully aware of the characteristics of the other agents. This type of imperfect information will be most relevant here and we discuss it in some detail.

One important role of future contracts is to provide price signals that can be used by the producers and distributors to allocate real resources. More specifically, futures prices collect and interpret the underlying economic information about conditions of supply and demand and so may influence storage and inventory decisions. In the following, we shall discuss how the issue of manipulation is linked with that of the efficiency of futures markets, and also the different concepts of efficiency that emerge.

The extent to which one can rely on futures prices conveying accurate information about the market's characteristics is relevant for the efficiency of futures markets (Edwards' section 5 and 6). Agents' characteristics, such as preferences, influence demand, and demand affects futures prices. Therefore, when agents' characteristics are unknown, each agent may give strategic signals to the market about these characteristics, in an attempt to shape the pricing structure to his advantage. For instance, a net sale may be considered a signal of an agent's preference. An agent may choose this signal strategically to influence prices according to his preferences. A strategy for each agent i is then a net sale s_i, which is taken as a signal for the agent's preference. This signal will affect market prices at the equilibrium. One can formulate precisely in this context the issue of manipulation. We say that a game with imperfect information is manipulable when for at least some player i, the outcome of the game that obtains when this player gives a signal $\bar{s}_i$ that misrepresents his characteristic s_i (preference) is better (according to i) than the outcome that obtains if he gives a correct signal about his preference. That is, denote by

$$(s_1, \ldots, \overset{\wedge}{s_i}, \ldots, s_k)$$

a $k - 1$ tuple of strategies of all players but i, where $\wedge$ denotes that the corresponding strategy is deleted; $>_i$ denotes "preferred to" by the ith player; X is the outcome space, and the player's strategies are in S.

A game g is manipulable if for some strategy of player i, and some $k - 1$ tuple of strategies of all other players but i, denoted

$$(s_1, \ldots, \overset{\wedge}{s_i}, \ldots, s_k) \, \varepsilon S^{k - 1}$$

the outcome

$$g(s_1, \ldots, \bar{s}_i, \ldots, s_k) >_i g(s_1, \ldots, s_i, \ldots, s_k)$$

where s_i is the true characteristic of the ith player, and $\bar{s}_i \neq s_i$.

This concept of manipulability formalizes the notion that it is individually optimal for some player to misrepresent his characteristics, at least in some cases. As already noted, informational efficiency requires the accurate transmission of information by prices. Therefore, if individual deception leads to different prices than those reflecting the true market conditions, it could translate into a loss of efficiency for the market as a whole. The issue of manipulation is therefore linked to that of market efficiency. This link, however, is not simple, and is discussed in more detail in the following sections. In particular, we shall define a class of games along the lines discussed here and study their manipulability in the last section.

We now give a brief overview of existing results on the manipulation of games that seem useful for the study of manipulation in futures markets. The first results in the theory of manipulation appeared in Gibbard (1973). A certain type of game is called "straightforward" when the individual has no incentive to misrepresent his characteristics in his choice of strategy. The informational structure of straightforward games is such that players do not communicate at all. We now discuss briefly the concept of game solution in relation to the degree of communication among players because it will help formulate the problem with precision.

Imperfect information may take several forms. An agent may be unaware of the other agents' characteristics, but he may be able to observe their strategic moves. This is different from a game where agents are unaware of each other's characteristics and are also unable to observe each other's moves.

The effects of different informational structures is seen more readily through the concept of solution or equilibrium. For example, in a game where each player knows nothing about the other's characteristics and is also unable to observe their strategic moves, the typical concept of a solution is that of dominant strategy equilibrium. In this concept, adopted by Gibbard, each player is playing his dominant strategy—that is, p_i for the ith player, which ensures him of the best possible outcome no matter what other players may be playing. Formally, s_i is a dominant strategy for i if for any $k - 1$ tuple

$$(s_1, \ldots, \overset{\wedge}{s_i}, \ldots, s_k) \ \varepsilon \ s^{k - 1}$$

and for all strategies $\overline{s} \neq s_i$ in S, then

$$g(s_1, \ldots, s_i, \ldots, s_k) \overset{>}{\ _i} g(s_1, \ldots, \overline{s}, \ldots, s_k)$$

A straightforward game is one in which giving the correct signal about one's characteristic is a dominant strategy for each player, and this gives rise to a dominant strategy equilibrium of the game. Gibbard's theorem can now be simply summarized, even though a few definitions are needed for stating it with precision. For a wide family of games, the only straightforward games are dictatorial. Dictatorial games are those in which the outcome is always identical to the preferred outcome stated by one of the players, called the "dictator." Dictatorial games do not provide an adequate representation of markets.

This result establishes that most nondictatorial games are manipulable, in the sense of not being straightforward. The phenomenon of manipulability appears therefore rather widespread. However, closer examination of Gibbard's result shows that the conditions of his theorem may be quite restrictive. His games generally have no dominant strategies. Therefore, in particular, correct signaling cannot be a dominant strategy equilibrium. Therefore, his games fail to be straightforward may be because they do not have any equilibrium. His result may appear to be mostly a statement about the stringency of the concept of dominant strategy equilibrium and of the assumption that there is absolutely no communication between the players. In addition, Gibbard assumes that no restriction exists on the players' a priori preferences.[3]

Several later articles viewed manipulation results in a wider, and perhaps more realistic perspective (Laffont and Maskin 1980; Chichilnisky and Heal 1981, 1982). We draw from this latter literature in this discussion. The first widening was to recognize that players do observe each other's strategic moves, even though they may ignore each other's true characteristics. Second, it is seldom the case that agents have all possible characteristics, so that it suffices to study market games where the players have characteristics within a subclass of all characteristics.

The first point, about the observability of each other's strategies, leads one immediately to a different concept of solution (or equilibrium) of the game. The concept generally used in games where individuals take into account each other strategic moves is that of a Nash equilibrium. A Nash equilibrium is defined as a vector of strategies

$$(s^*_1, \ldots, s^*_i, \ldots, s^*_k)$$

where strategy p^*_i is such that the ith player maximizes his utility given all other player's strategies. Formally:

$$\text{For all } i, g (s^*_1, \ldots, s^*_i, \ldots, s^*_k) = \max_{s_i \varepsilon S} \{u_i(g(s^*_1, \ldots, s^*_i, \ldots, s^*_k)) \}$$

where u_i is a real valued utility function on outcomes representing the preference of the ith player.

A Nash equilibrium is a familiar concept in the study of market behavior; it is usually referred to as a noncooperative solution. The concept is used, for instance, for the study of markets whose agents have some degree of market power, such as monopolistic competitors. In this context it is called the Cournot solution or Cournot equilibrium. From now on we shall adopt this concept of a solution, which appears to be more realistic in the case of futures markets.

Efficiency and Manipulation

The examples in the last section made an implicit assumption about market behavior: that some agents' supply/demand behavior reflects on market prices. Obviously, in any general equilibrium model, market prices reflect the aggregate supply and demand, which is obtained by adding up individual's supply and demand functions. An individual's behavior therefore affects the equilibrium market prices. However, it is an assumption of the theory of competitive markets that each agent acts as if he has no influence at all on prices—that is, no market power. Our treatment of futures markets as noncooperative games with imperfect information therefore deviates from the standard competitive model in two respects. One is the lack of perfect information. The second aspect is that some of the players are aware that they may have some market power and may be able to influence prices. The concept of futures markets used here is in this sense closer to that used in the chapters by Anderson and Sundareson and by Kyle in this book.

We now turn to the issue of efficiency discussed in the last section. We explained that the manipulation of a futures market may be used in defining the efficiency of this market because the market prices in this case may not convey accurate information about market conditions. There may be another source of inefficiencies, this one related to the overall allocation of resources. If individuals play the market strategically as a noncooperative game and reach a Nash equilibrium solution, this solution need not be an efficient allocation of resources, even when information is perfect. It is well known that Nash equilibrium solutions do not always yield Pareto optimal allocations among the players. In this chapter, however, we concentrate on informational efficiency, which arises more frequently in the study of financial as well as futures markets.

Using the concept of a game introduced in the previous section, we give a formal example of the behavior of futures markets as noncooperative games with imperfect information. Again, we assume that each agent announces a net demand schedule, which is characterized by a number of parameters, and can therefore be viewed as a vector in euclidean space. This vector is a signal of his true net demand function emerging from the optimization of individual preferences. Each component of the vector may, of course, be either positive or negative, depending on whether the agent buys or sells the particular commodity indicated by that component.

We can assume without loss of generality that the initial net amount traded when the market opens is the vector q_0 in R^{nm}, where m denotes the number of delivery dates, and n the number of commodities. Opening futures prices p_0 are therefore described by a positive nm dimensional vector. A signal for agent i is a net demand schedule, a vector denoted Δq_i. It is convenient, but not essential, to assume that q_i also has dimension nm—that is, $q_i \varepsilon R^{nm}$. Because in futures markets no immediate payment is necessary at the moment of contract—that is, there are no budget constraints—in principle a signal can be any vector in R^{nm}, with some coordinates positive and others negative. In the final section we shall also refer to cases where the agents have budget constraints, which limit their signals to a subset of R^{nm}.

In its simplest and most general form, we conceive of the game as a function that assigns to individual net demand schedule signals a market price, which is a positive vector in R^{nm}—that is

$$g(\Delta q_1, \ldots , \Delta q_k) = p \ \varepsilon \ R^{(nm) \ +}$$

Equivalently, we may consider the outcome as a change from initial to final prices—that is, we may rewrite the game in the form

$$g(\Delta q_1, \ldots , \Delta q_k) = \Delta p = p - p_0$$

This formalization is useful because we obtain more symmetry. The strategies of the players are vectors in R^{nm}, and the outcomes are vectors in R^{nm} as well. The game form or payoff function is therefore a function

$$g : (R^{nm})^k \rightarrow R^{nm}$$

where k is the number of players. In general, of course, the image of g will be a subset of R^{nm}.

We now focus on one class of games within this context, which is used later to explore the incidence of manipulation. The goal of each player is to attain a price change as close as possible to Δp^*_i, the ideal price change for this agent given his true (current or expected) market position. For example, assume that there are two periods and that each component of the price vector denotes the price for the same good in each of the two periods. Assume that in the first period the agent goes long for delivery of good a on the second period, and furthermore, that it is his private information that he does not wish to hold good a on or after the second period. Then if this agent can induce by strategic signaling a change in market prices that keeps future prices for good a at the first period, denoted $p_1(a)$, as low as possible, and second-period spot prices for a, denoted $p^2(a)$ as high as possible, he may be able to squeeze the market for delivery at the second date, provided he purchases enough in the first period for delivery at the second. His goal is then to obtain that change in price Δp^*_i that maximizes the ratio

$$\frac{p_1(a)}{p^2(a)}$$

For instance, if the agent's net position is long, his ideal price ratio in this market would be zero. In other cases—such as those with two or more delivery dates—one may consider the ideal price as representing instead futures prices at different delivery dates. If an agent holds a portfolio with different delivery dates, the ideal prices for this agent will in general be a vector whose components are positive. How an agent may influence prices to approximate his ideal price is described in the last section.

We now assume that prices are affected by the behavior of a subset of players who have market power P Prices will change in the same general direction of the excess demand vector of the players in P. More precisely, if Δq_i is the demand signal of the ith agent with market power, then Δp will be in the convex set of directions determining the signals Δq_i for all i in P. In particular, when all quantity signals are identical to each other—for example, to Δq (that is, everyone signals the same net demand)—then the change in prices will also be in the same direction. That is

$$\Delta p = \lambda \Delta q$$

for some positive number λ.

We can now describe the strategic behavior of the players. The optimal Nash strategy of the ith player, given that all other players in P are playing strategies Δq_j, for $j = 1, \ldots, k, j \neq i$, is that strategy $\overline{\Delta q_i}$ that yields a price change as close as possible to an ideal outcome Δp^*_i. Formally, the Nash strategy of the ith player is $\overline{\Delta q_i}$ if

$$g(\overline{\Delta q_1}, \ldots, \overline{\Delta q_i}, \ldots \overline{\Delta q_p}) - \Delta p^*_i =$$
$$\min_{\Delta q \in R^{nm}} (g(\overline{\Delta q_1}, \ldots, \Delta q, \ldots, \overline{\Delta q_p}) - \Delta p^*_i)$$

where $P = \{1, \ldots, p\}$, and the minimum is taken with respect to the standard euclidean distance in R^{nm}.

A Nash equilibrium set of strategies $(\Delta q_1^*, \ldots, \Delta q_p^*)$ is one in which for each player i, the strategy Δq_i^* is optimal, given that player j is playing strategy Δq_j^*, for $j = 1, \ldots, p, j \neq 1$. There is manipulation only if the Nash equilibrium strategy of agent i, Δq_i^*, which he chooses strategically to attain the best outcome in the game g, is a misrepresentation of i's net demand Δq_i, obtained under competitive assumptions from utility maximization at the competitive equilibrium market prices. If some player gains by misrepresenting his market position—for example, if it influences prices to move in a different way than they would do if he was to represent his position accurately—the informational efficiency of futures prices in predicting subsequent spot prices will be diminished. In the last section, we show that in this type of market game manipulation will take place generally—that is, each player will in general obtain a more favorable price move by misrepresenting his position (theorem 2). We can further refine the result by showing that when the outcomes of the game are directions of price changes, then under these conditions there exists always one player who can attain whatever direction of price change he desires by manipulation (theorem 1).

The results of theorems 1 and 2 show that although we have dropped the restrictions of Gibbard's theorem and consider more plausible games where agents do take into consideration each other's strategic moves, the problem of manipulation is still present. The next section will study alternatives to the examples of games discussed here and explore the role of disclosure in the context of repeated games.

Disclosure and Repeated Games

We have discussed examples of the incidence of manipulation in futures markets viewed as noncooperative games with imperfect information. In this section we analyze the strategic behavior that arises when players play the game repeatedly, even ad infinitum. The incidence of manipulation is likely to decrease when the game is played by the same agents repeatedly because each player's strategic behavior is observed by the other players. Once manipulation is exposed and the player is identified, future signals from this player may be interpreted differently. In particular, it is possible that by playing the game repeatedly, the manipulative player will reveal his true market position through his strategic behavior. If this is the case, the longer-run informational efficiency of the futures market as a repeated game may be recovered, despite the possible incidence of manipulation in each one-shot game.

Several factors may stand on the way of the full disclosure of an individual's position through his strategic behavior. However, at least in certain examples one can give sufficient conditions to guarantee that an optimal strategy in a repeated game is to reveal one's true market position. Such examples will be seen to require some form of disclosure or loss of anonymity. However, disclosure or loss of anonymity may be associated with barriers to entry, which decrease the market's allocative efficiency. Therefore, the gains from informational efficiency of repeated games may be accompanied by efficiency losses from barriers to entry. A mixed policy to optimize this tradeoff may be called for.

Ideally, we would consider the games discussed in the last section as played repeatedly. However, this view would lead to games on infinite dimensional strategy spaces. Therefore, we study now a simpler example of one-shot games that will then be repeated indefinitely. This is analogous but different from a one-shot game studied by Akerloff (1970). An extension of our game to a supergame—that is, the game obtained by repeating this one-shot game ad infinitum—is obtained. A precedent is Heal (1976) who extended Akerloff's game to a supergame and produced the first results in the area of incentives in repeated games. Because we repeat the game indefinitely, it is simpler to assume that only two strategies are available to each player, one representing truthful demand A and the second misrepresenting it for calculated strategic advantage B.

Our game differs from those of Akerloff and Heal in several ways. Heal requires that a "good quality" good obtained through trade have an intrinsic value for the player, a value that is the same for both players and is independent from what the other player's strategy is. Thus, his game has only four parameters: the value of obtaining a "good quality" good, the value of departing from a "good quality" good, and the same two values for "bad quality" goods. Here, we need instead eight parameters because there is no intrinsic value here to a truthful strategy. This value is determined by the market response, which depends of course on the other player's strategy.

We assume that there are two players, 1 and 2, and define eight parameters as follows. When players 1 and 2 play both strategy A, the outcome for 1 is α_{11} and for 2 is β_{11}; when 1 and 2 both play B the outcomes are α_{22} and β_{22}; when 1 plays A and 2 plays B, the outcomes are α_{12} and β_{12}, respectively, and finally when 1 plays B and 2 plays A, they are α and β_{21} respectively. We now define this game formally. The game form g is a function

$$g: \{A,B\}^2 \rightarrow \{(\alpha_{11}, \beta_{11})\ (\alpha_{12}, \beta_{12})\ (\alpha_{21}, \beta_{21})\ (\alpha_{22}, \beta_{22})\} \subset R^2$$

where $\{A, B\}$ is the set of strategies of each player, consisting of two strategies, A and B. The set of outcomes is contained in R^2. Each different set of strategies is assigned one outcome—for example, by construction

$$g(A, B) = (\alpha_{12}, \beta_{12})$$

We can represent the same game also in the more familiar matrix form:

$$
\begin{array}{cc}
 & \text{Player 2} \\
 & \begin{array}{cc} \text{strategy } A & \text{strategy } B \end{array}
\end{array}
$$

$$
\text{Player 1}\quad
\begin{array}{c}
\text{strategy } A \\
\text{strategy } B
\end{array}
\left(
\begin{array}{cc}
\alpha_{11}\ \ \beta_{11} & \alpha_{12}\ \ \beta_{12} \\
\alpha_{21}\ \ \beta_{21} & \alpha_{22}\ \ \beta_{22}
\end{array}
\right) = g
$$

By analogy with the previous game we may assume that the truthful outcome $(\alpha_{11}, \beta_{11})$ is Pareto-efficient—that is, that any other outcome which has a higher value for one of the players will necessarily have a lower value for the other. We shall also discuss cases where $(\alpha_{11}, \beta_{11})$ is not Pareto-efficient.

The next step is to find the non-cooperative solutions of this one-shot game. We are concerned with the cases where the game can be manipulated and wish to investigate how the repetition of this game may improve matters. The game can be manipulated when the outcome of playing strategy B (deceit) is an improvement over that of playing strategy A (stating one's truthful position). We may assume without loss of generality that the deceitful player is 1. Then if

$$\alpha_{21} > \alpha_{11} \text{ and } \alpha_{22} > \alpha_{12}$$

player 1 will always play strategy B (deceit). Player 2 will therefore always choose between β_{21} and β_{22} only. Under the assumption that $\beta_{22} > \beta_{21}$ (that is, it is preferable to respond to deceit with deceit), the only Nash equilibrium of this game is the pair of strategies (B, B) with payoff $(\alpha_{22}, \beta_{22})$. This will happen even though the truthful (A, A) strategy vector may yield a Pareto superior outcome—that is, even if $(\alpha_{11}, \beta_{11}) > (\alpha_{22}, \beta_{22})$, where $>$ is the standard vector order in euclidean space R^2. The Nash equilibrium—that is, noncooperative behavior of the agents—may lead to Pareto inferior outcomes if each player has an incentive to deceive the other in the one-shot game. Such a market would not be informationally efficient because at the equilibrium, we expect deceitful behavior of the agents.

Now assume the game is played repeatedly. Consider the following infinite strategy Γ for player 1: to real his correct position A in the first period, and in the tth period to play B if and only if player 2 has been deceitful in some previous periods $s < t$. Define Ω to be the symmetric policy for player 2. We can now compute the discounted future payoff of this strategy for both player. The playoff of Γ to player 1 is 2 plays Ω is

$$\alpha_{11} \sum_{t=1}^{\infty} \Delta^t \qquad (6.1)$$

where $0 < \Delta < 1$ is the discount factor. Similarly, the payoff to 2 of Ω if 1 plays T is

$$\beta_{11} \sum_{t=1}^{\infty} \Delta^t \qquad (6.2)$$

Now, if player 2 plays strategy Ω, can player 1 benefit by departing from strategy A? Assume that from $t = 1$ to $t = T$, 1 plays A, and for $t \geq T + 1$, 1 plays B. Then if 2 follows strategy Ω, 2 will play B from $t = T + 2$ onward, and therefore, the best 1 can do is to play B from there onward also. Therefore, the highest payoff to 1 of departing from strategy T at time $T + 1$ is

$$\alpha_{11} \sum_{t=1}^{T} \Delta^t + \alpha_{21} \Delta^{T+1} + \alpha_{22} \sum_{t=T+2}^{\infty} \Delta^t \qquad (6.3)$$

We can now compare the payoff to strategy Γ for player 1, to the payoff to this deviation from Γ. This is, we compare equations 6.1 and 6.3. It is easy to check that the payoff of equation 6.1 exceeds that of 6.3 if and only if

$$\Delta < \frac{\alpha_{11} - \alpha_{21}}{\alpha_{22} - \alpha_{21}}$$

Therefore, for sufficiently small discount rates Δ, the pair of strategies Γ, Ω is always a Nash equilibrium of the repeated game. This shows that for small discount rates—that is, when players value their future trades sufficiently— one possible solution to this game is that each player acts according to his true position without attempting to manipulate the outcome.

We therefore may attain informational efficiency if the discount rate is sufficiently small. Moreover, it can also be shown that for any discount rate, a Pareto-efficient solution of the game is an equilibrium of the supergame. Therefore, the truthful strategy (A,A) leads to a Pareto-efficient allocation. It follows that in such cases one may add Pareto efficiency of resource allocations to the informational efficiency of the solutions.

An interesting problem arises in those cases where the truthful strategy set (A, A) is informationally efficient but not Pareto-efficient. As discussed previously, this may arise in the Nash equilibrium of noncooperative market games even with perfect information, such as games of monopolistic competition. In such cases, it cannot be guaranteed that gaining more information about the market conditions (for example, through repeated games) will improve the outcome. More information may lead in some cases to all agents being worse off.

Finally, it should be pointed out that, in general, any Pareto-efficient allocation of a one-shot game will be a Nash equilibrium of the supergame. This result implies in particular that if the truthful strategy (A, A) is Pareto-efficient, it will always be a Nash equilibrium solution to the supergame.

Efficiency Gains and Losses from Disclosure

The previous section studied a one-shot game where the agents have an incentive to manipulate their signals to their advantage. It also showed sufficient conditions for this incentive to disappear when the game is repeated indefinitely. The intuitive reason is that when the game is repeated, the players build up reputations and may therefore internalize at least some of the losses that they may inflict on others in previous periods. The incentive to manipulate is therefore decreased. We exhibited two sufficient conditions for attaining a manipulation-free outcome. One is that the truthful strategies define a Pareto-efficient equilibrium. The other is that the agents have relatively low discount rates for the future. Clearly, the extent to which future trades matter will be reflected by more concern for one's current commercial reputation. These results lead us naturally to question the conditions under which a futures market can be considered a repeated game. This will be the first subject of this section. The second will be to explore the implications of this on efficiency.

One factor that emerged clearly in the discussion in the last section is that some form of strategic retaliation is necessary to prevent repeated manipulation. Clearly, such a strategy would require that the manipulating agents be identified. For example, if manipulation is followed by exit from the market, and perhaps reentry under a different brand name, manipulation may go unchecked and be repeated indefinitely.

To formalize this concept, one reformulates the repeated game defined previously to take exit into account. Depending on the returns outside of the game, one may be able to formulate precisely the optimal exit policy of a manipulative agent. For example, assume that the returns outside the game are x dollars per period. Consider the following strategy ξ for player 1. Player 1 plays the game straight for T periods, then it manipulates it on period T, and leaves the market on period $T + 1$. Then the payoff to 1 of strategy ξ, under the assumption that player 2 will not manipulate unless 1 does (that is, strategy Ω) is

$$\alpha_{11} \sum_{1}^{T-1} \Delta^t + \alpha_{21} \Delta^T + x \sum_{t=T+1}^{\infty} \Delta^t \qquad (6.4)$$

We may now compare the payoff of strategy Γ for player 1, with the payoff of two other strategies: manipulating and staying in the market, and manipulating and exiting. Clearly it will be preferable for 1 to follow strategy ξ rather than the straight strategy T if and only if

$$\Delta > \frac{\alpha_{11} - \alpha_{21}}{x - \alpha_{21}} \qquad (6.5)$$

Notice that the choice of cheat and exit strategy becomes more attractive in two cases:

1. The higher is the rate of discount of the future payoffs.
2. The higher is the payoff x outside the market, and this is independent from the stopping time.

Obviously, x must be larger than α_{22} because otherwise player 1 would never contemplate leaving the market. Also x must be smaller than α_{11} for this player to want to play at all. Therefore strategy ξ will generally be preferred to manipulating forever and will also be preferable to playing straight with high rates of discount of future payoffs.

As a result, there is the concern that at any point of the game a player may manipulate and then exit. Unless a player can be fully identified in terms of his history of trades, one cannot expect the players to reveal truthfully their market positions so that newcomers, who have no market history, would normally be suspect. With full disclosure, a wedge is driven between oldtime players and newcomers, which effectively restricts entry.

When more sophisticated strategies are considered, it can be expected that a natural concept of entry fee may arise—that is, the cost associated with developing a good market reputation for the newcomers. The formalization of such a concept would seem useful to compute the efficiency losses associated with restricted entry arising from disclosure. Or, equivalently, it may measure the efficiency gains from anonymity, in the form of free entry. Therefore, a measure of the informational efficiency gained by disclosure (in which case we may have a repeated and manipulation-free game) and the efficiency losses due to restricted entry caused by full disclosure would seem required.

Results for One-Shot Games and Applications

In this section we prove results on the manipulation of games with imperfect information. At the end of the section we shall also discuss their possible applications for the analysis of futures markets.

Let us assume that there are $k \geq 2$ players with market power. We shall examine their Nash strategies and the corresponding outcomes of a non-cooperative game. The game is defined by a game form g, a strategy set S in R^n for each player, and an outcome set X in R^n. Each strategy is a vector representing a net demand schedule for n commodities. The game form is a continuous function $g: (R^n)^k \to X$, which assigns to each k-tuple of strategies an outcome that is a direction of price change D_p in R^n, or else no change at all—that is, the vector $(0, \ldots, 0)$.

We shall assume that each player knows g, X, and S, and that they observe each other's moves; player i's preferred direction of price change is denoted Dp_i^*. To provide a simple proof of our next result, we shall look at the special case $k = 2, n = 2$. The results in this section hold true for higher dimensional cases, but the proofs require more complex tools of algebraic topology.

THEOREM 1. *Consider a game $g: (R^2)^2 \to R^2$ defined as above. Assume that prices move in the direction of a convex combination of the changes in net demands of the agents. There then exists a player who is always able to secure, as a Nash equilibrium outcome, his preferred direction of price change, for any (nonzero) strategies the other is playing. To attain this outcome, this player will generally misrepresent his true (net) demand, but his strategic net demand vector need never have a higher absolute value than that of the other player.*

Proof. Because g maps strategies into directions of price changes, and such directions are in a one-to-one correspondence with points in the unit circle S^1 of R^s, we may consider $g: (R^2)^2 \rightarrow S^1$. We shall now restrict ourselves to nonzero strategies, so we may look at $g: (R^2 - \{0\})^2 \rightarrow S^1$

We study next the restriction of the map g to the set $(S^1)^2 \subset (R^2 - \{0\})^2$—that is

$$g : (S^1)^2 \rightarrow S^1$$

We may define the degree of g restricted to the diagonal set $D = \{(x_1, x_2) \varepsilon (S^1)^2 : x_1 = x_2\}$, because D is homeomorphic to the circles S^1 in R^2 (Chichilnisky 1981).

The condition that price changes in the direction of positive linear coordination demands implies that when all individual demands are co-linear, they move in the same direction. Thus g restricted to D is the identity map, so that deg $g/D = 1$. Similarly we study the degree of g on each of the following subsets:

$$T_1 = \{(x, y): x = x_0, y \varepsilon S^1\}$$

and

$$T_2 = \{(x, y): y = y_0, x \varepsilon S^1\}$$

The degree of g restricted to T_1 and to T_2 is either zero or one, due to the convexity condition (Chichilnisky 1982b)—that is

$$0 \leqslant \deg g/T_1 \leqslant 1 \tag{6.5}$$

and

$$0 \leqslant \deg g/T_2 \leqslant 1 \tag{6.6}$$

Now, because D is homotopic to $T_1 U T_2$ within $(S^1)^2$, it follows that

$$\deg g/D = \deg g/T_1 \, U T_2 = \deg g/T_1 + \deg g/T_2 \tag{6.7}$$

Since deg $g/D = 1$, this implies by equation 6.5 and 6.6 that of the two degrees on the right side of equation 6.7, one must be zero, and the other one.

Assume without loss of generality that deg $g/T_1 = 1$ and deg $g/T_2 = 0$. This implies that when player 2 plays y_0 in S^1 for any outcome D_p^* in S^1 there exists an $x(y_0)$ in S^1 such that $g(x, y_0) = D_p^*$. By continuity of g, this is also true for any other y in $S^1, y \neq y_0$. This proves that the first player can always find a Nash strategy that ensures him of his preferred outcome, no matter what strategy player 2 plays. The argument is now easily extended to strategies in R^2.

For any y in R^2, consider the circle $S^1(y)$ centered in the origin, passing through y. Because g is defined on R^2, in particular g is defined on $S^1(y)$, and thus the preceding argument applies to this circle—that is, to the map

$$g/_{S^1(y) \times S^1(y)} : S^1(y) \times S^1(y) \to S^1$$

This proves that for the game $g: (R^2)^2 \to S^1$, the Nash response function of player 1 has always D_p^* as its outcome—that is, $g(x(y), y) = D_p^*$, $\forall D_p^*$ in R^2. Because the Nash equilibrium is in the intersection of both response functions of the players, the proof of the theorem is complete.

The following is an example of a game g as in theorem 1.

Example 1: A special case of Walras games of misrepresentation of preferences. This example draws on the literature on market manipulation (see Hurwicz 1972, 1979). We consider first a pure exchange market with two persons and two goods. Given an initial endowment W_i and a price p, each agent determines a utility-maximizing bundle $z^*(p)$. As the price p varies, the geometric locus of $z^*(p)$ in the commodity space constitutes the offer curve of this agent.

One may consider the game where each individual chooses strategically an offer curve to maximize his strictly convex preference subject to a budget constraint depending on W_i. Given a pair of such strategies, denoted h_1 and h_2, the outcome of the Walras game is defined by the determination of the market clearing prices for h_1 and h_2 and the subsequent selection of the corresponding Walras equilibrium allocation. In the case of multiple solutions, one is chosen.

Hurwicz has shown that the set of Nash allocations of the preceding game, which corresponds to equilibria in Nash strategies, coincides with the interior of the lens L^* constituted by the true offer curves. In general, therefore, manipulation of the market will take place, in the sense that the Nash solutions of the Walras game when agents play strategically is different from the set of Walrasian equilibrium market allocations.

We consider now a special case of the preceding game.

Given inital endowments W_i and preferences U_i, $i = 1, \ldots, k$ (k agents), let $\Sigma(W_i, U_i)$ be the set of Walrasian equilibria of the pure exchange economy described by $(W_i, U_i)i = 1, \ldots, k$. We assume that initial endowments (W_i) are given, and that the preferences U_i, $i = 1, \ldots, k$, may vary over a family of preferences parameterized by vectors in R^n (n goods).

This is a restricted domain assumption. For example, for $n = 3$, $k = 2$ let $U_1 = \min(a_1x,\ b_1y,\ c_1z)$ and $U_2 = \min(a_2x,\ b_2y,\ c_2z)$, so that U_1 is fully described by the three = dimensional vector (a_1, b_1, c_1) and U_2 by (a_2, b_2, c_2). Alternatively consider a faimily of Cobb-Douglas utilities $\{U_i = (x^\alpha, y^\beta, z^\gamma)\}$ each utility U_i indexed by a vector in euclidean space, namely $(\alpha, \beta, \gamma) \ \varepsilon R^3$.

We shall assume that there exists a continuous map ϕ from utilities to equilibria

$$\{U_i\} \xrightarrow{\phi} \sum (U_i,\ W_i)$$

where ϕ assigns a Walrasian equilibria to each utility U_i in a continuous fashion. Because the utilities U_i's are assumed to be characterized by vectors in R^n, then the map ϕ can be written as

$$\phi : (R^n)^k \rightarrow \sum (.\,;W_i),$$

where $\phi\ (r_1^1, \ldots, r_n^1, \ldots, r_j^k)$ is a Walrasian equilibria of the pure exchange economy $(r_1^1, \ldots, r_n^1, \ldots, r_n^k;\ \{W_i\})$ with initial endowments $\{W_i\}$ and preferences $\{U_i\}$ represented by the nk vector of parameters $(r_1^1, \ldots, r_n^k)$.

If we now consider the equilibrium price p^* supporting the Walrasian equilibria allocation $\phi(r_1^1, \ldots, r_n^k;\ \{W_i\})$, then we obtain from ϕ a continuous map

$$g : (R^n)^k \rightarrow R^n$$

assigning to $(r_1^1, \ldots, r_n^k)$ the equilibria price of $\phi(r_1^1, \ldots, r_n^k,\ \{W_i\})$. This map satisfies the conditions statement of theorem 1, defining a game form $g\colon (R^n)^k \rightarrow \mathbf{R}^n$. The strategy of the ith player is therefore an n-dimensional vector $(r_1^i, \ldots, r_n^i)$ in R^n representing his preference, or corresponding demand schedule. Each individual vector will represent a variation from an initial vector of parameters $(r_1^0, \ldots, r_n^0)$. Individual strategies are variations over a given preference or initial demand schedule. We now make the following additional assumption:

Regularity assumption: The equilibrium price p^* varies continuously as a function of individual demands in the direction of the convex combination of changes in individual demands. This condition can be described intuitively by saying that the equilibrium price moves in a certain direction whenever individual utilities change so as to assign higher utilities to commodity bundles in that direction. This condition can be weakened significantly, for instance to request that the map of from $(R^n)^k$ into R^n has degree 1 over certain subsets. In view of our two assumptions, the game form as defined by the Walras game satisfies all the conditions of theorem 1, and therefore the results of theorem 1 apply to this example.

We may also refer to cases where, because of constraints, the players may not play all possible net demand vectors as strategies. In the two-dimensional case, we may consider therefore that the strategies open to each player are restricted to a box in R^2, denoted Z^2. The manipulation of such games was studied in Chichilnisky and Heal (1982), and we quote here those results.

THEOREM 2. *Let g be a regular[4] game with strategies in Z^2 for each player, and outcomes in a convex set of R^2 (that is, the price space). Then g is nonmanipulable in Nash equilibrium only if g is locally simple—that is, locally a constant or locally dictatorial. Furthermore, locally constant or dictatorial games are nowhere dense in the family of continuous game forms g: $Z^2 \rightarrow R^2$. Therefore, generically, games g: $Z^2 \rightarrow R^2$ are manipulable.*
For a proof see theorem 2 and proposition 5 of Chichilnisky and Heal (1982).

We now give a corollary of theorem 1 that will be used in the following application to futures markets:

COROLLARY 1. *Let g: $(R^2)^2 \rightarrow R^2$ be a game as in theorem 1. Then there always exists a player that can ensure that the price of one of the goods will move in the opposite direction of his net demand vector for this good, at least in some ranges of his demand.*
Proof. This follows from the proof of theorem 1. The fact that deg/$T_2 = 0$ implies, together with the convex hull condition, that the set of values of g on the set T_2, that is

$$\{g(x_0, y) : y \varepsilon S^1 (x_0)\}$$

does not cover T_2. That is, as the net demand vector y of the second agent describes clockwise the circle $S^1 (x_0)$, the outcome must move counter-clockwise at least for some values of y. Therefore, as net demand of player 2 increases for one good, the price change moves in the opposite direction. This completes the proof.

We now explore an application of theorem 1 and its corollary 1 to a particular example of manipulation of futures markets, related to what is sometimes called a market squeeze (for a discussion and definitions, see for example Kyle, chapter 5, this volume).

Example 2: Market squeezes and the competitive fringe. For this example we must specify in more detail the institutional framework of the problem. We shall assume that there are two types of agents, those with market power and those without it. The latter are called the "competitive fringe." They are distinguished in operational terms by the fact that when operations are contractual but not physical (that is, no physical goods are exchanged, only contracts), the prices are determined by the market behavior of the players with market power. However, if as delivery date arrives physical deliveries take place, then the price changes are influenced by the physical volumes of demands and supplies of all players, including those without market power, until physical markets clear. We shall assume, as usual, that price changes move in the same general direction as aggregate excess demands.

In our example, there is one good a and two periods. We shall consider two prices: $p_1(a)$ denotes the futures price of a at period 1, and $p^2(a)$ represents the spot price of a at period 2. Obviously, with perfect information and no manipulation these two prices should be equal but for storage costs. As we will see, however, where there exist agents with market power in period 1, it will be possible (under certain conditions) to drive a wedge between these two prices to the advantage of the manipulative agent.

We shall consider a case where the first period is very close to the delivery date (or second period), so that the clearing house is not able to close the wedge through its periodic monitoring operations. Assume that there are two players with market power denoted 1 and 2 and a competitive fringe of undetermined size. Assume that the direction of price change is as before in the convex hull of player 1 and player 2's net futures contract demand for good a (to be delivered at date 2). Then corollary 2 establishes that at least for one agent, say player 1, it will be possible in some cases to increase its demand for a (to be delivered at date 2) and go sufficiently long without at the same time increasing, or even while decreasing, the futures price at which he contracts in period 1.

An intuitive explanation of this case could be as follows. If in previous periods agent 1 had traded with an agent with market power denoted 2, and 2 went sufficiently short, then in period 1, the second agent could prevent the futures price of a from rising—for example, while agent 1 goes long by buying only from the competitive fringe. Because we assumed that until physical trade takes place, the competitive fringe does not affect market prices, futures prices for a remains low, even as player 1 goes sufficiently long that his demand exceeds physical supplies in period 2. The manipulation is now completed. As period 2 arrives, if player 1 purchased more than the total physical quantities available, then obviously the spot price of good a will rise in period 2. This increase will give a net gain to player 1 if he accepts monetary compensation for the lack of delivery. This gain, of course, will only be meaningful if player 1 did not actually buy futures in good a because he needed good a in period 2; contrary to what he expressed about his demand for a in period 1, he does not actually need to consume a in period 2, so he can materialize the gain of the price wedge he produced through manipulation.

This result has two key elements. First, as provided by theorem 1 and corollary 1, in period 1 one agent may increase his futures demand for good *a* and go sufficiently long without increasing his futures price in contracts at period 1. The competitive fringe that went short in the aggregate in period 1 for delivery in period 2 will affect spot prices in the second period, because then delivery is enforced, so that the other physical scarcity of quantities traded affects spot prices.

A closer look at agent 1's strategy suggests that this agent may do well to buy first from those agents with the most market power. If they go short, they may help prevent increases in futures prices, thus allowing player 1 to continue to buy from the competitive fringe at lower prices and increase his long position significantly just up to the date where delivery must take place.

Notes

1. Forward markets do not mark to market as futures markets do.

2. For an institutional example of this tradeoff between ease of entry and manipulation, see "Antitrust Study of U.S. Bond Trading," *The New York Times*, April 4, 1983.

3. That is, a priori each player may have any possible preference among different commodities. The game is supposed to be straightforward with respect to any arbitrarily given set of players, each of which may have any possible preference.

4. A regular game is one whose game form $g : R^{nk} \to R^n$ satisfies generic transversality conditions; see Chichilnisky and Heal (1981).

References

Akerlof, G. (1970). "The Market for Lemons," *Quarterly Journal of Economics*.

Chichilnisky, G. (1982a). "Incentive Compatible Games: A Characterization of Strategies and Domains," Working Paper 139, Department of Economics, Columbia University.

———. (1982b). "Social Aggregation Rules and Continuity", *Quarterly Journal of Economics*.

———. (1981). "The Topological Equivalence of the Pareto Condition and the Existence of a Dictator," *Journal of Mathematical Economics*, 1981.

——— and Heal, G. (1982). "A Necessary and Sufficient Condition for Straightforwardness." Working Paper 138, Department of Economics, Columbia University.

———. (1981). "Nash-Implementable Games." Working Paper, University of Essex.

Edwards, F.R. (1982). "The Regulation of Futures Markets: A Conceptual Framework," Working Paper CSFM–23. New York: Center for the Study of Futures Markets, Columbia University School of Business.

————. (1982). "Comparative Analysis of Clearing Associations," presented at the Conference, "The Industrial Organization of Futures Markets: Structure and Conduct," New York: Center for the Study of Futures Markets, Columbia University.

Gibbard, A. (1973). "Manipulation of Voting Schemes: A General Result," *Econometrica*.

Grossman, S.J. (1977). "The Existence of Futures Markets; Noisy Rational Expectations and Informational Externalities." *Review of Economic Studies*.

Heal, G. (1976). "Do Bad Products Drive Out Good?" *Quarterly Journal of Economics*.

Hurwicz, L. (1979). "Outcome Functions Yielding Walrasian and Lindahl Allocations at Nash Equilibrium Points," *Review of Economic Studies*, April, 1979.

————. (1972). "On Informationally Decentralized Systems" in *Decision and Organization*, ed. C. McGuire and R. Radner. New York: North-Holland.

Johnson, L.I. (1960). "The Theory of Hedging and Speculation in Commodity Futures." *Review of Economic Studies*.

Laffont, J., and Maskin, E. (1980). "A Differential Approach to Dominant Strategy Mechanisms." *Econometrica*.

Stein, J.L. (1961). "The Simultaneous Determination of Spot and Futures Prices." *American Economic Review*.

Stiglitz, J. (1980). "Risk, Futures Markets and the Stabilization of Commodity Prices." Working Paper CSFM–25, Center for the Study of Futures Markets, Columbia University.

Comment

Richard E. Kihlstrom

Professor Chichilnisky has proposed a framework for the analysis of manipulation in financial markets. In this comment, I propose an alternative framework for the study of these questions. In the limited space available here, it is only possible to introduce this alternative model and to indicate briefly the nature of the results obtainable. A more complete exposition is contained in Kihlstrom and Postlewaite (1983).[1]

The model described in this comment represents a stylized securities market in which a dominant trader receives inside information. The question we consider is will this trader attempt to profit by keeping this information from becoming public and, if so, what are the welfare consequences of this behavior? The particular securities market to be considered is a market for the exchange of contingent wealth claims. Specifically, there are assumed to be two states and two traders. One trader M is a monopolist who chooses the price at which exchange takes place. The other trader C behaves as if he were a competitor. Each trader maximizes the expected utility of wealth. We denote the monopolist's (competitor's) utility of wealth function by u_m [u_c]. A priori (that is, before the monopolist receives his inside information, he believes that the probability of state s is π_s, for $s = 1$ and 2. The competitor begins with the same beliefs. If we let x_s^m (x_s^c) represent the number of contingent claims to wealth in state s held by M (C), the corresponding a priori expected utility of M (C) is

$$U_m^\pi(x^m) = u_m(x_1^m)\pi_1 + u_m(x_2^m)\pi_2$$

$$(U_c^\pi(x^c) = u_c(x_1^c)\pi_1 + u_c(x_2^c)\pi_2)$$

In these expressions, $x^m = (x_1^m, x_2^m)$ (or, for the competitor $x^c = (x_1^c, x_2^c)$).

Each trader begins with an initial allocation of contingent claims. Specifically, trader M (C) begins with $\omega^m = (\omega_1^m, \omega_2^m)$ (or $\omega^c = (\omega_1^c, \omega_2^c)$). If p is the relative price of state 2 claims in terms of state 1 claims and if trade takes place a priori—that is, when C's beliefs are described by $\pi = (\pi_1, \pi_2)$, then C will choose x^c to maximize $U_c^\pi(x^c)$ subject to

$$x_1^c \geqslant 0, \ x_2^c \geqslant 0$$

and

$$(x_1^c - \omega_1^c) + p(x_2^c - \omega_2^c) = 0$$

We let

$$h^\pi(p) = (h_1^\pi(p), h_2^\pi(p))$$

denote C's vector of a priori demands for contingent claims. $h^\pi(p)$ is the vector x^c that solves the maximization problem just described. At p, C offers to supply the vector

$$t^\pi(p) = \omega^c - h^\pi(p)$$

of contingent claims. C's a priori offer curve, O^π, is the locus of vectors $t^\pi(p)$ obtained by allowing p to vary between 0 and ∞. It is assumed that the monopolist knows C's offer curve when he chooses p. If the monopolist were to choose p before acquiring inside information, he would choose p^π where p^π and $^\pi x^m$ maximize $U_m^\pi(x^m)$ subject to

$$x^m = \omega^m + t^\pi(p)$$

and

$$x_s^m \geq 0, \text{ for } s = 1 \text{ and } 2$$

The resulting equilibrium allocation of contingent claims received by M and C would be

$$^\pi x^m = \omega^m + t^\pi(p^\pi)$$

and

$$^\pi x^c = h^\pi(p^\pi)$$

respectively.

This equilibrium is described in figure 6A–1. In this diagram, the initial allocation is $\omega = (\omega^m, \omega^c)$. The equilibrium contingent claims allocation is $^\pi x = (^\pi x^m, ^\pi x^c)$ and p^π is the inverse of the slope of the line, between ω and $^\pi x$. The competitor's offer curve is O^π and I_m^π is the monopolist's indifference curve through $^\pi x^m$.

Having described the equilibrium that arises when the monopolist chooses p without the benefit of inside information, we now consider the case in which p is chosen after the inside information is obtained.

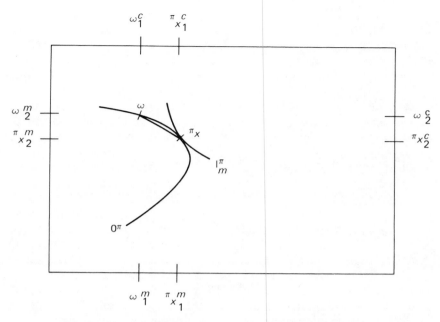

Figure 6A–1. Equilibrium without Inside Information

Formally, the information is an observation of a random variable $\bar{z}$ whose distribution depends on the true state s. Specifically, $\bar{z}$ can take either of two values, z_1 or z_2. If $\bar{z}$ is observed to equal z_s, we interpret this as a prediction that state s is the true state. We denote the probability that $\bar{z} = z_t$ given that s is the true state by $h(z_t|s)$ and we assume that

$$h(z_t|s) = \begin{cases} \theta & \text{if } t = s \\ 1 - \theta & \text{if } t \neq s \end{cases}$$

To capture the idea that the prediction is reliable but not necessarily perfectly so, we assume that $1 \geq \theta \geq \frac{1}{2}$.

When $\bar{z}$ has been observed to equal z_1, the monopolist's expectations are revised and his prior π is replaced by the posterior

$$\mu(z_1) = (\mu_1(z_1), \mu_2(z_1))$$

where

$$\mu_1(z_1) = \frac{\theta \pi_1}{\theta \pi_1 + (1 - \theta)\pi_2}$$

and

$$\mu_2(z_1) = \frac{(1 - \theta)\pi_2}{\theta\pi_1 + (1 - \theta)\pi_2}$$

Observe that $\theta > \frac{1}{2}$ implies

$$\mu_1(z_1) > \pi_1 \quad \text{and} \quad \mu_2(z_1) < \pi_2$$

If, furthermore, $\theta = 1$, the prediction is perfect and $\mu_1(z_1) = 1$ while $\mu_2(z_1) = 0$

After $\bar{z}$ has been observed to equal z_1, the monopolist's expected utility is

$$U_m^{z_1}(x^m) = u_m(x_1^m)\mu_1(z_1) + u_m(x_2^m)\mu_2(z_1)$$

Because

$$\mu_1(z_1)/\mu_2(z_1) > \pi_1/\pi_2$$

we must have, for all x^m,

$$\text{MRS}_m^{z_1}(x^m) = \frac{u_m'(x_1^m)\mu_1(z_1)}{u_m'(x_2^m)\mu_2(z_1)} > \frac{u_m'(x_1^m)\pi_1}{u_m'(x_2^m)\pi_2} = \text{MRS}_m^{\pi}(x^m)$$

Similar remarks apply when the monopolist observes $\bar{z} = z_2$. In this case, the monopolist's expectations are described by the posterior $\mu(z_2) = ((\mu_1(z_2), \mu_2(z_2))$, where

$$\mu_1(z_2) = \frac{(1 - \theta)\pi_1}{(1 - \theta)\pi_1 + \theta\pi_2} < \pi_1$$

and

$$\mu_2(z_2) = \frac{\theta\pi_2}{(1 - \theta)\pi_1 + \theta\pi_2} > \pi_2$$

His expected utility at x^m is

$$U_m^{z_2}(x^m) = u_m(x_1^m)\mu_1(z_2) + u_m(x_2^m)\mu_2(z_2)$$

In this case,

$$\mu_1(z_2)/\mu_2(z_2) < \pi_1/\pi_2$$

and, as a result,

$$\text{MRS}_m^{z_2}(x^m) = \frac{u_m'(x_1^m)\mu_1'(z_2)}{u_m'(x_2^m)\mu_2'(z_2)} < \frac{u_m'(x_1^m)\pi_1}{u_m'(x_2^m)\pi_2} = \text{MRS}_m^{\pi}(x^m)$$

If the monopolist can use observations of $\tilde{z}$ as the basis for his choice of p, the choice he would make when he observes that $\tilde{z}$ equals z_1 will in general differ from the choice he would make when he observes that $\tilde{z}$ equals z_2. If, for example, the monopolist could somehow keep the competitor from learning the realization of $\tilde{z}$, his choice for p when $\tilde{z} = z_i$ would be p^i where p^i and $^ix^m$ maximize $U_m^{z_i}(x^m)$ subject to the constraints

$$x^m = \omega^m + t^{\pi}(p)$$

and

$$x_s^m \geqslant 0 \quad \text{for } s = 1 \text{ and } 2$$

At this price, C and M would receive the allocations

$$^ix^c = h^{\pi}(p^i)$$

and

$$^ix^m = \omega^m + t^{\pi}(p^i)$$

respectively. These allocations, described in figure 6A–2. In this diagram, I_m^i is the monopolist's indifference curve through $^ix^m$. It corresponds to the utility function $U_m^{z_i}$. In figure 6A–2, p^i is the inverse of the slope of the line between ω and ^ix, where ω is as before and

$$^ix = (^ix^m, {}^ix^c)$$

As asserted, $p^1 \neq p^2$. In fact, p^2 exceeds p^1—that is, state 2 contingent claims are relatively more expensive when $\tilde{z} = z_2$ than when $\tilde{z} = z_1$, because state 2 is more likely when $\tilde{z} = z_2$ than when $\tilde{z} = z_1$.

If the monopolist can use observations of $\tilde{z}$ as the basis for his choice of p and x^m while keeping knowledge of $\tilde{z}$ from the competitor, he can obtain $^1x^m$ when $\tilde{z} = z_1$ and $^2x^m$ when $\tilde{z} = z_2$. His ex ante expected utility is therefore

$$V_m(\theta) = U_m^{z_1}(^1x^m)\phi_{z_1} + U_m^{z_2}(^2x^m)\phi_{z_2}$$

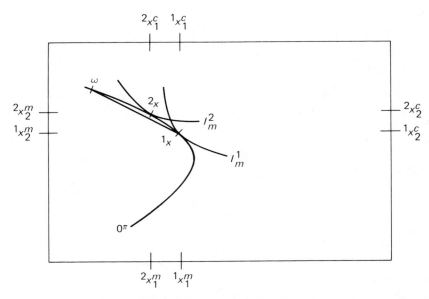

Figure 6A–2. Equilibrium with Inside Information

where

$$\phi_{z_1} = \theta\pi_1 + (1 - \theta)\pi_2, \quad \phi_{z_2} = (1 - \theta)\pi_1 + \theta\pi_2$$

and ϕ_{z_s} is the ex ante (that is, marginal) probability of observing $\tilde{z} = z_s$. It is easily shown, using standard arguments (see, for example, Marschak and Miyasawa 1968), that $V_m(\theta)$ exceeds $U_m^\pi(^\pi x^m)$, the expected utility the monoplist achieves without information.

When the monopolist has privileged information and is able to keep it from the competitor, he is better off than without information. Because $p^1 \neq p^2$, it is unrealistic to assume that the competitor remains uninformed if the monopolist uses his inside information when choosing p. As a consequence, the equilibrium just described is unlikely to arise. To describe a more plausible equilibrium, we should assume that if the monopolist uses the information that $\tilde{z} = z_i$ when choosing p, the competitor will also know that $\tilde{z} = z_i$ when making his demand decision. A competitor who knows that $\tilde{z} = z_i$ will maximize the expected utility

$$U_c^{z_i}(x^c) = u_c(x_1^c)\mu_1(z_i) + u_c(x_2^c)\mu_2(z_i)$$

The demands of a competitor who maximizes $U_c^{z_i}(x^c)$ subject to the constraints

$$(x_1^c - \omega_1^c) + p(x_2^c - \omega_2^c) = 0$$

and

$$x_s^c \geq 0 \quad \text{for } s = 1 \text{ and } 2$$

are denoted by $h^i(p) = (h_1^i(p), h_2^i(p))$. The vector of contingent claims supplied by such a competitor is

$$t^i(p) = \omega^c - h^i(p)$$

The a posteriori offer curve of C when he knows that $\bar{z} = z_i$ is O^i, the locus of vectors $t^i(p)$ obtained by allowing p to vary between zero and infinity.

When the monopolist knows that $\bar{z} = z_i$, his x^m and p choice will be constrained by O^i. He will therefore choose $\hat{p}^i$ where ${}^i\hat{x}^m$ and $\hat{p}^i$ maximize $U^{z_1}(x^m)$ subject to the constraints

$$x^m = \omega^m + t^i(p)$$

and

$$x_s^m \geq 0 \quad \text{for } s = 1 \text{ and } 2$$

The resulting allocation will be ${}^i\hat{x} = ({}^i\hat{x}^m, {}^i\hat{x}^c)$ where

$${}^i\hat{x}^m = \omega^m + t^i(\hat{p}^i)$$

and

$${}^i\hat{x}^c = h^i(\hat{p}^i)$$

The allocations ${}^1\hat{x}$ and ${}^2\hat{x}$ are described in figure 6A–3.

The offer curves O^1 and O^2 are related as shown because, for all x^c,

$$\text{MRS}_c^{z_1}(x^c) = \frac{u_c'(x_1^c)\mu_1(z_1)}{u_c'(x_2^c)\mu_2(z_1)} > \frac{u_c'(x_1^c)\pi_1}{u_c'(x_2^c)\pi_2} = \text{MRS}_c^{\pi}(x^c)$$

$$> \frac{u_c'(x_1^c)\mu_1(z_2)}{u_c'(x_2^c)\mu_2(z_2)} = \text{MRS}_c^{z_2}(x^c)$$

In Figure 6A–3, $\hat{I}^i$ is the monopolist's indifference curve through ${}^i\hat{x}^m$, corresponding to $U_m^{z_i}$. The price $\hat{p}^i$ is the inverse of the slope of the line between ω and ${}^i\hat{x}$. In figure 6A–3, $\hat{p}^2$ exceeds $\hat{p}^1$.

If the monopolist uses the information provided by the observation $\bar{z} = z_i$ when choosing p and if the competitor infers that $\bar{z} = z^i$ by observing the monopolist's p choice, then the monopolist's ex ante expected utility is

$$\hat{V}_m(\theta) = U_m^{z_1}({}^1\hat{x}^m)\phi_{z_1} + U_m^{z_2}({}^2\hat{x}^m)\phi_{z_2}$$

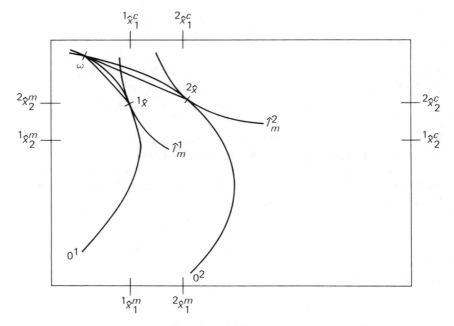

Figure 6A–3. Inside Information Revealed

Although, as noted earlier,

$$V_m(\theta) > U_2^{\pi}(^{\pi}x^m)$$

it is not necessarily true that

$$\hat{V}_m(\theta) > U_m^{\pi}(^{\pi}x^m)$$

Thus, when the competitor can infer z_s by observing the price chosen by the monopolist, the monopolist may be worse off ex ante when he receives privileged information than when he doesn't. One example in which $\hat{V}_m(\theta) < U_m^{\pi}(^{\pi}x^m)$ occurs when $\theta = 1$; that is, when the information is perfect. In this case, $\mathrm{MRS}_m^{z_1}(x^m) = \mathrm{MRS}_c^{z_1}(x^c) = \infty$ for all x^c and x^m so that O^1 and $\hat{I}_m^1$ are as shown in figure 6A–4. When this case occurs, state 2 claims are worthless to both the monopolist and the competitor; the only desirable good is x_1. As a consequence, no trade is possible, $^1p = 0$ and the utility of the monopolistic outcome to each player is the same as the utility of the initial allocation. (The monopolistic outcome can, of course, equal any allocation in the Edgeworth box on O^1 and $\hat{I}_m^1$.) In particular, the monopolist's utility is $u_m(\omega_1^m)$. Similarly, when $\bar{z} = z_2$, $\mathrm{MRS}_m^{z_2}(x^m) = \mathrm{MRS}_c^{z_2}(x^c) = 1/(^2\hat{p})$ $= 0$ and O^2 and $\hat{I}_m^2$ are as shown in figure 6A–4. In this case, state 1 claims

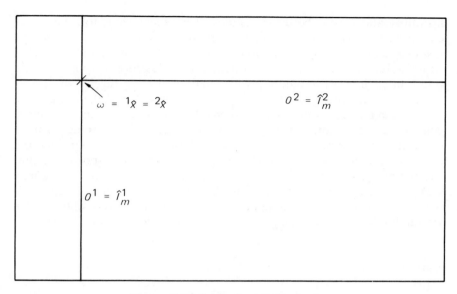

Figure 6A–4. Perfect Information

are worthless to both M and C and the monopolistic allocation is again indifferent to the initial allocation for both traders. Thus, when $\bar{z} = z_2$, the monopolist's utility is $u_m(\omega_2^m)$. Because $\theta = 1$ implies that $\phi_{z_1} = \pi_1$ and $\phi_{z_2} = \pi_2$

$$\hat{V}_m(\theta) = U_m^\pi(\omega^m) < U_m^\pi(_x\pi^m)$$

This example extends in an extreme form the idea of Hirschleiffer's example (1971) to a monopolistic setting. Hirschleiffer showed that in a competitive economy social information could have no value. In this example, the monopolist's privileged information is conveyed by his price choice and becomes social information. Thus, when trade takes place, both traders know the state. In this way, the information destroys the market and makes trade impossible. The elimination of the market makes both C and M worse off.

In the example just described, the monopolist can always choose not to use his privileged information and thereby avoid the associated loss in utility. As noted, this deceptive strategy makes both traders better off. We have thus exhibited a very simple case in which it pays for a dominant trader with privileged information to follow a deceptive strategy designed to keep his privileged information from becoming public and in which deception is socially optimal.

However, although the monopolist is better off ex ante if he does not use his information, he is better off ex post if he does. Thus, to achieve the equilibrium in which the monopolist ignores his information, it must be possible for the monopolist to credibly commit himself ex ante to such a strategy. If no such binding commitment is possible, the monopolist will not find it in his interest to ignore his information after he receives it.

In this example, deception took a very simple form; the monopolist simply didn't use his information. It is possible, however, to consider a more general class of deceptive strategies that permit the dominant trader to make partial use of his privileged information. These strategies require that the dominant trader randomize his choice of p. When the monopolist randomizes optimally—that is, chooses an optimal strategy of deception—he may make partial use of his information. An analysis of optimal deception is beyond the scope of this comment. A more complete analysis of deception via randomization is contained in Kihlstrom and Postlewaite (1983).

Note

1. Research support from the National Science Foundation is gratefully acknowledged. The author also wishes to note that although he is responsible for the exposition of these remarks, they describe research that he is carrying out jointly with Andrew Postlewaite. A more complete exposition of this work is described in Kihlstrom and Postlewaite (1983).

References

Hirschleiffer, J. (1971). "The Private and Social Value of Information and the Reward to Inventive Activity," *American Economic Review*, vol. 61, pp. 561–574.
Kihlstrom, R., and A. Postlewaite (1983). "Equilibrium in a Securities Market With a Dominant Trader Possessing Inside Information," CA-RESS Working Paper 83–05, University of Pennsylvania.
Marschak, J., and Miyasawa (1968). "Economic Comparability of Information Systems," *International Economic Review*, vol. 9, pp. 137–174.

7

The Clearing Association in Futures Markets: Guarantor and Regulator

Franklin R. Edwards

One of the least understood institutions in futures markets is the clearing association, or the clearing house corporation. Ironically, it is a key institution in futures markets; the functions it performs transform what would otherwise be forward contracts into highly liquid futures contracts. Through its rules and regulations and credit-monitoring activities the clearing association also plays a major role in maintaining the financial integrity of the entire industry. It, along with organized exchanges, forms the institutional bedrock foundation on which futures markets are organized.

Clearing associations are not well understood for two reasons. They are complex institutions, and information about what they do and how they do it is not easy to come by. The little that has been written about them does not describe them in sufficient detail to illuminate their contribution to futures markets. In addition, there are, as we shall see, many different clearing associations in futures markets, and they do not all function the same way. These differences clearly create confusion.

The chief purpose of this chapter is to clarify the role of clearing associations and possibly to correct some of these misunderstandings. As such, a large segment of the chapter describes what these institutions do and compares the rules and regulations and practices that they have adopted. Like all descriptive studies, however, it is difficult, if not impossible, to understand and to evaluate what we observe without a conceptual framework within which to fit the factual pieces of the puzzle. Another objective of this chapter, therefore, is to construct a framework for viewing clearing associations that can elucidate both their existence and the way they have chosen to operate. A final objective is to examine some of the principal current public policy issues that relate to clearing associations.

I have been generously assisted in the preparation of this paper by many people, too numerous to mention by name. I am particularly grateful to the managements of the clearing associations covered in the paper, who spent hours talking with me. In addition, Irving Redel thoroughly read a first draft and provided constructive criticism on almost every section of the paper, and Steve Selig corrected a number of the legal and regulatory aspects of the paper. The fault for any errors and important ommissions lies entirely with me, and not with those who painstakingly tried to enlighten me. I also wish to thank Columbia University's Center for the Study of Futures Markets for financial support.

The Clearing Association: Functions and Structure

Functions

Clearing associations perform two important functions. First, they attempt to ensure the financial integrity of futures transactions by directly guaranteeing some contracts and by establishing an elaborate self-regulatory mechanism to maintain the financial integrity of all clearing members. Second, because clearing associations become a party to all futures contracts, they provide a simple and convenient mechanism for settling futures contracts: by offset. The legal and contractual role of clearing associations permits them to cancel one party's obligation if that party enters into an offsetting transaction. This kind of settlement procedure is not possible in a forward market, for example, where there is no clearing association. (Settlement by delivery also is simplified by the clearing association, which acts as an allocator of deliveries to qualified longs, thereby providing a low-cost delivery mechanism.) Thus, the structure, rules and regulations, and procedures of clearing associations are designed to enable them to perform these two functions. However, as we shall show, there are sharp differences of opinion about precisely the kinds of structure and rules that are needed.

A further source of misunderstanding about the role of clearing associations in futures markets may be that there are clearing associations in banking markets as well, but which, while having the same name, perform a quite different function. Although both kinds of institutions perform a banking function by facilitating the transfer of funds between contracting parties and their agents, clearing associations in banking never become legal parties to transactions, do not act as guarantors in any way, and do not operate as a pervasive self-regulatory institution. Nor are they involved in facilitating settlement by delivery, which has no counterpart in banking. In futures markets, clearing associations are not a mere processing convenience; they are an integral part of what a futures contract is, and an essential aspect of these markets.

Structure

All organized futures exchanges in the United States have an affiliated clearing operation that clears futures trades made on that exchange. There are, therefore, eleven separate clearing operations in the United States (see appendix 7A). Some are organized as separate not-for-profit corporations, where membership is limited to members of the affiliated exchange, and others as stock corporations. However, all clearing organizations organized as separate corporations refund or rebate excessive income (or clearance fees) before the end of their respective fiscal years so that they do not have substantial annual retained earnings. Five other clearing associations are part of the exchange itself.[1] In all cases, firms approved to clear trades (or clearing members) must meet financial requirements that are more onerous than the membership requirements of the affiliated exchanges.

Membership in a clearing association may be attractive for two reasons: there is prestige associated with it, and it may be profitable. Because all trades on an organized futures market must be cleared, exchange members who are not members of a clearing association must still clear through a clearing member. Thus, in clearing nonclearing exchange members' transactions, clearing members obtain certain benefits: direct fee income from nonmembers whom they clear for; avoiding payment of such fees themselves; complete anonymity for their trading activities; and, very often, the investment income on the margin deposits posted by nonclearing members' customers. Against these benefits the clearing member must weigh the costs of membership, of which the major ones are the financial and reporting obligations and the restrictive regulations that go with membership.

In general, the clearing association is managed by officers independent from the affiliated exchange. However, this management is responsible to a clearing corporation board of directors, elected by the members of the clearing association.[2] The members of the board usually reflect, either formally or informally, the diverse interests of the related exchange—clearing floor brokers or traders, commission houses, trade hedgers, and so forth. It is the board's responsibility to set the policies and procedures of the clearing association; it is management's responsibility to implement those policies.

The Clearing Association in Operation: An Example

The best way to understand the role of clearing associations is to work through a simple hypothetical example. Although many such examples are possible, the one in the following discussion is, I believe, sufficiently rich to elucidate the critical function of the clearing association.

The hypothetical depicted in figure 7–1 has nine parties: a clearing association, two clearing member FCMs (futures commission merchants), a nonclearing FCM, and five individual customers (or traders), of whom two are customers of the nonclearing FCM and three are customers of the two clearing FCMs. For simplicity, all transactions are assumed to be in the identical futures contract.

The various positions of each party are as follows. With respect to the two customers of the nonclearing FCM, one is long 150 contracts and the other is short 140 contracts. Thus, the nonclearing FCM, which must clear

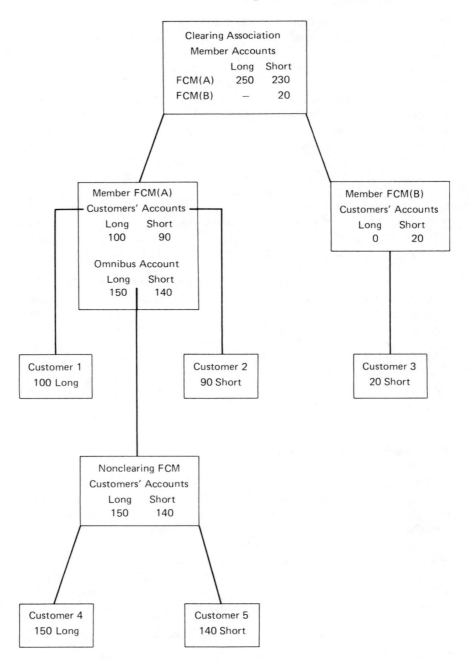

Figure 7–1. The Role of Clearing Associations

through a clearing member FCM (assumed to be firm A), has a net long position of 10 contracts with FCM(A), on an omnibus basis.[3]

In addition to having the nonclearing FCM as a customer, FCM(A) has two other individuals as customers: one has a long position of 100 contracts, and the other a short position of 90 contracts. Thus, in clearing (or recording) these transactions with the clearing association, FCM(A) ends up with a net long position of 20 contracts with the clearing association (10 in its own customer accounts and 10 in its omnibus account). Clearing member FCM(B) has only one customer, who has a short position of 20 contracts. FCM(B), therefore, has a net short position of 20 contracts with the clearing association.

In becoming a legal party to all futures transactions, the clearing association always has a balanced position—that is, an equal number of long and short contracts in all contracts traded on the affiliated exchange. (In most cases, of course, neither FCMs nor customers will hold such a balanced position.) In addition, clearing associations deal only with their members and not with nonmember FCMs or other traders. Thus, clearing association obligations extend only to members.

A central activity of the clearing association is to collect security deposits (or margins) on the futures contracts that it clears. These deposits ensure that parties to futures contracts will be able to fulfill their obligations at the expiration of the contract. Although this procedure may be implemented in different ways, for purposes of this example we make seven assumptions:

1. The clearing association collects margin deposits from members on a net basis.
2. Clearing FCMs collect margins from their customers on a gross basis.
3. The initial price of the futures contracts in our hypothetical example is $10 per contract.
4. The initial minimum margin required by the clearing association of members is $1 (10 percent of the contract's initial price).
5. The initial minimum margin required by member FCMs of their customers also is $1, but may be higher at the discretion of the FCM.[4]
6. All contracts are marked to the market daily, and variation margins are paid in (or withdrawn) the next morning, both by FCMs via clearing associations and by customers via FCMs.
7. There is a daily price limit of $1 in either direction.[5]

Given these assumptions, we can see that hypothetical FCM(A) collects at least $480 of margin deposits—$250 from the longs and $230 from the shorts. A gross margining system requires that both longs and shorts post margins. The nonclearing FCM must post margins with the clearing FCM on a gross basis (CFTC Regulation Section 1.58). FCM(B) collects $20 of margin deposits from customer 3. It is quite possible, and even likely, of course, that the two clearing FCMs may demand higher customer margin deposits than the required minimum of $500, depending on the financial characteristics of the customer. The exact amount required is a matter of negotiation between the FCM and his customer.

The clearing association is assumed to collect margin deposits on only the net position of each clearing member. The net position is 20 contracts long for FCM(A) and 20 contracts short for FCM(B). Thus, the Clearing Association collects from clearing members a total of $40. Of the total customer margin deposits of $500, therefore, the clearing association holds $40 and member FCMs hold the remaining $460.[6] (If the clearing association were to require gross margining, as some do, it would hold the entire $500.)

Now suppose that the price of our contract increases by $1, or changes from $10 to $11 during the day. The longs will have profits of $1 on each contract, and the shorts a $1 loss on each contract. Thus, FCMs will require a variation margin of $1 from each of their customers holding short positions: FCM(A) will require an additional total margin of $230, and FCM(B) an additional $20. Customers holding long positions, however, may wish to withdraw their profits, and may demand payment of $250 from FCM(A) (FCM(B) has no long customers.) FCMs, therefore, perform a banking function by transferring funds from some of their customers (the shorts) to others (the longs), at the same time continuing to maintain the original level of total margin deposits.

Similarly, the clearing association will require FCM(B) to post a variation margin of $20, because it has a net short position of 20 contracts, and FCM(A) may withdraw $20 from the clearing association. (This variation margin payment system is automatic in U.S. clearing organizations.) Thus, the clearing association performs a banking function by transferring $20 from members with short positions to members with long positions (just as FCM do for their customers), while continuing to maintain the initial required margin of $40.

The extent to which clearing associations perform a guarantor function can now be seen more clearly. In particular, so long as the magnitude of the daily changes in the price of a futures contract does not exceed the amount of the initial margin deposits, the margin deposits held by the clearing association and its clearing members are always sufficient to meet the financial obligations of both buyers and sellers of futures contracts. In our example, for instance, even if the shorts failed to meet their variation margin calls because they were bankrupt, the profits of the longs ($250) could still be paid to them out of the margins already posted by the shorts. Thus, the profits of either the shorts or the longs are guaranteed up to the amount of the margin posted. Further, at the instant of default, the clearing association and its clearing members will customarily liquidate the shorts' position by entering into an offsetting transaction, reducing their open interest obligations.

To summarize the implications of our example, both buyers and sellers of futures contracts are protected against the nonperformance of the other party by a procedure whereby each of them posts initial margin deposits with an FCM and then pays or receives on a daily basis from that FCM any losses or gains occurring as a result of market price movements on the futures contract. Similarly, clearing FCMs post initial margins with their own clearing associations and pay in or receive daily losses or gains. The amount of customer margin deposits held by clearing FCMs as opposed to the clearing association depends on the type of margining system in use: net or gross. In all cases, however, when there is a default customers with profits look to their respective FCM to obtain what they are owed; the clearing FCMs look in turn to their clearing associations to obtain any profits that they are owed on their net position with the clearing association. Thus, in our example, where there was a default by the shorts, the clearing association would guarantee only the 20 contracts that constituted FCM(A)'s net long position with it. FCM(A) would be the guarantor on the other 230 long customer contracts.

The fact that the clearing association's guarantee extends only to clearing members and possibly then only to the net position of clearing members is not always well understood. However, this arrangement makes sense. The opposite side of the net open position held by a clearing member is held by other clearing members over whom that clearing member has no control. In our example, the counterpart of FCM(A)'s net long position of 20 contracts is held by FCM(B). FCM(A) has no way of knowing whether FCM(B) is conducting its business in a prudent manner—that is, collecting customer margins in a timely way, not taking excessively risky positions, and so forth. Thus, the clearing association is in the position of guaranteeing all clearing members to each other, and in doing so it removes the necessity for each member to know and to investigate the party holding the other side of its net open position. To perform this role the clearing association necessarily becomes the regulator and monitor of all clearing members so that it can protect itself and fulfill its guarantor obligations.

Who is responsible for the other contracts held by clearing members over and above their net open positions with the clearing association? In our example, FCM(A) holds 230 long contracts and 230 short contracts in addition to the 20 long contracts that constitute its net position. Excluding their net positions held with clearing associations, therefore, clearing members always have balanced customer positions. Thus, as long as they prudently monitor the creditworthiness of their customers, and maintain the appropriate margin levels, they do not normally have any risk exposure on this position. Further, each clearing member can require greater margins from their customers if the member thinks it is necessary, collect variation margins in a timely fashion, monitor customer positions, and take whatever measures are necessary to manage his risk exposure.

If clearing associations were to guarantee all futures contracts, not only the net open positions of their clearing members, there would no longer be a market incentive for customers to evaluate the financial integrity of the FCMs they choose to deal with. Indeed, customers would probably look only for the cheapest FCM, and not worry about the ability of the FCM to meet its financial obligations, because they could rely on the clearing association guarantee. The result could very well be a general dilution in the credit worthiness of FCMs and an increase in the cost to the industry of ensuring the financial integrity of futures markets.[7]

Thus, in futures markets there are really two guarantors: clearing associations and FCMs. The solvency of both is essential to the stability and integrity of futures markets. A key function of the clearing association, therefore, is to regulate clearing members to ensure their solvency. This chapter focuses on the regulations and procedures used by clearing associations to achieve this end.

Potential Pitfalls

The margining system described in the previous section may not be adequate to protect customers under certain circumstances and conditions. For example, if FCMs do not keep customer margin deposits paid up on a daily basis, such deposits may not be sufficient to cover default losses. Because FCMs are required by exchange rules to do so, however, I simply note this as a potential weakness.[8]

Second, if initial margin deposits are too small to cover the movements in futures prices that actually occur, customer default losses may exceed security deposits. Obviously, initial margins must be set high enough to cover potential price movements. Given this need, it is not uncommon for exchanges to set daily price limits and then for initial margins to be based (at least partially) on such limits. This procedure raises the obvious problem that if real prices change by more than the allowed futures daily price limits, margins will not be adequate. Further, because no trading will take place at the price limit, it may be difficult for FCMs and clearing associations to liquidate defaulting customers' positions, so that ultimate losses may substantially exceed initial margin deposits.

Third, in the event of either a sharp run-up in price or a sharp sell-off in the market (as would occur in the collapse of a speculative bubble), it may be difficult or even impossible to liquidate defaulting customers' positions. In such circumstances ultimate losses may not only exceed customer margin deposits but may be so large as to trigger the bankruptcy of a clearing FCM and even a clearing association.[9]

To protect traders against situations where losses may exceed margin deposits, most clearing associations have adopted a host of self-insurance devices to guarantee performance. They have established guarantee funds and have erected elaborate procedures for assessing solvent members to cover the obligations of insolvent members. These schemes are discussed more fully later. In addition, when default losses do exceed margin deposits, the solvency and integrity of clearing member FCMs become critical because it is they who must satisfy customer claims, not clearing associations. The bankruptcy of major clearing FCMs will almost certainly mean that the losses of some customers will have to be borne by other customers. To keep this from happening, clearing associations commonly impose requirements and restrictions on their members, such as minimum capital requirements, reporting requirements, "super" margin requirements, and position limits. Although these limits are designed primarily to protect the integrity of clearing associations, an obvious secondary effect is to make clearing members better able to meet losses in excess of margin deposits, should they occur.

Thus, although initial margin deposits and a system of daily variation margins are the first line of defense against defaults by customers, clearing associations also perform a critical self-regulatory role. They regulate their members to ensure the financial integrity of clearing firms. This function is probably the most important role they perform as guarantor of futures markets.[10]

The Structure and Regulatory Framework of Major Clearing Associations

Table 7–1 is a summary comparison of seven major clearing associations. Six are in the United States; the seventh, the International Commodities Clearing House Limited (ICCH), is in London. The six U.S. clearing associations together clear more than 96 per cent of all U.S. futures trades, while the ICCH clears for most of the major futures exchanges located outside of the United States.[11] The following discussion incorporates the information in table 7–1 and some related issues.[12]

Organizational Structure

Three of the six U.S. clearing operations are organized as separate, not-for-profit clearing corporations, and three are part of an associated futures exchange (the Chicago Mercantile Exchange, the New York Mercantile

Table 7–1
Comparative Analysis of Clearing Associations

Organizational Structure and Solvency Regulations	COMEX	Chicago Mercantile	Chicago Board of Trade	Coffee, Sugar, and Cocoa	N.Y. Mercantile	MidAmerica	International Commodity Clearing House
Organizational structure	Separate affiliated corporation	Clearing association part of exchange	Separate affiliated corporation	Separate affiliated corporation	Clearing association part of exchange	Clearing association part of exchange	Separate corporation owned by six banks
Minimum capital requirements for membership	$1 million net capital	CFTC minimum, but clearing house committee may set higher requirements	$200,000 stated capital; or $50,000 adjusted net capital; or 4 percent of funds required to be segregated, whichever is larger	$1 million net capital	$500,000 net capital	$100,000 net capital	£100,000 to 1 million, depending on commodity
Financial reporting requirements	In compliance with CFTC	In compliance with CFTC	In compliance with CFTC	In compliance with CFTC	In compliance with CFTC	In compliance with CFTC	Annual reports, quarterly net worth
Guaranty fund requirements	$200,000 to $2 million based net worth	$50,000		$100,000 to $500,000 based on net capital	$50,000		
Primary assets used by members to fulfill contribution to guaranty fund	U.S. government securities and bank letters of credit	U.S. government securities and negotiable CDs of accepted banks	NA	U.S. government securities and bank letters of credit	U.S. government securities	NA	NA
Margin requirements—calculation	Net	Gross	Net	Combination of net and gross[a]	Gross	Net	Net on Larger side of a position

Original Margin	Increases with position size	Constant for all position sizes	Constant for all position sizes	Increases with position size	Increases with position size	Constant for all position sizes	May change with position size, at discretion of ICCH
Payment form	Cash, U.S. government securities, of credit	Cash only on CME; also letters of credit on IMM and OIM	Cash, U.S. government securities, letters of credit	Cash, U.S. government securities letters of credit	Cash, U.S. government securities[b]	Cash, U.S. government securities, letters of credit, bullion	Cash, foreign currency, U.K. treasury bills, letters of credit
Investment of margin funds	Interest accrues to clearing association	Interest accrues to clearing members[c]	Interest accrues to members	Interest accrues to clearing association	Interest accrues to clearing members	Interest accrues to clearing members	Interest accrues to ICCH
Variation margin payment form	Cash only	Cash only	Cash only	Cash only	Cash only	Cash only	Same assets acceptable for initial margin
Position limits	Tied to net capital	No fixed position limits, but clearing committee may require more capital the larger the position at its discretion[d]	No fixed position limits, but clearing may impose them on individual members at its discretion	Tied to net capital	Tied to net capital	No fixed position limits	No fixed position limits, but at the descretion of the ICCH
Daily price limits[e]	Yes	Yes	Yes	Yes	Yes	Yes	Depends on specific Exchange[f]
Procedure in event of default: attachable assets and assessment procedure	CM assets Association's guaranty fund Association's surplus funds Pro rata assessment on CM's cleared trades Limited to lower of 25 percent of	CM assets Exchange's trust fund Guaranty fund Exchange's surplus funds Unlimited pro rata rata on net capital, cleared trades, and open	CM assets Association's surplus funds No assessment of members permitted	CM assets Association's guaranty fund Association's surplus funds Pro rata assessment on CM's cleared trades and open interest	CM assets Association's guaranty fund Exchange's surplus funds Unlimited, shared equally by all members of exchange	CM assets Exchange's surplus funds Unlimited, shared equally by all exchange members	CM assets ICCH's capital

(Continued)

Table 7-1 (Continued)

Organizational Structure and Solvency Regulations	COMEX	Chicago Mercantile	Chicago Board of Trade	Coffee, Sugar, and Cocoa	N.Y. Mercantile	MidAmerica	International Commodity Clearing House
	CM's net capital or $10 million Not more than one assessment every ten days[g]	interest		Limited to lower of 25 percent of net capital or $10 million			
Number of members	76	100	155	68	85	35	450
Size of guaranty fund (July 1982)	$75 million	$29 million[h]	NA	$24 million	$2.5 million[i]	NA	NA
Size of surplus funds (July 1982) (either CM or exchange where relevant)	$2.5 million	$30 million	$14 million	$7 million	$6 million	$6 million	£16 to £20 million
Annual contract volume (1981)	13,293,049	24,527,020	49,085,763	3,562,613	1,781,407	2,588,540	4,883,398[j]
Percentage of total U.S. futures trading (1981)	13.49	24.89	49.82	3.62	1.81	2.63	

Note: NA = not applicable; CM = cleaning member.
[a]Net on FCM proprietary accounts; on FCM customer accounts it is net plus the smaller side of gross.
[b]Varies with commodity: for potatoes, only cash is acceptable; for petroleum products, letters of credit are also acceptable.
[c]Except for investment of discount on U.S. Treasury Bills, interest on which accrues to Clearing Association.
[d]There are fixed position limits only for agricultural commodities.
[e]Limits are set by respective exchanges; are different for different commodities; and are usually not imposed in delivery month.
[f]Most Exchanges have intra-day limits: when they are hit the market closes for 30 minutes, after which trading is resumed.
[g]A Clearing Member has the option of resigning from Clearing Association in periods between assessments.
[h]Includes a $24 million trust fund and a $5 million guarantee fund.
[i]When new rules are instituted, fund will rise to about $5 million.
[j]Does not include options.

Exchange, and the MidAmerica Exchange). Those organized as separate corporations are run by independent managers responsible to a board of directors made up of elected members of the clearing corporation. Where the clearing function is part of the exchange itself it is managed by exchange officers responsible to the board of directors of the exchange. When the clearing operation is organized as a separate corporation, exchange members are insulated from the obligations of the corporation and its clearing members; otherwise, they are not.

The ICCH is organized quite differently: it is owned and controlled by six major British banks, none of which are members of an organized futures exchange. It is a profitmaking enterprise, where the owners put their capital at risk in the expectation of earning a profitable return. It is the only clearing association in Britain.

All clearing operations are, to a greater or lesser extent, sensitive to developments taking place on the related futures exchanges. When the clearing operation is part of an exchange itself, the relationship is obvious. Where it is organized as a separate corporation, its policies are still established by members of the affiliated exchange who control its board. In the case of the ICCH, although the controlling banks are not directly involved in the management of futures exchanges, they do nevertheless lend substantial amounts to participants in futures markets.

Margins

There are significant differences in the margining systems used by clearing associations. Some collect initial margins deposits on a gross basis (or according to the total number of contracts held by the clearing member); others on a net basis only (or on the difference between the total long and total short contracts). Also, the Coffee, Sugar and Cocoa Clearing Corporation collects members' customer-margins on a "net plus a smaller side" basis (whether the long or short side). All require lower margins on various straddle positions, where the expected loss is less.[13]

In addition, different kinds of assets can be used by members to satisfy initial margin requirements. Almost all clearing associations accept both cash and U.S. government securities. A increasing trend, however, is to accept letters-of-credit from major banks as well. To satisfy variation margins, all U.S. clearing associations require cash; only the ICCH accepts bank guarantees or letters-of-credit to meet variation margin calls.

Last, members can withdraw from all of the clearing associations their excess margins (or profits). On U.S. clearing associations, such withdrawal is automatic; on the ICCH it is not. The ICCH specifically requires its members to make written requests to withdraw their profits, and approval of such requests is not automatic. This provision probably accounts for ICCH's willingness to accept bank guarantees and letters-of-credit to meet variation margin calls.

There is considerable debate about whether a gross margin system is superior to a net system. Under either system, the total amount of minimum margin deposits collected from the customers of member FCMs is identical. However, in a net system, clearing members hold most of these funds; in a gross system, the clearing association holds all of the funds (assuming that clearing margins are equal to customer margins). If all clearing members properly segregate customer funds (as require by law) and collect variation margins in a timely fashion (as required by exchange rules), there is no meaningful difference between a gross and net system, at least with respect to the security provided by customer margin deposits. An argument that clearing associations should collect margin funds on a gross basis, therefore, is essentially an argument that clearing members cannot be fully relied on to collect and safeguard customers' funds. This stance seems susceptible to empirical examination.[14]

The situation is somewhat different with respect to members' own (or proprietary) accounts. Here, a system of gross margining will increase the security deposits posted by members with clearing associations (compared to a net system). The amounts involved will depend on the positions held by members and on the association's margin policies applicable to straddle and spread positions. However, it is doubtful that this difference will have much bearing on the soundness of clearing members. Clearing associations regulate their members in a number of other ways to ensure their solvency.

A gross margining system also may reduce the earnings of member firms because they may not then be able to earn as great an investment return on customer margin funds. This may have two results: it may require clearing FCMs to increase their commission income by raising customer fees (and therefore customer costs); and, to the extent that they cannot restore their income fully, it may make them more vulnerable to bankruptcy.[15] It is by no means clear that the potential benefits from the possible increase in safety resulting from gross margining will outweigh the potential social costs.

Another related issue is the use of bank letters-of-credit by members to satisfy initial margin requirements. In this case a default by one or more members must be met by the banking system. An important issue, therefore, is whether clearing associations can adequately evaluate the credit-worthiness of commercial banks. Banks do not normally disclose information that is sufficient to make such an assessment. Also, under the present system of eleven clearing associations, members may and often do belong to several clearing associations. Thus, neither clearing associations nor banks have a complete view of the use of bank letters-of-credit to satisfy futures market obligations. Bank regulatory authorities probably do not have such a view either. The integrity of clearing associations, and perhaps of futures markets, is increasingly dependent on the soundness of our major banks, a factor that is largely beyond the control of the futures industry's self-regulatory institutions. Some thought should be given to the implications of this development.

The ICCH epitomizes the use of bank guarantees. Clearing members can satisfy both initial and variation margins with bank guarantees, and the solvency of the clearing corporation depends in the final analysis on the willingness of the major British banks to stand by it. Central banks are more involved with futures markets than they may know.

Other Solvency Regulations

Four additional regulations imposed by clearing associations and exchanges are directed at keeping clearing members solvent. Most clearing associations have minimum capital requirements and position limits; exchanges set daily price limits on futures prices and establish minimum customer margins that all exchange members must observe. Each of these are discussed briefly in this section.

Minimum capital requirements have the obvious purpose of restricting clearing membership to the more financially substantive firms, and, as a consequence, of reducing the probability of member insolvency. Everything else equal, the greater a member's capital, the greater the loss (or variance of return) he can withstand.[16] The higher the capital requirements, however, the fewer clearing members there will be, and the less the competition. At present, existing capital requirements do not seem to be unduly restricting competition.

Position limits are directed at reducing the risk that any single clearing member can assume and, therefore, at limiting the risk exposure of the clearing association to any one of its members. They are, essentially, a requirement that risk be diversified. Some clearing associations have formal restrictions that are clearly enunciated in their rulebooks; others have only informal policies that are applied to members at the discretion of the clearing association management.

In general, position limits are tied to a member's capital: the greater his capital, the larger position he can take. Larger positions increase the variance of a member's earnings distribution, and therefore increase the probability of his insolvency (everything else equal). A requirement of greater capital counteracts this effect—it reduces the probability of bankruptcy, everything else equal.

A criticism of position limits is that they may diminish liquidity in futures markets, because at times they may prevent certain participants from trading. Further, reduced liquidity may increase execution costs and make it more difficult for clearing members to liquidate customer positions in the event of a default, increasing the potential losses to all clearing members. Flexible position limits, such as those tied to capital, minimize but do not eliminate these adverse liquidity effects. Although there is no hard evidence on these issues, the risk-reduction benefits of position limits probably outweigh the costs associated with their possible liquidity effects.

The regulations of clearing associations are supplemented by two futures exchange regulations that are indirectly related to solvency: daily price limits and minimum customer margin requirements. The benefits and costs associated with daily price limits on futures prices are considerably more indefinite than their proponents and critics would have us believe. Two benefits are commonly cited—first, that price limits impose on markets a cooling-off period, during which more rational traders will come to dominate. Without price limits, it is argued, excessive speculative activity would result in more customer defaults. The imposition of daily price limits, therefore, is premised on the assumption that over short periods speculative activity is destabilizing, or that it increases the variance of futures prices. Needless to say, there is little evidence to support or deny this contention.

The second benefit cited is that price limits enable traders to better meet variation margin calls by giving them additional time to raise funds, and by making more predictable the amount of cash they may need during any given period of time. Limits also give the clearing association time to collect member margins and FCMs time to collect customer margins. Against these potential benefits must be weighed the temporary market illiquidity that price limits may create. When price limits are hit, markets close and liquidity is substantially diminished. The magnitude and incidence of the losses associated with this locked-in effect, however, are difficult to assess. In particular, in such instances there may be a liquidity window in the spot month of the contract because price limits are not usually imposed on spot months.[17]

The last related solvency regulation is minimum customer margin requirements imposed by futures exchanges on exchange members (of which a subset are members of the affiliated clearing association). These requirements, presumably, are directed at keeping competition among FCMs from pushing initial customer margins to too low a level, or to levels at which default losses would be unacceptably high. The rationale for minimum customer margins may be the interdependencies that exist in futures markets. If customer defaults are not covered by their margin deposits, FCMs may sustain losses that could threaten their viability. And if FCMs were to default, it could shake confidence in futures markets, sharply curtailing trading and adversely affecting market liquidity.

All FCMs, both clearing and nonclearing, enjoy the fruits that stem from public confidence in the integrity of futures markets. Although the clearing association lies at the heart of this confidence, the soundness of FCMs is, as we have seen, equally important. Nonclearing FCMs, which are not subject to the regulations of clearing associations, may have some incentive to take excessively high risks for the sake of short-run gains. Specifically, by requiring very low margins from customers such as FCM may seek to increase customer demand for its services to increase its current fee income. However, when customers fail to meet their margin calls, the FCM may simply default rather than meet its obligations. If this were to happen all FCMs would suffer the consequences of a reduction in public confidence. That is, there are negative externalities associated with the insolvency of even nonclearing FCMs. Thus, exchange-imposed minimum customer margins are intended to reduce the likelihood of such insolvencies or to keep them to an acceptable level.

Self-Insurance Arrangements

Many clearing associations have self-insurance arrangements to meet potential losses that may occur if some of their members were to become insolvent. Five of the seven clearing associations surveyed had either funded or unfunded schemes (or both); two (the Chicago Board of Trade and the ICCH) had no self-insurance arrangements. By funded I mean the existence of guarantee funds and trusts funds, where clearing members have already paid in assets or obtained independent bank guarantees. By unfunded programs I mean the various ex post assessments schemes that permit associations to assess members to make up default losses. The advantage of the former, of course, is that it leaves no doubt about the willingness and ability of members to meet their obligations when defaults occur, at least to the extent of the guarantee fund's coverage. No historical evidence suggests, however, that members would not meet ex post assessments.

Funded insurance programs increase the costs of clearing members and therefore may either increase customer costs or diminish members' profits (or both), everything else equal. If such arrangements are seen by traders as being safer, however, there may be a net benefit for clearing members.

Since the 1980 Silver Bubble two trends are evident: the increased use of funded self-insurance schemes, and the adoption of limited-liability ex post assessment schemes in place of the traditional "good to the last drop" liability system. Members have limited their liability either through changes in the Associations' rules or by forming separate corporate affiliates for clearing purposes.

Costs

The focus of this chapter is on safety and soundness. An important aspect of clearing operations that is not covered is the efficiency of clearing associations. If greater safety results in higher clearing costs, which in a competitive environment will be passed on to customers, such costs must be weighed against the gain in safety.

Without concrete evidence on clearing costs, two factors seem worth mentioning. The first is the impact of size or scale. Because of the technology that underlies the clearing process, there are clearly some economies of scale in operations. Costs per trade should be lower the greater the contract volume, everything else equal. Just how much lower can only be determined by a sophisticated cost study of clearing associations (which, to my knowledge, has never been done).

The second factor is the role of profits. Of the clearing associations covered in this chapter, only the ICCH is a profitmaking enterprise. All others are not-for-profit institutions that return excess earnings, should they occur, to members.

Do profitmaking clearing associations necessarily mean that users of futures markets will have to bear higher transaction costs, because higher clearing costs are required so that the clearing corporation can make a profit? No. If the amount of invested capital is the same for both a not-for-profit and a profitmaking clearing association, transaction costs should be the same, everything else equal. Members of a not-for-profit association must, one way or another, pass on these costs to customers so that they too can earn a fair (or normal) rate of return on their invested capital. Of course, if the profitmaking clearing corporation also were to have some degree of monopoly power, it might then be able to extract a higher than normal return. But even this situation does not necessarily mean higher transaction costs. If the cause of the monopoly power was a large scale of operations, perhaps because the clearing corporation cleared for many exchanges, it is possible that the cost reductions from economies of scale may offset the monopoly pricing effect.

These are empirical issues, however, about which very little is known. Considerably more research is needed before a judgment can be made about which clearing structure is the most efficient.

Is a Clearing Association Essential to a Futures Market?

Clearing associations in the United States are joint ventures among market participants organized to facilitate the transfer of funds among traders, enable settlements by offset, and ensure the integrity of futures transactions through a system of direct guarantees and solvency regulations aimed at maintaining the soundness of clearing members. As such, they are a key institutional aspect of futures markets.

Could futures markets exist without them? In fact, a well-known futures market, the London Metal Exchange (LME), has operated for nearly 100 years without one. Although it has employed the ICCH since June 1979 to monitor the daily indebtedness of its members, the ICCH does not perform the role of a traditional clearing association. In addition, in the United States the existence of futures markets predated the formal establishment of clearing associations.

Trading on the LME is among principals (ring brokers) only. In the event of a default, traders look solely to these principals for contract performance. To ensure such performance by the brokers, the LME relies on a system of lump-sum guarantees and a compensation fund. In particular, its new members must have capital of at least £500,000, must make a contribution in cash to the compensation fund equal to the average sum currently attributed by the exchange to each of its existing members, and must post bank guarantees of £100,000 to the fund. In addition, the open indebtedness of ring brokers is closely monitored and is continually related to their capital and the guarantees they have given. If necessary, the monitoring committee has wide discretion in the actions it can take to ensure compliance. As a result, the LME also has a system of self-regulation and self-insurance directed at maintaining the financial integrity of its members and of the contracts made on the exchange, but it is a system without a clearing association.

However, an important transaction cannot be effected on the LME but can be on every other futures exchange with a clearing association: settlement by offset. Contracts traded on the LME are standardized (as on other futures exchanges), and can be made for any day up to 90 days forward (but no further). But it is not possible on the LME to eliminate totally a position prior to the settlement date—each contract is a bilateral obligation between principals. There is no clearing association that is a legal party to all contracts and that can enable offset transactions. Although LME traders can at any time remove the price risk on their positions by entering into other offsetting contracts with the appropriate maturity (because the maturity can be of any length up to 90 days), they cannot eliminate all credit risk. In the event of a default by a principal prior to maturity, traders become simple general creditors of that principal. In contrast, closing out a position by offset on a futures exchange eliminates all risks and all legal involvement for the trader.[18]

The ability to settle contracts by offset is a critical element of a futures market. Most contract settlements in futures markets in fact take place this way. Without offset, futures contracts are not liquid financial instruments, and will not attract the same degree of market participation. Once the critical role of settlement by offset is recognized, it is easy to understand why clearing associations have become guarantors and self-regulators. If they are to perform this settlement role effectively, there must be no doubt in the minds of traders about the ability of clearing associations to meet their obligations. Further, to ensure their financial integrity they must regulate and monitor their members so that members remain solvent and are able to meet their own obligations.

A subsidiary issue is whether clearing associations are the most efficient institutional arrangement by which futures exchanges can provide the level of financial integrity they desire. The LME, although not permitting settlement by offset, still has a system to ensure the financial integrity of the exchange and its members (through guarantees, compensation funds, and exchange regulations). Exchanges develop such systems presumably because they increase the attractiveness of trading on the exchange and generate more business and greater profits for members.

To put this issue in another perspective, it can be assumed that futures exchanges wish to produce the optimal level of contract safety, and that this level will depend on the costs of producing such safety and the public's responsiveness to additional amounts of safety. If the use of a clearing association can produce a given level of safety more efficiently (or cheaply) than can alternative schemes, users of futures markets will benefit because their costs will be lower. Alternatively, if clearing associations are more efficient, it can be shown that under reasonable assumptions customers will obtain a greater level of safety than they would otherwise.

An analysis of the circumstances under which the use of a clearing association is the most efficient mechanism for producing safety is beyond the scope of this chapter. Such an analysis, however, would probably show that the important factors are the kind of trading that is desired, the nature of the market participants, the scale of trading, and the structure of competition.

In summary, clearing associations serve an essential function in modern futures markets. Without some version of them, futures markets could not function with as much liquidity as they do today. Further, given the frequency with which they are used, clearing associations are probably the most efficient institutional vehicle for providing the desired level of liquidity and financial integrity in futures markets.

Some Unresolved Issues

There are a number of important unresolved issues related to clearing associations. Some of these involve questions about the role of government regulation; others are industry matters.

Consolidation of Clearing Associations

In the United States, there are eleven organized futures exchanges, each with its own clearing operation, all operating independently of one another, with different rules and regulations. In England, one clearing association serves some ten different futures exchanges. Should U.S. clearing associations be consolidated into a few, or even a single, clearing corporation?

The possible benefits of consolidation are reasonably clear. First, there would probably be some economies of scale in operations, but just how much is unknown. Second, to the extent that clearing membership is expanded, risks can be diversified more. This benefit should not be exaggerated, however, because most large clearing firms are already members of all the major clearing associations. Third, because many clearing firms are members of more than one clearing association, consolidation can eliminate costly duplicative surveillance and auditing functions.[19] Fourth, it will result in better information about members' aggregate positions. At present, there is little exchange of information among clearing associations. Fifth, consolidation would permit greater risk sharing than now occurs, so that overall guarantee fund requirements could be lowered; or, alternatively, the same level of protection could be maintained at a lower cost to members. Sixth, the interdependencies among clearing associations would be better appreciated and perhaps better handled if they were consolidated. Specifically, demands made by one clearing association on its members may have adverse effects on other clearing associations because its members may belong to other clearing associations as well. There is presently no overview of such repercussions. Seventh, consolidation would result in uniform rules that would reduce the information and transaction costs of clearing members who now trade on many exchanges.

The negatives associated with consolidation are less clear, but may still be significant. First, consolidation may reduce competition. It will obviously reduce the number of clearing associations, and will probably reduce the number of clearing FCMs. To take a worst-case scenario, if there were only one clearing association, its members could set monopoly clearing prices that would be passed through to nonclearing firms and traders and ultimately to customers. Under the existing institutional arrangement of many clearing associations, clearing costs (and therefore trading costs) are one factor (albeit a small one) that potential users of futures markets may take into consideration when deciding which exchange to trade on. Thus, the impact of consolidation on competition in the clearing function needs to be assessed carefully. Second, although consolidation may spread risks, it may arguably make the entire futures industry vulnerable to a catastrophic event in a single commodity. Such an event might now bankrupt only one clearing association; with a consolidated clearing association, it may bring down everyone.

In view of these competing considerations, one solution may be partial consolidation: consolidation into not one but two or three clearing corporations. This proposal may capture most of the benefits of consolidation but still preserve a sufficient degree of competition. Alternatively, partial consolidation (or cooperation) along certain functional or operational lines may be feasible, although it clearly will not capture all of the potential benefits. In particular, risk-sharing via a pooled industry guarantee fund would result in reduced costs as well as greater protection for everyone. All of this, however, abstracts from the many historical, political, and human obstacles to consolidation.

Private Insurance

Clearing associations generally do not insure any of their exposure with private, independent insurance companies. To do so would be another way of diversifying their risk. The most likely role for private insurers, if they have any interest at all, is as limited co-insurers with the clearing association. The usual function of insurance is to insure risks that are independent of one another or that are random events. Where losses are subject to cataclysmic events, such as nuclear war, insurance is not feasible. Similarly, insurance against events in futures markets such as the collapse of a speculative bubble are probably not insurable. The random and occasional failure of a customer, an FCM, or a clearing member is insurable. Thus, clearing associations may be able to obtain private insurance up to a specified loss, but not beyond that amount. Indeed, even if open-ended insurance could be obtained, one would have to wonder about its reliability. Insurance companies go bankrupt too.[20]

Private insurance companies also would be best suited to be a co-insurer, insuring, say, 50 per cent of the losses. This level would preserve the proper incentives for clearing associations to monitor, police, and regulate their members to assure solvency. Otherwise, private insurers would have to perform these functions, and it is unlikely that they could do it as effectively. Whether even this limited role for private insurers is feasible depends, of course, on relative costs. Can insurers better diversify default risk in futures markets than can clearing members? Are there further economies of scale to be gained? In short, it is not at all obvious that introducing private insurers would be advantageous. Indeed, there is no apparent reason why we should rely more on the solvency of insurance companies (and on the ability of insurance regulators) than upon the soundness of clearing associations.

Limited vs. Unlimited Liability of Clearing Members

Knowing a clearing association's rules, regulations, procedures, and total funds available to meet defaults, and even the ability of its management, although essential, is not enough to make a comparative assessment of its relative soundness. Something also must be known about the actual or potential risk exposure of clearing associations. Further, this exposure varies from day to day as the open positions of members and their customers change and as market conditions change. Information about trading positions is commonly kept confidential so that competing traders cannot take advantage of it. Indeed, a benefit of having an independent clearing operation is that clearing members know that when they reveal their trading positions to it such information will be treated confidentially. It is unlikely, therefore, that clearing associations will ever be in a position to make public the kind of information that would be required for outsiders to evaluate their overall risk in dealing with a particular association.

Without an outside evaluation (or market test) of their soundness, the safety of clearing associations must necessarily rest solely with their managers and with the governing clearing members. Thus, it is essential that these responsible parties have incentives consistent with the welfare of both the industry and the public. A traditional device employed in the futures industry for ensuring the proper incentives is to make clearing members unlimitedly liable for all losses that may occur because of a default by any member.

The trend toward limiting member liability marks a significant break with this tradition. This trend is happening in two ways: by changes in membership rules that directly limit liability to specific amounts, and by the growing use by members of lower-capitalized clearing affiliates. This trend bears careful watching. It is vital that we maintain clear and sufficient economic incentives for members to monitor, police, and enforce their own rules and regulations.[21]

Explicit vs. Discretionary Rules

In recent years a split has developed among clearing associations with respect to their regulatory approaches. Some, particularly those in New York, have adopted quite formal and explicit rules and regulations; others, especially in Chicago, have retained the traditional discretionary philosophy.

An example of this difference is their disparate approaches to position limits. The New York associations have established position limits that are explicitly related to a member's capital. Clearing members know at the outset that if they want to hold positions greater than those specified in the rules they will have to increase the amount of their capital (or reduce the size of some of their positions). In contrast, the Chicago associations frequently have no fixed position limits, or none that are set forth in the association's rules and that are applied indiscriminately to all members. The imposition of such limits is left to the discretion of the clearing association (or to the clearing management or to a clearing committee) and will depend upon the general circumstances and perhaps a particular trader's situation. Thus, the Chicago associations would seem to have greater flexibility to deal with specific cases as they arise.[22]

The pros and cons of these alternative approaches are fairly clear. On the one hand, formal and explicit rules give clearing members (and their customers) more predictability. They know at the beginning what the rules are, and therefore what can be demanded of them. This minimizes regulator uncertainty, and should lower transaction costs. (However, on occasion, formal rules may increase such costs by requiring that unnecessary or even counterproductive rules be imposed.) On the other hand, discretionary rules give clearing associations greater latitude to protect members and can be tailored to the circumstances. Thus, the gain in customer predictability is at the cost of clearing association flexibility.

Exactly where the balance should be struck is difficult to judge. However, one thing is certain. The growing differences in regulatory philosophy and approach among clearing associations are and will continue to be a source of confusion, both to firms that are members of many associations and to their customers.

Is There a Role for Government?

Aside from having general oversight responsibility, government regulation presently plays no role in assuring the solvency of clearing associations. Should it? Is there an externality that associations are somehow failing to internalize? Do associations set margin deposits, position limits, capital requirements, and guaranty fund requirements that are too low or at levels producing a level of clearing association soundness below that which is consistent with the public's welfare?

Clearing members have a direct and obvious stake in the soundness of their associations. They have a significant personal liability in the event of a default, and their entire livelihood depends on the prosperity of futures markets, of which public confidence is a key ingredient. They also are in the best position to evaluate the costs of additional rules to increase soundness, as well as to appraise the effects of these costs on the users of futures markets. If public confidence in futures markets is less than optimal, it would seem to be in the interest of clearing members to establish rules that will increase it. Thus, at least on the surface there is no reason to suspect that clearing associations will adopt a standard of soundness inconsistent with the public's welfare. Alternatively stated, there do not appear to be any major externalities.[23]

Another argument commonly used to support greater government involvement in self-regulated industries is that there are potentially destructive conflicts of interest. At times, it is feared, self-regulators may take unfair advantage of outsiders. In futures markets, in particular, self-regulators are themselves heavy users of the market, and may at times have trading positions that clash with their regulatory responsibilities.

This issue is in all self-regulated industries and is obviously not a simple one. However, there are probably fewer areas for potential conflicts on clearing organization boards than on contract market boards. In any case, the potential for conflicts, I believe, calls only for some form of government oversight responsibility, not for more direct government participation. Clearing associations must, nevertheless, continually examine their procedures with an eye to eliminating potential conflicts of interest. There are clear benefits to a self-regulatory system that must be balanced against the occasional inequities which may arise because of conflicts of interest.[24]

Finally, it may be argued that government has, at least implicitly, a responsibility as the lender of last resort. An unusual and unanticipated event, or an occasional episode of speculative excesses (not unknown in the history of financial markets), may threaten the viability of clearing associations and perhaps even the entire financial system. In such circumstances, it is argued, government regulators, and the Federal Reserve in particular, must be prepared to step in and diffuse the crisis.

Although such a disaster is always a possibility, however remote, few industries have done more to protect against its occurrence than the futures industry. The entire focus of this chapter has been on the elaborate safeguards that have been erected in futures markets to prevent such a collapse. As futures markets expand in size and scope, I also would expect these safeguards to be adjusted accordingly. In summary, none of the foregoing arguments suggest a need for more government regulation of clearing associations.

Notes

1. The five are the Chicago Mercantile Exchange, the New York Mercantile Exchange, the MidAmerica Exchange, the Minneapolis Grain Exchange, and the New Orleans Commodity Exchange. See appendix 7A.

2. Where the clearing operation is part of the exchange, it is managed by officers of the exchange, who are responsible to the board of directors of the exchange itself.

3. The account is carried in the name of the originating FCM; the underlying customers are unknown to the receiving or clearing FCM.

4. Exchanges require that exchange members impose minimum margins on their customers: clearing associations establish them for clearing members. FCMs are free to impose margins on their customers higher than the exchange minimum. In addition, CFTC Regulation Section 1.58 re-

quires an FCM that maintains an omnibus account at another FCM to collect initial and maintenance margins on a level no less than that established for customer accounts by the rules of the applicable contract market. Finally, to simplify, no distinction between original (or initial) margins and maintenance margins is made in the above example.

5. Minimum initial margins are often set in a way that reflects daily price limits, but there is no necessary relationship. The use of daily price limits, and their relationship to initial margins, is discussed later in this chapter.

6. The customer margin funds held by FCMs must be placed in segregated customer accounts. 7 U.S.C. Section 6d(2); *CCH Commodity Futures Law Reporter,* Section 1071, at pp. 1564–1565.

7. An instructive parallel may be the Federal Deposit Insurance Corporation (FDIC) guaranteeing commercial bank deposits. In our case, the clearing association would be in the role of the FDIC, and FCMs in the role of banks. The effect of FDIC deposit insurance on diluting the soundness of banks is well understood. See, for example, Sam Peltzman, "Captial Investment in Commercial Banking and Its Relationship to Portfolio Regulation," *Journal of Political Economy* (78:1), January 1970, p.3.

8. A subsidiary issue is determining when the clearing association and the FCM obligations begin to run: when the trade is cleared, or when the customer posts margin (which is often a day later)? Typically, clearing organizations require that original margin on new positions be paid on the morning after the position is established. Variation margin may be called at any time during the day; if additional variation margin is due, it too is payable the next morning. In general, the time within which a customer must meet a margin call is determined by a combination of the customer's agreement with his FCM, exchange rules, and CFTC Regulation Section 1.17, which imposes capital charges if margins are not made in a timely fashion.

9. Although no U.S. clearing association has ever failed to meet its obligations, in 1974 the Bourse de Commerce de Paris, the clearing organization for the Paris futures markets, did default. The French clearing organization is now the Banque Centrale de Compensation.

10. Nonclearing FCMs are not regulated by clearing associations. However, nonclearing FCMs that are contract market members are subject to regulation by the relevant contract markets, and FCMs that are not members of any contract market are regulated by the National Futures Association. The CFTC, of course, has jurisdiction over all FCMs.

11. The ICCH provides full services to all market associations on the London Commodity Exchange Co. Ltd.: the London Cocoa Terminal Market Association Ltd., the Coffee Terminal Market Association of London Ltd., the London Rubber Terminal Market Association Ltd., the Gafta Soybean Meal Futures Association Ltd., the United Terminal Sugar Market Association Ltd., The London Vegetable Oil Terminal Market

Association Ltd., and The London Wool Terminal Market Association Ltd. In addition, it provides full services to the London Potato Futures Association Ltd., to the newly organized London International Financial Futures Exchange, and to the Sydney Futures Exchange Ltd.; and, through subsidiaries, it clears for the Hong Kong Commodity Exchange and the Kuala Lumpur Commodity Exchange, and has a reciprocal arrangement with Banque Centrale de Compensation, the French clearing organization in Paris.

12. This information was compiled from clearing association rulebooks and publications and through personal interviews with the managements of the associations covered in table 7–1.

13. All clearing associations can and do change the structure of their margin requirements from time to time, depending on market conditions. However, on December 3, 1980, as an example, the N.Y. Coffee and Sugar Clearing Association required an original margin of $6,500 a contract on a net position of 1,000 or fewer contracts of no. 11 sugar, but only $2,500 a contract on a straddle position in the same contract. Lower margins are required on straddle positions because there is less exposure.

14. Another complication is that clearing organizations, depending on the margin system they are using, may not impose similar original margin requirements (relative to risk or to their exposure). I understand that such margins tend to be lower where margin is collected on a gross basis.

15. Which of these two effects will dominate depends on the state of competition in the market for FCM services.

16. Although capital requirements may be redundant in a theoretical world of perfect capital markets where all firms have ready access to credit, this is probably not the scenario that would characterize an insolvency situation in futures markets.

17. There also is the danger that customers may think of price limits as some sort of safety net that minimizes their maximum potential losses. They could not, of course, be more mistaken.

18. Closing out a position with the same ring broker, which may be preferable from a credit risk perspective, may put the trader at a competitive disadvantage. Even this procedure does not insulate the traders' profits, however.

19. New York clearing associations have already agreed to effectively consolidate such functions for firms dealing on the New York exchanges.

20. I have been informed that efforts by clearing associations to obtain private insurance to cover massive failure have been unsuccessful, even with very large deductibles.

21. Another argument against unlimited liability is that it imposes unacceptable costs on clearing members, and may as a consequence reduce the numbers of members, as well as cause them to limit their liability in other ways.

22. The ability of clearing managements to use such power, of course, also depends on the nature of their clearing organization and their position in it. In some cases explicit rules may enhance rather than diminish the power of clearing officials to impose restrictions on their members because these officials may not have a strong political base within their own exchanges. In addition, depending on their specific by-laws and rules, clearing associations with explicit rules may still be able to deviate from rules under a broad range of circumstances.

23. Although some observers have argued that customer margin requirements are set too low, the focus of their argument has not been the solvency of clearing associations. In addition, this argument is more relevant to the minimum margins set by futures exchanges. For a discussion of these arguments, see my recent paper "Futures Markets in Transition: The Uneasy Balance Between Government and Self-Regulation," January 1983.

24. Ibid.

Appendix 7A
Organized Futures Exchanges and Associated Clearing Associations in the United States

Futures Exchanges

Chicago Board of Trade

Board of Trade of Kansas City, Missouri

Chicago Mercantile Exchange

Coffee, Sugar and Cocoa Exchange, Inc.

Commodity Exchange Inc.

MidAmerica Commodity Exchange

Minneapolis Grain Exchange

New Orleans Commodity Exchange

New York Cotton Exchange

New York Futures Exchange

New York Mercantile Exchange

Clearing Associations

Chicago Board of Trade Clearing Corporation

Grain Clearing Company of Kansas City, Missouri

Chicago Mercantile Exchange*

Coffee, Sugar and Cocoa Exchange Clearing Corporation

Commodity Exchange Clearing Association Inc.

MidAmerica Commodity Exchange*

---

*Clearing operation is part of the exchange.

Minneapolis Grain Exchange*

New Orleans Commodity Exchange*

New York Cotton Exchange Commodity Clearing Corporation

New York Futures Clearing Corporation

New York Mercantile Exchange

---

*Clearing operation is part of the exchange.

Comment

James M. Stone

The Columbia Center for the Study of Futures Markets is making a fine contribution to this rarified field, both through its support of the *Journal of Futures Markets* and through the conference that led to this book. Frank Edward's chapter, like that of Pete Kyle (chapter 5) breaks new ground. Where Kyle's work represents a theoretical advance, Edward's exploration of the clearing process is thoroughly practical. Clearing is one of the least understood aspects of the futures trading system; Edwards' work, which clears up some of the misconceptions, is surely welcome.

This chapter strikes me as making two distinct contributions. The first, a long descriptive essay, distills and analyzes the clearing function and its mechanisms. To the best of my knowledge, it is the most lucid piece available on that topic. The second is a brief collection of assertions on major issues of public policy. The author candidly admits they are gut reactions and do not automatically follow from the text. I am most comfortable viewing the whole as a sound contribution to an understanding of the role of clearing with an addendum raising some issues fit for further exploration by the center.

I can not resist, however, giving my own equally unsupported views on the points of controversy. One issue raised is whether gross margining should be required. As Edwards has properly stated, if the clearing houses paid interest on funds they held, the issue would be largely one of whom do you trust. Gross margining places relatively less reliance on the financial health and business judgment of the various clearing members and more on the clearing association itself. Net margining places trust with the FCMs. Recent history has shown that clearing members occasionally do exercise poor judgment, particularly when facing financial difficulty or when very large customer accounts are involved. The result can be injury not only to the member firm itself and its customers but to the strength and soundness of the entire system.

Edwards's principal argument against gross margining is that it might impede financial diligence. He fears it would threaten the competitive incentive for clearing members to maintain good reputations for financial health in the hope of attracting customers. The assumption that customers choose their clearing members on the basis of the member's fiscal integrity is not, in my view, robust. Many public customers, and particularly smaller ones, do not even know which firm is clearing their trades. There is not much evidence, such as from the advertising used by futures commission merchants, that public customers would be interested in the clearing firm's financial condition even if they did know its identity. And those customers who did wish to be informed would not be able to discover the necessary information for an assessment, because large position exposures and margining arrangements with other large accounts is closely held and confidential. The analysis Edwards envisions should probably have been identified only with the largest and most sophisticated of customers.

On the questions of consolidation of clearing associations, I find Edwards's reasoning fairly comprehensive. He has addressed the benefits to be gained by pooling the resources and the risks into larger units. An additional benefit of consolidation might be the pooling of information on position concentration that now eludes any individual clearing associations. If I have any dispute with Edwards on this matter it is on whether there really are any advantages to competition among rival clearing associations. As he notes, they are very important self-regulators, and I am unaware of any theoretical case for competition among regulators.

Edwards's overall conclusion—that is the present level of regulation of clearing associations is appropriate—rests on his assertion that there are "no major externalities" involved. This statement is puzzling because it seems clear enough that the framework in which the owners of clearing associations operate is the maximization of trading within constraints of safety; the public's concern is for maximum solvency assurance with far less of a stake in volume. The result may be an emphasis by the associations on rules that promote day-to-day volume at the expense of crisis protection while the preferable social perspective may be the opposite. I remember all too well that shortly after the silver crisis, one expert wrote that any demands on FCMs for clearing house assessments would result in phone calls to their lawyers, not their bankers.

Because my own views on these policy points are widely known, let me offer a few predictions rather than restate my personal preferences. First, with respect to gross margining, I expect to see an increasing movement in that direction even without a push from government. The FCM community is no longer a small comfortable family. We received very few adverse industry comments when the commission recently required gross margining on the part of nonmember FCMs. As the total cumulative count of insolvencies rises, so will the demand for either gross margining or a customer insurance mechanism or both. Second, on the unification of clearing organizations, administrative and operational economies will push toward a partial consolidation. Within a few years we will probably see fewer clearing houses, although the politics of clearing will most likely prevent a complete consolidation. Third, I predict that federal government involvement in setting commodity futures margins will grow—not for the reasons I would wish, but rather to satisfy a demand for parity with the increasingly similar instruments regulated under the securities margining regime. It was one thing to distinguish corn from common shares. It will be harder to distinguish options on stock indices from options on stock index futures.

Comment

Hans R. Stoll

Active U.S. futures markets meet two general conditions. First, the underlying commodity is standardized and in large supply. The traditional requirements of storability and deliverability are no longer mandatory (for example, the existence of futures in fresh eggs and the use of cash settlement in stock index futures). Second, an active secondary market is made possible by the clearing house that handles the mechanics of trading by offset and acts as a guarantor of transactions, thereby ensuring the financial integrity of the trading system and making possible trading among strangers. Without the clearing house, trading would take place in a forward market directly between two parties. Reversal of forward contracts is cumbersome. As evidence of the benefits of the clearing house and organized exchanges, one can cite the tremendous growth in Chicago Board Options Exchange trading as compared with OTC options trading. The OTC options market offers virtually no secondary market and transaction costs are high. Investors attempting to reverse contracts before maturity are at the mercy of the option originator. Certain forward markets, such as the interbank forward exchange market, work well because the participants are major institutions that are not strangers to each other. Nevertheless, delivery is much more common than in a futures markets.

Edwards has written an excellent chapter and I have no major criticisms. It makes clear the importance of the clearing house and provides valuable information on how clearing houses are organized and function in different futures markets. There are a few points I would like to touch on.

His chapter shows that the financial integrity of a futures market is guaranteed by regulation of the members of the clearing house. First, clearing house members are subject to regulations that are intended to minimize the chance of default (member margins and super margins, position limits, capital requirements, and reporting requirements). Second, the clearing house establishes a guarantee fund or makes arrangement for ex post assessment in the event of default of any of its members. (The relatively small size of most of the guarantee funds reported in table 7–1 is quite surprising.)

Its most striking aspect (and of futures markets) is the emphasis on protecting firms rather than on protecting customers. This may be a semantic distinction because a market in which firms never fail also protects customers. The securities markets, in which regulations emphasize the protection of customers, have probabily not had a more successful record of guarding against the failure of brokerage firms. Nevertheless, it seems important and relevant to examine in more detail the position of the customer.

257

I was surprised to learn that the customer does not have a contract with a clearing house. Instead he has a contract only with his futures commission merchant (FCM). If the FCM fails, what recourse does the customer have? Presumably the customer has priority in a bankruptcy on his initial margin deposit, which is supposed to be segregated. But what if the margin deposit has been illegally used by the FCM, and what if the FCM has failed to supply the necessary variation margin that belongs in the customer's account?

A customer in a clearing house member firm has some protection against bankruptcy because the clearing house regulates its members to minimize the change of bankruptcy. What is the position of the customer of a nonclearing house firm? I was surprised to learn that futures markets do not appear to impose any minimum capital requirements or similar rules on its members. In securities markets such rules have been imposed by the exchanges and by the Securities and Exchange Commission.

It appears that the ultimate source of financial integrity of futures markets lies in the system of margins. The margin supplied by the customer to his broker and by the broker to the clearing house are intended to ensure that contractual commitments will be met. Two issues arise. First, should one rely on only one mechanism for maintaining the financial integrity of the system? Will the system protect against poor bookkeeping, back office jams, or crooks? I do not mean to imply by this question that federal regulators should necessarily impose additional financial requirements on FCMs. Indeed, every futures market has a tremendous incentive to ensure its financial integrity and, therefore, the financial integrity of its members. This is not an area in which one would ordinarily suppose federal regulation would be necessary. On the other hand, the lack of additional mechanisms for protecting customers suggests that futures markets may want to modify their regulations to provide greater assurance to customers.

A second issue that deserves greater investigation is the basis for setting the margins. This question is particularly difficult because the appropriate margin is a characteristic of the investor rather than of the transaction. The appropriate margin on a long position in a futures contract depends on whether that contract is hedged and on the total portfolio position of the customer holding the contract. A customer with a well-diversified portfolio is in a much less risky position than is a customer whose entire wealth is committed to the futures contract. Although some important work has been done in this area by Lester Telser (1981) additional research is clearly warranted.

Aside from the role of the clearing house in maintaining the financial integrity of futures markets, Edwards examines industrial organization issues of a more traditional sort. In this regard, it seems to me that more data could usefully be provided on the size and timeseries behavior of clearing house fees and on the level of services. He addresses an issue of industry structure; namely, the benefits and costs of consolidating clearing houses. There are obvious economies of scale in centralizing clearing of all transactions in a given futures contract. However, the benefits of clearing different contracts in a single clearing house are not nearly so straightforward. As Edwards points out, the clearing house is perfectly hedged and is margined with respect to both its long and short positions. It therefore has no need to diversify against commodity price risk (as an investor might want to). The concern is that a clearing house member may default on its contractual obligations. Separate clearing houses—one for each futures market—insulate against such a default on a particular futures market. Consolidation of clearing houses might subject the entire industry to financial difficulty (as Edwards notes). In addition, consolidation of clearing houses might reduce the total margin in the industry because it might be argued that offsetting contracts in similar commodities traded in different futures markets should be subject to lower margin.

In summary, the two points that have concerned me are (1) whether regulation of the financial integrity of futures markets in the interest of exchange members adversely affects customers, and (2) whether consolidation of clearing houses is desirable. Regardless of one's position on these questions (my tentative answer to both questions is no), each deserves more careful consideration. However, these issues, in large part, go beyond the main purpose of this chapter and should not detract from the significant contribution it makes to our understanding of the structure and functioning of clearing houses in U.S. futures markets.

Reference

Telser, Lester (1981) "Margins and Futures Contracts," *Journal of Futures Markets* (1:2), pp. 225–253.

8 Self-Regulating Commodity Futures Exchanges

Garth Saloner

Trading on commodity futures exchanges is subject to a plethora of regulations. They range from questions of exchange government and membership to the details of which commodities will be traded, when they may be traded, and minimum and maximum daily price fluctuations. Although supervision of U.S. exchanges falls under the jurisdiction of the Federal Regulatory Agency for Futures Trading, to a large extent the commodity exchanges are self-regulating.

Given the large volume of commodities that are sold through these exchanges, the question of the impact of this self-regulation on the welfare of the participants is of corresponding importance. Because of the large volume of transactions, the speed with which traders can respond to changes in market conditions, and the large number of potential traders, these markets are often put forward as working examples of the ideal of perfect competition. However, to evaluate the welfare implications of the self-regulating bodies and to decide what kind of outside regulation, if any, is called for, an understanding of the effect of self-imposed regulation is required.

This chapter has two objectives. The first is to provide a simple model of self-regulating commodity exchange. Although the model presented here is too simple to base strong welfare statements and regulatory imperatives on, it does suggest that the issues are important and are worthy of further investigation. Further, the model emphasizes the importance of replacing the neoclassical Walrasian auctioneer by its real-life institutional counterpart. The costs of transacting when market power is held by intermediaries may result in a suboptimal quantity of output and a very different distribution of income than when these transactions costs are not present.

The second objective of the chapter is to illustrate that when certain institutional details are taken into account, equilibria may exist that do not exist when these details are ignored (or their characteristics may be substantially altered). In particular, a familiar result in the industrial organization literature is that a Bertrand equilibrium when there is excess capacity

I would like to thank Ron Anderson for suggesting the topic and for useful discussions. Partial support for this research from the Center for the Study of Futures Markets, Columbia Business School, is gratefully acknowledged.

results in a marginal cost-pricing rule (and associated losses when there are fixed costs). The model presented here illustrates that the rules of organization within a single commodity exchange may result instead in a zero-profit equilibrium.

The Model with A Single Exchange

We consider a commodity that is perfectly inelastically supplied by a large number of identical farmers. Let the amount supplied by each farmer be q_i units and the total supply be Q units. Although supply is assumed to be completely deterministic, the demand for the commodity when harvested is uncertain at the time of planting. Thus the inverse demand function is given by $P(q, \tilde{\varepsilon})$ where q is the amount demanded and $\tilde{\varepsilon}$ is a stochastic term with distribution function $F(\tilde{\varepsilon})$ representing the uncertainty. We think of the income derived by the farmers from the sale of the crop as contributing a sufficiently large part of their total incomes that they are risk-averse to the price outcome. Letting the vector X denote other arguments of the farmers' utility functions, we define the farmer's certainty-equivalent $\bar{P}$ implicitly by

$$U(\bar{P}q_i; X) = \int_\varepsilon U(P(q, \tilde{\varepsilon})q_i, X)dF(\tilde{\varepsilon})$$

the farmer is indifferent at the time of planting between a certain price P that is, or the gamble represented by the uncertain future price. The expected price is given by $P^* \equiv \int_\varepsilon P(q, \tilde{\varepsilon})dF(\tilde{\varepsilon})$. We have $P^* > \bar{P}$ by the assumption of the farmers' risk-aversion.

We assume the existence of a group of risk-neutral speculators. These individuals, presumably because they are able to diversify away the idiosyncratic risk associated with the commodity or because they can hold sufficiently small quantities of it, are prepared to purchase a futures contract for the commodity at the time of planting for the expected price P^*. The gains from trade (the value of the insurance to farmers) from matching farmers (hedgers) with speculators is thus given by $P^* - \bar{P}$ per unit. The question to be examined is how a self-regulating commodity exchange distributes these gains from trade among the hedgers, speculators, and the exchange itself.

To begin, we suppose that it is prohibitively costly for individual farmers to search out individual speculators and to enter into private futures contracts.[1] Thus farmers can either bear the risk associated with the price uncertainty by waiting until the commodity is harvested and selling it on the spot market or else they can sell the commodity forward through the futures exchange. The supply and demand for the commodity at the time of planting are therefore as given in figure 8–1.

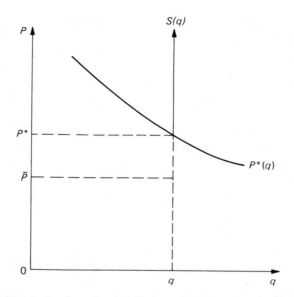

Figure 8-1. Supply and Demand of Futures Contracts

In this section we examine the case where a single exchange board has the monopoly over trades in futures contracts. The exchange has fixed costs of F per period; F represents not only the start-up costs of providing the physical premises but also the costs of screening potential speculators. The board is assumed to act to maximize the total profits of its members (traders), to have the freedom to regulate the number of members N and to specify a sharing rule by which individual members will be charged for the joint fixed cost of the exchange F. Thus a constitution for the exchange consists of the pair $\{N, \Phi(\cdot)\}$ where $\Phi = \{\Phi_1, \ldots, \Phi_N\}$ is the rule specifying the amount of the fixed costs each trader is to pay. We do not restrict the arguments that $\Phi(\cdot)$ can take. For example, Φ could specify that the fixed costs will be shared equally by the members or in proportion to their respective volumes of trade.

The N traders are assumed to be profit-maximizing and to face private fixed costs f and constant marginal costs (normalized to be zero), as well as the costs levied by the board, and to have a capacity for k trades per period. To avoid integrability problems we assume that $N^* \equiv Q/k$ is an integer. Trader i is assumed to be free to charge any commission c_i per trade. This commission can be interpreted as a bid-asked spread. We assume that traders act noncooperatively in setting the commissions. Obviously, hedgers and speculators favor the trader with the lowest commissions.

The N traders are therefore involved in a game that is formally equivalent to that of the Bertrand game of an industry consisting of firms compet-

ing in prices with individual capacity constraints. The only difference is that
here they face additional joint fixed costs. It is well known that the Bertrand
game with capacity constraints either admits of no pure strategy Nash
equilibrium or, if fixed costs are sunk, has an equilibrium in which the firms
set price equal to marginal cost and make losses equal to their fixed costs. As
will be shown, the presence of the joint fixed costs alters the picture
considerably.

Let $\Pi^i(c_i, c_{-i})$ denote trader i's profits when he charges commission c_i
and the vector of the other trader's commissions is c_{-i}. Then given the
constitution $\{N, \Phi\}$, a pure strategy Nash equilibrium is defined in the usual
way to be an n-tuple $\{c^*_1, \ldots, c^*_N\}$ such that $\Pi^i(c^*_i, c^*_{-i}) \geq \Pi^i(c_i, c^*_{-i})$
for all i and all $c_i \neq c^*_{-i}$.

We impose four restrictions on Φ:

1. Nonnegativity: $\Phi_i \geq 0$ for all i
2. Budget balance: If $\Sigma^n_{i=1}(\Pi^i + \Phi_i) \geq F$ then $\Sigma^n_{i=1}\Phi_i = F$
3. Anonymity: If traders i and j have concluded the same volumes of trades
   than $\Phi_i = \Phi j$
4. Joint liability: If $\Sigma^n_{i=1}\Pi^i < 0$ then $\Pi^i < 0$ for all i.

Conditions (1) and (3) are straightforward. The budget-balance condition ensures that the joint fixed costs are paid if the exchange members
jointly have sufficient profits to cover them. The joint liability condition
requires that the traders be jointly and severally liable for all joint fixed
costs. This condition disallows the exchange from proclaiming bankruptcy
while individual members have made profits. Put another way, it requires
that in the event that some traders declare bankruptcy, the other traders will
be called on to cover the fixed costs. As we will show, these institutional
details prevent the kind of cutthroat competition that results in unprofitable
prices in the Bertrand model.

The outcome of the noncooperative game between the traders and the
relationship between this outcome and the constitution $\{N, \Phi\}$ are summarized in the following proposition:

PROPOSITION 1. *Under any constitution that satisfies nonnegativity, anonymity, joint liability, and budget-balancing, the unique pure strategy Nash equilibrium is given by:*

$$c^*_i = \begin{cases} P^* - \bar{P} & \text{for all } i \text{ if } N \leq N^* \\ \dfrac{N}{Q}\left[f + \dfrac{F}{N}\right] & \text{for all } i \text{ otherwise} \end{cases}$$

Proof. The case $N \leq Q/k$ is trivial. If $c_i > P^* - \bar{P}$, hedgers will choose to
sell their output on the spot market. Therefore, $P^* - \bar{P}$ serves as a natural

upper bound on c and can be interpreted as the monopoly price. When $c = P^* - \bar{P}$ traders not only receive the monopoly price but also work to capacity k. Clearly none will have an incentive to deviate. Now suppose $N > N^*$; that is, $Q > kN$. Consider trader j and suppose $c_i = c^* = N/Q\,[\,f + F/N\,]$ for all $i \neq j$. If trader j sets $c = c^*$ he earns $\Pi^i = c^*N/Q - f_i - \Phi_i$. This result implies that all the traders have identical trades and by anonymity, $\Phi_1 = \Phi_2 = \ldots = \Phi_N$. But then budget-balancing implies $\Phi_i = F/N$ for all i. Therefore $\Pi^i = Q/N\,[N/Q\,(\,f + F/N)\,] - f - F/N = 0$. Suppose j sets $c > c^*$. Then since Q/k is an integer, $Q/k \geq N + 1$. Hedgers and speculators prefer the traders charging c^* who will therefore consummate all the trades because they have sufficient capacity. Accordingly, trader j earns $\Pi^j = -f - \Phi_j$, which is negative because $\Phi_j \geq 0$ by nonnegativity. Now suppose j sets $c < c^*$. Since j is the low-commission trader he is able to trade k units at a charge of c per unit. Trader j therefore has revenues of ck. The traders other than trader j have total revenues of $[Q - k]c^*$. Thus total exchange revenue is $Qc^* - k(c^* - c) = N\,[f + F/N] - k(c^* - c)$. But total fixed costs are $N[f + F/N]$. Accordingly, since $c^* > c$ and $k > 0$, total profits $= N[f+F/N] - k(c^*-c) - N[f + F/N]$ are negative. But then the joint liability condition ensures that no trader makes a profit. In particular $\Pi^j(c_j, c^*_{-j}) < 0$.

In equilibrium, commissions are set at the monopoly level provided there is not aggregate excess capacity. When there is aggregate excess capacity, commissions are set at the zero-profit level. At this level each trader is operating with excess capacity. The usual incentive to undercut the commission slightly is eliminated by the presence of joint liability. Although the individual trader's revenue would certainly increase with a sufficiently small cut in his commission, this action would drive his colleagues into bankruptcy, leaving the deviater to pay a larger share of the fixed costs. The joint liability condition softens the usual Nash behavior. Traders have to be concerned with the impact of their own actions on other traders' profits. The Nash equilibrium here therefore bears some resemblance to the equilibrium concept used by Wilson (1977) in the context of insurance markets. In that model, an insurer contemplating introducing a new contract was required to look forward and take into account the fact that insurance contracts currently offered would be withdrawn if they became ex post unprofitable once the new contract was introduced. That feature of looking forward is endogenized here by the presence of joint liability.

The noncooperative equilibrium is the same regardless of the form of the sharing rule. Moreover, because the outcome is symmetric, anonymity ensures that, regardless of what the arguments of $\Phi(\cdot)$ are, in equilibrium Φ reduces to an equal-sharing rule with each trader paying F/N of the fixed costs.

Given the unique noncooperative outcome for each level of N and assuming that establishing an exchange is profitable at all, a board wanting to maximize total exchange profits would set $N = N^*$ and any Φ satisfying conditions 1 to 4.[2] The result is that $c_i^* = (P^* - \bar{P})$, total output is sold through the exchange, and all the gains from trade are appropriated by the traders. Hedgers are completely insured in equilibrium but the premium they pay for this insurance is such that they are indifferent between selling their commodity forward and waiting to sell it on the spot market. Nonetheless, the outcome is Pareto efficient. This result drives solely from the assumed perfect inelasticity of supply and ceases to hold when this assumption is dropped later in the chapter.

The model may appear to depend critically on the assumption that traders have fixed capacity k for the output they are able to trade and that they have constant marginal costs for trades up to k. A more reasonable assumption would be that in addition to a fixed cost f each trader i has variable costs—say $T(Q_i)$—which exhibit increasing marginal costs in the amount of output Q_i, traded by trader i—that is, $T'(Q_i) > 0$ and $T''(Q_i) > 0$. In fact, allowing for this more general form does not alter the results. Let Q_i^m be such that $T'(Q_i^m) = P^* - \bar{P}$—that is, Q_i^m is the output that a trader would supply if he was unconstrained by competition. Then define N^* so that $N^* = Q/Q_i^m$. Now we can proceed as before. The corresponding proposition follows.

PROPOSITION 2. *Under any constitution that satisfies nonnegativity, anonymity, joint liability, and budget-balancing, the unique pure strategy Nash equilibrium under increasing marginal costs is given by*

$$c_i^* = \begin{cases} P^* - \bar{P} \text{ for all } i \text{ if } N \leqslant N^* \\ \dfrac{N}{Q}\left[T\left(\dfrac{Q}{N}\right) + \dfrac{F}{N} + f \right] \text{ for all } i \text{ otherwise} \end{cases}$$

Proof. The argument when $N \leqslant N^*$ is the same as before. Now consider $N > N^*$. As before, no trader has an incentive to raise c_i. Suppose a trader lowers c_i to c_i^o. The trader will choose to trade some amount Q_i^o. Clearly for this to be profitable—that is, for $c_i^o Q_i^o > Q/N c_i^*$—it must be the case that $Q_i^o Q/N$. Exchange profits are now

$$\Pi \equiv c_i^o Q_i^o + c_i^* (Q - Q_i^o) - F - nf - T(Q_i^o) - (N - 1)T \left(\frac{Q - Q_i^o}{N - 1}\right)$$

Now $c_i^o Q_i^o < c_i^* Q_i^o$ because $c_i^o < c_i^*$. Also, with increasing marginal cost the least costly way for N traders to supply Q units is for each to supply Q/N units—that is

$$T(Q_i^m) + (N - 1)\, T\left(\frac{Q - Q_i^m}{N - 1}\right) > NT\left(\frac{Q}{N}\right)$$

Therefore, $\pi < c_i^* Q - F - nf - NT (Q/N) = 0$ by the definition of c_i^*. But then the joint liability condition requires that $\pi^i < 0$.

As both versions of the model show, once excess capacity is present commissions fall sharply. This result suggests that the free entry of competing exchanges would very rapidly drive commissions down, resulting in at least some gains from trade for hedgers in equilibrium. As the following section demonstrates, however, this is not the case.

Multiple Exchanges

In this section we examine the nature of the equilibrium when there are multiple competing exchanges. For simplicity, we examine the case of two exchanges and traders with fixed capacity although it is clear how the model generalizes. As before we consider a two-stage game. In the first stage each exchange i selects a constitution $\{N_i, \Phi_i\}$. With the constitutions thus chosen the traders then play noncooperatively in the second stage. For given constitutions the equilibrium is characterized in the following proposition.[3]

PROPOSITION 3. *Given constitutions* $\{\Phi_1, N_1\}$ *and* $\{\Phi_2, N_2\}$ *with* Φ_1, Φ_2, *satisfying nonnegativity, budget balance, anonymity, and joint liability for each exchange, the unique pure strategy Nash equilibrium is given by:*

$$c_i = \begin{cases} P^* - \bar{P} & \text{for all } i \text{ if } N_1 + N_2 \leq N^* \\ 0 & \text{for all } i \text{ otherwise} \end{cases}$$

Proof. As before, the case where $N_1 + N_2 \leq N^*$ is straightforward. There is no excess aggregate capacity and accordingly the monopoly price can be charged. In the event that there is excess aggregate capacity—that is, $N_1 + N_2 > N^*$—the zero-profit level can no longer be maintained as a non-cooperative equilibrium. The reason is clear. Previously a trader had no incentive to undercut this level because any increase in revenue was gained at the expense of his fellow exchange traders. Because this loss in their revenue resulted in their inability to pay their fixed costs, which in turn had to be borne by the deviating trader, his incentive to deviate disappeared. Here, however, a deviating trader increases his revenue not only at the expense of his fellow exchange traders but also in part at the expense of the rival exchange traders. Joint liability requires that the deviater pay the fixed costs that his fellow exchange traders are unable to pay but not to those that rival traders cannot pay. Accordingly, an incentive to deviate still exists that will drive the price down to marginal cost (which has been normalized to be zero).

In the first stage, therefore, the boards of the exchanges would never want to pick constitutions that had $N_1 + N_2 > N^*$. It is clear if the boards operate noncooperatively in selecting their constitutions, any pair $\{N_1^*, N_2^*\}$ such that $N_1^* + N_2^* = N^*$ will constitute Nash equilibrium choices.[4] Although there may be many such $\{N_1^*, N_2^*\}$ pairs that satisfy this condition, they all have the same basic properties. As before, the monopoly price is charged in equilibrium, hedgers are completely insured but pay a premium of $P^* - \bar{P}$, and total output is sold through the exchanges. Furthermore, additional fixed costs of F are borne.

Thus although the exchanges are behaving noncooperatively, each selects a constitution that, given the constitution the other has chosen, ensures that no aggregate excess capacity exists. This results in the same total number of traders N^* operating in equilibrium with the same commission levels as in the single exchange case. The multiple exchanges serve to increase the total costs of transacting without exerting any additional competitive influence on commissions.

The Model with Elastic Supply

The results derived in the previous two sections appear to depend crucially on the assumption that the good is perfectly inelastically supplied. Certainly, the proofs invoke this assumption on several occasions. As this section illustrates, however, the basic behavior of the model is not altered when this assumption is relaxed. However, the Pareto efficiency of the single exchange disappears and much stronger welfare conclusions can be drawn.

Let $S(q)$ be the aggregate supply function for farmers. Thus S denotes the futures price net of transactions costs necessary to induce an output of q. Let $P^*(q)$ be the demand function for speculators as before, and let $c(q) \equiv P^*(q) - S(q)$. The $c(q)$ function defines the maximum commission that can be charged in order for an output of q to clear the market and therefore represents the demand function facing the exchange. Clearly $c(q)$ is decreasing in q if $P^*(q)$ and $S(q)$ are decreasing and increasing in q respectively. The output level q^c, which is defined implicitly by $c(q^c) = P^*(q^c) - S(q^c) = 0$ has special significance—that is, it is the output that would emerge in the standard Walrasian equilibrium where transactions costs are absent.

We will assume that the profit function facing the exchange, $\pi(q) \equiv qc(q) - F - Nf$, is quasiconcave in q. Several benchmarks are worth defining. Let q^m be the maximizer of $\pi(q)$. As before, to avoid integrability problems we will assume that $N^* \equiv q^m/k$ is integer-valued. For each $N > q^m/k$ let $c_\circ^N$ and $q_\circ^N$ be such that $c_\circ^N(q_\circ^N)q_\circ^N - F - Nf = 0$—that is, $c_\circ^N$ is the zero-profit commission when N traders charge the same commission. We assume that there is some size exchange that is profitable—that is $\pi(q^m) > 0$. These features are illustrated in figure 8.2.

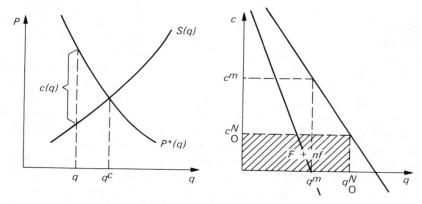

Figure 8–2. The Model with Elastic Supply

The elasticity of supply adds one additional complication. Suppose that all traders charge the same commission, say c^m. If one deviates to a lower commission, hedgers and speculators would prefer to trade through the deviating trader. As is usually the case in such situations, some method of rationing is required. One method that is commonly used and that makes a great deal of sense in this setting is to assume that trades are rationed proportionately. Thus if the trader deviates from c^m to c^o, the demand from the traders still charging c^m is $q^m - [q^m / c^{-1}(c^o)]k$. That is to say, because the trader cannot distinguish trades that have been induced by the lowering of price from trades that would have taken place at the old price, he completes a random selection of trades.

With this machinery in hand we can demonstrate the following proposition.

PROPOSITION 4. *Under any constitution that satisfies nonnegativity, anonymity, joint liability, and budget-balancing, the unique pure strategy Nash equilibrium is given by*

$$c_i^* = \begin{cases} c^m \text{ for all } i \text{ if } N \leq N^* \\ c_o^N \text{ for all } i \text{ otherwise} \end{cases}$$

Proof: As before, the case $N \leq N^*$ is straightforward. Suppose then that $N > N^*$. Clearly no trader has an incentive to raise his commission for the same reasons as before. Suppose that trader i lowers his commission to $c_i < c_o^N$. Let $c^{-1}(c_i) \equiv q_i$. Total exchange profits are given by

$$c_i k + c_o^N \left(q_o^N - \frac{q_o^N}{q_i} k \right) - Nf - F$$

But by definition of $c_\circ^N$ we have $c_\circ^N q_\circ^N - Nf - F = 0$. Therefore, exchange profits are $c_i k - c_\circ^N q_\circ^N / q_i k$. This is positive if and only if $c_i q_i > c_\circ^N q_\circ^N$. However, by the quasiconcavity of $\pi\ (q)$ this never holds for $q_\circ^N < q_i$, and hence never holds for $c_i < c_\circ^N$ by the monotonicity of $c(\cdot)$.

As was the case in the previous analysis, profits drop off sharply when N exceeds N^*. Accordingly, an exchange would limit the number of traders to N^*. The resulting outcome is drawn in figure 8–3. As figure 8–3 illustrates, the welfare effects of the exchange's action is similar to the imposition of a value-added tax of c^m. Output is reduced from q^m to q^c resulting in a deadweight loss equal to the cross-hatched area. In addition, there are the redistributive aspects that were present in the previous sections. The hedgers are fully insured but the entire risk premium when output q^m is c^m is appropriated by the exchange itself. The exchange's revenues are given by the shaded area which is composed of the traders' profits and the fixed and variable costs.

This outcome can be compared with the Pareto optimum. Total welfare is given by

$$W \equiv \int_0^q [P^*(q) - S(q)]dq - F - \left(\frac{q}{k}f \right)$$

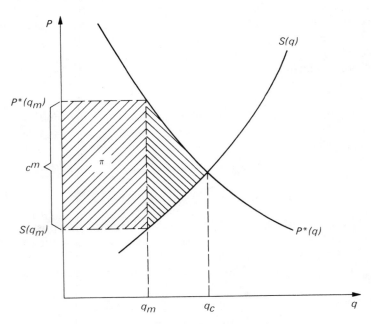

Figure 8–3. Welfare Analysis

Suppose this is maximized at q^{po}. Differentiating W with respect to q yields the first-order condition.

$$P^*(q^{po}) - S(q^{po}) = \frac{f}{k}$$

This simply requires that the marginal social welfare be equated to the marginal transactions cost.[5] Note that $\pi(q^{po}) = c(q^{po})q^{po} - Fq^{po}/k = -F$ because $c(q^{po}) \equiv P^*(q^{po}) - S(q^{po}) = f/k$. Thus the Pareto-optimal exchange makes a loss. Note that $dW/dq|_{q^m} = c(q^m) - f/k > 0$ since $\pi(q^m) > 0$. Therefore $q^{po} > q^m$.

We can also compare the output in the Pareto-Optimal exchange with a second-best optimum in which social welfare is maximized subject to the constraint that the exchange at least break even. Let this output be q^{sb}, that is

$$q^{sb} = \underset{q}{\text{argmax}} \int_0^q [P^*(q') - S(q')]dq' - F - \left[\frac{qf}{k}\right] \text{subject to } c(q)q$$
$$- F\frac{q}{k}f \geq 0$$

Note that $dW/dq|_{q^m} > 0$ and $\pi(q^m) > 0$ imply that $q^{sb} > q^m$. Proposition 5 follows.

PROPOSITION 5.

$$q^m < q^{sb} < q^{po} < q^c$$

Proof. $\pi(q^c) = -F - q^c/k \, f$, $\pi(q^{po}) = -F$, $\pi(q^{sb}) = 0$ and $\pi(q^c) > 0$. Therefore, $\pi(q^c) < \pi(q^{po}) < (q^{sb}) < \pi(q^m)$. Because $\pi(q)$ is monotone decreasing on $[q^m, q^c]$ the result follows.

Profit-maximizing commissions result in a suboptimal level of output. Even an exchange constrained to break even sets its commissions too high so that it can cover its fixed costs. Finally, the Walsarian output that results when commissions are set equal to zero is too large because it results in output being produced where the marginal social gain before marginal transaction costs are exceeded by the transactions costs themselves.

Conclusions

This chapter explores the welfare effects of trading in commodities taking place through organized futures exchanges. The model strongly suggests that the ability of a futures exchange to regulate the size of its membership endows it with substantial monopoly power and that this power is not eliminated by the presence of competition between exchanges. This monopoly power enables the exchange to appropriate the full risk premium that the farmers are prepared to pay for insurance. As a result, if the farmers' aggregate supply function is increasing in price, a suboptimal quantity of the output will be provided in equilibrium.

Because of the potential importance of this finding, additional research to enrich this model is needed. A number of possible avenues exist. The role that the exchange plays in alleviating the moral hazard problems that exists when hedgers attempt to enter into private contracts with speculators needs to be explicitly modelled. Second, the model presented here has an extremely simple informational structure. Largely as a result, it is immaterial to all the parties concerned whether the traders trade on their own account or merely act as intermediaries. A richer informational structure is necessary to examine the impact of the ability of traders to trade on their own account. I hope to take up these and other issues in future research.

Notes

1. For models that examine search costs see, for example, Diamond and Maskin (1979) and Salop and Stiglitz (1977).

2. Each additional trader up to a total of N^* adds profits of $k(P^* - \bar{P}) - f > 0$ if the exchange is profitable at all. For all $N > N^*$ profits are zero.

3. A formal proof has been omitted in favor of the intuitive discussion that follows.

4. This assumes of course that $Q[P^* - \bar{P}] \geq (N_1^* + N_2^*)f + 2F$ so that two exchanges can profitably coexist and that N_1^* and N_2^* are chosen such that

$$[Q/(N_1^* + N_2^*)](P^* - \bar{P}) > N_i^* f + F \text{ for } i = 1, 2$$

so that neither exchange operates at a loss.

5. This treats the number of traders as a continuous variable.

References

Diamond, P., and E. Maskin. (1979). "An Equilibrium Analysis of Search and Breach of Contract, I: Steady States," *Bell Journal of Economics* (Spring) pp. 282–318.

Salop, S., and J. Stiglitz. (1977). "Bargains and Ripoffs: A Model of Monopolistically Competitive Price Dispersions," *Review of Economic Studies*, 44 pp. 493–510.

Wilson, C. (1977). "A Model of Insurance Markets with Incomplete Information," *Journal of Economic Theory*, 16 (December) pp. 167–207.

9

Theories of Contract Design and Market Organization: Conceptual Bases for Understanding Futures Markets

Robert M. Townsend

Why are there organized futures markets? Do such markets constitute an optimal social arrangement? Should society encourage the development of such markets or control their operation? Of course, this chapter does not pretend to offer a definitive answer to these questions. But it does argue that a number of relatively recent efforts in the theory of general economic equilibrium can help us to explain the existence of organized futures markets and help us to pose and to answer normative questions. The purpose of this chapter, then, is to review those efforts and advance some new frameworks— all with the hope of furthering subsequent research efforts.

To motivate the general equilibrium models presented here, it is useful to review first the standard Arrow-Debreu general equilibrium model and to comment on its ability to explain the existence of organized futures markets. Two polar and somewhat characterized views are presented that motivate the intermediate view adopted in this paper. Next, I review the present case for the regulation of futures markets, as presented by James M. Stone, former chairman and current commissioner of the Commodity Futures Trading Commission. Again, Stone's views serve to pose more sharply some of the normative (policy) issues. These discussions are followed by the models themselves and some concluding remarks.

Do We Live in an Arrow-Debreu World?

Imagine an economy with a finite number of firms. These firms have well-behaved technologies for transforming a finite number of factors of production into a finite number of produced goods. Production takes place both at a point in time (for example, labor is used to manufacture consumption goods) and over time (for example, labor is used to manufacture consumption goods) and over time (for example, there are nontrivial investment capabilities). Finally, firms' production technologies are subject

---

Helpful comments from Lester Telser and John Blin are gratefully acknowledged. The author assumes full responsibility for any errors as well as for the views expressed herein.

to random disturbances or shocks (for example, good or bad weather affects crop yields). The firms of the economy are owned by households. The households themselves are endowed with factors of production and have well-behaved preferences over such factors not supplied (such as leisure) and over consumption of produced goods. Again, endowments and preferences may be random.

Now imagine that at the beginning of time all firms and households get together to plan what to do. Under one possible planning scheme, a neutral auctioneer calls out prices specifying per unit credits and debits for sales and purchases in terms of some abstract unit of account or numeraire. That is, firms make commitments (that is, they enter into contracts) to hire inputs and to produce consumption goods contingent on various possible events (such as the entire histories of the technology, endowment, and preference shocks). Firms maximize profits, the valuation of their plan under the accounting system. Households make commitments to sell factors of production and to purchase consumption goods under various possible events or contingencies, subject to the budget constraint that the valuation of their purchases not exceed the valuation of their sales. The auctioneer finds prices of factors of production and consumption goods such that all plans are consistent. Then, as time evolves and states of nature are realized, all contracts are honored.

Under a second planning scheme, there are various possible auctioneers who compete with one another. In fact, one may imagine that any households that want to can offer to buy and sell commodities at specified prices. One can conjecture that the outcome of the second scheme will be the same as the outcome under the first scheme, at least if the number of households and firms is large.[1]

Finally, we might weaken the requirement that everyone meet together at an initial planning date, as if everyone were in the same physical location. Instead, imagine that there is a perfect telecommunications system at the initial date and all households and firms are armed with costless and unlimited computers. Still, households and firms are imagined to make commitments to brokers who compete with one another. The outcome should again be the same.

Of course, the economy just described is the Arrow-Debreu general equilibrium model, or at least a contemporary version. Perhaps some would argue that the Arrow-Debreu model is irrelevant, that it has no relationship to actual markets and institutions. On the other hand, others might argue that the Arrow-Debreu world is essentially the world in which we live. It is true that transactions are entered into over time, but the outcome is equivalent with the outcome of the world with complete Arrow-Debreu markets as just described. Frictions, it is argued, are unimportant; money (checking accounts) is not needed in a world with free access to mutual funds, for example. The only challenge, according to this second view, is to determine the appropriate sequence of trades and combination of financial instruments, trades, and combinations that allow one to attain the Arrow-Debreu competitive equilibrium allocation.

Naturally enough, the paper adopts a third view. The Arrow-Debreu model is not so wild, despite the apparent absence of observed institutions and markets. After all, we do want highly stylized models; the Arrow-Debreu model is a useful starting point. But the Arrow-Debreu model is missing important frictions or obstacles to trade, obstacles that are not so easily circumvented. The idea, then, is to try to model those frictions and to let observed contracts and institutions emerge endogenously. In this way one might hope to explain futures markets. And in proceeding in this way, keeping track of preferences, endowments, and technologies, one might hope to do explicit welfare analyses. That is, such frameworks provide natural structures in which to pose organization and regulatory issues. This chapter, then, tries both to help us to understand the properties and limitations of the standard Arrow-Debreu model and to review a number of recent efforts in the theory of general economic equilibrium that introduce explicit trading frictions.

Should Society Control the Operation of Futures Market?

To pose the normative and policy issues more sharply, it will prove useful to review the case for regulation of futures markets as presented by Stone (1981). First, Stone proposes that

> Government regulation has commonly been brought to bear in situations where one person is entrusted with other people's money. The trust characteristic of the futures trade and consequent opportunities for customer loss though insolvency and illicit conversion of funds contribute to the first leg of what I will call the tripod of reasons to regulate. . . . As in banking, insurance, and elsewhere, the public authorities feel a need to minimize this risk. . . (by) maintenance of special segregation accounts for customer funds as well as minimum capital requirements. Reinforcing the first leg of the tripod is the extreme difficulty of the customer in assessing the value of the futures contract and the quality of service rendered. . . . [T]he natural intricacy of price determination in any contingent goods market leads further to the customers' problem. Finally, it is difficult to distinguish even in retrospect between the effect of incompetent or unscrupulous activities on the part of a broker or trader and the impacts of accepted market contingencies. Government encourages good faith (of the retailer) . . . by providing disclosure rules, punishing deceit, and providing a civil forum.

Stone then goes on to say:

> The second leg of the regulatory tripod is the potential for abuses of concentration by large position holders in the futures marketplace. From the inception of futures markets it has been well understood that contingent asset markets with quantities sold not limited to expected physical supply are vulnerable to squeezes and other abuses of market power. . . . The threat that some individual or group will hold a position surpassing deliverable supply is a danger constantly overhanging the futures markets. . . . The exchanges themselves provide a first line of defense against congestion and manipulation. Their historical performance, however, is uneven. When key exchange members themselves or their most valued customers are the large position holders, the record of self-regulation is inadequate. . . . Regulatory review . . . of proposed contract specification and trading rules is useful . . . . Speculative position limits help provide a constraint on excessive market size and market power. The Commission's large trader reporting requirements allow constant monitoring.

And, third, Stone remarks:

> The third leg of the tripod is the inclination toward monopoly or oligopoly on the part of exchanges and clearing organizations. . . . That tendency can be traced to powerful scale economies in operating technology, liquidity, and product acceptance, as well as from quasigovernmental rulemaking powers with which an exchange is imbued. . . . Government recognizes the reality of natural monopolistic inclinations by its grant of a franchise to contract markets.

Stone has much to say about approval of new contract applications:

> statute and regulation provide for an economic purpose test, a burden of proof upon the exchange that its proposed contract will be of some demonstrable value to commerce. . . . Futures contracts with no economic or commercial purpose look suspiciously like (gambling) arrangements. . . . Commercial purpose is served when a futures market will do a more effective price job than the preexisting cash markets. . . . Efficiency depends largely upon the knowledge and behavior of participants in a marketplace . . . hedging and price discovery . . . are for the most part corollaries of (the commercial purpose) test . . . . It is relatively easy to make a case for commercial value in the grain futures markets. . . . The atomized nature of cash grain markets and the diversity in those markets with respect to quality rendered elusive the development of an efficient central cash market in most grains. . . . A contrasting and more difficult case for commercial value analysis arises in the financial futures markets.

Stone concludes his essay by noting the paucity of an economic literature on futures market regulation.[2] But Stone's arguments and observations allow one to draw some links to some efforts in the theory of general economic equilibrium.[3] Again, the idea is to conduct standard welfare analysis in tightly specified general equilibrium models, with and without trading frictions, to see if some of Stone's arguments might be validated or overturned. Of course, there is no presumption a priori that government regulation of the type envisioned (or practiced) by Stone is warranted. Again, that is left as an open question. We shall return to some of these issues in the conclusion to this chapter.

Spanning, Futures Markets, and the Theory of General Economic Equilibrium

As Stone (1981) notes in his review of Arrow (1981), the standard theory of general economic equilibrium, as developed by Arrow (1964) and Debreu (1959), among others, helps us to understand what commodities need to be traded, in general, to ensure economic efficiency—that is, to achieve a Pareto-optimal allocation of resources. That theory is also a natural starting point for this essay because it includes no frictions or informational asymmetries; one would like to gain an understanding of futures markets without unnecessary complications, or at least to see if this is possible.

To begin, then, we shall consider the economy that is implicit in Arrow's discussion (1981). Imagine an economy inhabited by a finite number of households who live for a finite number of periods. Each household has preferences over finite-dimensional vectors of possible consumption commodities at each date as represented by a well-behaved utility function. Imagine also, for simplicity, that there is no production.

One can consider in Arrow's economy two possible trading regimes. In the first regime there is a complete set of competitive, date-contingent commodity markets. That is, there is a price system that specifies the number of units of money which must be surrendered, say to an exchange authority, for claims to each possible commodity at each possible date. Households take the price system as given and sue their initial allotment of money incomes to purchase such claims. Then, as the economy evolves over time, claims are honored and hosueholds consume accordingly. This trading regime can be interpreted as one with a complete set of futures markets, with maturities at every possible date. One the other hand, as Arrow notes, there is no trade in spot markets at any date, a somewhat damning feature.

In the second trading regime, hosueholds can trade their money incomes for claims on money at each possible date. Then, as the economy evolves over time, households receive their claims on money and use the money income to purchase commodities in the usual way. This trading regime can be interpreted as one with a complete set of active spot markets with the initial-date price system specifying the term structure of interest rates.

As Arrow argues, these two trading regimes are equivalent in terms of the final consumption bundles that are allowed in perfect-foresight competitive equilibria. That is, at equilibrium prices, the set of complete date-contingent commodity markets spans the same space as the set of complete bond markets with spot commodity trades. And, of course, under mild regularity conditions, the final allocation of consumption bundles is Pareto-optimal.

This observation is somewhat damning for commercial-purpose tests of futures markets. As Stone (1981) notes, it seems to imply that apart from bonds, futures markets are not needed. And, again following Stone, bonds futures would seem not to be needed because they are just futures on futures and introduce no new time element into the contingent-asset menu. However, one should be careful with these interpretations.

To proceed, we shall consider a private-ownership version of Arrow's economy, perhaps more consistent with Debreu (1959). In this version households have exogenously specified endowment vectors and there is no money as such. In the first exchange regime, then, there is a complete set of date-contingent commodity markets in which households trade claims on consumption goods, at specified prices, and there are no spot markets. In the second regime there is a complete set of initial-date markets in which households can trade claims on some numeraire, and there are complete and active spot markets at each date.

Obviously it is problematical as to how to interpret the claims on the numeraire in the second exchange regime. If one (arbitrary) commodity is taken as a numeraire, then the second exchange regime requires a futures market in one arbitrary commodity, with active spot markets. If one normalizes prices in the usual way, on the unit simplex, then the second regime seems to require some kind of index futures. The point, of course, is that one should not overinterpret the second exchange regime in the nonmonetary economy and, by the same token, one should not overinterpret the second exchange regime in Arrow's monetary economy. Without a theory of money—that is, a theory that prices money as a separate commodity—numeraires are indeterminate and so are the predictions of the theory. It is thus premature to use the theory for commercial-purpose tests of bond futures, for example. We shall return to this point again in the following sections.

Thus far there has been no mention of uncertainty, an aspect long thought to be essential to the existence of futures markets. But it is the fundamental insight of Arrow (1964) and Debreu (1959) that social uncertainty introduces no new complications into the theory of general economic equilibrium. One need only index commodities by fully observed states of nature, and theorems on the existence and optimality of competitive equilibrium, say for the first exchange regime, readily apply. But such social uncertainty would now seem to be damning to the existence of futures markets, for such markets allow the trade of uncontingent claims on commodities, whereas the theory would seem to predict the existence of markets in contingent claims on commodities, contingent on states. But it can be argued, following another insight of Arrow, that unconditional futures markets with active spot markets may well span the space of possible returns after all.

Arrow's insight (1964) is that one does not need, in general, a complete set of state-contingent commodities to achieve optimal allocations. To be specific, imagine an economy with one consumption date and S possible states of the world, and suppose, with Arrow, that households are endowed with money at some initial preconsumption date. Then the analogue to the second exchange regime is as follows. At the preconsumption date, households trade money for S possible securities, with security s promising to pay one unit of money if state s occurs and zero otherwise. Then, when states of nature are realized, delivered claims on money are used to purchase commodities in spot markets in the usual way. The allocation of consumption bundles that can be achieved in this way is equivalent with the allocation which can be achieved in complete, state-contingent commodity markets, and again the allocation is Pareto-optimal.

In lieu of these Arrow-type securities, now consider an exchange regime in which households trade unconditional claims on commodities in the preconsumption markets, claims that are valid independent of the state of nature that is realized, and suppose again the possibility of active spot market in every state. For such a futures market regime, Townsend (1978) has established an extension of Arrow's theorem, for a nonmonetary private-ownership economy. That is, if there are at least as many commodities as states of nature, and if the relevant matrix of equilibrium spot-market prices is full rank, the set of allocations that can be achieved with complete state-contingent commodity markets is equivalent to the set of allocations that can be achieved with the futures market regime. The point, of course, is that an unconditional claim on a commodity has a return contingent on the state, as spot prices can vary with the state. Under the rank conditions, the space of such returns is equivalent with the space spanned by Arrow-type securities.

This theorem seems to deal more kindly with the existence of futures markets than the comments of many authors concerning the absence of state-contingent securities or commodities. But the standard theory of general economic equilibrium would still seem to be missing many essential elements. First, the futures market regime may well be equivalent with the complete market regime, but there is nothing in the theory which predicts one over the other. Indeed, Ekern and Wilson (1974) and Radner (1974) have argued that equities or shares have a spanning property in a certain model, and Ross (1976) has made a similar argument for options. In general, financial structure is not pinned down by the theory. Putting this another way, there are no essential dynamics and no theory of financial assets such as money. Second, the theory does not make a distinction between futures markets and forward markets. All the markets are very much centralized. Third, there is no scope for an analysis of private information; uncertainty is social, not private. To evaluate Stone's first policy premise, and to some extent the second, one seems to need an abstraction in which private information is critical. Some of these concerns are addressed in the following sections, beginning with the explicit introduction of private information into the standard Arrow-Debreu paradigm.

Competitive Markets with Private Information

Expanded Commodity Spaces and Optimal Contract Design

To begin the discussion, imagine a world that allows for uncertainty in almost all aspects of economic life. Suppose, for example, each individual's endowment of consumption goods and factors of production is drawn from a well-specified probability distribution. Similarly, suppose production technologies are subject to random shocks, as are preferences or tastes. If the economy evolves over time, then suppose these shocks to endowments, technologies, and preferences are drawn from well-specified stochastic processes. Finally—and the key part of the specification—suppose that period by period each individual alone sees the realizations of his own endowments, preferences, and technology shocks.

In this world with asymmetric information, we may well imagine conducting economic analysis in the usual way—that is, in the obvious commodity space, with standard constructs or paradigms. After all, the addition of uncertainty does not alter the set of underlying commodities in the economy. Thus we might inquire, for example, about the operation of futures markets when deliverable supply of wheat is uncertain, with crop yields known only to the individuals themselves. But here again the indexation insight of Arrow and Debreu may well be applicable for both positive and normative purposes. That is, we might index commodities by all realizable states of nature or shocks and attempt to conduct standard competitive analysis in the enlarged commodity space.

There is, of course, a potential problem with this approach. Some states of nature (shocks) may be known only to the individuals themselves. If, for example, a contract specifies payment to a second party under contingencies known only to the first party, the first party may well claim that no such contingencies have ever occurred (see Arrow 1974 and Radner 1968). In short, in the terminology of Hurwicz (1972), allocations achieved by complete competitive contract markets, markets in completely indexed commodity bundles, may not be incentive-compatible.

To address these incentive information problems directly, we need to define first the set of allocations that are indeed achievable (both feasible and incentive-compatible) despite the existence of asymmetric information. And to avoid confounding the problems of asymmetric information with the problems of limited communication, we shall suppose that communication as such is unlimited, and that there are no other trading frictions.

Thus imagine that all individuals in the economy can communicate and trade with one another at no cost. That is, imagine that at the beginning of each period, after the realization of privately observed shocks to preferences, endowments, and technologies, each individual can send a message to some center or centralized market. There may be some a priori restrictions on the set of possible beginning of period messages for each individual. Next, in accord with some prespecified rule or outcome function, the beginning of period messages determine within period transfers may well be functions of messages sent at earlier dates. Finally, suppose each individual takes as given the sequence of a priori feasible messages spaces, one space for each period; the set of outcome functions, one for each period; and the period-by-period strategies used by all other individuals in the economy, mappings from previous (fully observed) messages and current (privately observed) shocks to current messages. Then each individual faces a well-defined decision problem and can determine a maximizing period-by-period strategy as well. These strategies then determine within period transfers or allocations as functions of realized shocks. It is imagined that in this process each individual makes full use of all available information. So we may term the outcome we have just discovered as a Bayesian-Nash equilibrium. (For a more formal treatment see Myerson 1979; Harris and Townsend 1977; 1981; and Townsend 1982).

If we examine the period-by-period allocations that result from a Bayesian-Nash equilibrium for any one of the class of resource allocation processes—that is, for any specification of message spaces and outcome functions—it becomes evident that those allocations satisfy certain restrictions. It is as if allocations were indexed by possible announcements of privately-observed shocks and are such that each individual announces privately observed shocks truthfully.[4] No such restrictions apply if more than one individual sees the same shock, or if privately observed shocks are completely deducible (for example, suppose endowment shocks were perfectly correlated across two individuals). In such cases, information is essentially public—individuals can be induced in a Nash equilibrium of some game to reveal the truth (this assumes no collusion, of course). But information that is truly private does have implications for resource allocation—arbitrary state or shock-contingent allocations are not necessarily achievable.

What implication does this rather abstract discussion have for the operation of competitive markets? To answer that question, we shall consider two rather extreme specifications. First, imagine a pure exchange economy with two types of individuals a and b and two underlying commodities 1 and 2. Households of type a have an endowment vector $(8, 30)$ of the first and second commodities respectively and preferences as represented by the utility function

$$U_a = x_{a1}x_{a2} + \theta_a x_{a1} + 3x_{a2}$$

Here (x_{a1}, x_{a2}) is the consumption bundle and θ_a is a parameter drawn from a well-known distribution, namely $\theta_a = 8$ with probability $\beta = .5$ and $\theta_a = 32$ with probability $1 - \beta = .5$. Households of type b have an endowment $(10, 10)$ and utility function

$$U_b = x_{b1}x_{b2} + \theta_b x_{b1} + 9x_{b2}$$

where $\theta_b = 12$ with probability $\alpha = .44$ and $\theta_b = 48$ with probability $1 - \alpha = .56$. The parameter θ_i is known to households of type i just prior to the time of trading, but not the parameter $\theta_j, j \neq i$. Finally, suppose there are a large (infinite) number of traders of each type.

Now suppose that there is a competitive (spot) market in which exchange of the two commodities can take place after the revelation of individual preference shocks. Then it is straightforward to compute competitive equilibrium allocations and utility levels for each of the four possible specifications of preference shocks. Allocations and utility levels are displayed in tables 9–1, and 9–2, respectively. Integrating down the columns of table 9–2, using the prior distribution over $\theta_b = (12, 48)$, namely $(\alpha, 1 - \alpha)$, one can compute the expected utility level of households of type a just before the opening of the market conditioned on the two possible values of θ_a. Similarly, integrating across rows in table 9–2, using the prior distribution over $\theta_a = (8, 32)$, namely $(\beta, 1 - \beta)$, one can compute the expected utility levels of households type b, just before the opening of the market conditioned on the two possible values of θb.

It may now be asked whether the competitive equilibrium parameter-contingent allocation is Pareto-optimal relative to the preferences of households just before trading. That is, is there an alternative parameter-contingent allocation that is better for households type a, conditioned on either value of θ_a, relative to its prior $(\alpha, 1 - \alpha)$ on values of the parameter θ_b, and similarly for households type b. A negative answer to the optimality question is provided by the Pareto-superior parameter-contingent allocation and levels displayed in tables 9–3 and 9–4, respectively.

Table 9-1
Competitive Equilibria with Spot Markets
Allocations

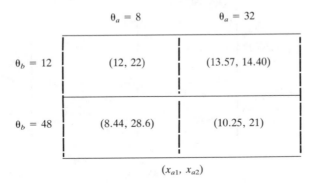

	$\theta_a = 8$	$\theta_a = 32$
$\theta_b = 12$	(12, 22)	(13.57, 14.40)
$\theta_b = 48$	(8.44, 28.6)	(10.25, 21)

(x_{a1}, x_{a2})

Table 9-2
Competitive Equilibria with Spot Markets
Utilities

	$\theta_a = 8$	$\theta_a = 32$
$\theta_b = 12$	426	672.85
	342	396.97
$\theta_b = 48$	394.82	606.25
	670.46	690.25

U_a/U_b

That the parameter-contingent allocation of table 9-3 is implementable is an implication of the preceding discussion above—there are many households of type a, so the parameter θ_a is essentially public information, and similarly for a parameter θ_b. The possibilities for preallocation communication (which here are unlimited) allow the competitive equilibrium allocation to be dominated.

This example has two implications. First, competitive spot markets as we usually model them may not be Pareto-optimal if there is asymmetric (but not private) information in the economy at the time of trading, though

Table 9–3
Parameter Contingent Allocations

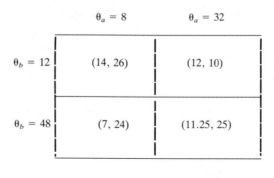

(x_{a1}, x_{a2})

Table 9–4
Parameter Contingent Allocations

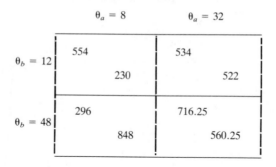

U_a/U_b

allocations are, of course, Pareto-optimal ex post by classical results. Second, there may be some gain to operating spot markets of a different kind, and there are certainly gains to operating a forward market before the revelation of preference shocks. In both instances commodities or contracts might be indexed by individually observed states of nature (again the preference shocks). This repeats the message of Arrow and Debreu. But it seems such contracts would need to be indexed to the announcements of all traders, including other traders of the same type, to provide incentives for correct revelation. By the same token, it is important that traders of the same type not collude in their announcements in an attempt to conceal their information. One is reminded of Stone's second policy premise, where potential abuses are associated with the concentration of information.

But how might standard competitive markets operate if there is information in the economy which is truly private? To examine this question, we shall consider a second, somewhat extreme specification. Imagine in particular an economy with one consumption date and ℓ possible commodities. Each individual has a strictly positive, ℓ-dimensional endowment vector e in the consumption period and preferences over ℓ-dimensional consumption vectors c as represented by a well-behaved utility function $U(c, \theta)$. Here the parameter θ is interpreted as a shock to preferences at the beginning of the consumption period, observed by the individual alone. For simplicity, suppose θ can take on a finite number of values in some set (H). Suppose also that there is no aggregate uncertainty, that is, let λ (θ) be the fraction of households in the population who experience shock θ in the consumption period, some fixed constant. Knowing this, but little else, each individual regards $\lambda(\theta)$ as the probability of experiencing shock θ in the consumption period, with the expectation as of some prior planning period.[5]

In this economy, individuals will want to trade forward contracts in some planning period market, but they will want those contracts to be contingent on privately observed outcomes.[6] This may seem untenable, but it need not be so. Imagine a contract that calls for the exchange of one commodity for another, in specified amounts at specified prices, but that allows for options which are effected entirely by the individual. For example, the individual might default on the commitment entirely or offer only partial fulfillment. Indeed, we might well imagine that the amount of actual payment by the individual is determined in a probabilistic manner, as some legal system adjudicates claims, or that payment to the individual under another option is random as existing commodity supplies are rationed.[7] But whether or not the actual outcome is random, the individual will act in his own best interest, choosing which option to effect subsequent to the revelation his underlying circumstance—his shocks θ. This induces a natural ordering on outcomes relative to his θ-contingent utility function. Indeed, following the results of Harris and Townsend (1978, 1981), Myerson (1979), and Townsend (1982) described earlier, we may adopt an abstract, canonical representation for a contract, supposing that households make direct announcements of their shocks θ and that contracts are such that these announcement are made truthfully.

More formally, then, the previous economy with planning period contracts and individually effected contingencies is described as follows. First, for simplicity, restrict attention to a finite number of possible consumption bundles c. Then let $x(c, \theta)$ assign probability to consumption bundle c conditional on the announcement θ. The expected utility of the representative household is then

$$u(x) \equiv \sum_{\theta} \lambda_{\theta} \sum_{c} x(c, \theta) U(c, \theta)$$

The consumption possibilities set is

$$\bar{X} = \{x:\ x \geq 0, \sum_c x(c,\theta) = 1 \text{ for each } \theta$$

and

$$\sum_c x(c,\theta)U(c,\theta) \geq \sum_c x(c,\phi)U(c,\theta) \quad \theta, \phi\}$$

Thus $\bar{X}$ ensures that the $x(\cdot,\theta)$ are probability measures and that preference shocks are revealed truthfully. Thus $\bar{x}$ defines the set of allowable contracts.

Imagine that any contract in $\bar{X}$ can be purchased in a competitive, planning period market, as if each of its components were priced separately. That is, let $p(c,\theta)$ be the price of the $x(c,\theta)$ component in terms of some abstract unit of account. Each individual is effectively endowed with some contract ξ in $\bar{X}$, a vector of probability measures putting mass one on the endowment e for all $\theta \in \Theta$, that is $\xi(e,\theta) = 1$ for all $\theta \in \Theta$ and $\xi(c,\theta) = 0$ for all $c \neq e$, $\theta \in \Theta$. Thus the individual maximizes utility $u(x)$ by a choice of a contract x in $\bar{X}$ subject to the budget constraint

$$\sum_\theta \sum_c p(c,\theta)x(c,\theta) \leq \sum_\theta \sum_c p(c,\theta)\xi(c,\theta)$$

One might also imagine there are intermediaries (firms) in the economy that make plans (in the planning period) to buy and sell consumption goods. An intermediation choice $y(c,\theta)$ specifies the number of units of the bundle c that the intermediary plans to deliver or sell to the market for use by households announcing they are of type θ. Thus, if $y(c,\theta)$ is negative, there is a plan to take in or buy resources. The intermediation set Y is defined by

$$Y = \{y(c,\theta): \sum_\theta \lambda(\theta) \sum_c cy(c,\theta) \leq 0\}$$

so that the intermediary can not deliver more than it takes in. Note that Y displays constant returns to scale, so we may act as if there were only one intermediary. The intermediary takes prices as given and maximizes profits

$$\sum_\theta \sum_c p(c,\theta)y(c,\theta)$$

constrained by the set Y.

Finally, a competitive equilibrium is a specification of contract choice $x(c,\theta)^*$, intermediation choice $y(c,\theta)^*$ and a price system $p(c,\theta)^*$ such that first, the contract choice is utility-maximizing given the price system; second, the intermediation plan is profit-maximizing given the price system; and third, markets clear—that is $x^*(c, \theta) - y^*(c, \theta) = \xi(c, \theta)$ for each c and θ. It may be verified that the third market-clearing condition in conjunction with intermediation set Y is equivalent to the condition that the economy-wide average consumption not exceed the economy-wide average endowment. That is

$$\sum_\theta \lambda(\theta) \sum_c x(c, \theta)c \leq e$$

The competitive contract markets just described may seem difficult to interpret. After all, as with standard competitive analysis, nothing has been said about the price determination or market assignment processes. That is, it is not clear from where prices come or who trades with whom, so one might be tempted to argue that this is not a useful abstraction. But imagine a market made up of a number of brokers who compete with one another, specifying the terms of contracts and calling out terms of trade or prices. These brokers attempt to attract household customers, pooling risks and in effect acting as the intermediaries just described. Of course, these brokers-intermediaries are really just households themselves, trading on their own account. One might well imagine, then, that the outcome of this process will resemble the competitive equilibrium allocation and price vector as the number of households (and potential brokers) gets large.[8]

Prescott and Townsend (1982a) have established both the existence and optimality of competitive contract market equilibria in environments that include the one just described as a special case. Indeed, the general analysis allows for ex ante privately observed diversity, and arbitrary (finite) number of trading dates, and private information at each date. In general, the equilibirum contracts will involve random components; they are used to discriminate (distinguish) among households with privately observed heterogenous characteristics. Finally, the analysis reduces to standard Arrow-Debreu general equilibrium theory when the information structure is private but not sequential.

The positive and normative implications of the work are apparent. From a positive standpoint, it seems we might expect to observe competitive markets in contracts with individually effected contingencies.[9] From a normative standpoint, it seems such markets would have desirable characteristics. This may have a direct bearing on commercial purpose tests.

There is, however, an important qualification to this entire discussion. If households with characteristics that are distinct and privately observed at the time of initial trading do not enter the economy-wide resource constraints in a homogenous way, there can be problems for the existence and optimality of competitive contract markets. Such problems will occur in the preceding example if there is some statistical dependence in preference shocks, so that households have some asymmetric information on their own future shocks at the time of initial trading. Indeed, as Prescott and Townsend (1982b) argue, these are precisely the problems that lead to difficulties in the insurance market models of Rothschild and Stiglitz (1976) and Wilson (1977) and the signaling models of Spence (1974). It seems clear from these results, and from what is now an enormous literature, that our standard conception of what might constitute a competitive market in such situations may well have to be altered. Thus there may indeed be some scope for intervention or control, though that question is still open. But by the same token, these problems do not emerge if trade occurs in forward contracts before the arrival of private information.

In conclusion, I have argued that when there is private information, standard views on what are natural commodities or contracts to be traded may need to be altered. We have made some progress in understanding when there may be problems for the operation of competitive markets under private information and whether those problems can be remedied by contract design or maturity structure. Still, there remain many observations and issues that cannot be addressed by the constructs of this section. For example, many of the issues raised by Stone's first policy premise remain unaddressed. The reason is also apparent: Despite the existence of private information, the competitive markets described in this section are highly centralized—the communication technology allows a great deal of information to be transmitted and, consequently, there is a great deal of implicit coordination across individual traders. For example, there is no possibility for markets for individual insurance as distinct from forward markets. Neither can the constructs of this section address issues of market formation and the role of price discovery mentioned in Stone's fourth policy premise, nor can they address issue concerning monopoly power on the part of exchanges or issues of self-regulation on the part of exchanges, as in Stone's third policy premise. Finally, the constructs of this section still do not allow money or the existence of financial assets in the usual sense of the term. Thus, we turn next to alternative means of breaking up the Arrow-Debreu paradigm—namely, limited communication.

Coordination Problems in
Decentralized Models of Exchange

*Uncoordinated Trade and the Gains
from Market Formation*

It seems useful to begin this section with a model in which there are no centralized markets whatever—traders search for one another in a random fashion, and exchange takes place on a haphazard basis. A characterization of the equilibrium of that model makes clear the type of coordination problems that can emerge—there are multiple equilibria, and the equilibria are in general nonoptimal. We shall then retain some of the search frictions of that model, but allow a centralized exchange. As might be expected, the problems disappear but new issues are raised.

Diamond (1982) constructs a model that poses the coordination issue nicely. Imagine a tropical island with many individuals. When unemployed, each individual strolls the beaches examining palm trees. Some trees have bunches of coconuts, but the height of the bunch above the ground varies from tree to tree. More generally, individuals are imagined to learn of production opportunities as if opportunities were generated by a Poisson process, with arrival rate a. That is, $a \cdot \Delta t + \sigma (\Delta t)$ is the probability of finding a production opportunity during interval of time Δt, where $\sigma (\Delta t)$ is a second-order term that is negligible relative to Δt for small Δt. Thus a is interpreted as the probability of finding a production opportunity per instant of search. Each opportunity has y units of output and costs c units to produce. Output y is the same for all projects but c varies across projects with cumulative distribution G.

Now suppose individuals cannot eat the fruit of their own labor. So having climbed a tree, the employed individual sets out in search of a trading partner to trade nuts for nuts. But trading partners are encountered at random, and one is more likely to encounter a trading partner the higher is the fraction of individuals on the island who are also searching for trading partners. More generally, suppose that the arrival of trading partners is also a Poisson process with arrival rate $b(u)$, with $b' < 0$, where u is the fraction of the unemployed population searching for trees.

The only decision in this model is the height of trees to climb—that is, some critical c^* above which production opportunities are foregone. The higher is c^*, the greater is the instantaneous cost. On the other hand, with nuts in hand, eventual consumption is made possible, with the utility of consumption discounted at rate r; the utility function is otherwise linear, increasing in consumption and decreasing in costs c. Thus, as might be expected, the more likely is an encounter with a trading partner, the greater is the gain from having nuts in hand, and thus the higher will be the choice of critical value c^*.

It is now apparent how this model can generate multiple equilibria. If everyone decides to climb relatively high trees (that is, engage in costly production), a large fraction of the population will be searching for trading partners in a given instant. This, in turn, can rationalize the decision to climb high trees. On the other hand, equilibria with relatively low levels of economic activity are viable as well. More formally, with parameter a interpreted as the fraction of unemployed individuals in the population who encounter production opportunities in any instant, $G(c^*)$ as the fraction of such individuals who decide to produce in that instant, and $b(u)$ as the fraction of employed individuals who encounter a trading partner in any instant, the unemployment rate satisfies

$$\dot{u} = b(u)(1 - u) - auG(c^*) \qquad (9.1)$$

with the maximizing critical value c^* satisfying

$$c^* = \frac{by + a\int_0^{c^*} c}{r + b + aG(c^*)} \qquad (9.2)$$

Plotting equation 9.1 at $\dot{u} = 0$ and 9.2 yields figure 9–1 (after Diamond 1982). Any crossing of the two curves in figure 9–1 constitutes a stationary equilibrium.

It is also now apparent why equilibria are nonoptimal. No individual takes into account that his decision to climb a tree and search for a trading pattern has a beneficial impact on the others who are also searching. That is, $b'(u) < 0$, but each individual takes $b(u)$ parametrically. The model has positive externalities. More formally, take the social welfare critierion to be discounted average (per capita) utility,

$$W = \int_0^\infty e^{-rt} Q(t) dt$$

where

$$Q(t) = b(u)(1 - u)y - au \int_0^{\hat{c}^*} cdG,$$

and where $b(u)(1-u)$ is interpreted as the rate of sales in the population at each instant in time, with consumption y per sale, and with $auG(c^*)$ as the

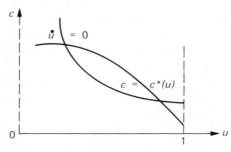

Figure 9–1. Diamond's Search Model: Multiple Equilibria

average rate of production, with an average cost $\int_0^{c*} G/G(c^*)$ per unit of production. Then the maximization of W with respect to c^* yields

$$c^* = \frac{by - b'(1 - u)y + a\int_0^{c*}cdG}{r + b - b'(1 - u) + aG(c^*)} \tag{9.3}$$

Generally, equations 9.2 and 9.3 are inconsistent. In fact, at an equilibrium level c^*, $\partial W/\partial c^* > 0$ so that locally there is too little activity in the economy.

Diamond's model raises clearly an essential coordination issue. How is a decentralized equilibrium to be effected? Any such equilibirum has self-fulfilling expectations, but there are multiple equilibria. So how is it that individuals come to know that others are climbing high trees, so that the unemployment rate is low, for example. The search process seems to suppose a complete absence of communication across individuals.

As Diamond emphasizes, this coordination problem arises because of the undirected nature of the search process. To see this more clearly, suppose that somehow or other all individuals believe that others are taking their nuts to a centralized exchange market at a known location.[10] Retaining some of the frictions of search for trading partners, suppose each individual with a nut to sell arrives at the exchange market as if under a Poisson process, with arrival rate b some constant. Then it is readily verified that there is, in general, a unique equilibrium, because the maximizing c^* is no longer an implicit function of the unemployment rate (see figure 9–2).

It is also immediate from equations 9.2 and 9.3 with $b' \equiv 0$ that the unique equilibrium is the unique social optimum. Finally, note that $(1 - u)b$ is the nonzero fraction of agents in the population who arrive at the exchange center in any instant, so there is continually some market activity. Having arrived, though exchange is instantaneous and empty-handed, individuals then reinitiate the search for production opportunities. As a result, there is nontrivial frictional unemployment. (For that outcome, we may just have well let $b = 1$.)

To suppose the existence of on centralized exchange market in Diamond's model is to beg an obvious question related to the coordination problem. How is it that individuals come to know that others are traveling, when employed, to a specific location? Again, communication among individuals is apparently precluded a priori. The model without a centralized exchange seems to cry out for such institutions, but we do not have a theory that explains how such institutions come about. As it turns out, related issues are raised by Mortensen (1974) in which there are a finite number of possible locations for exchange markets. The welfare analysis in Mortensen is even more problematical.

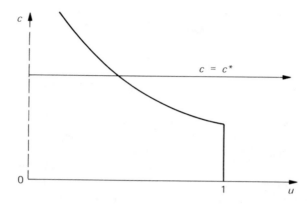

Figure 9–2. Diamond's Search Model: Unique Equilibrium

A Problem of Cross-Market Coordination

Imagine with Mortensen a pure exchange economy with ℓ commodities, m potential markets, and n traders. Each trader has a nonzero endowment vector of commodities and has preferences over consumption vectors as represented by a continuous, strictly concave, and strictly increasing utility function. For our purposes, we shall suppose there is only one trading date, though Mortensen gives his model a more dynamic interpretation. Finally, we shall restrict attention to a special case of Mortensen's model and suppose that every trader can choose to participate in any (one) market and that every commodity can be traded (potentially) in each market.

Each of the markets is assumed to function in the standard way, as if there were a Walrasian auctioneer given the traders who choose to participate in that market. Thus there arises an ℓ-dimensional price vector that clears the market in all commodities, given the excess demand functions of each of the traders who have congregated there. But choice of markets is endogenous—each trader can choose at most one market at the beginning of the period before knowing the choices of others.

Now suppose that for some reason or other a given trader imagines that all others are choosing markets at random, say each market with probability $1/m$. Then given the price formation and allocation rules, all markets look alike to the given trader a priori. And thus he too may just as well choose a market in this random fashion. In short, we have just described a Nash equilibrium in market-choice strategies. Alternatively, suppose the given trader imagines that all others are choosing some one particular market. Then the given trader will generally want to choose that same market (at least there can not be a better strategy). The reason for this is clear. If a trader chooses a market in which no one else participates, the price formation and allocation rules imply that he will end up consuming his endowment. Thus we have described a second Nash equilibrium in market-choice strategies.

It thus seems that if market formation is endogenous, in the sense that it is in Mortensen's model, there can arise multiple equilibria. And, as intuition might suggest, an equilibrium with random market-choice strategies can not be Pareto-optimal. Suppose we were to give to each trader that allocation which is the mean of his random allocations in the Nash equilibrium with random strategies. Then the new economy-wide allocation is feasible and, with risk aversion, Pareto dominates the equilibrium allocation.

The existence of multiple equilibria in Mortensen's model raises again the question of how any equilibrium is to come about without extramarket control or coordination. And the undesirable randomness associated with at least some equilibria would seem to give impetus to coordination efforts. But some caution is in order, for the obvious policy intended to coordinate market choices and remove undesirable randomness may not benefit all traders. One might contemplate, for example, in Mortensen's economy, the legal prohibition of trade in all markets save one, if somehow or other such an agreement could be effected (recall again that a priori communication is precluded). It is trivial that there can be no randomness in the resulting allocation; we have merely replicated the second equilibrium described above. Indeed, as all trade takes place in a standard Walrasian market, the resulting allocation will be Pareto-optimal.

But that allocation need not Pareto-dominate the random allocation of the first equilibrium. To see this, consider first a somewhat extreme case and suppose that the prices of a centralized Walrasian equilibrium are such that at least one trader does not trade at all. In contrast, the Nash equilibrium with random market-choice strategies by all traders will produce a random price in each market (and a dispersion of prices across markets ex post) and thus would offer in general the possibility of beneficial trade with positive probability, as Mortensen notes. This result is clearly more general, and the result bears repeating. In the absence of centralized markets, a move in the direction of centralization need not be uniformly welfare—improving.[11] Some traders may be hurt. We might expect them to oppose such a move.

Again, Mortensen's model suggests a need for some extramarket coordination if any of a number of essentially equivalent markets can operate simultaneously. That is, some (centralized?) decision may be needed on which markets ought to be active. And if some are already in operation, an equitable scheme might involve some compensation to existing or potential traders, not to mention brokers. We might well ask whether these coordination problems would disappear in a setting in which the number of markets is fixed and in which traders have no choice among markets whatever. As it turns out, there still can be problems if decisionmakers face nontrivial intertemporal decisions. Indeed, these problems bear on the issue of the existence of organized exchanges, much as Telser (1981) has argued.

Liquidity, Coordination, and the Existence of Organized Exchanges

Telser (1981) argues that organized futures markets exist, as distinct from forward contracts, because of liquidity considerations. He draws an analogy between futures contracts and money and suggests that we would not want futures in all commodities. He also argues that organized exchanges that allow more anonymous dealing among traders enhance the liquidity of futures contracts. Not surprisingly, many of Telser's arguments have formal analogues in some recent work on endogenous inside and outside monies.

To begin, imagine a world with just two trader types and one consumption good. Suppose that all traders of type A begin life with zero units of the consumption good and face an endowment sequence that alternates period by period, say $(0, 1, 0, \ldots)$. Similarly, suppose that all traders of type B begin life with one unit of the consumption good and face the endowment sequence $(1, 0, 1, \ldots)$. All traders have identical preferences, described by the time-separable discounted utility function

$$\sum_{t}^{\infty} = \beta^t U(c_t^i)$$

where c_t^i is the number of units of consumption of a trader type i at date t. There is supposed to be no storage and no production.

Suppose now that there are a fixed number of markets and that each trader visits one market in each period of his life in a fixed sequence. In particular, imagine that each trader is traveling on some spatial plane, as if on a highway or turnpike, either east or west, as indicated in figure 9–3. The arrows indicate the direction of travel and the spikes indicate markets. The numbers 0 and 1 index the endowment of a trader at the indicated position. Initially, at $t = 0$, there is one representative agent at each position, and each trader moves forward one market in each period.

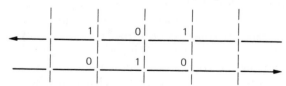

Figure 9–3. Markets with Anonymous Traders

This model is constructed in such a way that when two traders meet in at any market at any date they are completely anonymous; that is, the two have never seen each other before and will never see each other again. An implication of this is that there can be no private debt. No IOU can be redeemed by any issuer. Thus, there can be no inside financial assets. There are no objects that when acquired provide liquidity in subsequent periods and no objects that give the ability to purchase the consumption good in hard times when the endowment is low.

Some such liquidity can be provided with fiat money. In particular, suppose there were pieces of paper in the previously described economy that represent outside indebtedness, pieces of paper that are never redeemed. Still, on the expectation that this money will maintain its value relative to the consumption good, some of it can be acquired in good times when the endowment is high and passed along in bad times. Indeed, Townsend (1980) establishes for precisely this model that there exists a monetary equilibrium with that property. Again, money provides liquidity in a world where traders are anonymous. It allows mutually beneficial trade, an improvement over barter (here barter is equivalent with autarky).

We may now ask whether privately issued securities might also provide liquidity in a slightly modified world in which traders are not so anonymous. Suppose, in particular, that the previously described turnpike is connected end to end, as if traders were on a merry-go-round or circle. Then, as discussed in Townsend (1980, section 5), there is an equivalent canonical model in which traders meet one another repeatedly (see table 9–5). Indeed, one may as well allow endowments and preferences to be more general and consider an example economy in Townsend and Wallace (1982), in which there are four trader types. In it, traders type 1 and 2 are paired at date 1, in some location 1, and traders 3 and 4 are paired at date 2, in some location 2. Traders 1 and 4 stay at their respective locations during each period, and traders 2 and 3 alternate locations period by period. Finally, for simplicity, it may be supposed that the economy lasts only 4 periods.

Table 9–5
A Townsend-Wallace
Economy

Date	Location 1	2
1	(1,2)	(3,4)
2	(1,3)	(2,4)
3	(1,2)	(3,4)
4	(1,3)	(2,4)

Privately issued securities are viable. Indeed there is now the possibility of direct bilateral loans for the traders who are paired at dates 1 and 3 and at dates 2 and 4. In a sense, these loans provide some liquidity. On the other hand, they are always held by the original acceptor until the redemption date. They may be thought of as forward contracts. More interesting perhaps is the possibility of securities that are traded before redemption dates, such as a promise issued by trader 1 at date 1 and location 1 to pay the consumption good at date 4 in location 1. This security or futures contract is passed from trader 1 to trader 2 at date 1, from trader 2 to trader 4 at date 2, from trader 4 to trader 3 at date 3, and presented for redemption by trader 3 at date 4. That is, with each of our traders types taken as representative of a large number of identical individuals, this model can be interpreted as implying the existence of active secondary (or futures) markets.

Townsend and Wallace (1982) establish for this example economy that the existence of active secondary markets in general. But they also encounter another apparent coordination problem. The consumption allocations of any perfect foresight equilibrium can be supported with a variety of security trades, trades that seem to require some communication or coordination at a time across the two spatially separated markets. It is enough, for example, that traders 1 or 2 issue 4-period securities at date 1, or that traders 3 or 4 do so. If both pairs do so, then the amounts should be constrained to satisfy a certain equation, but there seems to be no reason for that to occur. Indeed, it is hard to see how it can occur in the absence of communication across markets, communication that was apparently precluded a priori. As with the multiplicity of the models of Diamond and Mortensen, this result is highly suggestive of the need for some (centralized?) decision on which security markets should be active and which not or for some institution that coordinates trade across markets. And here at least the welfare analysis is straightforward; one equilibrium is as good as any other. The only issue is how an equilibrium is to be attained.

One last point can be made in the context of the present model. Suppose the economy posed in table 9–5 lasts just 2 periods. Then, again, there can be no privately issued securities as no security can be redeemed. And of course this is so even if, for example, traders 1 and 4 would like to borrow from traders 2 and 3, respectively, in an entirely symmetric fashion. But now suppose that somehow or other traders 1 and 4 form a syndicate or trading cooperative and that a commitment made by any member of the cooperative is equivalent with a commitment made by all. Then trader 1 might borrow from trader 2, making a commitment for the syndicate (1, 4) to pay back the loan and similarly for traders 4 and 3. That is, trader 1 borrows on his own account from the syndicate (1, 4) and 2 lends to the syndicate (1, 4). The books of the syndicate balance. Then at the second date, when traders 2 and 4 meet, 4 honors the commitment (of 1) and similarly for trader 1. That is,

4 pays back the syndicate (1, 4) by in effect paying 2. Again, the books of the syndicate balance.

Of course, with the formation of such syndicates, the 2-period loans increase in liquidity. They more represent money because they are used in exchange with a person who is anonymous. More generally, in the Townsend-Wallace terminology, the formation of syndicates leads to more chains of pairings that lead from an issuer (or his trading syndicate) at some specified date and location to the issuer (or his syndicate) at the designated redemption date and location. In short, syndicates serve as go-betweens or intermediaries; one does not have to track down the original issuer, or a third party who will be linked eventually (or indirectly) with the original issuer, to break a commitment.

The formation of trading syndicates raises another issue, however. Are large syndicates, which otherwise would seem to be advantageous, necessarily associated with market power or elements of imperfect competition? That is, some coordination or communication appear to be beneficial in this environment with frictions or barriers to trade. But this coordination should not be done collusively, in the sense that Adam Smith had in mind. One is reminded of Stone's third policy premise.

In a sense, though, this discussion of exchange syndicates is premature. In the Townsend-Wallace (1982) model, as well as the model of Mortensen (1974), markets or trader-pairings are specified a priori and are not subject to alteration. That is, there can be centralized communication within markets or pairings but there is supposed to be no communication across markets. To discuss exchange syndicates, then, or market formation more generally, or indeed to discuss the formation of extramarket control devices, one seems to need a model in which trading frictions exist but can be overcome at some cost—that is, a model with variable but costly communication. In what follows, two such models are presented. (However, these models are particularly stylized and are only intended to suggest results that might follow in more elaborate setups.)

On Limited Communication, Self-Regulation, and Exchange Rules

First, we describe a model with costly matching (see Mortensen 1982, and the antecendents in Diamond 1980; Diamond and Maskin 1979; and Mortensen 1979, among others). It is also closely related to the Diamond (1982) model presented previously in this chapter.

Imagine a world with two trader types, n_i of type i, $i = 1, 2$. Each unmatched trader of type i seeks an unmatched trader of type j to exploit some joint opportunity or to engage in exchange. Let λ_i denote the search intensity of an unmatched trader of type i, where $\lambda_i dt + \sigma(dt)$ is the probability of contacting an agent of the opposite type during a short time dt long (here $\sigma(dt)$ is a second-order term). Thus λ_i is interpreted as the probability of such contact, made by trader type i per unit time or per instant. Assuming contacts are made at random, $q_j = (n_j - m)/n_j$ is the probability that the trader contacted by i is unmatched, where m is the number of matched pairs. Consequently, the probability of a successful contact made by i per instant is $\lambda_i q_j$. Now number $(n_j - m)$ traders of type j are also searching for a match with intensity λ_j. Thus, a trader of type i may be contacted in this manner with probability $[(\lambda_j)(n_j - m)]/n_i = [n_j q_j \lambda_j]/n_i$. Adding probabilities, the probability of successful contact for an unmatched trader of type i (however generated) is

$$\frac{q_j}{n_i}[n_i \lambda_i + n_j \lambda_j] \equiv h_i(\lambda_1, \lambda_2)$$

Here it is apparent that the probability of successful contact varies positively with the search intensity of traders of the opposite type.

The instantaneous (per unit time) cost of search intensity λ_i for trader type i is $c_i(\lambda_i)$, where $c(\cdot)$ is a nonnegative, increasing, strictly convex function. The benefit of search depends on both the random time to match, which is endogenous, a function of λ_1 and λ_2, and the division of the value of the match. As regards the latter, suppose the capital surplus of any match is divided equally between the two members, as it would be in Nash's solution to the obvious bilateral bargaining game. Thus, letting V_i denote the value of utility payoff of continued search in the present model for a trader of type i—that is, the discounted present value or utility payoff for any unmatched trader of type i, the value of a match for a trader of type i is $V_i + \frac{1}{2}(B - V_1 - V_2)$ where B is the direct joint payoff of gain from a match, some constant. Thus, if the future match takes place at date t, the discounted present value is

$$\Pi_i(t) \equiv e^{-rt}[V_i + \frac{1}{2}(B - V_1 - V_2)] - c_i(\lambda_i)(1 - e^{-rt})/r$$

where r is the discount rate. And thus, with the random time to match as negative exponential

$$V_i(\lambda_i, \lambda_j) = \int_0^\infty \Pi_i(t) h_i(\lambda_1, \lambda_2) \exp(-h_i(\lambda_i, \lambda_2)\, t)\, dt$$

(Here both the number of participants, the n_i, and the fractions of unmatched agents of type i, the q_1, are taken as fixed and stationary.)

In a noncooperative equilibrium, each trader of type i takes the search intensity of the other type, λ_j, as given. Thus a Nash equilibrium is a specification of search strategies $(\lambda_1^*, \lambda_2^*)$ such that

$$V_i(\lambda_i, \lambda_j^*) \leq V_i(\lambda_i^*, \lambda_j^*) \quad \text{for } i = 1, 2$$
$$j \neq i$$

As in earlier work, Mortensen finds that a noncooperative equilibrium is necessarily inefficient. That is

$$\left. \frac{\partial V_i(\cdot)}{\partial V_j} \right|_{\lambda^*} > 0$$

The intuition is straightforward: The value of the game to both agents increases with search intensity because time to match falls and both agents share in the surplus when a match forms.

Mortensen (1982) also establishes that this externality can be internalized if the trade type responsible for the match, say type i, is given the entire surplus of the match less a compensation to the other trader equal to the latter's foregone value of continued search—that is, is given $B - V_j$. Then, not surprisingly, the noncooperative equilibrium with this new allocation rule will maximize the joint wealth of the typical unmatched pair and in that sense is optimal.

As Mortensen notes (1979), these results raise a troublesome enforcement issue. Under the second allocation rule, no trader when contacted by another has an incentive to agree to the specified division of the surplus. Nor is it clear how unmatched traders can precommit to one another because they are indeed unmatched. Thus, in the present model, there again seems to be a suggestive role for additional coordination, some agreement concerning a priori rules of exchange. The model does not suggest how such an agreement might come about.

Thus far we have avoided an analysis of the effect of competition among members of one class of traders for potential exchange with members of the other class. Perhaps one's intuition is that such competition would be beneficial. But in the context of a model with limited and endogenous communication, that need not be the case as a model of Boner (1981), following Butters (1977) points out.

Imagine after Boner a static pure exchange economy with two commodities and two classes of traders, say bidders and searchers. Each class has a continuous and strictly increasing utility function that may vary across types. In addition, the endowment allocations are extreme. The bidders have all of one commodity, the searchers all of another.

Each of the set of bidders can send a message (advertise) an admissible trade in the two consumption goods. Any individual message is received by at most one of the searchers, and falls on each searcher with the same or uniform probability. Each searcher chooses a utility maximizing bid from the set of bids received (randomizing if there are ties).

Boner seeks to characterize a noncooperative Nash equilibium in the choice of messages or bids. He discovers a sense in which noncooperative equilibria necessarily involve random strategies among the bidders, leading to a nonatomic bid distribution. But the Pareto optima for the economy, allowing for coordination of bids, are typically atomic bid distributions. Thus, competition among bidders would seem to be socially inefficient. We again see a potential gain for cooperation among advertisers or brokers in models with limited communication or costly exchange. But again unlimited cooperation at the very least implies a skewed distribution of income (welfare). It is not clear that self-regulation would be socially desirable. Of course, one might note that in Boner's model the bidders are given an exogenous communication advantage.

Concluding Remarks

The enforcement of contracts, property rights, and rules concerning the operation of competitive markets has long been regarded as a proper role for government. But which contracts, rights, and rules? This chapter argues that we might well address such questions in the context of highly stylized general equilibrium models of the economy. In effect, such models offer a laboratory in which we can inquire as to the effect of trading frictions, such as imperfect information and limited communication, and attempt to pinpoint features of the economy that may prove crucial.[12] The idea is to search for an optimal social arrangement in the context of models with such frictions and to take as the role for government the enforcement or implementation of such an arrangement. In short, following Lerner (1944), government should do no more than enforce the collective sentiment of the individual citizens.

Is there an active role for government to play? The decentralized models given previously seem to suggest a coordination role for government, but exactly what that role should be remains unclear. After all, it is never said how some outside agency can come to play a coordination role that is infeasible for private individuals. Indeed, the government cannot do that in the models as specified. More generally, it seems useful to bear in mind Lerner's distinction between control (that is, the implementation of the social optimum in a thorough manner but with a minimum of complexity in regulation) and contemporary regulations as he perceived them in industrial countries. The question of whether regulatory agencies are indeed organized in the social interest is still open, but rigorous welfare analyses along the lines of this chapter may help to begin to answer that question.

Two areas of future research seem deserving of immediate attention. First, we need models in which third parties or groups of agents play explicit intermediary roles in exchange. Indeed, that result was suggested by Mortensen (1979) as a way to internalize the externalities associated with his matching process. And many of the other models described here suggest a gain to cooperation among individuals, something that is impossible in the models as formulated. In the end, we seem to be led to a model in which groups or exchange syndicates compete with one another and perhaps to some modified version of the core as a useful equilibrium notion.[13]

Second, the models of this paper do not yet seem capable of addressing many of the issues raised in Stone's first policy premise. Private information alone is not enough, as I make clear earlier. More decentralization is needed. A synthesis of models with private information and limited communication would seem to be a promising direction for future research.

Notes

1. See Townsend (forthcoming) and the literature cited therein.

2. No attempt is made here to survey the literature on futures markets or futures market regulation (see the references cited in Telser 1981 and the volume containing Arrow 1981 and Stone 1981 for a start). Edwards (1981) also argues that we should be clear about which frameworks we have in mind when contemplating futures market regulation.

3. Again, no attempt is made here to offer a complete review of all relevant general equilibrium models. The models offered here are intended to be suggestive and to provoke further thought.

4. Here and later attention is restricted to economies with privately observed shocks to preferences. These may be interpreted as shocks to an underlying household production function. General extensions to explicit technology and endowment shocks are possible, but more awkward.

5. For a formal justification of this specification see Bewley and Radner (1980).

6. Of course, trade in spot markets would be mutually beneficial ex post, but spot trades alone do leave ex ante risk and the desire for some kind of insurance. Hereafter, following the usual Arrow-Debreu treatment of uncertainty, ex post spot markets are precluded without loss of utility.

7. To some extent actual futures contracts have these characteristics. See note 9.

8. Again, this conjecture is based on Townsend (forthcoming).

9. Indeed, a futures contract is not a simple, noncontingent agreement to buy or sell a specified commodity. For potatoe or for crude oil futures, the buyer or seller have various options, including the method, place, and exact date of delivery. If the agreed-on delivery specification proves impossible in crude oil futures because of an act of God or various specified events, a new set of options comes into effect. In potatoes futures, default terms are included. Default charges depend on contract value (last settling price for the delivery month), though they can be waived or reduced by the exchange if delinquency in performance is viewed as beyond the control of the delinquent party or if there are mitigating circumstances. Margin calls must be met within a reasonable time and if not met give the carrying broker the right to close out all or part of the open trades until any remaining unliquidated contracts are fully margined.

10. The possibility of organized location-specific markets was suggested by Robert E. Lucas, Jr., in a discussion of Diamond's paper in a conference on transactions costs at the University of Pennsylvania.

11. Again, this is the theory of second-best.

12. Lucas (1980) makes the case for this scientific method in analyzing business cylces.

13. Again, see Townsend (forthcoming).

References

Arrow, Kenneth J., (1964). "The Role of Securities in the Optimal Allocation of Risk Bearing," *Review of Economic Studies*, vol. 31 (April), pp. 91–96.

———. (1974). "Limited Information and Economic Analysis," *American Economic Review*, vol. 64, pp. 1–10.

———. (1981). "Futures Market: Some Theoretical Perspectives," *Journal of Futures Markets,* vol. 1

Bewley, Truman F., and Roy Radner, (1980). "Stationary Monetary Equilibrium with a Continuum of Independently Fluctuating Consumers," Northwestern University *Working Paper* (October).

Boner, Roger, (1981). "Noncooperative Bidding and the Pareto Ranking," manuscript, University of Maryland.

Butters, Gerald. (1977). "Equilibrium Distributions of Sales and Advertising Prices," *Review of Economic Studies*, vol. 44 (October).

Debreu, Gerard. (1959). *Theory of Value: An Axiomatic Analysis of Economic Equilibrium*. New Haven: Cowles Foundation.

Diamond, Peter A. (1982). "Aggregate Demand Management in Search Equilibrium," *Journal of Political Economy*, vol. 90, no. 5 (October).

————. (1980). "Wage Determination in Search Equilibrium," MIT Working paper 253.

————. and Eric Maskin (1979). "An Equilibrium Model of Search and Breach of Contract, I: Steady States," *Bell Journal of Economics*, vol. 10, pp. 282–316.

Edwards, Franklin R. (1981). "The Regulation of Futures Markets: A Conceptual Framework," Working Paper no. CSFM-23, Columbia Business School (September).

Ekern, S., and R. Wilson. (1974). "On the Theory of the Firm in an Economy with Incomplete Markets," *Bell Journal of Economics* (Spring) pp. 171–180.

Harris, Milton, and Robert M. Townsend. (1977). "Allocation Mechanisms for Asymmetrically Informed Agents," Carnegie-Mellon University Working Paper 55–76–77.

————. (1981). "Resource Allocation Under Asymmetric Information," *Econometrica* (January).

Hurwicz, Leonid. (1971). "On Informationally Decentralized Systems," in *Decision and Organization*, ed. R. Radner and B. McGuire. Amsterdam: North Holland.

Lerner, Abba P. (1944). *The Economics of Control*. New York: Macmillan.

Lucas, Robert E., Jr. (1980). "Methods and Problems in Business Cycle Theory," manuscript, University of Chicago (March).

Mortensen, Dale T. (1974). "Search Equilibrium and the Core in a Decentralized Pure Exchange Economy," manuscript, Northwestern University (August).

————.(1979). "The Matching Process as a Non-Cooperative/Bargaining Game," Discussion paper 384, Northwestern University (May).

————. (1982). "Property Rights and Efficiency in Mating, Racing, and Related Games," *American Economic Review* (December).

Myerson, Roger B. (1979), "Incentive Compatibility and the Bargaining Problem," *Econometrica*, vol. 47 (January), pp. 61–74.

Prescott, Edward C., and Robert M. Townsend (1982a). "General Competitive Analysis in an Economy with Private Information" (revised September 1982).

————. (1982b). "Optima and Competitive Equilibria with Adverse Selection and Moral Hazard" (revised October 1982).

Radner, Roy. (1968). "Competitive Equilibrium Under Uncertainty," *Econometrica*, vol. 36, pp. 31–58.

Ross, Steven A. (1976). "Options and Efficiency," *Quarterly Journal of Economics*, (February), pp. 75–89.

Rothschild, Michael, and Joseph Stiglitz. (1976). "Equilibrium in Competitive Insurance Markets: An Essay on the Economics of Imperfect

Information," *Quarterly Journal of Economics*, vol. 90, (November) pp. 629–649.

Spence, A. Michael. (1974). *Market Signaling: Information Transfer in Hiring and Related Screening Processes*. Cambridge: Harvard University Press.

Stone, James M. (1981). "Principles of the Regulation of Futures Markets," *Journal of Futures Markets*. vol. 1, no. 2.

Telser, Lester G. (1981). "Why There are Organized Futures Markets," *The Journal of Law and Economics*, vol. 24 (April) pp. 1–22.

Townsend, Robert M. (1978). "On the Optimality of Forward Markets," *American Economy Review*, vol. 68.

———.(1980). "Models of Money with Spatially Separated Agents," in *Models of Monetary Economies*, ed. John H. Kareken and Neil Wallace. Minneapolis: Federal Reserve Bank of Minneapolis.

———.(1982). "Optimal Multiperiod Contracts and the Gain from Enduring Relationships Under Private Information," *Journal of Political Economy* (December).

———. *Theories of Intermediated Structures*, Carnegie-Rochester Conferences Series on Public Policy, forthcoming.

———. and Neil Wallace. (1982). "A Model of Circulating Private Debt," staff report 83, Federal Reserve Bank of Minneapolis (August).

Wilson, Charles. (1977). "A Model of Insurance Markets with Incomplete Information," *Journal of Economic Theory*, vol. 16, pp. 176–207.

Comment

Lester G. Telser

Professor Townsend's paper touches on many of the important and classical problems of economic theory. It shows the close connections between these problems and those which arise in the theory of futures markets. Townsend begins by asking whether we can have a pure futures economy without any spot markets. This question first began to be discussed in the debate about the feasibility and efficiency of a centrally planned economy. Barone was the first to pose the question in modern economic theory and there are important contributions by Lange, Hicks, and Lerner. Hicks in particular drew to the attention of economists to the relationship between spot and futures markets. The existence of uncertainty made it necessary to have spot markets, according to Hicks. This results from the desires of those who have entered into futures contracts to reverse their commitments by transacting in the spot market because events they have not foreseen make this desirable. Therefore, according to Hicks, it was not possible to eliminate all the consequences of a lack of coordination in a sequence of spot markets by having futures markets in their place. It would be helpful if Townsend had included a discussion of Hicks's contributions to this problem.

Townsend correctly points out that Arrow and Debreu gave a theoretical solution to this problem of uncertainty by introducing the concept of state-contingency contracts. Townsend gives the impression that futures contracts in particular are not state-contingent and, more generally, that there are few actual instances of state-contingent contracts. I find myself in disagreement. Many if not all insurance contracts are state-contingent contracts. The party issuing the insurance—that is, the one who sells the contract—agrees to make a payment to the buyer of the contract, the one who obtains the insurance, under prescribed conditions. The biggest obstacle to the more widespread use of these contracts is moral hazard. It may be very costly to determine whether or not there has been fraud so that the insured party has more or less deliberately brought about the event that would cause the issuer of the insurance to make payment.

Take fire insurance on a house, for example. The issuer of the insurance usually imposes an upper bound on the amoung of the payment he will make in case there is a fire that is below the market price of the house. The reason is obvious. Similarly, other conditions set limits on the obligations of the parties to a futures contract. Usually they give the circumstances under which one of the parties no longer has the obligation to fulfill the contract. Therefore, futures contracts do have elements in common with state-contingent contracts. Indeed, virtually all transactions have these elements.

I have been following Townsend's terminology by referring to these as futures contracts. It would have been helpful had Townsend explained in greater detail the distinction between forward and futures contracts—a distinction crucial for understanding the role of an organized market, as I have argued in several articles. A forward contract is between two specific parties and may not be bought or sold without the consent of the other party. For example, General Mills might buy wheat forward from Continental Grain. This forward contract will specify a large number of particulars including the specific type of wheat; when and where it will be delivered and by what means, say truck or rail; how payment will be made and on what terms; and so on. General Mills may not sell this contract to another party and thereby extinguish its obligation to fulfill the terms of its forward contract nor may Continental Grain buy a contract from a third party and thereby satisfy its commitment to General Mills. In addition, those who negotiate the terms of these forward contracts must be knowledgeable experts on the commodity. They must know the grades and qualities of the commodities they handle and they must know the needs of their employers or principals. We may summarize by asserting that a forward contract is not a fungible instrument.

In contrast, a futures contract is fungible. It is not a transaction between two specific individuals. The buyer and the seller do agree on the price and quantity. But this agreement establishes an obligation to the organized exchange in the form of the clearinghouse of the exchange. The buyer has an asset, which is the liability of the clearinghouse, whereas the seller of the futures contract has a liability, which is an asset of the clearinghouse. Either the buyer or the seller can extinguish this instrument with the clearinghouse by making the appropriate offsetting transaction. The buyer can sell the futures contract to anyone at a mutually agreeable price then prevailing on the floor of the exchange. The seller can close his commitment to the clearinghouse by finding a buyer with whom a mutually satisfactory trade can occur at the then prevailing price. Neither the original seller nor the original buyer needs to know anything about the subsequent transactions. As a consequence, a futures contract is a highly fungible instrument. A futures contract stands to a forward contract in the same sense that currency stands to a check. In a trasnaction settled by currency the creditworthiness of the buyer is not relevant. The seller need only be sure that the currency is genuine—not counterfeit. However, if payment is made by check then the seller requires some assurance that the check will not bounce.

The fungibility of the futures contract and the greater liquidity of this type of contract relative to a forward contract is not its only important distinguishing feature. It also enables the principals of the transactions to use agents who can carry out their instructions while knowing far less about the particular details of the principal's situation. Reconsider General Mills.

Say it wishes to sell wheat futures contracts. It can give instructions to its agents who will carry them out on the floor of the exchange in the form of price and quantity. The agent does not need to know anything about the kind of wheat that General Mills uses or needs. All the agent needs to know is the minimal acceptable prices and the quantities that General Mills wants to sell. The abstract nature of the futures contract not only adds to its fungibility but it also permits specialization and thereby a reduction of cost.

Townsend does not discuss the theory aimed at explaining certain important aspects of prices on organized exchanges. In such exchanges prices change from one transaction to the next. At each transaction there is a rapid auction occurring among the traders and as soon as there is mutual agreement on price and quantity between a buyer and a seller, this price becomes public knowledge. But then what information can be gleaned from the prices because they change from one transaction to the next? Would it be better to have a few fixings per day as in the London gold market? Some of the relevant theories for studying these questions refer to the efficient market hypothesis. It might have been desirable to allocate some space to these questions and reduce the space taken up with the search models. The relevance of the search models to futures markets is not clear except for one fairly obvious point.

An organized market constitutes a single place where traders can meet and do their business. It is not necessary for them to wander aimlessly about some region looking for each other. Indeed, over a wide range of operation an organized market obtains economies of scale. The traders know where to go not only to reduce their search costs but also to increase liquidity—that is, individuals can have confidence of finding a ready market when they wish to transact and know that the prices will not reflect the effects of individual transactions. In this way the trades in the market itself gives a close approximation to the theoretical ideal of a perfectly competitive market.

Townsend's argument—that moving from random search among the traders dispersed in space to a focal point, an organized market, where all may meet and trade makes some traders better off and others worse off—is obscure. There is no coercion. A trader need not go to an organized market to make his trades if this would make him worse off than his available alternatives. Therefore there is surely a presumption of gains at least to all of the direct participants in the organized market.

The choice of a single place to have the market poses no difficulties. Unlike the simplified model of sophomore economics, in the world people can discuss how to arrange their affairs and design markets to satisfy their desires, which causes no loss owing to collusive manipulations. Here I disagree with Adam Smith. It is false and misleading to assert that whenever businessmen come together to discuss arrangements for setting up an organized market that the public will suffer. It is misleading to call organized exchanges natural monopolies. A single market is the most efficient—that is, the least costly—way of handling the transactions the businessmen wish to make. There is no loss of efficiency that accompanies a monopoly. On the contrary, the loss of efficiency would occur if erroneous notions of competition were to prevent the concentration of trade in a given commodity into a single place. Because the prices arrived at in an organized market convey information to everyone, including outsiders who do not trade in these markets, there is a free rider program. The exchange, its members, devise rules to protect themselves and help ensure their survival. Among these are rules to prevent members from making trades off the floor.

At several places in his paper, Townsend alludes to problems that he seems to believe require outside intervention. These problems are often merely casual remarks that do not reflect the same degree of care and thoughtfulness that he shows on almost every page. The question of how well government bureaucrats can regulate the exchange is a serious one that requires thoughtful consideration. It is an injustice to well-meaning regulators to toss off the instances where problems arise as casual asides. The exchanges themselves, especially the older ones that have encountered a wide variety of problems during their lifetimes (more than 130 years in the case of the Chicago Board of Trade), make up rules and police their members. This is not to say that the rules are never broken and that all violations are detected and punished. Yet it is true that self-regulation has the undoubted advantages that those who stand to lose the most for infractions have the greatest incentive to punish them. No one has devised a comparable system that gives third parties the same incentive of reward and punishment as presently exists in the organized exchanges.

About the Contributors

Simon Benninga teaches in the Faculty of Management of Tel Aviv University and in the Finance Department of the Wharton School.

Graciela Chichilnisky is professor of economics at Columbia University. She has worked both on mathematical economics and on international trade.

Jean-Pierre Danthine teaches at the University of Lausanne. His papers on futures markets have been devoted to hedging, speculation, and private information.

Franklin R. Edwards is professor of business at Columbia University and director of the Center for Futures Market Studies. His speciality is financial regulation.

Carl A. Futia is currently a consultant on financial markets at Futures Strategies Corporation. He was formerly on the staff of Bell Laboratories where he worked in the area of mathematical economics.

James Hayes is an economist at the Chicago Board of Trade. He has been closely involved with the development of the CBT's futures contracts for the petroleum complex.

Thomas E. Kilcollin is chief economist at the Chicago Mercantile Exchange. He holds a Ph.D. in economics from the University of Chicago.

Richard E. Kihlstrom is professor of finance at the University of Pennsylvania. He has worked on the theory of markets with imperfect information.

Albert S. Kyle teaches at Princeton University. In addition to writing on mathematical economics, he has traded futures at the Chicago Board of Trade.

David M.G. Newbery teaches at Churchill College, Cambridge. Until recently he was on the staff of the World Bank where he carried out a number of studies on commodity market stabilization.

Louis Phlips is a professor at the Center for Operations Research and Econometrics at the Catholic University of Louvain. His contributions to industrial organization include *The Economics of Price Discrimination*.

Robert W. Rosenthal is a game theorist who has worked particularly on problems of imperfect information. He teaches at the Virginia Polytechnic Institute and was formerly at Bell Laboratories.

Stephen W. Salant has made many contributions to theoretical industrial organization, including a study of the speculative disruption of price stabilization programs. He is an economist at the Rand Corporation.

Garth Saloner is assistant professor of economics at the Massachusetts Institute of Technology. He works on applications of game theory to industrial organization.

Hans R. Stoll is professor of finance at Vanderbilt University. He has done a number of studies of futures markets.

James M. Stone was formerly commissioner and chairman of the Commodity Futures Trading Commission and is now an executive at the insurance firm Fairfield and Ellis. He holds a Ph.D. in economics from Harvard University.

Mahadevan Sundaresan teaches finance at Columbia University. He has worked on intertemporal models of futures market prices.

Lester G. Telser teaches at the University of Chicago and has made numerous studies of futures markets.

Robert M. Townsend is professor of economics at Carnegie Mellon University. He has written a number of theoretical studies on financial intermediaries.

Lawrence J. White is a senior economist at the U.S. Department of Justice and is on leave from New York University. He specializes in industrial organization.

About the Editor

Ronald W. Anderson is an associate professor at the Graduate School of Business of Columbia University. He is the author of a number of studies on hedging, speculation, and price behavior in futures markets as well as econometric studies of U.S. agriculture. He is an associate editor of the *Journal of Futures Markets*.